Steven Brill

Tailspin

Steven Brill has written for *The New Yorker*, *Time*, *The New York Times Magazine*, *Esquire*, *New York*, and *Fortune*. He founded and ran Court TV, *The American Lawyer* magazine, ten regional legal newspapers, and *Brill's Content* magazine. Brill is the author of *Time*'s March 4, 2013, special report "Bitter Pill: Why Medical Bills Are Killing Us," for which he won the 2014 National Magazine Award for Public Interest, and the 2015 bestseller *America's Bitter Pill*. He has regularly appeared as an expert analyst on NBC, CBS, and CNN. He teaches journalism at Yale, where he founded the Yale Journalism Initiative to enable talented young people to become journalists. In 2018, he cofounded NewsGuard, which rates the legitimacy of online news sites. He lives in New York City.

Tailspin

TAILSPIN

The People and Forces Behind America's
Fifty-Year Fall—and Those Fighting to Reverse It

Steven Brill

Vintage Books
A DIVISION OF PENGUIN RANDOM HOUSE LLC
NEW YORK

FIRST VINTAGE BOOKS EDITION, APRIL 2019

The Library of Congress has cataloged the Knopf edition as follows:
Names: Brill, Steven, 1950– author.
Title: Tailspin : the people and forces behind America's fifty-year fall—
and those fighting to reverse it / Steven Brill.
Description: First edition. | New York : Alfred A. Knopf, 2018. |
Includes bibliographical references and index.
Identifiers: LCCN 2017051857
Subjects: LCSH: Social change—United States. | Political culture—United States. |
Equality—United States. | Democracy—United States. | United States—Social
conditions—1960–1980. | United States—Social conditions—1980– | United
States—Politics and government—1945–1989. | United States—Politics and
government—1989– | BISAC: POLITICAL SCIENCE / Public Policy / General. |
POLITICAL SCIENCE / Public Policy / Economic Policy. | POLITICAL SCIENCE / Civics
& Citizenship. Classification: LCC HN59 .B75 2018 | DDC 306.0973—dc23
LC record available at https://lccn.loc.gov/2017051857

Vintage Books Trade Paperback ISBN: 978-0-525-43201-2
eBook ISBN: 978-1-5247-3164-9

In memory of my parents,
and to Cynthia, Emily, Sophie, and Sam

In memory of my parents,
and to Cynthia, Emily, Sophie, and Sam

Contents

Tailspin

The Protected and the Unprotected

Is the world's greatest democracy and economy broken? Not compared to the Civil War years, or to the early 1930s. And not if one considers the miracles happening every day in America's laboratories, on the campuses of its world-class colleges and universities, in offices and lofts full of developers creating software for robots or for medical diagnostics, in concert halls and on Broadway stages, or at joyous ceremonies swearing in proud new citizens. And certainly not if the opportunities available today to women, non-whites, and other minorities are compared to what they faced as recently as a few decades ago.

Yet measures of public engagement, satisfaction, and confidence—voter turnout, knowledge of public policy issues, faith that the next generation will have it better than the current one, and respect for basic institutions, especially the government—are far below the levels of a half century ago, and in many cases have reached historic lows. So deep is the estrangement that 46.1 percent of American voters were so disgusted with the status quo that in 2016 they chose to put Donald Trump in the White House.

It is difficult to argue that the cynicism is misplaced. From the relatively small things—that Americans are now navigating through an average of 657 water main breaks a day, for example—to the core strengths that once propelled America, it is clear that the country has gone into a tailspin since the post-war era, when John F. Kennedy's New Frontier was about seizing the future, not trying to survive the present.

The celebrated American economic mobility engine is sputtering. A child's chance of earning more than his or her parents has dropped from 90 percent to 50 percent in the last fifty years. The American middle class, once the inspiration of the world, is no longer the world's richest.

Income inequality has snowballed. Adjusted for inflation, middle-class wages have been nearly frozen for the last four decades, and discretionary income has declined if escalating out-of-pocket health care costs and insurance premiums are counted. Yet earnings by the top one percent have nearly tripled. The recovery from the crash of 2008—which saw banks and bankers bailed out while millions lost their homes, savings, and jobs—was reserved almost exclusively for the top one percent. Their incomes in the three years following the crash went up by nearly a third, while the bottom 99 percent saw an uptick of less than half of one percent. Only a democracy and an economy that has discarded its basic mission of holding the community together, or failed at it, would produce those results.

Most Americans with average incomes have been left largely to fend for themselves, often at jobs where automation, outsourcing, the near-vanishing of union protection, and the boss's obsession with squeezing out every penny of short-term profit have eroded any sense of security. Self-inflicted deaths—from opioid and other drug abuse, alcoholism, and suicide—are at record highs, so much so that the country's average life expectancy has been falling despite medical advances. Household debt by 2017 had grown higher than the peak reached in 2007 before the crash, with student and automobile loans having edged toward mortgages as the top claims on family paychecks.

The world's richest country continues to have the highest poverty rate among the thirty-five nations in the Organisation for Economic Co-operation and Development (OECD), except for Mexico. (It is tied in second to last place with Israel, Chile, and Turkey.) Nearly one in five of America's children live in households that their government classifies as "food-insecure," meaning they are without "access to enough food for an active, healthy life."

Beyond that, few of the basic services seem to work as they should.

America's airports are an embarrassment, and a modern air traffic control system is twenty-five years behind schedule. The power grid, roads, and rails are crumbling, pushing the United States far down international rankings for infrastructure quality. Despite spending more on health care and K–12 education per capita than any other developed country, health care outcomes and student achievement also rank in the middle or worse internationally. The U.S. has the highest infant mortality rate and lowest life expectancy among its peer countries, and among the thirty-five OECD countries American children rank thirtieth in math proficiency and nineteenth in science.

American politicians talk about "American exceptionalism" so habitually that it should have its own key on their speechwriters' laptops. Is this the exceptionalism they have in mind?

The operative word to describe the performance of our lawmakers in Washington, D.C., responsible for guiding what is supposed to be the world's greatest democracy, is pathetic. Congress has not passed a comprehensive budget since 1994. Like slacker schoolchildren unable to produce a book report on time, the country's elected leaders have fallen back instead on an endless string of last-minute deadline extensions and piecemeal appropriations. Legislation to deal with big, long-term challenges, like climate change, the mounting national debt, or job displacement, is a pipe dream. It is as if the great breakthroughs of the past, marked by bipartisan signing ceremonies in the White House—the establishment of the Federal Trade Commission, Social Security, interstate highways, the Food and Drug Administration, Medicare, civil rights legislation, the EPA—are part of some other country's history.

There are more than twenty registered lobbyists for every member of Congress. Most are deployed to block anything that would tax, regulate, or otherwise threaten a deep-pocketed client. Money has come to dominate everything so completely that those we send to Washington to represent us have been reduced to begging on the phone for campaign cash four or five hours a day and spending their evenings taking checks at fund-raisers organized by those swarming lobbyists. A gerrymandering process has rigged easy wins for most of them, as long as they fend off primary challengers in their own party—which assures that they will gravitate toward the polarizing, special interest positions of their donors and their party's base, while racking up mounting deficits to pay for goods and services that cost more than budgeted, rarely work as promised, and are never delivered on time.

The story of how all of this came to be is like a movie in which everything seems clear only if it is played back from the start in slow motion. Each chapter unfolded slowly, usually without any clue of its ultimate impact. The story is not about villains, although there are some. It is not about a conspiracy to bring the country down. It is not about one particular event or trend, and it did not spring from one single source.

Excellent books and scholarly treatises have been written about the likeliest suspects: the growth of income inequality, the polarization and paralysis of American democracy, the dominance of political money, or the recklessness that precipitated the financial crash of 2008–9 and the ensuing failure to hold anyone accountable. The story of America's breakdown is about all of that, and more. And there is a theme that threads through and ties together all of these subplots: The most talented, driven Americans chased the American dream— and won it for themselves. Then, in a way unprecedented in history, they were able to consolidate their winnings, outsmart and co-opt the government that might have reined them in, and pull up the ladder so more could not share in their success or challenge their primacy.

By continuing to get better at what they do, by knocking away the guardrails limiting their winnings, by aggressively engineering changes in the political landscape, and by dint of the often unanticipated consequences of the breakthroughs they pulled off in legal rights, financial engineering, digital technology, political strategy, and so many other areas, they created a nation of moats that protected them from accountability and from the damage their triumphs caused in the larger community. Most of the time, our elected and appointed representatives were no match for these overachievers. As a result of their savvy, their drive, and their resources, America all but abandoned its most ambitious and proudest ideal: the never perfect, always debated, and perpetually sought-after balance between the energizing inequality of achievement in a competitive economy and the liberating, community-binding equality of power promised by democracy. In a battle that began a half century ago, the achievers won.

The result is a new, divided America. On one side are the protected few—the winners—who don't need government for much and even have a stake in sabotaging the government's responsibility to all of its citizens. For them, the new, broken America works fine, at least in the short term. On the other side are the unprotected many, who rely on government, as they always have, to protect and preserve their way of life and maybe even improve it. That divide is the essence of America's tailspin. The protected overmatched, overran, and paralyzed the government.

The unprotected need the government to provide good public schools so that their children have a chance to advance. They need the government to provide a level competitive playing field for their small businesses, a fair shake in consumer disputes, and a realistic shot at justice in the courts. They need the government to provide a safety net to assure that their families have access to good health care, that no one goes hungry when shifts in the economy or temporary setbacks take away their jobs, and that they get help to rebuild after a hurricane or other disaster. They need the government to assure a safe workplace and a living minimum wage. They need mass transit systems that work and call centers at Social Security offices that don't produce busy signals. They need the government to keep the political system fair and protect it from domination by those who can give politicians the most money. They need the government to provide fair labor laws and to promote an economy and a tax code that tempers the extremes of income inequality and makes economic opportunity more than an empty cliché.

The protected need few of these common goods. They don't have to worry about underperforming public schools, dilapidated mass transit systems, or jammed Social Security hotlines. They have accountants and lawyers who can negotiate their employment contracts, or deal with consumer disputes, assuming they want to bother. They see labor or consumer protection laws, and fair tax codes, as threats to their winnings—winnings that they have spent the last fifty years consolidating by eroding these common goods and the government that would provide them.

That, rather than a split between Democrats and Republicans, is the real polarization that has broken America since the 1960s: The protected versus the unprotected. Enhancing the common good versus maximizing and protecting the elite winners' winnings.

It may be understandable for those on the losing side to condemn the protected class as gluttons who are comfortable rationalizing the plight of the unprotected as their fault for not being self-reliant. That explanation, however, is too simple, and it misses the irony and true lesson of what has happened. Many of the winners are people who have lived the kind of lives that all Americans celebrate. They worked hard. They tried things that others didn't dare attempt. They usually believed, often rightly, that they were writing new chapters in the long story of American progress.

The breakdown came when their intelligence, daring, creativity, and resources enabled them to push aside any effort to rein them in. They did what comes naturally—they kept winning. And they did it with the protection of an alluring, defensible narrative that shielded them from pushback, at least initially. They won not with the brazen corruption of the robber barons of old, but by drawing on the core values that have always defined American greatness—meritocracy, free markets, innovation in technology and finance, the rule of law, the First Amendment, even democracy itself. They didn't do it cynically, at least not at first. They simply got really, really good at taking advantage of what the American system gave them and doing the kinds of things that America treasures in the name of the values that America treasures. The problem is that, ultimately, these best and brightest got too good at it.

This story starts with a new definition of the best and brightest. In the 1960s, colleges and universities, and then the country generally, began to apply a long-treasured, although usually ignored, American value—meritocracy—to challenge the old-boy network in determining who would rise to the top. That made those at the top smarter and better equipped to dominate what was becoming a knowledge economy. It was one of the twentieth century's great breakthroughs for equality. As you will read, I was a beneficiary of the change and also played a role in embedding it in the legal industry. It had the unintended consequence, however, of entrenching a new aristocracy of rich knowledge workers who were much smarter and more driven than the old-boy network of heirs born on third base.

From the 1970s on, they upended corporate America and Wall Street with inventions in law and finance that created an economy built on deals that moved corporate assets around instead of building new assets. They created exotic, and risky, financial instruments. They organized hedge funds that turned owning stock into a minute-by-minute bet rather than a long-term investment. They invented proxy fights, leveraged buyouts, and stock buybacks that gave lawyers and bankers a bonanza of new fees and maximized short-term profits for increasingly unsentimental shareholders, but deadened incentives for the long-term development and growth of the rest of the economy.

They overwhelmed regulatory agencies with battalions of lawyers, who brilliantly weaponized another core American value whose expanded reach had been pushed in the 1960s by legal scholars on the left as a new civil right: the guarantee, embodied in the concept of "due process," that the rule of law, not the whims of rulers, would always prevail. In the hands of thousands of Washington lawyers drawn from the new meritocracy, due process came to mean not just that the government couldn't take away land or freedom at will, but that an Occupational Health and Safety Administration rule protecting workers from a deadly chemical used on the job could be challenged and delayed for more than a decade and end up being hundreds of pages long, filled with clause after clause after clause whose meaning the lawyers could contest.

A landmark suit brought by consumer rights activist Ralph Nader gave corporations that owned drugstores a First Amendment right to inform consumers by advertising their prices. However, it morphed into a corporate free speech movement that produced one court decision after another allowing unlimited corporate money to overwhelm democratic elections.

Beginning in the 1970s, the First Amendment right to petition the government was deployed to allow businesses to storm Washington with thousands of lobbyists to press their case with members of Congress and their staffs and at regulatory agencies and executive branch departments. Free speech also became a winning battle cry for corporations seeking to avoid regulations governing marketing, the sale of personal data, and product labeling, including the safety labels on the same drugs whose prices Nader had won retailers the right to advertise.

Progress in post-war diplomacy, international banking, and supply chain networks massively expanded opportunities for global trade, which American union leaders championed in the 1960s. Amid the optimism following the war in which their country saved the world, they assumed their workers would be unbeatable in international competition. It took less than a decade for them to realize that for those who worked with their hands, trade was a threat, not an opportunity, because the companies they worked for could shift jobs into cheaper labor markets overseas.

Technological innovation produced even more job displacement for the rank and file. As epitomized by textile maker J.P. Stevens's epic battle against union attempts to organize its workers, the wages of workers who remained were suppressed by their employers' fierce defiance of New Deal labor laws and their cynical realization that paying even the most expensive platoons of lawyers to hold off the National Labor Relations Board was far cheaper than obeying the law. The result was the virtual end of unions in the private sector, which extinguished not only the economic power of rank-and-file workers but also the political muscle that unions had once provided to balance out business interests.

Although even Republican economists from the 1970s on predicted that massive job training programs would be necessary in the age of automation and global trade to keep the working class from falling by the wayside, those programs never became more than ineffective sops meant to placate the minority of politicians who complained about job displacement. With Washington overrun by political money channeled into campaign contributions and lobbying, power resided with those more worried about keeping trade up and taxes down than about the prospect of a forgotten working class.

The best evidence of the protected-unprotected divide is that the most vulnerable of all—the poor—were left with safety net programs that are not nearly what they could be if those with the power cared. Politicians at least now pay lip service to the plight of the middle class, but they rarely talk about the poor, much less do enough to help them. This can only be explained by their fear that the middle class might see any attention paid to those below them as further evidence that their elected officials have abandoned them.

Those who were winning in the finance-dominated economy and in a democracy warped by First Amendment–powered political money invested those winnings into still more dominance. This allowed them to take advantage of power vacuums created by another avenue of ostensible progress that began in the 1970s: the reform of Washington institutions and American politics to make everything more democratic. These reforms in the name of democracy undermined democracy. Taking the selection of candidates away from political bosses and giving it to the people, through primaries and caucuses, enhanced the importance of political money. It also produced candidates more likely to appeal to the most committed, and extreme, members of their party, who were most likely to vote in primaries or caucuses. That in turn began to produce the polarization that now dominates American politics, and which paralyzes government. For the protected—those who don't want government to intrude on how they are doing business, and who do not depend on the services government provides—this is a positive, not a negative.

The new magic of data analytics exacerbated polarization by allowing candidates on either side to target messages to their most avid supporters, focusing on their personal hot-button issues. This increased turnout among the committed, but ended the old politics of appealing to undecided moderates with more mainstream policies.

Politics was made less mainstream and nastier by other technology advances. C-Span gave a new wave of politicians, epitomized by Georgia congressman Newt Gingrich, a national television audience and the incentive to go on the attack. Cable television and then the Internet and then social media allowed people to read and see whatever reinforced what they already believed. The days of the country sharing the same set of facts by watching the news unfold on broadcast television were over. It is not surprising that the micro-focused elected leaders who emerged from this new media world could not get together to address runaway health care costs, the decaying infrastructure, immigration reform, working-class job displacement, or the rampant speculation on Wall Street that crashed the economy.

As government was disabled from delivering on these vital issues, the protected were able to protect themselves still more. For them, it was all about building their own moats. Their money, their power, their lobbyists, their lawyers, their drive overwhelmed the institutions that were supposed to hold them accountable—government agencies, Congress, the courts.

The most obvious example is how they were able to avoid accountability when the banks they ran crashed the economy by trading trillions in fraudulent securities tied to risky or even certain-to-fail mortgages. The CEOs had been able to get the courts to treat their corporations like people when it came to protecting the corporation's right to free speech. Yet after the crash the same CEOs got prosecutors and judges to treat them like corporations when it came to personal responsibility. The corporate structures they had built were so massive and so complex that, the prosecutors decided, no senior executive could be proven to have known what was going on. The bankers kept their jobs and their bonuses.

While these moats protected the powerful from the government's job of holding them accountable to everyone else, national defense became perhaps the one aspect of government about which all Americans shared a sense of common purpose. Everyone worries equally about an enemy missile. As a result, national defense works well; everyone is well protected.

National defense does not work, however, when it comes to how America buys it. Defense procurement, and government contracting generally, are a national embarrassment of cost overruns, waste, and excess profits enjoyed by a band of entrenched Beltway contractors. Those contractors, the lobbyists they employ, and the members of Congress who receive their campaign contributions, or who make them bring jobs to their districts, benefit from the broken system. They have an interest in preserving it that far exceeds everyone else's interest in fixing it. For the taxpayer who sees an occasional headline about a cost overrun, government waste may be part of a general complaint about Washington. But it is not a preoccupation. For the richest taxpayers, who pay so much less proportionately in taxes (and who may have business interests that align with the overpaid contractors), it is a non-event.

The same is true of breakdowns in important government operations, such as the one highlighted by a 2014 scandal involving the covering up of long waiting lists for veterans seeking care at Veterans Administration hospitals. The public cared briefly because of the headlines and the obvious outrage of treating servicemen this way. The ones who really cared were the veterans, who didn't have the power they would have had if the United States still had a draft and everyone was equally affected by soldiers being abused this way. The other group that cared a lot were the civil servants at the Veterans Administration under attack for their misconduct. But they had their own moat. They had civil service protections born out of the same treasured but abused core value, due process, that business lobbyists used to gum up the federal regulatory system. Civil service laws required that they be afforded what had become almost impregnable due process protections before they could be fired or disciplined. Civil service is another great American reform that in the last fifty years became another great American moat.

Except for the most civic minded among them, corporate executives—who spend millions to lobby against employment laws forcing even a fraction of these due process protections on their companies when they hire or fire their own employees—are not likely to worry about the straitjacket their government faces in recruiting talent or in training or in dismissing the untalented. Nor do they care much that their government doesn't produce a budget or performance metrics, or pay enough to hire and keep competent people in jobs managing billions of dollars' worth of programs.

Similarly, there is an imbalance of passion and interest when it comes to perhaps the most obvious common good: the nation's infrastructure. America's deteriorating roads and power grids, and broken mass transit systems, are daily reminders of how the protected have undermined the government's ability to fulfill its most basic purpose. Support from both parties for investing in infrastructure used to be as routine as Congress issuing a Flag Day proclamation. However, a power base, supplemented by an ideological base, has jelled over the last fifty years around the cause of keeping taxes low and government small and, as a general matter, blocking any significant bipartisan solutions even to the most obvious government responsibility— maintaining and improving the bricks and mortar that allow a country to function. Additional hurdles have been added by environmentalists and community groups that may favor new roads or an expanded mass transit system as a general matter, but not a project in their neighborhoods. They have been able to use the truncated, multi-agency approvals process—in other words, more due process—to delay projects for decades, or to make getting them approved so difficult and so expensive that they get shelved. The environmental impact statements mandated by the passage of the Environmental Protection Act in 1970 were required under the law to be "concise, clear, and to the point." These documents now routinely run hundreds of pages, with hundreds more in appendices. They take years to write, and routinely face court challenges.

Like the deterioration of America's infrastructure, America's overall decline has been a slow-moving story. Each development unfolded gradually, rarely making headlines. As with the First Amendment victory for drugstores, there was often little warning that one element or another of the unfolding story would end up producing anything other than unalloyed progress.

Each element reinforced the others. The whole became larger than the sum of the parts. In that sense, one could call this great unraveling of American exceptionalism a perfect storm, but one that paradoxically featured what appeared to be bright skies all along the way—milestones in innovation in all the arenas that make America great.

Although the chapters that follow each focus on one element of the breakdown, the elements were interrelated. For example, the rise of meritocracy that created a newly entrenched aristocracy of knowledge workers powered the transformation of America into a finance-dominated economy. That in turn created still more demand for financial engineers and lawyers, which further entrenched the meritocracy and widened income inequality. Similarly, the emergence of the First Amendment as a tool enabling unlimited money to finance campaign contributions and to pay for lobbyists to dominate Washington allowed business interests to prevail in multiple battles against the middle class, including fights over unionization. That further marginalized the political clout of the middle class, which allowed those at the top to win still more advantages in Washington and to build moats to protect themselves still more. Polarization, which was fueled by well-meaning democratic reforms and the rise of political money, crippled the government, which allowed those moats to be left unchallenged and the country's most basic needs—including re-attaching the middle class to the American Dream—to remain unaddressed. At the same time, the collapse of government into a swamp of contractors, lobbyists, entitled civil servants, and bickering, panhandling politicians fueled public cynicism about government as a solution for anything, which exacerbated polarization and played into the hands of those who do not need government to protect them and who benefit when the government is hamstrung and does not sufficiently tax or regulate them.

It seems like a grim story. Except that the story is not over. In every arena that the achievers commandeered to create the protected-unprotected divide, there are now equally talented, equally driven achievers who have grown so disgusted by what they see that they are pushing back. There are college presidents breaking down the barriers of the newly entrenched meritocracy. Others are making eye-opening progress with training programs aimed at lifting the poor and those displaced by automation or trade back into middle-class jobs. Legal scholars are developing new doctrines to get the courts to deal with what they see as a runaway corporate free speech movement, while new non-profit organizations supported by disillusioned politicians from both parties are fighting for campaign finance reforms and pushing legislation that would limit the influence of lobbyists by reining in their checkbooks. Increasingly well-funded non-profits staffed by creative thinkers and undaunted fighters with sterling résumés and hard-knocks experience are going after continuing abuses and lack of accountability on Wall Street. Others are preparing blueprints for civil service reform and other improvements in how the government is managed, and hashing out plans aimed at tax reform, better budgeting and contracting, and infrastructure investment—all of which can attract bipartisan support if and when those in Washington finally get pushed to act.

Although their work is often frustrating, the worsening status quo seems to energize those who are pushing back. They believe that things have gotten so bad, or will soon get so bad, that the pendulum that throughout American history swung between excess and reform but became stuck at excess in the 1970s, will soon be unstuck. They believe that when Americans reach a level of frustration and anger that is fast approaching, they will overrun the lobbyists and cross over the moats. They are certain that when the country's breakdown touches enough people directly and causes enough damage, the officeholders who depend on those people for their jobs will be forced to act. Some even see President Trump's election, largely powered by a disgusted working class, as evidence of that. All see the new activism following his election as stronger evidence.

They are doing what they do despite developments in America that seem to be galloping in the opposite direction not because they are gluttons for frustration, but because they believe that America can be put back on the right course. In a variety of arenas, the people you will meet here are laying the groundwork for disgust to be channeled into a restoration.

This, then, is the story of how America got here and how America can get back. It is about the overachievers who upended much of the American Dream as they pursued their own, and about how others with equal drive and talent have come forward to restore that flickering dream. The story begins with a well-meaning reform that made the American Dream a reality for people like me, but that, like so many elements of the tailspin, had unintended consequences.

Meritocracy Becomes the New Aristocracy

I was always uncomfortable at Deerfield Academy, because I never felt I belonged. I had ended up there almost as a lark. In 1964, I was a bookworm growing up in Far Rockaway, a working-class section of Queens. One day, I read in a biography of John F. Kennedy that he had gone to something called a prep school, named Choate. None of my teachers at Junior High School 198 had a clue what that meant, but I soon figured out that prep school was like college. You got to go to classes and live on a campus, only you got to go four years earlier, which seemed like a fine idea. The idea soon seemed even better because I discovered that some prep schools offered financial aid.

I toured three of them. First up was Phillips Andover, which I didn't like because the admissions officer actually asked *me*—a straight-A student at JHS 198—whether I thought I could handle the work. I looked at Hotchkiss, which turned me off because I was told that boys on financial aid had to wait on tables in the dining room for those who paid full freight.

Then came Deerfield, in western Massachusetts, where everyone waited on tables and the headmaster, Frank Boyden, told my worried parents, who ran a perpetually struggling liquor store, that his financial aid policy was that they should send him a check every year for whatever they could afford. I didn't know that only about 5 percent of the Deerfield boys were actually given financial aid, just that Boyden made the place seem really egalitarian.

It wasn't. Deerfield has changed, but then it was almost completely a place for well-rounded rich kids. Boyden had only recently decided to tinker with the mix a bit by adding a few scholarship boys, including some Jews like me, and even a few African Americans.

I got the message the first week when one of the kids in our dorm, who lived on Park Avenue, asked where I lived. When I said Queens, it didn't register, so I explained that if he had ever flown out of Kennedy or LaGuardia airports he'd been to Queens. (A relative of his in our class knew where Queens was because his family owned the Mets, who play there.)

A few days later, I failed an exam for the first time ever because our Ancient History teacher had the temerity to give us a quiz on the day's homework with no warning. My classmates mostly came from private schools where spot quizzes were part of the drill; no teacher at 198 would have ever done that.

My clothes weren't as nice and I wasn't nearly as glib or worldly as my classmates seemed to be. A kid sitting in Ancient History laughed in astonishment one morning when I couldn't pronounce Mesopotamia. That was the least of my problems when it came to oral expression. I also had a terrible stutter, which had receded quite a bit after elementary school, but roared back when I got to Deerfield.

The sense of not belonging came to a head about a month into that first term when the proctors in our dorm—one bound for Harvard, the other for Princeton—hosted a doughnuts-and-cider party one afternoon. They began by asking each of us to tell the group where we wanted to go to college. When I stuttered out, "Uh, Yale or Harvard, I guess," the room erupted in laughter.

Three years later, although I still didn't feel like I fit in at Deerfield, my grades had long since recovered from those first weeks because once I knew I could get quizzed, I prepared obsessively. Which is why I found myself sitting in the headmaster's office one afternoon in the fall of my senior year. Boyden had given it over to a man named R. Inslee Clark, Jr., the dean of admissions at Yale. Clark looked over my record and asked me a bunch of questions, most of which, oddly, were about where I had grown up and how I had ended up at Deerfield. (He seemed intrigued by the JFK/Choate serendipity.) Then he paused, looked me in the eye, and asked if I really wanted to go to Yale—if Yale was my first choice. When I said "Yes," Clark's reply was instant: "Then I can promise you that you are in. I will tell Mr.

Boyden that you don't have to apply anywhere else. Just kind of keep it to yourself."

What I didn't know then was that I was part of a revolution being led by Clark, whose nickname was Inky. I was about to become one of what would come to be known as Inky's boys and, later, girls. We were part of a meritocracy revolution that flourished at Yale in the mid-1960s, and had its roots in the development of standardized aptitude tests that colleges began to require in the late 1930s as part of the application process.

Clark had been made admissions director in 1965 by Yale president Kingman Brewster, himself a scion of the old aristocracy (*Mayflower* descendant, Yale College, Harvard Law School). Brewster, a member in good standing of a group of well-heeled progressive Republicans, was determined, he famously explained at a cocktail party, not to continue "to preside over a finishing school on the Long Island Sound." Through the 1950s, Yale had accepted most alumni sons who applied and had otherwise loaded the college with boys from the most prestigious prep schools, despite the fact that they achieved academic honors, such as Phi Beta Kappa, in proportions far lower than the minority who came from public schools. Alumni played a major role in screening applicants and used a scoring sheet that measured "the all-around boy." It even included a checklist of desired physical characteristics.

Alumni interviewing prospective applicants were warned about falling for people like me: As Jerome Karabel recounted in *The Chosen*, an indispensable history of admissions at elite universities, the alumni vetters were urged not to "hesitate to admit a lad with relatively low academic prediction whose personal qualifications seemed outstanding, rather than a much drabber boy with higher scholastic predictions."

With his hiring of Inky Clark, Brewster set out to change that. Clark began by making the Yale admissions team's visits to the top feeder prep schools something other than a glad-handing ritual aimed at keeping the pipeline filled. He stunned and angered officials at perhaps the nation's most select prep school, Andover, when he declared that Yale would no longer take underachievers, even from Andover; finishing in the bottom quarter there would not be enough to be considered by Yale.

For Clark, then, I became something of a two-fer—a way not to anger Deerfield, yet stick to his guns on looking for those drabber but high-achieving boys.

As recounted by Brewster biographer Geoffrey Kabaservice, when Clark and Brewster had presented their plan to the Yale Corporation, the university governing body, which included some of the school's most prominent alumni, one member said, "Let me get down to basics. You're admitting an entirely different class than we're used to. . . . You're talking about Jews and public school graduates as leaders. Look around at this table. These are America's leaders. There are no Jews here. There are no public school graduates here." Brewster's determination, as well as the friendships he enjoyed among the board members, was such that the corporation not only went along with his plan, but approved a policy of need-blind admissions—meaning people like me would be admitted without any consideration of whether they needed financial aid, and would be guaranteed that aid.

In Clark's first year, admissions from the leading prep schools plummeted, while the entering class's SAT scores were the highest in history. Yale alumni howled in protest, and many made good on threats to withhold contributions. However, although alumni sons (and, beginning in 1969, daughters) would continue to be favored, as would athletes, their advantages continued to be reduced, and the trend of lower admission rates of alumni offspring and higher achievement scores in the entering classes continued through the 1960s and 1970s. Yale was not alone. The 1960s were a time of progressive awakening in many arenas, as institutions of all kinds lowered their barriers. Meritocracy was replacing aristocracy. Or was it?

Forty-eight years after Inky Clark gave me my ticket on the meritocracy express in 1967, a professor at Yale Law School (from which I had graduated after completing four years at Yale College) jarred the school's graduation celebration. Daniel Markovits, who specializes in the intersection of law and behavioral economics, told the graduating class that their success getting accepted into, and getting a degree from, the country's most selective law school—long associated with progressive politics and public service—actually marked their entry into a newly entrenched aristocracy that had been snuffing out the American Dream for almost everyone else.

Markovits's speech began with the upbeat observations typical of such occasions. After seconding the dean's declaration that the members of the class of 2015 at the country's most elite law school were "the finest new law graduates in the world," Markovits, a popular teacher who had been selected by the students to be their graduation speaker, reviewed what he called the "rat race" they had won: super-achievement from grade school through college (and, in many cases, rat races even to get into elite grade schools and high schools). That meant, he said, that, "you are sitting here today because you ranked among the top three-tenths of 1 percent of a massive, meritocratic competition.

"But the competition is new," he added, explaining how Kingman Brewster had led the movement that replaced old-boy favoritism with the merit-based contest that they had just won.

Markovits listed all of the benefits—stature, satisfying careers, the ability to have enormous public policy impact, and, of course, the opportunity for great wealth—that winning this "excruciating" competition offered. Then his talk turned darker.

"Elite lawyers' real incomes," he said, "have roughly tripled in the past half-century, which is more than ten times the rate of income growth experienced by the median American. Moreover, this explosion in elite lawyers' incomes is not an eccentric or even isolated phenomenon," he added, offering a sobering picture of how the meritocracy movement had changed the nature of wealth:

> Instead, it fits into a wider pattern of rising elite labor incomes across our economy. You probably know that the share of total national income going to the top 1 percent of earners has roughly doubled in the past three decades. But it is perhaps . . . more surprising still to learn that the top 1 percent of earners, and indeed even the top one-tenth of one percent, today owe fully four-fifths of their total income to labor. That is unprecedented in all of human history: American meritocracy has created a state of affairs in which the richest person out of every thousand overwhelmingly works for a living.

In short, the new aristocracy were those who worked the hardest and smartest, not those who inherited the most.

"Elite lawyers' incomes," he continued, "will place you comfortably above the economic dividing line that comprehensively separates the rich from the rest in an increasingly unequal America."

Then Markovits explained the counterintuitive downside of the new meritocracy—why the new source of wealth might actually be more entrenched than inherited wealth: "Perhaps most critically, your lawyerly skills will finance training your children—through private schools and myriad other enrichments—to thrive in the hyper-competition that you have yourselves, in effect, just won.

"This, then," the professor continued, "is where things stand. We have become a profession and a society constituted by meritocracy. Massively intensified and massively competitive elite training meets massively inflated economic and social rewards to elite work. You, in virtue of sitting here today, belong to the elite—to the new, super-ordinate working class."

Then the professor delivered his gloomy bottom line.

"This structure, whatever its virtues, also imposes enormous costs," he told the class of 2015. "Most obviously, it is a catastrophe for our broader society—for the many (the nearly 99 percent) who are excluded from the increasingly narrow elite.

"Brewster and others embraced meritocracy self-consciously in order to defeat hereditary privilege," he continued, "but although it was once the engine of American social mobility, meritocracy today blocks equality of opportunity. The student bodies at elite colleges once again skew massively towards wealth."

Markovits elaborated in a way that made sense to all the parents and offspring in the audience who had benefited from exactly what he now described: "These facts will shock, as they are designed to do," he said, "but a moment's clear reflection should render them unsurprising and even inevitable. The excess educational investment over and above what middle-class families can provide that children born into a typical one-percenter household receive"—including private school, music or tennis lessons, résumé-building work-study summers abroad, tutoring for the college or law school admissions tests—"is equivalent, economically, to a traditional inheritance of between $5 [million] and $10 million per child. Exceptional cases always exist—as some of you sitting here prove—but in general, children from poor or even middle-class households cannot possibly compete—when they apply to places like Yale—with people who have imbibed this massive, sustained, planned, and practiced investment, from birth or even in the womb. And workers with ordinary training cannot possibly compete—in the labor market—with super-skilled workers possessed of the remarkable training that places like Yale Law School provide.

"American meritocracy has thus become precisely what it was invented to combat," Markovits concluded, "a mechanism for the dynastic transmission of wealth and privilege across generations. Meritocracy now constitutes a modern-day aristocracy, one might even say, purpose-built for a world in which the greatest source of wealth is not land or factories but human capital, the free labor of skilled workers."

If anything, Markovits had understated the problem.

A student survey carried out at Yale Law School in 2012 revealed that, despite the school's need-blind admissions policies and generous financial aid packages, 4 percent of students self-identified as "lower working class," and 8 percent identified as "lower middle class," or within the bottom 40 percent of family incomes. Another 27 percent identified as "middle class." However, half identified as "upper middle class," or within the top 5 percent, and another 11 percent identified as "upper class." That added up to 61 percent coming from families in the top 5 percent and just 12 percent from the bottom 40 percent.

The relative loneliness of those who came from the bottom of the income ladder was such that two years before Markovits's speech a group of Yale Law students had formed a group called First Generation Professionals, whose goal was to push the administration to be more sensitive to issues their more well-heeled classmates, who dominated the student body, didn't have to think about: providing aid to cover travel expenses for job interviews, for example, or offering counseling on how to handle interviews and professionally related social situations.

A member of the Yale Law class that graduated the year after the student survey was taken was J. D. Vance, the author of the 2016 best seller *Hillbilly Elegy*. Markovits's speech seemed to be channeling Vance's book before he wrote it—and before it came to be regarded as a telling chronicle of the class divisions that ailed America in 2016. Vance described Yale as a place where "people could say with a straight face that a surgeon mother and engineer father were middle class," a place so different from the world he came from that when he arrived, "I felt like my spaceship had landed in Oz."

Indeed, almost everyone, according to the student survey, was a product of the kind of educated home that Vance hadn't known and that Markovits had said provides so many advantages: 92 percent reported that one of their parents had a college degree, with 54 percent saying that one parent had a graduate or doctoral degree. Nationally, about a third of American adults have college degrees.

A survey at Harvard College in 2015 examining the demographics of elite undergraduates produced similar results. Although an undergraduate with an annual family income of less than $65,000 pays no tuition at Harvard, just 9.5 percent of the students reported family incomes below $40,000, while 54 percent reported incomes of over $125,000.

Beyond the most exclusive schools, the trend has spread across college campuses generally. In 1970, the college graduation gap between adults over twenty-four who had come from families in the top quarter of family incomes and those from families in the bottom quarter was 34 percent—40 percent versus 6 percent. By 2013 it was 77 percent versus 9 percent.

The richer offspring, drawing on their parents' resources and coaching, have clearly mastered the meritocracy rat race that education leaders like Kingman Brewster and Inky Clark launched in the 1960s as a substitute for the old-boy pipeline.

As for Markovits's more surprising point—that the change in rules that increasingly enable "merit" to outrank old-school ties and other connections has produced a *more* entrenched aristocracy that has led to *more* overall income inequality—there is compelling data that the playing field has, indeed, tilted generally across the population. Much of it is by now familiar because growing income inequality has become a popular political issue. Still, the specifics are stark.

The year 1970 ended a streak of forty-one years (stretching back to 1929, the year of the stock market crash) when middle-class family incomes grew *faster* than upper-class incomes in the U.S. In other words, it was an era in which income inequality was steadily reduced. In 1971, the trend started going the other way and has accelerated (except for a slight pause in 2015). Specifically, in 1928, the top 1 percent accounted for 24 percent of all income. In 1970 the one-percenters' share of the wealth was down to about 9 percent, the result of multiple economic dynamics and government policies, including the New Deal reforms and the post-war growth in the 1950s and 1960s of the country's manufacturing base and, with it, private sector unions. However, by 2007 the one-percenters' share was back up to 24 percent, and except for a brief decline during the Great Recession it has remained at about that level.

Meanwhile, the bottom 90 percent of earners went from sharing 52 percent of all income in 1928 to 68 percent in 1970. That share for the bottom 90 percent started dropping back after 1970. It had fallen to 49 percent by 2012, the first time the share ever dipped below half. It has stayed at about that level or slightly below since. The trend accelerated precipitously in the recovery following the Great Recession because the recovery passed over most of America. Incomes for the top 1 percent rose 31.4 percent from 2009 to 2012, but crept up a barely noticeable .4 percent for the bottom 99 percent. The moats built by those who were largely responsible for the Great Recession, or at least prospered in the run-up to the crash, worked. They survived the damage suffered by everyone else. As a result, a 2016 study by the Stanford University Center on Poverty and Inequality reported that the "U.S. has the highest level of disposable income inequality among rich countries."

In America, the standard answer to concerns about such inequality has always been that unequal results are the trade-off that comes with a vibrant, competitive capitalist system, the saving grace of which is that its vibrancy allows anyone with talent and drive to move up the ladder. In other words, inequality is a snapshot of a whole population that doesn't capture the inspiring moving picture of individuals' income mobility. Yet as the enrollment demographics at the best schools suggest, that, too, has become more a fantasy than a dream for most. A 2016 study by professors at Stanford, Harvard, and Berkeley found that "children's prospects of earning more than their parents have fallen from 90 percent to 50 percent over the past half century."

The *wealth* of the upper class has not grown nearly as fast as annual *earnings*—which is the point Markovits was making when he talked about the greatest source of wealth being "human capital," or talent put to work, rather than land or an inheritance. In terms of income mobility, that makes things worse. For many, inherited wealth is like sand in an hourglass. Either through profligate spending by ne'er-do-wells or the perpetual divisions of the wealth among generations of inheritors, it often dissipates. However, human capital can last, and with all the extra resources offered to its offspring as they begin their competition in the rat race, it can be passed on to those who will be smart enough and work hard enough to protect it.

POWERING THE CASINO ECONOMY

The meritocratic elite that began emerging in the 1960s became the vanguard of what we now call the "knowledge economy"—a world in which brawn (or the investment in and organization of brawn in manufacturing) has increasingly been replaced by brains as the American economic engine. Except for engineers inventing software, the knowledge economy mostly put the new meritocratic elite to work as lawyers, bankers, executives, and consultants creating new ways to trade and bet on stock and other financial instruments, and new ways to rearrange or protect assets, rather than grow them. In that sense, the knowledge economy should probably be called the financial economy—and, given all the betting rather than building involved, perhaps even the casino economy. The rise of the meritocratic elite both drove the rise of the casino economy *and* thrived in it, and then kept expanding to meet its growing demands.

Markovits had told the graduating class that unlike those with landed or inherited wealth, "those with such valuable human capital must comprehend yourselves on instrumental terms. Your own talents, training, and skills—your self-same persons—today constitute your greatest assets, the overwhelmingly dominant source of your wealth and status. To promote your eliteness—to secure your caste," he warned, "you must ruthlessly manage your training and labor." In other words, the new meritocratic elite had to keep working hard, and if they wanted to maximize the "return" on their human capital, they had to work at—and protect—the places that would pay the most for it, which more often than not meant some corner of the casino economy.

This, then, is how meritocracy perversely enhanced entrenchment. A different, more talented group of people were entrenched and more able to staunch income mobility. Those with blue-chip college degrees or degrees from top law or business schools had always gone in large numbers to work at prestige banks, businesses, consultancies, and law firms. Now the ones who flocked there were more likely to be more talented and tougher—because they were more likely to have gotten there through brains and hard work, not connections. They would be better at winning, and better at building moats to protect their winnings.

An old-school Wall Street law firm that, like the Yale of old, had treated its partnership more as an extension of the country club than an assemblage of the best and brightest (and hardest workers) would now hire the "drabber boys," as well as the minorities and the women, who were coming out of the best law schools and who had the most drive and the most talent to create tax shelters, invent new types of financial instruments, engineer corporate mergers, or defend anti-trust or consumer protection claims. If they didn't hire that talent, their competition would, which meant they ultimately would have to do the same, or perish (as some did). As a result, most blue-chip law firms began to open up just as Brewster had opened up Yale.

Anyone who believes in merit and abhors discrimination would see that as progress. However, another result was that these firms became much smarter—and much better able to serve the large corporations that hired them, thereby helping to un-level the playing field.

Markovits explained it this way in a conversation a year and a half after his graduation speech: "The elites have become so skilled and so hardworking that they are able to protect each other better than ever before."

They also now have a better, more defensible story to tell. It is much easier to resent people who made their way up through connections than it is to resent those who get to the top because they work the hardest and jump highest and fastest over the hurdles they face on the way. Conversely, it may be easier for those at the top to feel sure that they belong there, that the system has worked fairly and doesn't need to be tinkered with. A contest open to all comers was held, and they won. A contest was then held for their kids, and they won, too. Isn't it more "fair" to have the winners be people who work hard and are talented, rather than people who inherited landed-wealth stock portfolios, or the right connections? "Fair" or not, if a country that draws its energy and sense of community from a prevailing expectation of upward mobility—the sense that anyone can make it—freezes a new class into safe perches at the top, let alone embeds a new class that has a more ingrained sense that it belongs there, there is a price to be paid.

In September 2015, three months after his speech to the Yale Law graduates, Markovits and economist Ray Fisman published an article in the journal *Science* that suggested that the meritocratic elites, even at a predominantly liberal stronghold like Yale Law School, were no less protective of their positions than their predecessors.

The authors did an experiment comparing two groups: Yale Law students and a sample drawn from what the authors described as a "broad cross section of Americans." Each group was asked to assume that they could distribute a pot of money between themselves and an anonymous other person. The amount of money in the pot would vary based on their choices, so that their distribution method would run along a continuum for outlays that were either more efficient or produced more equality. For example, distributing a dollar to the other person might only cost the first person a dime (making it efficient), but in another scenario, distributing five dollars to the other person might cost three dollars (producing more equality but less efficiency). Although the Yale Law group identified themselves as far more liberal politically than the group of average Americans, the Yale group opted for efficiency over equality much more frequently than the broad-based group.

"This lack of concern about inequality among the elite is not a partisan matter," Markovits and Fisman wrote. "Even when they self-identify as progressive Democrats, elite Americans value equality less highly than their middle-class compatriots." These results, they continued, "suggest that the policy response to rising economic inequality lags so far behind the preferences of ordinary Americans for the simple reason that the elites who make policy—regardless of political party—just don't care much about equality."

Their study was attacked in a *Washington Post* opinion column, headlined "Fisman's and Markovits' Bogus 'Class War'" and published fourteen months before the 2016 presidential voting. Writer David Bernstein, referring to two insurgents who seemed to be picking up steam in the 2016 presidential race during the summer of 2015, described the study as "alleging that the appeal of candidates like Donald Trump and Bernard Sanders can be attributed to a class divide in American political attitudes."

After citing polling data indicating that Americans did not favor wealth redistribution, Bernstein ended his column this way: "Markovits and Fisman conclude that Sanders' and Trump's 'disruptions of elite political control are no flash in the pan, or flings born of summer silliness. They are early skirmishes in a coming class war.' Fortunately, they are almost certainly wrong."

"By the time we thought seriously about answering him, we decided that his last sentence spoke for itself," Markovits later explained.

Markovits and Fisman's study suggesting that even those he described as elite liberals politically were not big on income equality suggests an explanation of a fundamental paradox of the last fifty years in America: That at the same time that the country made such great strides in liberal causes related to democracy and equal rights— women's rights, civil rights, voting rights, LGBT rights—the balance of economic power and opportunity became so unequal.

Looking further at elite lawyers is a good way to see how the growth of the knowledge economy and meritocracy reinforced each other. Until the 1970s, law was a relatively sleepy profession. From 1900 to 1970 the number of lawyers per capita in the U.S. remained about the same, despite the onslaught of new laws and regulations in the Teddy Roosevelt reform era and continuing during the Franklin Roosevelt New Deal. In the 1970s, however, demand for lawyers exploded, the result of legislative and other developments beginning in the 1960s—including corporate mergers and takeovers; a growing interest in tax shelters; new regulations related to consumer products, employment discrimination, worker safety, and the environment; and industry's determination to fight back against the rise of adversaries like Ralph Nader and environmentalist Rachel Carson, the author of *Silent Spring*. In just the 1970s, as the knowledge economy blossomed, the number of lawyers nearly doubled, and then increased by another 50 percent in the 1980s. In terms of dollars generated, by the mid-1980s the legal industry was bigger than steel or textiles, and about the same size as the auto industry. The new lawyers were increasingly concentrated in fast-growing, large law firms that served large corporations and were prepared to pay skyrocketing salaries to attract the best talent.

The competition among these firms to recruit new troops intensified, highlighted in 1986 when the Wall Street firm of Cravath, Swaine & Moore jumped the starting salary for newly minted graduates from $53,000 to $65,000. Cravath's competitors quickly matched what had become the new "going rate." The most established law firms had generally shared the Ivy League's culture of favoring pedigrees and connections, including the old schools' notion that well-rounded young men should even look the part. But even before Kingman Brewster and Inky Clark came to Yale, Cravath—despite boasting a client list as blue-chip as that of any firm in the country—had always been unusual among the white-shoe firms because of its habit of being so talent-hungry that it would occasionally hire brilliant but odd-duck young lawyers who often ended up being among their most successful partners.

Even back in 1968, the firm had caused an uproar on Wall Street when it boosted salaries for starting lawyers from $9,500 to $15,000. The same year, average household income was $7,700. By 2016, the going rate had jumped to $180,000. That year, average household income was $53,657. The incomes of these young lawyers, which had been 23 percent higher than the average family's in 1968, were now 235 percent higher. The elite first-year lawyers, who were in their mid-twenties, had advanced more than ten times as fast as the average family. Their starting incomes also had become 50 percent to 100 percent higher than what was earned by older, experienced lawyers who worked for less prestigious firms or for government, individuals, or consumers.

The talent went where the money was, even at Yale, which had always prided itself on minting public-service-oriented graduates. In 2015, the Yale Law class of 2010 reported that five years after graduation, 58.5 percent were working either at law firms or in businesses, including investment banks, while 34.5 percent were working for the government or doing what the graduates identified as "public interest" work. At another top law school, Columbia, 297 of 413 members of the 2015 graduating class reported the following year that they were working at law firms with 250 or more lawyers.

Among the top firms, stratification accelerated, according to specialties. Hundreds of $1-million-to-$5-million-a-year partners, backed by squadrons of best-and-brightest associates, carved out niches in everything from tax law to Foreign Corrupt Practices Act defense. Reuters reported that in 2013, the Washington offices of just a handful of elite firms had become so dominant in the biggest-league practice of all—appeals to the Supreme Court—that "66 of the 17,000 lawyers who petitioned the Supreme Court succeeded at getting their clients' appeals heard at a remarkable rate." They were six times more likely to get a High Court hearing than all the other lawyers who filed appeals combined. Of those "66 most successful lawyers," Reuters found, "51 worked for law firms that primarily represented corporate interests," and "in cases pitting the interests of customers, employees or other individuals against those of companies, a leading attorney was three times more likely to launch an appeal for business than for an individual."

Writing in the *Boston University Law Review* in 1988, Stanford law professor Robert Gordon described that growing meritocratic arms race as a development akin to the fall of Western civilization: "The decision by Cravath, Swaine and Moore to inflate the salaries of first-year associates, a move instantly imitated by other New York firms and later by firms in other cities, has been one of the most anti-social acts of the bar in recent history," he wrote. "It further devalues public service by widening the gulf—until recently not very large—between starting salaries in private practice and in government and public interest law. It drives impressionable young associates toward consumption patterns and expectations of opulence that will be hard to shake off if they want to change careers."

I played a role in this "anti-social" movement. In 1979, I started a magazine called *The American Lawyer*, which focused on the business of law firms. Although business publications routinely wrote about the ups and downs of General Motors, IBM, or Macy's, *The American Lawyer*'s coverage of the law business was initially condemned by lawyers (and in some circles still is), who preferred to think of themselves as professionals above these crass concerns. This was especially true of partners at the most established firms. They thought of their workplaces as collegial partnerships. Many even took pride that all partners were paid in lockstep according to their seniority at the firm, not according to how much revenue they brought it.

I understood that but also thought of these firms as big, powerful businesses, with intriguing questions lurking behind their uniformly elegant reception areas. Which ones were best managed, or had the most effective strategies for developing new lines of business? Which had the most talent and provided the best client service in which areas of law, and how did they do it? Which ones overcharged and which ones provided good value? I also viewed the law business from the standpoint of my Yale Law School classmates, who had had to decide where they wanted to work without basic information about their potential employers. Which firms had the best litigators, or the best mentors? Which offered the most opportunity to women or minorities? Which were more likely to promote associates to partnership because they were economically healthy and/or valued sharing the wealth more than others? Which had the fairest or most generous bonus systems for young associates? And, yes, which had the most interesting clients and a client base that provided the highest profits for partners?

That last question resulted in *The American Lawyer* launching a special issue every summer, beginning in 1985, in which we deployed reporters to pierce the secrecy of these private partnerships so that the magazine could rank the revenues and average profit taken home by partners at the largest firms. Suddenly, lawyers at each major firm, as well as their clients and prospective recruits, could see how firms that seemed so much alike compared as businesses.

When the first survey was published, I received a call from a former classmate who practiced at a large Los Angeles firm. He was outraged because he—and his wife—had now found out that another classmate who worked at another, seemingly fungible, L.A. firm made about 25 percent more than he did. Until then, they had been perfectly happy with his six-figure income. Not anymore. At that moment, his anger was directed at me, for providing him information that upended at least one aspect of his view of his career. Over time, it would also be directed at his firm—perhaps the management or maybe some laggard partners—for not producing a business that was as profitable as his classmate's.

Journalists take the obvious, if self-serving, position that their job is to provide accurate information about important subjects, and that how people use, or misuse, the information is not their responsibility. But there is no denying that the fallout from this report and those that have followed since *The American Lawyer* and other trade publications was significant and double-edged. The new flow of market information about these businesses made those who ran them more accountable to their partners, their employees, and their clients, but it also transformed the practice of law by the country's most talented lawyers in ways that had significant drawbacks.

True, collegiality had often been a code word for WASP enclave, and the new market pressures forced firms to embrace the new meritocracy, opening them to minorities and women and giving them the incentive to reward talent and hard work. But there was a downside to what Americans instinctively believe is a core value: robust markets made more competitive and efficient, in this case by the introduction of another core value—the free flow of basic market information. Starting with the founding of *The American Lawyer* and still accelerating today, as lawyers began to focus on the business side of their lives, these clubby partnerships became hard-edged businesses. They were roiled by defections, mergers, resentments over allocations of partner shares based on productivity, and even firings of partners. Many cut back on the pro bono work they did and pushed partners and associates to work longer hours, market harder, and in some instances cut ethical corners in order to satisfy the rainmakers in their ranks, who were being recruited by competitors and might jump ship if the firm's profits, and their take, did not continue to grow. That meant the emphasis had to be on serving those clients who could pay the most.

In fact, if law was going to become so much like a business, it became inevitable that some of the best and brightest were soon leaving their high-pressure legal jobs and going to equally stressful jobs in even more lucrative fields, where they could maximize their human capital still more. "No wonder lawyers exposed to such regimes are leaving them for investment banking and other businesses," Professor Gordon wrote. These refugees, along with thousands of the lawyers they left behind, were becoming the meritocracy that would turn the knowledge economy into the casino economy. They would become the troops who would transform America into a place where creating new financial instruments and making deals to move assets around would increasingly replace making things. They would thrive as they enabled the tail to wag the dog. Legal and financial engineering, once meant to be instruments for gathering and organizing the capital necessary for the research, development, and production of goods, itself became the product.

REVERSING THE TIDE

Fortified by the gloss of a narrative that features the smartest and hardest workers winning the race to the top and then, as devoted parents able to help their offspring win the same race, the position of the meritocratic aristocracy seems irreversible. Universities have made progress when it comes to enrolling more minorities and women, but, as Markovits asserted, not much when it comes to diversifying family incomes.

But there are exceptions.

Until Anthony Marx became president of Amherst College in 2003, he had never run anything in higher education. He hadn't even chaired the political science department at Columbia, where he taught. Yet Marx, who was forty-four at the time, did have a vision, one that would not have dawned on a more conventional university administrator. It was, he explained, born of his work in the 1980s as a founder of a secondary school in South Africa aimed at preparing blacks for college. "The results for these kids in South Africa with just one year, which is all we gave them, were astonishing," he said. "These were people who were purposefully uneducated. They were deliberately stopped from advancing, but at our great colleges and universities, another group—the economically disadvantaged—were simply neglected. Which is not much better, when you think about it."

Marx, who grew up in the northwest corner of Manhattan and went to the highly competitive Bronx High School of Science, did not take his initial interview with the Amherst board's presidential search committee seriously: "I didn't think I had a chance. I had no experience. I hadn't even gone to Amherst"—he had graduated from Yale and had a master's and PhD from Princeton—"and had no other connection to the school. They probably just had to interview a bunch of people before picking whoever they had in mind."

As a result, he recalled, "I decided to tell them what I really thought. . . . That Amherst was great, but that education should be about distance traveled, not gilding the lily by giving more advantages to those who already had lots of them. Ever since South Africa," he explained, "that has been my lodestar, getting education to those who need it the most."

It is an important distinction. All high-quality colleges and universities had financial aid programs aimed at diversifying their classes and giving some non-wealthy students opportunity. What Marx was talking about, however, was *reorienting Amherst to aim its resources at those who could benefit from them the most.* At the time, about 8 percent of Amherst students were in the low- and lower-middle-class income categories that qualified them for federal aid under the Pell Grant program or similar programs, even though about half of American families fell into that income category.

Marx told the committee that if he got the job, he wanted to change the demographics of the school, with more aggressive financial aid and more aggressive recruiting. Other than athletes, Amherst—an elite college of 1,800 students that is one of the most selective in the world—had never had to do recruiting. It would have to start, Marx told the committee, if it wanted to fulfill what he considered to be its true mission.

On that score, Marx came prepared. He had found Amherst's original charter, written in 1821, which declared that the school's purpose was to "educate indigent young men." "The board wasn't aware of that," he recalled, but they were intrigued, especially board chair Amos Hostetter, Jr. Hostetter is a cable industry pioneer who founded Boston-based Continental Cablevision. Known as one of the nice guys in what began as a rough-and-tumble industry, he ended up with more than $2 billion when he sold his business in the 1990s. Hostetter, said Marx, "clearly believed that when you're at the top of your game, as Amherst was, that's the time to try to do more."

"I told them that they were not being true to the Amherst dream, and that not being true to that vision makes the country feel broken to me, because we are creating an unjust leadership class," Marx continued, sitting at a conference table in an elegantly paneled, art- and book-lined office on the second floor of the New York Public Library, where he became president in 2011. "But that wasn't the only reason," he added. "I'm an educator, and I thought that the way to really

improve education at Amherst was to have the son or daughter of a
janitor talking to the son or daughter of a CEO in the dining room,
in a dorm, or in a history or politics class. Education is all about those
conversations."

Once he got the job, Marx reallocated resources. At Amherst—
whose endowment is one of the largest per student in the world—that
was not as challenging as it would be elsewhere. Still, there was grousing about funds redirected from a planned parking lot addition and
another athletic field. Potential complaints from alumni that more
students from low-income families would mean fewer places for
their children were eased by the fact that at the same time the school
planned to increase overall enrollment from 1,600 to 1,800.

The new money required more than additional financial aid. As
noted earlier, Harvard charges no student anything, even by way of
loans, if family income is below $65,000, yet enrolls few economically
disadvantaged students. The problem is that economically disadvantaged but high-achieving high school students don't know they can
attend for free. Most often, they enroll at the local state university,
thinking that the $10,000 a year they might have to pay (or maybe
less if they get scholarships) is a bargain, even though they could go to
Harvard (or Yale or Princeton and other top schools that have similar
aid policies) for free, and often receive aid for books, travel, and other
expenses, too. Low-income students that the best schools do manage
to enroll typically live in areas, principally major cities, where they go
to school with other students who are more sophisticated about the
college admissions process, and where there are guidance counselors
who can steer them to the most promising choices.

"We knew we had to go out to places we hadn't gone to," Marx
recalled, "and we had to get our alumni and students who came from
those places or knew people there to spread the word. I decided I
was going to throw the kitchen sink at it." He hired a consulting firm
to help with recruiting. Instead of using what he calls "make-work"
campus jobs aimed at giving semester-time income to students who
needed it, "we put them to work as mentors, by phone and email, to
high school kids we were trying to recruit. . . . One kid even got his
mother to call the skeptical mother of the kid he was mentoring, who
had seen our sticker price, to tell her that, yes, he could really come
here for free."

Marx even spread the word to the nation's two-year community colleges. "If we took twenty transfers from the million—literally a million—community college graduates, imagine how selective we could be," he explained. The grade point averages of those coming from community colleges ended up actually being higher than Amherst's overall average grades.

Were the low-income recruits given special advantages when it came to grades or board scores? "We didn't have to," Marx said. "In fact, we became more selective. Our SAT scores went up." However, Marx added, "We did acknowledge that it was just as impressive, if not more so, that a kid had worked five hours a day at the 7-Eleven during high school than that a kid had been flown by his parents to the Dominican Republic for a week one summer to help build houses."

The bottom line: When Marx left Amherst in 2011, 24 percent of the student body came from families with incomes low enough to qualify for Pell Grants, and the number has continued at that level or a bit higher as the word has continued to spread, and as his successor, Carolyn Martin, has continued the program. These 24 percent have done as well or better than their classmates, in part because Amherst established discussion forums and other programs to help them adjust to a culture that was second nature to their more well-to-do classmates. At the same time, Marx said, alumni support increased because "some felt they were now giving to a real philanthropy instead of just their old school."

Another relatively small but elite college—Vassar, in Poughkeepsie, New York—has followed Amherst's lead, with the same good results.

Can larger elite schools, like Yale or Harvard—which would have to find three or four times as many underprivileged, high-achieving high school students as Amherst does to match Amherst's percentage—do the same? They both have said they are trying, but they are not succeeding, in part because they continue to concentrate their efforts in the same urban areas where they can most efficiently reach potential targets, thereby creating a situation in which the same schools compete for a limited pool of prospects.

The median family income of a Yale College student was $192,600 in 2016, placing that median family in the top 18 percent of earners. (At Amherst, it was $158,200, putting that family in the top 22 percent.)

At Yale, 16 percent of the class admitted in 2017 were considered to be in the poor or lower-middle-class categories qualifying them for Pell or similar grants.

Yale admissions dean Jeremiah Quinlan said that his goal was to get the Pell Grant number to 20 percent, by continuing to use outreach programs. The efforts include, he said, 150 student "ambassadors" who reach back to their old high schools to encourage applicants, twenty thousand postcards targeted at high-performing, low-income students, and recruiting trips to urban areas. ("We can't go everywhere," Quinlan said.) He estimated that Yale spends "about a million dollars" on these efforts, on flying in applicants for visits, and on pre-freshman summer programs designed to acclimate low-income students to life at Yale. "At 20 percent, we'd be at the top of the Ivy League, which is my goal," Quinlan said.

Asked why he doesn't think he can reach Amherst's level of lower-income enrollment, which by 2017 was just over 24 percent (and still represented only about half of the percentage of American families in that income group), Quinlan said, "Amherst obviously feels that they can extend themselves to these students in a way that we can't, given all the other pressures on our process."

"We thought everyone would follow us," said Marx, "but the biggest brands didn't. I guess they know they have a great brand and are inclined to not risk it." One big brand, however, has followed Amherst's lead. Beginning in 2005, Princeton embarked on a campaign similar to the one Marx initiated, and, according to *The Washington Post*, a dozen years later the percentage of students at Princeton eligible for Pell Grants had climbed from 7 percent to 22 percent.

A NON-ELITE MOBILITY ENGINE

José Talon was not recruited by Yale, Princeton, or Amherst. Instead, although his journey had started in South America, he was lured into pursuing the American dream by a college in New York City that was a subway ride away. It is a school that has been an engine of American economic mobility for nearly 150 years, and that offers the same model now that it did then for how people can be given the tools to pull themselves up and make their way into an otherwise entrenched meritocracy. There is no excuse for other public universities not to be provided the resources and leadership to enable them to follow the same model.

When I met him in the spring of 2017, Talon was a senior in college. Six years before, having just come to the United States from Colombia, he could not speak a word of English. Sitting in a T-shirt and jeans in a windowless conference room at his college, he explained—in flawless English—that after graduation in a month he would be starting as an $85,000-a-year investment banker at the New York office of the Royal Bank of Canada. He landed the job after completing successful summer internships at Citibank and Goldman Sachs, where he worked, he said, on "trade and treasury solutions." Talon was planning to move out of the apartment he shares with his mother in Queens, but, he said, "I'll help her pay the rent, and help my sister with rent, too."

Talon was about to graduate from Bernard M. Baruch College, whose bricks-and-mortar facilities, squeezed onto Lexington Avenue from Twenty-second to Twenty-fourth Streets in Manhattan, are a world away from the movie-set Amherst campus in western Massachusetts. Sitting in the middle of the traffic-choked, eastern end of New York's Flatiron District, Baruch's main building, called the Vertical Campus, is a seventeen-floor structure, fourteen above ground and three below. It was built in 2001 to supplement three other Baruch outposts a block or two away, all 50 to 175 years old. Together, these inelegant buildings, barely distinguishable from a hulking, aging post office terminal sitting among them, serve ten times the number of students enrolled at Amherst.

Founded in 1874 as the Free Academy, the school became part of the City University of New York system in 1919, and was later named after Bernard Baruch, the financier and adviser to Presidents Woodrow Wilson and Franklin Roosevelt. On any given day or evening, the Vertical Campus's lobby and escalator teem with young people, who speak 130 different languages. There are 18,000 Baruch students, 15,000 undergraduates and about 3,000 in the graduate schools. Like Talon, all but about 300 are commuters. Like Talon, 85 percent hold part-time jobs. (He said he drove a cab.) Like Talon, about two thirds are enrolled in the school's business programs.

Talon had transferred to Baruch after two years at the Borough of Manhattan Community College, which is where, he said, "I taught myself English, and started to understand how things worked. I didn't even know what an SAT was." When he told fellow summer interns at Citibank—"a lot of Ivy League types"—that he had gone to BMCC, they asked him where it was, having no idea that it was almost next door to the Citi office tower where they worked, in Manhattan's Tribeca district. "It was a little intimidating to be with them at first," he said, "but I learned to fit in."

Sitting across from Talon, along with four of his other classmates, was Alexis Yam, a Baruch junior who also lives in Queens with her parents. She worked all four years during high school because her father, a Cambodian Khmer Rouge refugee, and her mother, from Burma, had lost their jobs during the Great Recession. Yam was about to spend her summer as a financial analyst at JPMorgan, where she expected to work following her 2018 graduation.

She told me she was interested in public finance and community development banking. She said it quietly, so much so that she seemed a bit shy to be trying to break into top-tier banking. Yet it turned out that Yam was so interested in her chosen specialties—and so un-shy when it came to her career—that she had spent months during the school year trying to find people who worked in those fields. She would email them, cold, via LinkedIn, to explain who she was and ask if she could meet for coffee to discuss their careers and get advice. Yam ended up arranging "thirty or forty meetings or sometimes phone calls," she said. "I feel like I know a lot now."

Once she makes enough money in banking, Yam said, she hopes to start or work at a non-profit, "so that I can give back."

"I'd rather stay in banking and be the person who donates money; I didn't come to America at seventeen and struggle like this to end up making $40,000 or $50,000 a year," José Talon interjected.

A third student, senior Jacob Jusupov, had worked summers as a lifeguard in Rockaway Beach, Queens, and during the school year as a salesman in Manhattan's diamond district. He was on his way to Cardozo Law School, having been given a full scholarship as part of Cardozo's program to fortify its ratings by recruiting applicants with exceptionally high scores on the law boards. Because the Baruch career development office had put him in contact with an alumnus who is a partner at Cravath, Swaine & Moore—the elite Wall Street firm that has traditionally set the "going rate" for high starting salaries—Jusupov hoped to practice corporate law there when he graduates.

The average family income of students entering Baruch in 2017 was $40,000 (or about a fourth of the Amherst families' incomes), with about a third having incomes at or below the poverty line, like the Yam, Talon, and Jusupov families. Fifty-one percent of the Baruch undergraduates, or more than 7,500, come from families with incomes of $40,000 or less.

"We have one of the lowest average family incomes of any school in the country," said Baruch president Mitchel Wallerstein, a former assistant defense secretary in the Clinton administration who came to Baruch in 2010 after serving as dean of the Maxwell School of Citizenship and Public Affairs at Syracuse University.

The average starting salary of the 85 percent of the Baruch 2016 graduating class who reported having jobs six months after leaving school was $50,100. "They will be earning more on their first day than their parents ever earned," said Wallerstein. "It's life-changing for them, and for their families."

Although the school has a liberal arts program, Baruch is much less about Shakespeare or Nietzsche than it is about accounting or currency trading. Wallerstein recalled that at Dartmouth, where he went to college, "the administration never worried a bit about what jobs students would get. That's not what the place was about. And it was like it was preordained that everyone would end up okay. Here, that is pretty much all we worry about."

"People who work here really feel like they are doing something important; we are moving people into the middle class or higher," said Mary Gorman, a Baruch vice president who runs the school's admissions and financial aid programs. "It's what I feel, and it's what I see even in the administrative staff. They see their sons and daughters when they look at these students."

"Historically, Baruch has always been the gateway to a different life," explained Wallerstein. "Only now the ethnicities are different. The school used to have many more Jews a hundred years ago. The backgrounds today are different, but the desire to succeed is identical." In 2017, Baruch was about 41 percent Asian, 32 percent white, 17 percent Hispanic, and 11.5 percent African American. Ninety percent came from New York State, most of whom lived in New York City's five boroughs.

For New York State students, the tuition was $6,600 for the two-semester school year, and that can be reduced to zero for those with

the most financial need. Because the cost is so low and the job placement rate so high, Baruch is one of the most selective public colleges
in the country. Twenty-five thousand students applied in 2017, and
7,000, or 28 percent, were admitted, with 1,500 enrolling. Many of
the applicants are transfers from New York's two-year community colleges. Seventy percent of those who enroll graduate within six years,
a success rate that is well above the 59 percent average in American
higher education, and most graduate with little or no loans to pay.

Although as Wallerstein pointed out, Baruch has a history of being
a gateway into the middle class, in recent years it has done much more
to get its students ready to ride the escalator. Many public colleges
and universities enroll large numbers of poor and lower-middle-class
families, but few succeed the way Baruch does in propelling so many
so far.

Like the handful of expensive private colleges and universities,
such as Amherst, that have lately made an effort to find economically deprived students who can meet their high admission standards
and earn a prestige degree, Baruch is selective, too, though nowhere
near as selective as Amherst, whose students have higher SAT scores,
and which admits 14 percent of applicants. However, by nurturing so
many thousands of high-achieving but admittedly less stellar students
(at least in terms of credentials derived from SAT scores), Baruch is
producing a flood of upward-bound young Americans.

True, many Baruch graduates start out and even end up in relatively average corners of the middle class—lower-level accounting
jobs or back-office work at the investment banks. That is why the
average starting income is only $50,100 in a group where many, like
José Talon and Alexis Yam, start out earning so much more. However,
that, too, has changed for the better in the last decade, said Wallerstein. As with Talon and Yam, Baruch has pushed increasingly large
numbers of its students into front-office jobs.

It hasn't happened by accident or just with pep talks urging them
to reach high (although there is quite a bit of that). The school has
developed a menu of programs that leaves little to chance and that
offers a road map for how more higher education institutions can
create a new kind of meritocracy that is not nearly as generationally
entrenched:

- There are classes on résumé writing and what the school calls "building brand."

- The school keeps closets full of suits for the men and business attire for the women, so that they can look the part when they have interviews.

- A series of workshops brings speakers, often alumni, to the school to talk to students about different industries.

- A staff of eleven counselors runs fifteen to twenty workshops a week during the school year to teach students what Ellen Stein, the head of the career development center, described as the "soft skills. We call it, 'Small talk, big deal.' How do you start a conversation at a cocktail party? What utensils do you use at a lunch? What is the bread plate for? How do you stay up on current events? What kinds of political topics should you maybe avoid? How do you network?"

- Students do rounds of mock interviews with counselors to go over how to present themselves, and do online mock interviews to critique each other.

- Outstanding freshmen are targeted for a "Peers for Careers" program beginning in their sophomore year. After thirty-one hours of training they become peer counselors for other students, helping them through mock interviews, résumé writing, and still more "soft skills" training.

- A Passport to Partnership tract guides the large cohort of students enrolled in Baruch's accounting programs.

- A pre-law program channels aspiring lawyers into special classes and visits to law schools and law firms, and provides a lawyer-mentor for each participant.

- A financial leadership program targets high-performing juniors who want to be bankers. They get an array of special services, including training in financial software, advanced accounting, financial modeling and analysis, presentation skills, and access to mentors and potential Wall Street employers. In 2016, all of the twenty-two graduating students in this program went to front-office jobs at investment banks, according to Stein, including one whose mother worked on the overnight cleaning crew at the bank that hired him.

- A real-time trading center (named for a donor-graduate who went on to become the chief financial officer of Time Warner) provides a simulated stock trading floor, equipped with stock tickers and terminals. Students go there to do the same kind of modeling and analysis of real-time data that they would do at what they hope will be their first jobs. "I want to work at a hedge fund," said Miriam, who was sitting at a terminal practicing making a projection using Bloomberg's advanced data analytics.

- A special program for the poorest incoming students, typically those whose families are on welfare, offers tutoring and workshops in study skills, time management, and oral and written presentations. "It turns out," says career services head Stein, "that they end up with higher grades than the average here."

- A heavily trafficked website (347,000 log-ons during the 2016–17 school year) catalogues and schedules these programs, and offers a searchable database of coming job fairs, interviews, and other opportunities, as well as information about alumni mentors and other resources.

In all, Baruch spends approximately $2 million of its $140 million annual budget on these and other programs devoted to getting its students jobs, a proportion of its overall budget that dwarfs the resources devoted to the same activities by any college or university budget I have ever looked at. "Everything we do," explained president Wallerstein, "is aimed at giving our students the resources and skills to get in front of the right people. The other half of it is that once they do, these employers see that they are hungrier—85 percent have worked while going to school. So, they really do want to recruit them."

According to data compiled in 2017 by *The New York Times* for its "Upshot" column, 79 percent of the students at Baruch whose families were in the bottom fifth of income when they enrolled ended up in the top three fifths of income by the time they reached their mid-thirties. Eight other state schools, such as the University of California at Irvine—which, with 31,000 students, is almost double Baruch's size and has the same percentage of low-income enrollees—had upward mobility levels equal to or slightly higher than Baruch's. They achieve it by deploying programs similar to Baruch's but geared to the school's particular geographic and economic orientation. UC Irvine has seventeen different types of workshops, including "Tech Interviewing Techniques," aimed at boosting students into the high-tech economy.

Breaking the entrenched meritocracy of the kind Professor Markovits decried at Yale is possible. It takes real resources and the unwavering use of them that go beyond complaining about how difficult it is to offer mobility in the face of so many applicants entering the race with the kinds of family-based advantages Markovits pinpointed. As schools like UC Irvine or Baruch face increasing—and appallingly counterproductive—pressure from state budget cutbacks, it would make sense for foundations and philanthropists who profess to be worried about equal access to the American Dream to direct resources toward them, rather than to already heavily endowed elite institutions. And they could do much more to support other large, public universities with funds aimed at replicating the efforts of those schools that are un-stalling the income mobility that was once so much a part of the American narrative.

As for those elite schools, they could follow Amherst's example and take it still further. Rather than taking donor money for another new building or esoteric academic program with the donor's name on it, they could convince a wealthy patron or two to fund an opportunity program that maximizes the reach of their already generous financial aid packages. They could spend much more on professional staff and recruiters to lure more qualified applicants from among the disadvantaged. They could market themselves far more aggressively through social media and other avenues, so that top students would be told, and reminded, that they could attend Harvard or Yale for free. They could even discount applicants' SAT scores based on whether they

assume the applicant had access to test preparation coaching (something many schools already do tacitly).

Amherst and Baruch demonstrate that meritocracy can still be
a driver of income mobility rather than a bulwark against it. The
fact that they are exceptions, however, is emblematic of the hole the
country has dug for itself when it comes to keeping the American
Dream alive. The unavoidable truth is that as a group my generation
of meritocrats became the creators and enablers of a new American
economy that widened the gaps between the have-a-lots and everyone else. Worse, this is one of those problems that is self-reinforcing.
The more the winners in the merit contest win, the more they can
feed their perfectly understandable instinct to make sure that their
offspring get the tools to win, too.

Breaking the cycle is possible, but it will not be easy.

CHAPTER 3

Casino Country

The rise of the meritocracy came at a time when the American economy was fundamentally changing. The upheaval was sparked by an alluring new economic theory that swept through Wall Street and corporate boardrooms in the 1970s. In the nearly fifty years since, it has reigned as the business world's mantra for justifying a dizzying array of legal and financial engineering that would be performed by the new wave of meritocrats, who would be celebrated, and rewarded, as brilliant innovators even as their work undermined the capacity of the country to produce economic security for average Americans.

In a hallway at the Aspen Institute's New York office there is a blowup of a *New Yorker* cartoon published in 2012. A man in a tattered suit and tie sits cross-legged, in the dirt, with his three children around a makeshift fire in the dark. A dust-filled skyline of half-collapsed buildings looms in the background. It looks like a scene from a disaster movie.

"Yes, the planet got destroyed," the man says to the children. "But for one beautiful moment we created a lot of value for shareholders."

The poster hangs outside the office of Judith Samuelson, a former banker who runs Aspen's Business & Society program, which since 2016 has included the American Prosperity Project. Behind the innocuous name is an agenda aimed at persuading the business community to reverse the dominating narrative of the last fifty years in finance and commerce—what Samuelson calls "the disease of short-termism that is destroying the American economy." For Samuelson and a growing collection of high-powered business sector leaders who have joined the cause in recent years, "short-termism" is defined as worrying about instant gratification for shareholders at the expense of everything else. Too much focus on the day-to-day price of their company's stock forces corporate executives to give short shrift to the long-term interests of the enterprise, underpay or underemploy their workforces, shortchange customers by skimping on product quality, and ignore what Samuelson calls "key externalities," such as the environmental damage that their companies might cause. "The era of shareholder primacy has to end," she argues.

Nobel laureate economist Milton Friedman, who died in 2006, would spin in his grave if he thought arguments like that, especially the concern for those "externalities," were picking up steam. Friedman—the champion of extreme deregulation and the free market privatization of longtime governmental functions, such as education—famously wrote an article in *The New York Times Magazine* in 1970 declaring that "The social responsibility of business is to increase its profits." The management of a corporation, he argued, worked for its shareholders and only its shareholders. If managers paid attention to that responsibility, and only that responsibility, the free market would function in a way that made everyone better off.

Friedman's manifesto could not have come at a better time to make a splash in the business community. Corporations were under fire from consumer advocates and environmentalists, among others, to be more socially responsible. They were also coping with high inflation and sagging profits. Adding to Wall Street's frustration was that many large corporations were buying up other companies and becoming conglomerates that gave the executives bigger businesses to run (and therefore bigger paychecks to run them), but were not producing better returns for shareholders.

There was impeccable logic behind Friedman's idea—and even a seemingly unassailable label that could be attached to it: shareholder democracy. Corporations are owned by shareholders, and shareholders are entitled to managements that are always working to maximize the price of their shares. As Friedman saw it, the focus on stock values that Aspen's Samuelson condemns as short-termism was the essence of shareholder democracy—the ability and willingness of shareholders to demand that the executives working for them perform, and to have the right to fire the managers or even sell their stock if they don't.

Friedman's shareholder rights battle cry soon picked up what became an unstoppable academic gloss. In 1974, Michael Jensen, a thirty-four-year-old economist who was a disciple of Friedman's, began circulating an article among scholars and business leaders that when published with coauthor William Meckling in 1976 would be titled, "Theory of the Firm: Managerial Behavior, Agency Costs and Ownership Structure."

Using seventy-seven pages of jargon and algebraic equations that one would expect from the *Journal of Financial Economics,* where their article appeared, the authors wrote that managers are mere "agents" of the shareholder-owners, but that as agents, rather than owners, they will often have different incentives than the owners do. They might want to make deals to buy companies that expand their empires but do not produce the best returns for the shareholders. Or they might be inclined to overspend on perks or staff, or invest in half-baked ideas. To minimize the cost of monitoring or otherwise controlling these agents, or the cost of them not acting in the shareholders' interests, the shareholders should try to align the agents' incentives with the owners. The way to do that, their monograph explained, was to tie the compensation of the agents as directly as possible to the shareholders' return on their investment in the shares. Therefore, managers should be compensated with stock or stock options rather than simply with salaries and vaguely calibrated bonuses.

The Jensen-Meckling article was widely praised in other academic journals and business publications. As it swept through consulting firms, business schools, and executive suites, its message became the new great thing in business strategy. Let managers live or die by their stock price, and all would be good.

Jensen, who was soon recruited to teach at the Harvard Business School, and Meckling followed up with a paper warning that the survival of corporations was threatened by government attempts to force them to pay attention to factors other than the shareholders' return. "Large corporations today," they wrote,

are being forced by law and by threat of law (euphemisti-
cally called social responsibility) to serve as a vehicle for
effecting almost any social reform which happens to take
someone's fancy—discrimination, poverty, training, safety,
pollution, etc. . . . . Corporations can, in the long run, behave
in a "socially responsible" way only to a very limited extent.
When it becomes clear that "socially responsible" behavior is
abrogating the rights of the owners, the values of corporate
ownership claims will fall (as they have) and corporations will
be unable to raise new capital, or will be able to raise it only
at very high costs.

There has always been an inherent tension in societies that are politically democratic and economically capitalist. The former is based on
equality; the latter is fueled by the participants' dreams of accruing
more wealth than the other guy. Maintaining political equality in a
land of wealth inequality involves a delicate balance. If the forces of
political equality prevail so totally that they do too much to equalize
wealth, such as with confiscatory taxes, the incentives and energy of a
capitalist system are eroded. If wealth inequality gets too extreme, the
power of the wealthy can be deployed to erode democracy.

The new focus on shareholder wealth at the expense, literally, of
everything else a corporation could do began a long process of upsetting the balance that had allowed democracy and capitalism to coexist in a way that satisfied most Americans. Shareholder democracy
turned out to be a threat to actual democracy.

The Jensen-Meckling articles came at a time when the nature
of stock ownership itself was changing radically, in a way that would
feed off of and accelerate what was about to become managers' obsession with their companies' stock price as the determinator of their
compensation.

This preoccupation was new. From the time the New York Stock
Exchange was formed in 1792 through the first half of the twentieth
century, companies typically offered stock in order to pool a founding
family's stake with investments from outsiders, who, like the founders, were usually players in the Wall Street community. The goal was
to solidify the company's capital base and use it to expand into new
markets or develop new products.

Companies could only begin offering stock on the exchange once they had established clear, steady records of profitability, usually over a decade or more. (General Electric, which sprang from a series of profitable electric companies founded by Thomas Edison beginning in 1878, did not go public until 1892.) The investment was meant to pay steady dividends while allowing the business to grow and the stock to rise based on that growth. It was a bet on the long-term value of the company, not the short-term price of the stock.

In the early 1970s, the public markets changed, sparked by the creation of the NASDAQ stock market in 1971. Smaller companies, often start-ups, had once been limited to raising money through stock offerings on a more closed over-the-counter market, involving one-on-one sales. The opening of the NASDAQ—enabled by advances in information technology that facilitated fast-paced trading of stocks around the world, and motivated by the rocketing fortunes of a few of the earliest start-up tech companies—allowed these smaller companies to go public with little revenue and often no profits. A NASDAQ listing offered founders and their earliest employees the possibility of striking it rich by cashing out early grants of stock or stock options, or at least establishing a public, liquid market value for those grants.

Instead of investing based on the expected earnings of established companies, the NASDAQ was all about a more binary bet on the stocks themselves—not just on whether the nascent businesses they represented would make it or not, but on whether enough people would expect them to make it. Thus someone could make a successful short-term bet that the stock would go up based on others' expectations.

All of this was happening at the same time that pension funds—a perk initiated in the 1950s and 1960s for private sector employees and then for public employees—began to accumulate large pools of money. Those funds needed to be invested wisely so that there would be enough money to pay out the defined monthly benefits specified in the employees' contracts when the workers retired.

In 1978, money began accumulating still faster in pension funds because a new provision of the tax law, 401(k), allowed employers and employees to contribute jointly to tax-exempt pension funds that would pay out based on how much money these funds earned from investments. So-called Keogh plans were also added, which allowed the self-employed to set aside tax-exempt funds for pensions. In 1960,

$86 billion was held by pension funds. In 1980, $1.03 trillion was sitting in pension funds available to be invested. In 2003 there was $11.4 trillion, including $4.7 trillion in those 401(k) and Keogh funds. By 2017, there was $26 trillion set aside in pension funds. In 1950, institutional investors, such as pension funds, owned about 6 percent of the stock in the largest corporations. In 2009, they would own 73 percent.

Those who controlled the funds, including the hedge funds and mutual funds that served the pension funds that did not invest on their own, cared less about the long-term success of the companies whose stocks they held than about whether, when the prices of the stocks they had picked were tallied every quarter, they would look better or worse than their competitors or even the other stock-pickers sitting next to them in their fund's office. They, too, were in it for the short term.

The change was revolutionary. In 1960, stock was held by its owner for an average of eight years and four months. In 1980, the average was two years, nine months. In 2016 the average was four months, and high-frequency, split-second trading of stocks, often done by quantitative hedge funds—another creation of the knowledge economy, which buy and sell stocks based on algorithms—was estimated to account for roughly half of all stock trades.

If shareholders were now in it for the short term, so, too, were the managers of the shareholders' companies. Their compensation increasingly depended, Jensen-style, on the quarterly or annual increase in the stock price. That in turn was typically based on a multiple of the company's quarterly or annual earnings, not on whether the company was making investments that might hurt those earnings in the short term but were sensible, necessary long-term investments.

Yet amid high inflation and an economy that was no longer booming as it had in the late 1960s, stock prices in the 1970s for anything other than the most glamorous go-go start-ups were generally stagnant. In response, a new brigade of lawyers and bankers emerged to hold managers accountable. They did it not only by following Jensen's doctrine and making their compensation rise or fall with the stock price, but also by inventing ways to use shareholder democracy to achieve the ultimate in accountability: throwing managers out of their jobs and replacing them with those who would more single-mindedly boost the short-term price of the stock.

The result would be the emergence of an economy where the most money was to be made not by building companies but by deploying thousands of the smartest knowledge workers of the new meritocracy to engineer new ways to rearrange who owned them and create new forms of debt and other financial instruments so that shareholders might score a quick win.

THE TAKEOVER FIGHTER

Joseph Flom was a pioneering soldier of the meritocracy. Long before meritocracy became the norm two decades later, Flom—short, obese, the son of struggling Jewish immigrants—talked his way into the Harvard Law School class of 1948. He didn't have a college degree because he had left night school at City College to join the Army, but he persuaded Harvard with an impassioned letter emphasizing his drive to be a lawyer and citing his stellar record at the selective New York City high school he had attended. He followed up the letter, he later explained, "by making a huge pain in the ass out of myself."

At Harvard, Flom ranked near the top of his class, made Law Review, and was regarded as a genuine, if odd, genius by his professors and classmates. Yet after graduation, no Wall Street firms offered him a job. He did not fit the mold. Until his death in 2011, it was something he resented and still talked about. Flom eventually found work helping three scrappy lawyers at a firm that handled whatever came their way. By the 1960s, he had developed a fascination with something called proxy fights—battles over the control of corporations, usually confined at the time to second- or third-tier companies—and made it his specialty.

These were the first contests for corporate control rooted in what would become the shareholder democracy movement. An investor would buy shares in a public company that he had targeted and then, guided by Flom, lodge a public campaign to get the other shareholders to give their proxies to him so that he could have enough votes to remove the incumbent board and its chosen executives. He would replace them with people who, he promised, would run the company better, align executive compensation with the stock price the way the Jensen doctrine dictated, and thereby boost the stock.

The battles were not polite. The raiders attacked the incumbents mercilessly, and the incumbents fought back by attacking the reputations and integrity of the raiders. Private investigators and public relations firms were key members of the fight teams. Cigar-chomping Joe Flom was the quarterback—the top strategist, as well as the obsessed, down-in-the-weeds expert on the applicable, arcane securities laws. He relished the fight, which lawyers from more prestigious firms regarded as occupying an underbelly of corporate law far beneath them.

Flom and proxy fights perked along, largely under the radar, until 1968, when a change in federal securities laws codified new rules to govern what proxy raiders could do. Rather than curb the practice, the fact that the new law acknowledged it and provided legal guidelines for engaging in the battle began to make it more respectable. "That was like the starting gun at a horse race," Flom recalled.

At the same time, Flom started tinkering with a new strategy, which came to be called a tender offer. Rather than have his clients buy a sizable but minority stake in a company and then seek enough proxies to gain a majority of the shareholders' votes, he would get his clients to raise enough cash—typically by arranging large amounts of debt, which Flom would help negotiate—to make a public offer to shareholders to buy their stock at a price well above what it was trading for on the stock exchange. If a majority of shareholders, who usually learned of the offer through an ad placed with no warning to the target company in the business section of major newspapers, tendered their shares, Flom's client would have the votes to throw out the incumbent board and management.

The emergence of tender offers as something respectable companies and their lawyers might pursue came in 1974 when International Nickel, or INCO, made a cash offer for ESB, a maker of car batteries. Morgan Stanley, the white-shoe investment bank, represented INCO and hired Flom. ESB, represented by Goldman Sachs, tried to head off INCO by finding a more friendly buyer, but INCO prevailed in what became a bidding war whose daily ups and downs played out across the business pages of major newspapers. On Wall Street, it was like reading the sports pages.

The tender offer floodgates opened. Within the next half decade, major public companies, including blue chips like American Express, McGraw-Hill, and Loews, got into the fray. As with the INCO battle, these early fights made headlines in the business pages because they were so out of character with the old clubbiness of Wall Street lawyers and bankers and their Fortune 500 clients, and because the thrusts and parries, including the personal attacks on the targets and raiders, were fun to read about.

They were a pale forerunner of things to come. There have been dozens of fights for corporate control every year since, and even more friendly mergers negotiated by CEOs worried about a hostile take-over. Flom got into the arena first, and with established law firms slower than the banks to seize on this new, high-stakes work, he enjoyed a near-monopoly position as the brawlers' lawyer of choice.

If one side always had Flom, the other side had to have some-one else. More often than not, Martin Lipton became that man. Lip-ton's life story began seven years after Flom's, and mimics it. He had immigrant Jewish parents. He finished at the top of his class at New York University Law School, but was not hired by any establishment firm when he graduated in 1955. He started his own firm with three NYU classmates with the same backgrounds. Although Lipton and Flom often switched sides, Flom was typically on offense while Lip-ton played defense.

I met Flom and Lipton in 1976, when I was writing for *New York* magazine. I'd been told about a trend that might make a great story: Two relative unknowns at two equally un-prominent law firms were dominating a new area of law that was bringing them and their part-ners millions in fees. The article, "Two Tough Lawyers in the Tender-Offer Game," which described their moves and countermoves in a fight over whether gunmaker Colt Industries would be taken over by a company called Garlock, depicted Flom and Lipton on their way to building what seemed likely to become two of the world's most suc-cessful law practices.

By then, Flom's firm, Skadden, Arps, Slate, Meagher & Flom, had grown from twenty-nine lawyers to ninety in five years, increasingly drawing on the new meritocracy emerging from the elite law schools. I quoted one envious lawyer at a Wall Street firm as marveling that the *Harvard Law Review* editor who couldn't find a job on Wall Street "has broken the link between the old investment banking firms and blue chip companies and their lawyers."

Lipton had crashed the party, too. He and his partners were doing so well and were so eager to cement their gains by attracting top talent that his firm, Wachtell, Lipton, Rosen & Katz, was offering starting salaries above the going rate. Both places were pressure cookers far beyond anything young lawyers experienced at the more established firms. "If you're going to get romantically involved," one of Flom's partners was quoted as warning an applicant, "don't work here. You'll never be able to sustain the relationship."

Three years later, in 1979, when I started *The American Lawyer* magazine, Flom ended up on the cover of the inaugural issue because Skadden, Arps was reported to have the highest average partner incomes of any large law firm in the world.

By 2016 Flom's firm had grown to 1,677 lawyers. It had diversified beyond mergers and acquisitions into some practice areas that were less lucrative, but lucrative enough to put the firm near the top in partner incomes, at $3.1 million. Lipton's firm had only grown to 261 lawyers in 2016 because the founders were determined to stick to premium-fee practices in mergers and acquisitions and a few other areas. It was firmly ensconced at the top of the income charts. Its partners earned an average of $6.6 million that year, epitomizing the new meritocracy aristocracy that Markovits had described to the Yale graduating class. By then mergers and acquisitions, related complex debt and bond deals, and the litigation that often accompanied these and other financial maneuvers had created hundreds of nearly as prosperous law firms, while ballooning the ranks of the still richer investment bankers.

"What we've seen is the financialization of the economy," Lipton said in 2016, reflecting on the last fifty years. "We created a whole separate economic activity of trading pieces of paper—which accomplishes nothing." As *Time* magazine economics columnist Rana Foroohar explained in her book, *Makers and Takers: The Rise of Finance and the Fall of American Business*, "Wealth creation within the financial markets has become an end in itself, rather than a means to the end of shared economic prosperity." One of Foroohar's most compelling data points: "The top twenty-five hedge fund managers in America make more than all the country's kindergarten teachers combined."

Beginning with his early efforts to ward off raiders, Lipton had become an increasingly vocal—some said, cranky—critic of the kind of short-termism that Judith Samuelson of Aspen decried. He was a leading adviser to her group, as well as a similar one formed in conjunction with the Davos World Economic Forum. Critics argued that Lipton was trying to find moral high ground for the cause of entrenched corporate clients who did not want to be held accountable for poor boardroom performance. However, the pace of deals, as well as the financial sleights of hand often behind them—plus the conduct of some of the raiders he contended with as the financialization accelerated—gave Lipton a lot of ammunition. More than that, he was not only identifying a change that had affected, and enriched, lawyers, bankers, and those in the boardroom. He was describing a tectonic change in what drove the American economy. News about takeover fights, mergers, and other machinations and the accompanying financial engineering may have been mostly confined to the financial pages, but in offices, factories, and households across the country there were broad, unsettling ramifications behind all the jargon and the stories adorned with photos of beaming men in suits celebrating their latest deal.

JUNK

The takeover boom and merger deals generally were fueled by another mid-1970s innovation in financial and legal engineering: the debt-financed takeover, or leveraged buyout. The prime innovator was Michael Milken.

Working at Drexel Burnham Lambert, a second-tier brokerage and investment bank, Milken—who would go to prison in 1991 for securities law violations—figured out that if companies had sufficient earnings or potential earnings, he could help what would become a group of buccaneer raiders, including Carl Icahn, Victor Posner, and Boone Pickens, borrow the money to buy them. The interest rates on what came to be called "junk bonds," which Milken specialized in, would be high because the risk would seem high. However, if the raider took over and made the right expense cuts and sold off the right pieces, and then cashed out, the result would be a home run. Besides, in the 1970s, investors were willing to take the risk on bonds that paid high interest, rather than park their money in banks or in safer bonds, whose payouts often didn't keep up with the era's high inflation rates.

Here is how it worked. A raider would pick out a company that had good cash flow but seemed to be lagging in earnings growth. Perhaps it had been too worried about the "externalities" that Milton Friedman and Michael Jensen abhorred and, therefore, hadn't used technology to replace enough workers, had not shipped enough jobs overseas, or was investing too much in research and development that had no immediate payoff. Or perhaps management was lazy or incompetent, or was wasting money buying businesses it didn't know how to run.

Whatever the case, suppose the target company had $100 million a year in cash flow that could be used to pay interest. Milken would find a raider who was convinced he could slash enough expenses at the company to get the cash flow to $140 million within two years. Assuming the stock was currently selling at a price equivalent to seven times its cash flow, a standard multiple at the time, purchasing all of the stock would cost $700 million at the current (and stagnant) stock price. If Milken could raise $800 million in debt and get the raider to put up just $50 million in cash, the raider could offer shareholders $850 million, or a 21 percent premium on the current $700 million stock price. Even if the interest on the debt was 11 percent, or $88 million a year, the raider could pay it out of that current $100 million cash flow and still give himself a $12 million dividend in the first year, not counting some extra cash he might get by selling off poorly performing divisions that had little or no cash flow.

In the second year with the cash flow of $120 million, and on its way to the $140 million target, the dividend (coming from cash flow that didn't have to be used to pay the $88 million interest on the debt) could be as high as $32 million. At the end of the second year, if the raider had achieved that $140 million in cash flow, he could then sell the company for $980 million, assuming the same seven-times cash flow (7 × $140 million = $980 million). He would then pay back the $800 million in debt and have $180 million left for himself, or $130 million more than he invested. Add the $44 million in dividends he took along the way and in two years he would have ended up with a $174 million return on the $50 million in cash he had invested.

Thanks to innovators like Milken—and backed up by platoons of bankers and lawyers from the meritocratic elite who crunched the numbers and drafted the reams of necessary documents—the raider was using $800 million of other people's money and only $50 million of his own to take over a big company and get $174 million back. He was executing a brilliant leveraged buyout.

There were two catches. First, if the raider's projections didn't work out, he would be forced to fire more workers and sell off more assets to pay the debt. He might even lose the whole company to the lenders if the cash flow couldn't cover the interest. Second, even if everything worked out, the win scenario still required job cuts, asset sales, and other dis-investments. Sometimes this was, indeed, a matter of enforcing long-overdue efficiencies to make the enterprise stronger. Other times, it would mean strip-mining what had been a viable business.

The deal flow that Milken and others organized became a tidal wave, as banks and investment funds poured money into debt instruments to finance these raids. Suddenly, leveraged buyouts made even the biggest companies vulnerable, giving the lawyers and bankers non-stop work on billion-dollar deals that dwarfed anything Wall Street had ever seen. At the turn of this century, deals that seemed unimaginable in the 1960s and jaw-dropping in the 1980s had become routine. And every significant bank and law firm on Wall Street and in major cities across the country and around the world were doing them.

Financialization advanced on other fronts. Investment banks and hedge funds, which are organized solely to bet on stocks and other securities, developed specialties in an old but now intensified stock market betting practice—deal arbitrage. They would purchase options to buy, or sell, the stock of a takeover target based on whether they thought the deal would go through or even be bid up higher in the coming days, or be blocked by the other side's lawyers or bankers or by government regulators on anti-trust grounds. Deal arbitrage was a pure—and purely vicarious—bet from the sidelines on the bets being made by the raiders. What the company in play actually produced did not matter.

Money, itself, became the focus of another betting parlor. In 1971, the collapse of the Bretton Woods international accords— which had locked in the relative value of major currencies since

1944—accompanied by President Richard Nixon's decision to let the value of the dollar float freely, created a new market for speculating in the fluctuation of exchange rates. With technology emerging to facilitate trades around the world instantaneously, knowledge workers had new pieces of paper (francs, dollars, pounds) to trade for other pieces of paper.

Trading pieces of paper was on its way to becoming America's prime economic activity, literally. In 1950, the financial industry accounted for 9 percent of all corporate profits. Since the beginning of the twenty-first century, except for a brief downturn during the Great Recession, finance's annual share of total American profits has hovered at about 30 percent, making it by far the largest industry sector in terms of profits produced. Meantime, manufacturing of durable goods, which accounted for 33 percent of profits in 1950, now accounts for about 12 percent. With that role reversal, a small group of elites has replaced the middle class, who once produced, warehoused, and shipped those manufactured products, as the backbone of America's economy. Even broadly defined to include insurance companies and the smallest banks, the financial sector's share of overall employment, including administrative workers and other support staff, has never exceeded 3 or 4 percent, and the lawyers doing their work probably number no more than another 0.2 percent.

THE ULTIMATE DE-INVESTING TOOL

In 1982, another advance in financial engineering began to set in motion a set of boardroom dynamics that would eat away still more at the American economic engine. There was little reporting about it at the time in the general press or on broadcast news. Yet to see how America got where it is today, it is important to understand the pivotal decision to allow what Wall Street called stock buybacks.

As part of a broader deregulatory agenda, President Ronald Reagan's Securities and Exchange Commission chairman, John Shad, pushed through a rule setting out liberal guidelines for corporations to repurchase their stock on the open market. Such stock buybacks had long been frowned on by regulators, who feared that companies could profit unfairly at the expense of their own shareholders by buying stock just before they knew good news about the company was to become public. More important, the regulators feared that buybacks would allow managers to manipulate the price of the stocks upward without doing anything to improve operations or profits.

For example, if there were five million shares of a company outstanding, the company could buy back a million of them, thereby boosting the price in two ways: First, the emergence of a new bulk buyer would create more demand for the stock, which would raise the price. Second, once the company had bought back the shares, there would be 20 percent fewer shares. That meant that even if the company's $100 million in earnings stayed the same, its earnings per share—the key benchmark for stock prices—would suddenly go up 25 percent ($100 million in earnings divided by four million shares instead of five million).

Shad, who had been vice chairman of the investment bank E. F. Hutton before President Reagan selected him as SEC chairman in 1981, was not worried about that. He told *The Wall Street Journal* that boosting the stock price was actually the goal. According to the *Journal*, Shad explained that "stock repurchases 'confer a material benefit' on a company's shareholders by fueling increases in stock market prices."

By 1982, with corporate boards increasingly following Jensen's cue and paying managements in stocks and stock options enriched by jumps in the stock price, those making the decisions to buy back shares would be the most immediate beneficiaries. Moreover, with raiders armed with all that new junk bond financing that they could use to offer shareholders a premium over current prices, and with shares increasingly held by unsentimental institutions that needed their stock picks to be validated every quarter, the use of buybacks to get the company's stock price up closer to whatever premium might be offered by a raider was a perfect moat—a great way for CEOs and their lieutenants to ward off a takeover.

In short, buybacks became irresistible in the new world dominated by three interrelated forces: the Jensen-inspired evangelism for making stock prices the yardstick for management compensation, the rise of short-term-focused institutional shareholders, and the threat of the debt-financed raiders.

The result turned the interplay of corporations and stock markets inside out. As already explained, corporations had traditionally issued new stock in order to invest in new products and new markets, and to hire people for new jobs. As they collected profit, after paying out some portion of it as dividends to shareholders, they reinvested the rest to grow the business, which the shareholders would benefit from over the long term through rising profits and dividends. Now management and boards (who also had stock-based compensation) were *dis*-investing. They were handing money back to some shareholders who wanted to cash out and magically raising the share price for everyone else, including themselves. In the process, they were putting off research and development or investments in new markets because the cash spent on buybacks couldn't be spent on these longer-term needs. They were also exacerbating income inequality by laying off workers or shifting jobs overseas so that they would have the cash to finance the buybacks that enriched the executives. In fact, buybacks packed the double whammy of cutting demand for rank-and-file workers, thereby stagnating their wages, while boosting the incomes of bosses who benefited so richly from stock awards and options. Thus, they became a major factor in widening the gap between CEO pay and the salary of the company's average worker. In 1970, the ratio was 20:1. In 2016, it was 300:1.

Writing for the Brookings Institution in 2015, economist William Lazonick reported that in the decade from 2003 to 2013, drug makers Amgen and Pfizer had each paid out buybacks and dividends to their shareholders amounting to more than 100 percent of their total earnings. Intel, IBM, Cisco, Microsoft, Hewlett-Packard, and Procter & Gamble had also dis-invested more than all of their earnings.

More generally, Lazonick reported in the *Harvard Business Review* that the "449 companies in the S&P 500 index that were publicly listed from 2003 through 2012 . . . used 54% of their earnings [during that period]—a total of $2.4 trillion—to buy back their own stock, almost all through purchases on the open market. Dividends absorbed an additional 37% of their earnings." That left only 9 percent "for investments in productive capabilities or higher incomes for employees."

Economist Andrew Smithers told author Rana Foroohar that he had calculated that in the 1970s, the decade before buybacks were allowed, American companies invested fifteen times what they gave back to shareholders in dividends.

Other data Lazonick gathered made the motive for the change clear:

> In 2012 the 500 highest-paid executives named in proxy statements of U.S. public companies received, on average, $30.3 million each; 42% of their compensation came from stock options and 41% from stock awards. By increasing the demand for a company's shares, open-market buybacks automatically lift its stock price, even if only temporarily, and can enable the company to hit quarterly earnings per share (EPS) targets.

An executive compensation reform aimed at the ballooning gap between top executives and everyone else that was pushed—and then allowed to be abused—in the 1990s by President Bill Clinton had exacerbated the problem. Clinton initiated a rule that any annual compensation to an executive above $1 million would no longer be a deductible expense when the company calculated its income tax obligation. However, any payments over $1 million that were *performance-based* would remain deductible. Options, or stock awards, and even cash bonuses based on the year-end stock price now had the government's blessing, thereby making stock buybacks that boosted stock prices even more enticing. To compound the problem, after being pressured by Republicans and many Democrats in Congress, the Clinton administration blocked a push by the Financial Accounting Standards Board and financial reform groups to get the SEC to require that the cost of stock options be clearly accounted for in a company's financial reports.

THE "ACTIVISTS"

Buybacks have continued to increase heavily in volume since Lazonick gathered his 2003–2012 numbers. Most recently, the Republicans' late-2017 tax cut legislation, which provided a trillion dollars over the next decade in tax cuts for corporations, ignited an unprecedented orgy of multi-billion dollar buybacks, confirming the prediction by critics of the legislation that the lion's share of benefits would go to the top tier of Americans who own stock in large corporations and to the executives who run them—and not to workers who might be hired if the tax cuts were used to invest in business expansion.

In addition to that immediate trigger, buybacks have become a favorite tool for appeasing and enriching a new breed of raiders.

In the last decade, raiders have taken on a new gloss, one that is even more consistent with the notion of shareholder democracy and that borrows the rhetoric of other democracy movements. Armed with cash from huge hedge funds that they control, the raiders now style themselves as "activist shareholders" engaged in campaigns to get even some of the largest and most successful companies to do better for their shareholders by "unlocking" the value they are hoarding.

After they insert themselves by paying a few hundred million dollars for 2 or 3 percent of a company's stock, they engage in high-profile, proxy-like campaigns. However, unlike the original Flom proxy raids, these assaults usually come with a specific set of demands for unlocking that value. A massive stock buyback is typically at the top of the list. When the company yields by purchasing huge amounts of its stock, the hedge funder usually sells his stake at the now increased price and goes away. Even Apple yielded, beginning in 2013, when it borrowed billions of dollars (rather than tap profits it was shielding overseas from U.S. taxes) to finance a massive buyback that was being pushed by, among others, raider Carl Icahn.

Whether Icahn's assault on Apple produced a positive or negative result for the company is beside the general point, which is that these kinds of drive-by shareholders have no accountability for the long-term damage that those who run the corporations they briefly own might do to please them.

Just before his inauguration, Donald Trump publicly interceded to block a plan by air-conditioning manufacturer Carrier to move jobs from Indiana to Mexico. The incoming president eventually pressured the company to let some of the jobs remain, albeit temporarily, but the company refused to reverse a decision not to invest in new facilities in Indiana.

At the time, Carrier's parent, United Technologies, was completing a $16 billion stock buyback program. The announcement of the plan in 2015 had sent "the conglomerate's shares higher even as it copes with declining sales and profits," *The Wall Street Journal* reported. The paper also quoted UT's CEO Greg Hayes—70 percent of whose $14.9 million compensation was based on the company's stock price—as conceding that the company's buybacks and recent sell-offs of assets were steps he had taken to anticipate what a raider might try to force on him. "We're the activists," Hayes told the *Journal*. "If an activist wants to come in and make a suggestion that we do it, we can say, 'Been there, done that.'"

Not all buybacks are destructive. Some companies—perhaps Apple is one—may have so much profit flowing in that they cannot invest all of it sensibly, and putting some of it back in the hands of shareholders for them to re-invest would make sense. However, if buybacks were again prohibited, that would force those businesses to concentrate their shareholder paybacks into dividends, which are taxed at higher rates than capital gains and which don't allow for the stock price manipulation that buybacks offer. Indeed, even when not under immediate attack from activist raiders but when profits are lagging, as was the case with United Technologies, executives now routinely use buybacks near the end of a quarter to boost earnings per share up to the targets that their board has set for them in order to be paid bonuses.

It adds up to such a short-term mind-set that by 2005 a survey of 401 large-company chief financial officers co-published by the Duke University business school and the *Journal of Accounting and Economics* reported that 80 percent of CFOs would cut planned spending on research and development, advertising, or maintenance in order to meet a quarterly earnings target. The result, according to a Harvard Business School 2016 report on American competitiveness, is that "Business investment is lagging. . . . The annual growth rate of quarterly private investment in intellectual property, structures and equipment remains weak, falling below historic rates."

BOOSTING BANK STOCKS BY GAMBLING WITH OTHER PEOPLE'S MONEY

We have seen how high-wire financial and legal engineering created enormous pressure on businesses to focus on short-term earnings and the corresponding day-to-day price of their stock. What if the key players in all of that financial engineering—the banks—could find ways to boost *their own* earnings by creating products that would add trillions to the volume of financial trading, but could be engineered so that those who created and traded in them could never lose? What if the giant traditional banks and the investment banks—which, along with traditional banks had now become public companies, facing the same pressures on their stock prices—could multiply the stakes at the casino, have a great chance of winning big, and have, at least in their minds, no chance of losing?

Enter Lewis Ranieri.

Brooklyn-born Ranieri's story reads like the bio of a Baruch College student, circa fifty years ago. Ranieri dropped out of St. John's College in Queens in 1968 to go to work in the mailroom at the Salomon Brothers brokerage house. By the mid-1970s he was working on one of the firm's trading desks, supervised by a banker who was developing a way to turn mortgages held by banks across the country into another new kind of financial paper. When the supervisor fell ill, Ranieri, who was then in his early thirties, took the idea and ran with it—so successfully that when *The New York Times* published an admiring profile of him in 1984 (which reported that he was responsible for 40 percent of Salomon's $415 million profit the year before), he was quoted as proclaiming, "I have more money than I ever knew existed. I never dreamed this big."

Michael Lewis, in his best-selling book *Liar's Poker*, described Ranieri's days as a young trader at Salomon:

> Lewie Ranieri was the wild and woolly genius, the Salomon legend who began in the mailroom, worked his way onto the trading floor, and created a market in America (and was starting a similar one in Britain) for mortgage bonds. Ranieri was Salomon, and Salomon was Ranieri. . . . He was evidence that the trading floor was a meritocracy. . . . [Ranieri] looked about as much like an investment banker as the average Italian chef. He was, in the words of one of his former partners, "a fat slob." But it simply did not matter.

By 2004, *BusinessWeek* would crown Ranieri one of the "greatest innovators of the past 75 years." He had turned humdrum mortgages into gold by inventing something called "securitization." It became and remains the pivotal piece of financial engineering that drove the financialization of America to the ultimate extreme—and drove much of the middle class over the edge.

Mortgages, of course, are contracts obligating a homeowner to pay a bank the interest and principal on the money the homeowner borrowed to buy a house. The homeowner's promise is backed, or secured, by the home. If he doesn't pay, the bank can take over the home and sell it to recover its money. Ranieri took thousands of mortgages and packaged them together into a new piece of paper that he sold as a new kind of security. Salomon Brothers would negotiate with banks to buy their mortgages and sell them to new investors all over the world. Those investors would be buying the right to the future cash flow from all the interest and principal owed by the homeowners. If the homeowners (who the investors, of course, knew little or nothing about) defaulted, the investors, working through intermediaries, could foreclose on the homes and sell them. Thus was born the "mortgage-backed security," or MBS.

Traditionally, banks could only provide mortgages with money available from what depositors gave them or what they could borrow from the Federal Reserve, which placed limits on how much they could be at risk. Now a bank could take $100 million of the mortgages it had already negotiated and sell them off—through Salomon or other investment banks that quickly entered the market—to hedge funds, other banks, or other investors. They could then use the money from those sales to provide new mortgages.

With the housing market sagging in the late 1970s, MBSs got off to a slow start. As the market began recovering in 1981, they took off, fueling a surge in home ownership.

A bank would sell these packaged mortgages at a discount on what the ultimate payout in interest and principal on the mortgage might yield, and Salomon would keep some of that discount for its trouble before it sold the MBSs to the new investor or investors. Those investors might trade them off at some point based on their guesses on whether mortgage interest rates were going up or down. The entire exercise was not a bet on the traditional criteria of a home's actual value and the creditworthiness of its owner, but on macroeconomic dynamics. If their package of mortgages had average rates that they thought would be lower than future rates, for example, they might sell them off to speculate on future mortgages.

As new mortgages were handed out by the banks with the

reclaimed money from the sale of the first MBSs, a bank could turn around and sell the second round of mortgages into another MBS, then use those proceeds for a third round of mortgage loans.

The large conventional chartered banks began to compete aggressively for the business of packaging and selling MBSs, as did Morgan Stanley, Goldman Sachs, and other investment banks. Like Salomon Brothers, they were now becoming public companies that had to worry about their share prices. Before, they had been partnerships where the bosses were responsible for covering any losses.

Soon, all the players on Wall Street were in the MBS business (which expanded to include repackaged car loans and credit card debt). Thousands of analysts and vice presidents were put to work finding, packaging, pricing, and selling them. Other squadrons of lawyers were deployed to do all the paperwork.

With all that new money available, rates on mortgages came down, and more people were able to buy homes. Ranieri told the *Times* in 1984—by which time Salomon had been involved in trading $270 billion worth of mortgage-backed securities—that the business "had a real social and economic benefit. We really did lower the cost of a mortgage. You can't help but feel good about that kind of thing."

There was a catch. Before MBSs, banks had to worry about whether a borrower might default and, if so, whether the house it would take back in foreclosure could be resold to recoup the money lost on the default. Now the bank was acting as a field sales force to find mortgage borrowers whose debt would be handed over, via Salomon and other banks, to all those new investors, who were buying the MBSs that contained the mortgages and might trade them off to others equally far removed from the borrowers and the homes that secured the mortgages. Financial engineering was separating decision makers from the consequences of their decisions.

In theory, the buyers of the MBSs had to worry about the soundness of the security they were buying. However, the package of mortgages in them was so large—and the thousands of individual properties, borrowers, and loan terms behind them so varied—that it was impossible to evaluate them in-house. Instead, they relied on the three major credit ratings firms—Standard & Poor's, Moody's, and Fitch Group. Their usual work involved closely examining the finances of a city to gauge the creditworthiness of a municipal bond

offering, or vetting the balance sheet of a corporation to rate its creditworthiness. The three firms claimed to have developed elaborate
algorithms to process all the variables and rate the risks in these huge
packages of mortgages, based on samples. Yet they competed heavily,
and they were chosen and paid by the banks that were packaging and
selling the MBSs. They mostly gave their highest ratings to whatever
MBSs they were asked to analyze.

"Major firms and investors blindly relied on credit rating agencies
as their arbiters of risk," reported the Financial Crisis Inquiry Commission, a federal commission empaneled after the Great Recession
to report on the causes of the crash. "The three credit rating agencies
were key enablers of the financial meltdown. . . . Participants in the
securitization industry realized that they needed to secure favorable
credit ratings in order to sell structured products to investors. Investment banks therefore paid handsome fees to the rating agencies to
obtain the desired ratings." The result, the commission found, was
an assembly-line process like this one attributed to Moody's, whose
largest shareholder was Berkshire Hathaway, the company controlled by Warren Buffett: "From 2000 to 2007, Moody's rated nearly
45,000 mortgage-related securities as triple-A. This compares with
six private-sector companies in the United States that carried this
coveted rating in early 2010. In 2006 alone, Moody's put its triple-A
stamp of approval on 30 mortgage-related securities [each containing
thousands of individual mortgages] every working day."

It wasn't that many of the traders at banks and hedge funds dealing in this paper weren't aware of how un-vetted they were. However,
a phrase shortened to "IBGYBG" became popular on Wall Street as
a testament to the culture of short-termism that brushed aside those
concerns. It stood for, "I'll be gone. You'll be gone"—before whatever
reckoning might come.

INSURING AGAINST RECKLESS GAMBLES

Two toxic ingredients that would be key factors in America's tailspin had come together: A preoccupation with financial engineering
aimed at enabling ever more aggressive betting on paper instruments
had combined with still more engineering that allowed for those

facilitating the bets to avoid accountability for the risks they were creating—risks whose consequences would ultimately be suffered far beyond the financial community. In fact, there would soon be a way for wary buyers of mortgage-backed securities to pass off their own risk completely.

The financial engineering hero this time was Blythe Masters, a twenty-five-year-old, Cambridge-educated banker in JPMorgan's London office. In 1994, Masters invented the credit default swap, or CDS.*

A CDS is a derivative—a security that derives its value from the value of something else. For example, if Jones runs an airline and is worried that the price of $100 million worth of jet fuel will go up 10 percent or more next year, he might spend a million dollars to buy a derivative that gives him the right to buy the fuel next year at today's price. The trader selling him the derivative would be betting a million dollars that the price of fuel will not go up, just the way an insurance company is betting that your house will not burn down. In terms of economic theory, this makes sense because Jones would rather focus on running an airline than worry about the ups and downs of oil prices, while the trader selling him the derivative is in the business of focusing on oil prices. Sensible economic theory, however, can be abused.

Tasked with finding new products for JPMorgan, Masters focused on holders of securities for whom a default would be like the price of jet fuel going up—something they wanted to insure against. Suppose someone could "swap" that risk, she thought, with someone else by paying the other party to assume that risk, just the way a homeowner pays an insurance company to assume the risk on her house.

Masters's first credit default swap deal involved JPMorgan paying the European Bank for Reconstruction and Development to assume JPMorgan's risk that Exxon would default on a $4.8 billion line of credit the bank had extended to the oil giant. There was little risk of default, but if the bank could hand off the risk that way, it would be free to make more loans because regulators, who worried about limiting the total risk on a bank's balance sheet, would no longer count the Exxon line of credit as money at risk.

Masters and her colleagues, who were a hard-driving, hard-

---

* Masters is portrayed masterfully in Gillian Tett's *Fool's Gold*, published by the Free Press in 2009, from which much of this information about her is derived.

partying go-go team of innovators at the old-line bank, quickly saw the possibility of a larger market—a mass market in billion-dollar products. Soon they were brokering deals for insuring MBSs, linking buyers, who held the mortgage-backed securities and wanted to buy insurance against defaults, and sellers, who were willing to be paid as little as a fraction of one percent of the paper value of all the billions of dollars of payments due on the mortgages in return for insuring the MBS holders against the risk. Before long, many banks were setting up units to sell the credit default swaps themselves, meaning they were insuring against the risk borne by other banks and financial institutions. One actual insurance company, American International Group, or AIG, emerged as the biggest CDS player of all.

For AIG, the business was better than actual insurance, because real insurance is regulated: Insurance companies have to prove, using actuarial tables that gauge risk, that they have the funds available to pay off a life insurance or homeowner policy. A credit default swap was not considered insurance by any of the regulators who could have interceded, in part because, until it was too late, none of them appreciated the volume of the bets being made. So, with no reserves required—and, therefore, only minimal risk calculated and deducted from the premiums paid on the swaps to determine actual profit—almost all of it could count as profit. It was found money that seemed to be dropping from the sky. In 2008, AIG would get the largest of the government bailouts following the crash: $182 billion, which, in turn, it would have to use to pay off all the investment banks and other investors that bought its credit default swap insurance to cover their MBSs, only to find that AIG had not reserved the money to pay for all the MBS defaults.

While Masters and JPMorgan were launching CDSs in 1994, Congress, under a sustained lobbying campaign by its contributors in the financial industry, was completing the unraveling of restrictions on the size of banks that had been put in place following the Great Depression. A new federal statute allowed banks to merge and to operate branches in all fifty states. By 2005 the ten largest banks would have a market share of 61 percent, compared to 21 percent in 1960. This made the consequences of their potential failure stemming from their bets on MBSs and CDSs that much greater.

The loosening of these restraints on banks also meant that they were becoming giant corporations that needed to win big bets in big markets to move the needle on their earnings and stock price. Six years later, in 2000, another lobbying triumph resulted in the complete elimination of the federal government's already weak regulation of derivatives trading. In keeping with the prevailing spirit of innovation, it was called the Commodity Futures Modernization Act.

A year earlier, President Clinton had signed a law repealing the Depression-era Glass-Steagall Act, which had prohibited chartered banks, which are backstopped by the government, from engaging in risky investment-banking-like activities such as trading in derivatives. The theory of Glass-Steagall had been that if government-protected banks engaged in these risky activities, the government would be responsible for cleaning up after those risks if the banks needed to be bailed out. In the different political climate that prevailed by the 1990s—even among dominant factions of Democrats in Congress and the Clinton administration—financial deregulation was championed as a way to unshackle the creativity of the financial engineers.

When it came to mortgages, the laissez-faire political winds were especially favorable because encouraging mortgage lenders to expand their customer base had become a liberal cause. It had been sparked by a mini-uproar generated in 1992 by a report from the Boston unit of the Federal Reserve Bank that African Americans and Hispanics were four times as likely to be rejected for mortgages. The Clinton administration and Congress pushed banks to fill the gap. The two government-sponsored behemoths that bought millions of mortgages to package into mortgage-backed securities—the Federal Home Loan Mortgage Corporation (known as Freddie Mac) and Federal National Mortgage Association (Fannie Mae)—were mandated to set ambitious goals to expand home-buying opportunities for low-income and minority families.

LIKE BETTING ON A PRIZEFIGHT

The financial engineering and the economic havoc it would cause was still not over. All of the activity around MBSs—the volume of which had reached into the trillions of dollars—fascinated hedge fund gamblers and other investors sitting on the sidelines. They wanted to get in on the action but were not in the business of buying or selling MBSs or CDSs for their own accounts, in most cases because they were wary of the assets—the homes and their debtor owners—behind the mortgages.

Enter the *synthetic* credit default swap, a variation on credit default swaps, which became popular once CDSs picked up steam with the rise in the real estate market in the early 2000s. A synthetic credit default swap was simply a bet that something would happen that the people making the bets had nothing to do with—in this case, that the mortgage-backed securities would pay out or would go bad. It was *synthetic* in that the buyer was insuring against a bad event (the defaults) that he had no actual interest in protecting against, and the seller was betting that the bad event would not happen.

It was like buying life insurance on the life of a stranger who you thought looked unhealthy, or insuring someone else's house against a fire because you knew the owner was a drunk who smoked a lot. That kind of vicarious insurance is almost always illegal. It is considered to be against public policy, because you would be incented to kill that stranger or steer him to an incompetent doctor, and because, well, it's just a bet, which is usually restricted to licensed casinos. Yet that is how dozens of investors who bought the synthetic credit default swaps made vast fortunes when the credit markets crashed, and how the hedge funds, banks, and other investors that sold them the synthetic credit default swaps suffered crushing losses.

Regulators didn't do anything about synthetic credit default swaps either. In 2005, the notional value, or the amount of money at risk, in all credit default swaps, real or synthetic, totaled $67 trillion. The actual value of the assets underlying all the securities (or loans) was only $15 trillion. That meant that the casino would have to pay $67 trillion for $15 trillion worth of losses, making it mathematically impossible that the vast majority of those buying this ostensible insurance were doing so to hedge against a risk that they might actually suffer. They were betting on something from the sidelines. It was like a Las Vegas crowd placing bets on their way into the arena to watch a boxing match.

All of this financial engineering was about eliminating accountability and responsibility by separating the actors from the consequences of their actions. As explained, Ranieri's introduction of securitization began a process by which investors who were buying his mortgage-backed securities, or MBSs, and were counting on borrowers not to default had no relation to those borrowers, much less any direct knowledge of their ability to pay or of the value of the home involved. And the banks or non-bank mortgage companies—a new industry that had emerged to make home loans from funds reaped by securitizing the mortgages they sold—did not have much incentive to worry about the loans they were making, because they were going to sell the mortgages in giant tranches to those investors.

Blythe Masters then made it so that the MBS investors didn't have to care either; they could buy her credit default swaps, which were sold by banks and AIG. Those selling the default swaps assumed they were taking in pure profit, because thousands of mortgages put together in one package had no chance of experiencing so many failures that the packages themselves would ever lose significant value requiring that this insurance be paid out. Or so they thought. Meanwhile, other gamblers on the sidelines could bet that the mortgages would default by buying synthetic credit default swaps from those willing to bet that the mortgages would not go bad.

THE RECKONING

"You had no incentive whatsoever to be concerned about the quality of the loan, whether it was suitable for the borrower or whether the loan performed. In fact, you were in a way encouraged not to worry about those macro issues. . . . I knew that the risk was being shunted off. I knew that we could be writing crap."

That is how Christopher Cruise, testifying in 2010 to the commission investigating the financial crisis, explained the mind-set of the people who were actually deciding on those mortgages. Cruise was employed as a consultant from 2002 through 2006 to train the thousands of loan officers hired by major banks and mortgage finance companies to give out mortgages. His testimony presents a stark picture of the consequence of what America became once financial engineering and betting on pieces of paper ascended as the country's dominant commercial activity. Supervised by managers and executives who were enjoying paydays beyond anything they had ever dreamed of, thousands of young Americans just entering the job force, who might have once worked in factories producing goods valued by their countrymen, were now cynically pushing paper that would bury millions of families under crushing debt.

"The subjects of compliance were of absolutely no interest to the loan officers that I trained," Cruise said. They were interested in "immediate production, immediate success. . . . It was a constant battle, number one, to keep them awake. Number two, to get them to come to the room and come back from breaks." When Cruise's training spiel did not "involve commission," he added, it was "extremely difficult to get them to stay in the room. . . . They wanted to know how they could do more deals and how they could make more money, not how they could comply with federal laws."

Among Cruise's major clients were mortgage lenders Ameriquest and New Century Financial. Ameriquest would be shut down in 2007 when it was buried by the defaults on mortgages that it was no longer able to sell off as mortgage-backed securities because default rates had become so high that investors were afraid to add to the MBSs they already had. New Century would be delisted on the stock exchange and forced into bankruptcy the same year.

Before they went under, they were the two largest lenders of subprime mortgages, which are mortgages carrying high interest rates because the borrowers have poor credit ratings. By 2002, the mortgage-backed securities market had become so feverish—in part because so much money was flowing in from China, which was eager to invest its massive trade surpluses—that handing off even subprime mortgages to investors was easy. That, plus the continued policy push to spread home ownership down the economic ladder, resulted in subprime mortgages and the high-flying stocks of the companies that sold them dominating the market.

The number three player was Countrywide Financial, a relative newcomer to the subprime race. Taking advantage of funds flowing from securitization rather than bank deposits, Countrywide had flourished as the country's largest provider of standard mortgages. In 2003, CEO Angelo Mozilo, the son of a Bronx butcher who had co-founded Countrywide in New York in 1969 and had since moved it to California, was determined to have the largest market share of *all* mortgages.

That compelled him, he later told the Financial Crisis Inquiry

Commission, to move aggressively into the subprime market. When he did, Countrywide's standards were thrown overboard. Mozilo didn't just jump into subprime lending. He added bells and whistles to the practice, such as expanding the use of adjustable rate mortgages, or ARMs, that lured borrowers in with initially low interest rates that would spike up after a year or two. Another innovation, "Option ARMs," let borrowers pick their initial monthly payments for the first few years, only to have to face double or triple the monthly payments later on. "Exploding ARMs" featured particularly low, often negligible initial payments. The increases to come later were detailed in the loan document, but in dense language that salespeople like those Cruise trained had little incentive to explain. Their commissions were geared to how profitable the loan looked on paper for Countrywide, not whether it made the most sense for the borrower.

Nor did the salesmen have any incentive to require paperwork from the borrowers that documented their incomes and, therefore, their ability to make loan payments. Cash down payments were reduced to as little as 5 percent of the sale price and sometimes even less, instead of the traditional 20 percent that was meant to ensure that in a foreclosure the mortgage holder would get a home worth as much or more than the loan. That did not seem like much of a risk at the time because, with the housing market fueled by all the loose mortgage money, home values seemed to be on a relentless trajectory upward.

Countrywide extended $1.5 trillion in mortgages from 2002 to 2005, and was able to sell off 87 percent of them to investors. From 2000 through 2008, Mozilo received more than $500 million in salary and stock-based bonuses, while his company graced *Fortune* magazine's list of America's most admired companies. At times, however, Mozilo blanched at the risky loans his salesforce was making. In one email, he warned his senior managers that they could bring "financial and reputational catastrophe." In another, he called the company's subprime loans "toxic." Yet he pressed on, continuing to make the loans and then push them off into securitization, until Countrywide's loan portfolio was so full of defaults or loans whose payments were in arrears that no one would buy them.

In 2008, Mozilo was forced to sell the company to Bank of America for just 15 percent of the market value that his stock had enjoyed four years earlier, although not before having cashed out $140 million in stock options in the two years before the sale. Mozilo was later sued by the SEC for fraud because Countrywide's SEC filings and other documents had assured investors in his stock and buyers of his mortgage-backed securities that his loan standards had remained high, even as he called them toxic in an internal email. He settled for a fine of $67.5 million. He was never charged criminally.

Until the end, Mozilo—like the politicians and regulators who had pushed the mortgage industry to help spread home ownership to the masses following the 1992 Boston Fed report about inequitable mortgage lending—maintained his stance as a true believer in mortgage democracy. Testifying before the Financial Crisis Inquiry Commission in 2010, he described how his company had put 25 million families into homes and prevented social unrest by providing ownership opportunities to minorities. Over forty years he had built, he said, "one of the greatest companies in the history of the country," one that had created sixty thousand jobs and had "a better stock record than Warren Buffett." Faced with all that new subprime competition, Mozilo testified, he was not about to close down his company rather than make the kinds of loans his competition was making. People were "going to get those loans anyway," he said.

What had gone wrong, in his view, was that with all that mortgage money available, housing prices kept going up, and housing became an investment more than a home: "Human beings are driven to try to improve their lives, and in a capitalist country you do that with money. Housing prices were rising so rapidly . . . that people—regular people, average people—got caught up in the mania of buying a home and knowing they could flip it. Homes suddenly went from being part of the American dream of housing a family to being a commodity." When housing prices started to fall at the same time that the required payments on those adjustable rate mortgages jumped, everything came crashing down. "I never considered," Mozilo explained, "that people would leave their homes and stop making payments simply because the value of the home went below the mortgage. That has never happened." In other words, the short-termism and gambling that started in the financial world had been spread, by the financial world, to middle America. Americans all became gamblers. A house was not a home. It was a bet.

THE PUSHBACK

Later, we will see how people like Mozilo were able to protect them-selves from financial ruin and criminal responsibility. We will also see that regulatory measures, such as the Dodd-Frank financial reform law passed in 2010, have not done enough to curb the short-termism and gambling mania that brought the Great Recession. Similarly, the obsession with quarterly stock prices—and with it, cutbacks in research and development, outsourcing of jobs, and stock buybacks forced by "activist" raiders—has not abated. In 2016, the value of stock buybacks and dividends returned to shareholders from the S&P 500 companies exceeded all of their operating profits.

That does not mean that people like Judith Samuelson at the Aspen think tank or takeover defense lawyer Martin Lipton are not still trying to persuade corporations to take the longer view. In fact, they are making progress. Their anti-short-termism movement has been spreading rapidly in recent years, picking up lots of new sup-porters in the academic and corporate worlds. Even Michael Jensen, the father of stock-based compensation theory, backtracked in 2005, writing an article titled "How Stock Options Reward Managers for Destroying Value and What to Do About It." (His prescription: give managers stock options that they can cash out only over the long term, with the payout adjusted up or down by the dividends paid to share-holders or the costs incurred by shareholders, including the cost of inflation, over that long term.) Jensen's retreat was followed five years later, in the wake of the financial meltdown, by a brutal and widely circulated monograph written by two economists who surveyed the wreckage his theory had wrought: Managers had taken advantage of "perverse incentives," wrote Frank Dobbin and Jiwook Jung, by gam-ing the stock option system to maximize their payouts while ignoring risk, decimating the long-term fortunes of their companies, and fend-ing off the kind of independent boards that could rein them in.

"I was misunderstood," Jensen said in an unpersuasive 2016 inter-view. "I was always worried about all the stakeholders—employees, customers, suppliers, debt holders, shareholders."

At the school where Jensen ended up becoming a marquee pro-fessor, the *Harvard Business Review* weighed in with a 2014 article by Dominic Barton, the managing director of consulting powerhouse

McKinsey, and Canadian Pension Board investment manager Mark Wiseman, warning that "short-termism is undermining the ability of companies to invest and grow, and those missed investments, in turn, have far-reaching consequences, including slower GDP growth, higher unemployment, and lower return on investment for savers." Barton, who was among the business leaders who had signed on to the Aspen American Prosperity Project "framework," told me that when he moved from working for McKinsey in Asia in 2009 to London he was struck by the difference in how business leaders in Europe and the West focused "only on the short term. In Asia," he recalled, "everyone understood that it takes eight or nine years for an investment to play out. When I got to London I made a point at the beginning to meet one or two CEOs every day. I was shocked at how short their time horizons were."

McKinsey has continued to publish data (trumpeted on the Aspen website and promoted in the business press) that show an alarming array of damage caused by short-termism: Despite the recovery from the Great Recession, investment by corporations in capital goods such as new equipment, or in research, has reached historic lows. Money for training employees to assume higher-skilled jobs has declined rapidly. China is now ahead of the U.S. in how much its corporations spend on research and development. So how does McKinsey deal with CEOs who are worried about potential raiders and hire the consulting firm to help boost short-term results? "We tell them there are good ways to boost the short term, and bad ways," Barton said. "And we also try to steer them to long-term investors, like some of the Asian funds, who understand long-term value."

Those like Barton who have taken up the short-termism fight in the business world have been doing so since 2016 under a variety of banners, in addition to Aspen. The Davos World Economic Forum has promulgated, under Martin Lipton's authorship, a "New Paradigm Roadmap for an Implicit Corporate Governance Partnership Between Corporations and Investors to Achieve Sustainable Long-Term Investment and Growth." It calls on boards to "guide, debate, and oversee a thoughtful, long term strategy" for corporations to set high standards for human rights, sustainability, and environmental and social responsibility. That sounds good, but it will always be difficult to tell which boardroom adherents are executives who just enjoy assuming the role of statesmen on the podium at Davos, or who don't want to be held accountable for their performance except over a long term that is long enough that they'll be gone after having enjoyed high-paying jobs without delivering commensurate performance.

Still, the anti-short-termism effort has picked up a broad range of credible supporters. One is Paul Polman, the CEO of Unilever—the manufacturer of consumer products such as Hellmann's mayonnaise, Ben & Jerry's ice cream, Dove soap, and Lipton tea. "Too many CEOs play the quarterly game and manage their businesses accordingly," Polman told *The Atlantic* when the Aspen initiative was announced and his involvement was listed. "But many of the world's challenges cannot be addressed with a quarterly mindset."

Unlike many other business leaders, even anti-short-termers, Polman defines his job and the responsibility of Unilever as more than worrying about the company's quarterly or even longer-term profits. Rather, he has been unabashed about his efforts aimed at assuring that Unilever is helping to make the world a better place, apart from how much it helps its bottom line. That means developing a fabric softener that uses less water or bottles that use less plastic, banning gender stereotypes from the company's advertising, and even jumping into issues like climate change and world hunger that might not have any effect on Unilever's particular fortunes. "If ultimately the purpose of a company is maximizing shareholder return, we risk ending up with many decisions that are not in the interest of society," he told *The Atlantic*. To lessen Wall Street's pressure on him and his team, Polman scrapped the practice of providing quarterly earnings predictions to stock analysts.

The kinds of "externalities" related to social responsibility that Milton Friedman and Michael Jensen dismissed have evolved in a way that has allowed Polman and others to argue that the interests of a business and of the larger world are increasingly aligned. The externalities are no longer as external to the well-being of a business, especially businesses like Unilever that count on having a good name with consumers, who can now read critiques of a company on social media or post their own. How companies approach climate change, for example, matters more than it once did, as does continued investment in product quality and customer service.

At the same time, as the consequences of short-termism—its

effect on investments in good jobs for the middle class, its role in widening the pay gap between the bosses and those who work for them, and what it has done generally to weaken the economy by limiting investment—have become more visible, short-termism's profile as a political issue has sharpened. In the 2016 American presidential election, the impact of stock buybacks as a damaging disinvestment tool was raised for the first time by one of the major nominees. "All too often," declared Hillary Clinton during the campaign, "the additional corporate revenue is going to stock buybacks and executive bonuses instead of benefiting consumers, employees, and the economy as a whole."

Although it is lately more in vogue, the idea that corporations should be worrying about consumers, employees, and the "economy as a whole"—often called the "stakeholder model"—is as old as the corporation itself. Lipton likes to point out that early corporations in Europe and then in the United States during colonial times were given their charters by the government to carry out specific endeavors meant to enhance the common good. Status as a corporation would give the proprietors special protection against personal liability as well as the ability to pool resources and manpower that could not easily be achieved by an individual proprietorship. It was not until the mid-nineteenth century that corporate charters began being handed out to anyone who asked, without the founders having to justify their need for this special status by specifying what their beneficial purpose was.

How the numbers have played out over the longer term also presents good arguments against short-termism. As early as 1980, Lipton asserted in an article in a legal trade publication that, more often than not, the quick premium offered to shareholders by raiders in takeover fights was illusory: "The 36 unsolicited tender offers that were rejected and defeated by the target between the end of 1973 and June 1979 (believed to be all such tender offers filed with the SEC during this period) show that the shares of more than 50 percent of the targets are either today at a higher market price than the rejected offer price, or were acquired after the tender offer was defeated by another company at a price higher than the offer price." More recent studies have fortified those findings that shareholders are better off waiting for the long term, although other studies have argued the opposite, and academics on each side of the debate regularly claim that the other side's data is cherry-picked or otherwise distorted.

The raiders' better argument, though, is simpler: shareholder democracy, as in, "Why not let the shareholders decide whether to take the offer, rather than let management deploy Lipton's legal maneuvers to block giving them the choice?" This raises the core question: Is a corporate board supposed to bow to the day-to-day wishes of shareholders, or should it act in what the corporation's leaders believe is the company's best long-term interests, or even in the best interests of all stakeholders—shareholders, employees, consumers, suppliers, and the community as a whole?

That stakeholder view seems to be making a comeback. Barton and many other business leaders are increasingly taking up the cause. And with the political climate turning against the kind of short-termism that computerized trading, hedge fund raids, and buybacks have exacerbated, regulatory reforms may become possible within a few election cycles. These include disallowing favorable capital gains tax treatment on stock sold within, say, three years of its purchase; putting an extra tax on computerized split-second trading in stocks, bonds, and currencies; limiting the power of raiders and fast-trading hedge funds by giving more weight in voting to shareholders who hold stock for a stipulated length of time, such as one or two years; and once again not allowing stock buybacks—a Reagan-era deregulatory experiment that has clearly been bad for the overall economy. All have been proposed by recent political candidates, particularly on the Democratic side, as changes that could reverse the damage of the last fifty years of financial engineering.

There is also the option of structuring the governance associated with public stock differently. Over the last decade, much has been written about how some of the country's most promising start-ups were hurt when they took their companies public. They then faced the pressure of having to explain quarterly earnings results to stock analysts and a broad group of non-founder investors, who might not be sympathetic to their vision of continuing to invest in developing the company's products. Of course, in many cases the pressure was a healthy counterforce against exuberant spending without a plan for attracting the revenue to match. In other instances, however, companies under this new pressure have had to abandon what might have been viable but longer-term strategies for success and sell themselves to larger companies that didn't pay enough attention or invest enough to fulfill the start-up's early promise. As a result, some of America's most successful start-ups, including Google and Facebook, decided that the only way to go public was to abandon the pretense of share-holder democracy. The founders insisted on public offerings that featured two classes of stock—one for the founders, and one for the public. The founders' shares would have the majority of votes, ensur-ing that while the public could bet on the success of the company, there would be no democracy when it came to defining or pursuing that success.

"If Facebook hadn't had a different class of stock for [founder Mark] Zuckerberg, it might well have been taken over soon after it went public because of the costly shift he made early on to mobile," explained Barton, referring to the social network's expensive but stun-ningly successful investment in creating a platform for ads on mobile devices.

Establishing dual classes of stock is not new. It is what the New York Times Company did in 1969, when the founding Sulzberger family wanted to raise money from public investors while assuring that they would remain in control, able to withstand any Wall Street pressures to sacrifice their vision of the company's journalism mis-sion. As a public company, the Times Company was still subject to the SEC's self-dealing, accounting, disclosure, and other rules, but, like Facebook, it was not susceptible to a raider-inspired democratic revolt. Shareholders who wanted to buy the stock had to be will-ing to accept that. "The fact that shareholders in the public markets have accepted that there is no shareholder democracy when it comes to companies like Facebook," said Samuelson, "is a really hopeful sign."

There is also a potential silver lining in the growing dominance of institutional shareholders. Institutions typically are holding and investing money for entities such as university endowments or pen-sion funds whose beneficiaries are thinking of the long term; most people with money in a pension fund worry more about what the funds will look like next decade than next month. There is already a growing movement under the umbrella of the Investor Stewardship

Group, which includes many of the largest institutional shareholders, to encourage company boards to think longer term. However, there is nothing in the group's charter about aligning that view with how those same institutions in the group reward their own people, who continue to be paid at most funds for their short-term stock picks. "That's the elephant in the room," Samuelson of Aspen told me. "It's something we're now starting to focus on. If that happens, real change will happen. The era of shareholder primacy will be over."

"Maybe about 5 percent of [institutional investors] reward their people on the long term," says McKinsey's Barton. "But I think that is changing, and my hope is that over the next five or ten years, that will be 50 percent. I think they will understand that if you're thinking about the long term, you have to invest in companies that worry about winning the trust of their customers, having a healthy talent pipeline, and, yes, think about long-term issues like climate so that they don't end up with stranded assets."

In 2017, for the first time, McKinsey's annual guide to "Measuring and Managing the Value of Companies" devoted an opening chapter to attacking short-termism, declaring, "Creating shareholder value is not the same as maximizing short-term profits." What followed was a practical argument, backed by numbers, examples, and graphs, that shareholders are better off if denied short-term sugar highs. "Managers must resist short-term pressure to take actions that create illusory value quickly at the expense of the real thing in the long term," the report concluded.

Harvard Business School professor Rebecca Henderson is not optimistic that this logic will prevail. She believes, she said, that there is "a 65 percent chance that we will continue down the current path—the rich will get richer and make so much money that they'll continue focusing on the short term. It's awfully tempting, especially at firms that do more operating than innovating, to come in and strip the assets and the employees, make a lot of money, and leave." In fact, Henderson, who seems to be a slave to real rather than convenient data, says that there is no conclusive evidence that "it's more profitable *for the company* to think long-term," in part because that could be an excuse for management not to make tough decisions. But, she said, "it is absolutely clear that the stakeholders' model"—worrying about the welfare of employees, suppliers, and the community as a whole, as well as the company—"generates more overall wealth and well-being."

That Henderson gives the stakeholder model even a 35 percent chance of prevailing over the next decade is, to her, a sign of progress. She said that in 2012, when she started teaching a course called "Reimagining Capitalism"—which covers whether and how corporations can help solve the world's problems instead of contributing to them—she would have put the odds at 10 percent. The growing enthusiasm for her course is part of what gives her more hope. In 2012, 28 of the business school's 1,800 second-year students enrolled. By 2017, 600 were enrolled, and another 120 had to be turned away. In just five years it had become the third most popular class at the school.

"It's the Business School's way of having one course that tries to solve the problems created by all the others," sniffed one of Henderson's cynical colleagues. "Remember, we're the school that promoted Jensen and everything that followed." Some of her students "may just be curious," Henderson conceded. "But I think a lot of them really want to do something different. These are twenty-seven- and twenty-eight-year-olds, who are really affected by everything going on out there. They understand that worrying about carbon or income inequality or innovation is their responsibility and that, whether investors like it or not, the world is going to force that responsibility on them."

We should remember that the innovators of what became the short-term-obsessed, casino economy were not villains. With some exceptions, the world does not divide that simply into black and white. Joe Flom, his raider-clients, the stock buyback engineers, Lew Ranieri and Blythe Masters, even Angelo Mozilo, didn't set out to do harm, let alone create a crash that cost America $20 trillion in lost gross domestic product and boosted the have-a-lots far above everyone else. Even those who broke the law didn't wake up in the morning determined to destroy the economy so they could make money. They simply responded—many with trailblazing ingenuity—to the incentives put in front of them and the culture of the times. Change the incentives and change the culture and the genius of their successors can be redirected. Short-termism, which has been so devastating to so many Americans, is not immutable.

THE VALEANT POSTER CHILD

Indeed, the market could correct itself when too many deals that seemed great in the short term go bust once tested by time. A leading candidate for the first in what may become many poster children for self-destructive short-termism is a drug company called Valeant.

By 2008, Michael Pearson, a Canadian-born Duke University graduate working at McKinsey, had built the consulting company's biggest practice (which is saying something). Working out of an office in New Jersey, near many of his clients, he advised some of the world's largest drug companies, including Johnson & Johnson, on how to maximize profit from their patented prescription drugs.

Pearson's advice to his clients was simple, but, dressed up with all of McKinsey's PowerPoints and whiteboards, it seemed profound: Raise the price of the drugs aggressively, which they could do because the patents assured a monopoly on these treatments, and boost sales by targeting potential new groups of patients, even if that meant moving into markets for which the FDA had not approved the use of the drug. For example, Johnson & Johnson would try to get doctors to recommend its blockbuster anti-psychotic, Risperdal, for use by children and the elderly, even though the FDA had determined that the drug had not been proven safe for children or the elderly.

Pearson also counseled that his clients could cut back on research and development. Instead, he urged, they should spend their money buying smaller drug makers that already had products in the development pipeline but lacked the funds to finish the FDA approval process and market the products sufficiently. (Asked about Pearson having hatched his short-term strategy out of his consulting experience at McKinsey, Barton, who now runs McKinsey, would only say, "That's not the kind of advice we give today.")

In 2008, Pearson decided to become a player himself. He started by leaving McKinsey and taking over a small California drug maker. By 2010, he had borrowed enough to pull off a merger with a larger Canadian company and moved his headquarters there, avoiding American corporate income taxes in the process. Pearson's new company, renamed Valeant, then went on a buying spree. He would borrow money or issue new stock, buy a company, raise prices, expand markets, and cut back on R&D. Then he would buy another company.

He took on as a partner William Ackman, a celebrated hedge fund investor. In one attempted deal, they tried to force Allergan, the maker of Botox, to agree to a sale. At the time, Ackman told stock analysts that Valeant's announced plan to strip 90 percent out of Allergan's research and development budget was "really the opportunity" he saw in his and Pearson's proposed takeover. Allergan's CEO hired Lipton to fight Pearson off. Lipton and Allergan won (although it was then purchased by another drug company in a friendly deal).

Pearson moved on to other prey. In 2015, after doing more than a hundred deals, Valeant's stock was up about 4,000 percent since Pearson had taken over. He had negotiated a compensation plan giving him stock and stock options that were worth $3 billion, and Ackman's $4 billion investment in Valeant was worth more than $12 billion. All of the bad press and congressional grumbling targeting Valeant for raising prices by 200 or 300 percent on its often crucial drugs did not seem to faze the owners. An exultant Ackman began calling Pearson "the Warren Buffett of the twenty-first century."

By mid-2016 the house of cards had collapsed. Valeant, having no new products in the pipeline and having run out of deals, was found to be cooking the books to inflate reported sales. Pearson was fired (with an $11.9 million severance package), and although he had sold nearly $100 million worth of stock when the company was riding high, all of the remaining options he had earned were worth nothing. Ackman ended up losing all of his fund's $4 billion investment. It had taken fewer than eight years for the short term to become the long term.

In the spring of 2017, the *Harvard Business Review* published an unusually scathing article by two impeccably credentialed authors holding up Valeant as the best example of why corporate boards ought to rethink their nearly fifty-year devotion to Friedman's and Jensen's doctrine. "Don't misunderstand," Professors Joseph Bower and Lynn Paine wrote:

> We are capitalists to the core. We believe that widespread participation in the economy through the ownership of stock in publicly traded companies is important to the social fabric, and that strong protections for shareholders are essential. But the health of the economic system depends on getting the role of shareholders right. The [Jensen] agency model's extreme

version of shareholder centricity is flawed in its assumptions [because fast-trading institutional investors, who dominate stock ownership and hold it on behalf of others, are not true "owners"], confused as a matter of law [because corporations get charters from the state to do more than serve shareholders], and damaging in practice [usually to the long-term interests of the company and more certainly to the overall economy]. A better model would recognize the critical role of shareholders but also take seriously the idea that corporations are independent entities serving multiple purposes and endowed by law with the potential to endure over time.

The article continued with a blow-by-blow description of all the damage Jensen's theory had done. Because the authors were two highly regarded, tenured Harvard professors, their takedown of Jensen, Valeant, and short-termism soon became the talk of the business community. *Fortune* editor Alan Murray touted it in his daily newsletter the morning it was published, writing to seventy thousand members of the business community that "At a time when capitalism is increasingly under attack, it's worth asking whether the system has taken a fundamentally wrong turn." Lipton sent a memo a week later to his firm's clients, calling Bower and Paine's work a "must read" that documented "the fallacies of the economic theories and statistical studies that have been used since 1970 to justify shareholder-centric corporate governance, short-termism and activist attacks on corporations" in which the authors "demonstrate the pernicious effect of the agency theory" promoted by Friedman and Jensen.

In an email to Aspen's Samuelson attaching a final galley proof of her article, coauthor Paine thanked Samuelson, saying that she "owed much to the pioneering work" Samuelson and her colleagues had done. Samuelson forwarded Paine's email to colleagues, saying, "Okay, I can die happy. :)"

Not yet. It won't be a straight or easy path to untangle short-termism. Unilever's stock has more than doubled since Polman took over in 2009, yet in early 2017, Polman had to fight off a $143 billion takeover bid by a private equity fund known for aggressive employee layoffs and cost cutting when it had purchased consumer products companies Kraft and HJ Heinz. Since then, Unilever has repeatedly been rumored to be the target of raiders salivating over how they might "unlock value." In April 2017, the conservative *National Review*—reacting to Polman's rejection of the Kraft-Heinz takeover, which had caused Unilever stock to fall back after the announcement of the bid had seen it jump 14 percent—channeled Milton Friedman in an article titled "Multinational Boss Fashions Himself King of the World."

"CEOs need not aspire to be Gordon Gekko," wrote Deroy Murdock. "But they need not strive to be Mahatma Gandhi, either. Polman fancies himself as the latter." The magazine quoted a shareholder as saying, "I would prefer if Mr. Polman furthered his societal ambitions using his own rather than his shareholders' money," adding, "Paul Polman could satisfy many people, not least himself, by standing down as Unilever CEO and announcing his candidacy for secretary general of the United Nations." The following week, Polman announced a plan to sell Unilver's margarine businesses and buy back $5.3 billion of its shares, while forgoing larger asset sales and employee layoffs. "Polman satisfied investors by tightening some of the bolts, but at least he didn't throw out the baby with the bath water," McKinsey's Barton said. Nonetheless, through the end of 2017, Unilever was still thought to be a prime takeover target, with *Bloomberg Businessweek* speculating that the Kraft-Heinz group was likely to make another try. Polman, though, expressed confidence that his version of what the magazine called the unfolding "arc of economic history" would prevail: "Do we choose to serve a few billionaires, or do we choose to serve the billions?" he told the magazine. "Over time, I think the billions will win."

CHAPTER 4

The Greening of the First Amendment

While Paul Polman and other business leaders faced down short-termism, and while the rest of the country suffered the damage that the legal and financial engineering associated with it had done to an economy and a social fabric that depends on a thriving, hopeful middle class, the political sphere saw a parallel upheaval that would intensify the inequality being produced by the new economy. Like athletes supplied a wonder steroid, it would allow the winners to use political muscle of a kind never seen in Washington or in the country's state capitals to enhance their winnings and disable government in a way that would protect what they had won, even what they had won by abusing or breaking the rules. It, too, was the product of best-and-brightest legal engineering. It, too, began in the 1970s, when a cherished American value was hijacked.

One afternoon in 2017, in a grimy, windowless room in an ordinary four-story building about four hundred yards from the Capitol dome, a congressman, whom we will call Jones, hunched over a desk dialing phone numbers listed on computer printouts that a determined young aide persisted in handing him, one after another. The printouts included assorted personal details related to the people he was dialing: spouse's name, children's names, last phone call or meeting and what was said, last campaign contribution. Although he was elected to focus on policy, sit through hearings, and debate or even write the laws his country lives by, calling people to ask for campaign contributions is what Jones did for four or five hours every weekday.

On a lamp next to his desk a Post-it note in his handwriting read, "I don't give a shit!" It was a tongue-in-cheek reminder, he explained, "that I have to stay focused. I have to suspend all humanity when I am doing this. If the guy at the other end of the phone says he's been sick, I can sympathize with him for a minute and act like I care, but as soon as I can, I have to get the conversation back on track, because I just can't afford to spend a lot of time. I can't let myself give a shit about his problems. I have to get a check from him. 'Your wife died? Oh, that's awful. She was such a terrific person. Is there anything I can do? Oh, I need to tell you that we're nearing the end of the quarter, so I really need you to max out with a check by Monday, so we can show a great quarter when we file.' That's the kind of person I have to be when I'm in this room."

Why does Jones—a smart, down-to-earth, good-humored, passionate public policy wonk who ran for office for all the right reasons—have to be that kind of person?

It is Martin Redish's fault, and the fault of the First Amendment.

In 1969, Redish, a third-year student at Harvard Law School who grew up in a middle-class family on Long Island, was eager to impress a faculty adviser who was, he said, "a cantankerous old guy, but someone who could write me a valuable recommendation. . . . My strategy was to think of something to write for my final paper that was different, contentious, even courageous. I desperately wanted to be an academic, and thought this was my entrée."

Redish had been interested in free speech issues since his sophomore year in high school, when the principal infuriated him by censoring an intemperate paragraph he had written for the school paper attacking the John Birch Society. Six years later, in the summer before his first year at law school, Redish wrote another paper about free speech—this time spelling out why flag burning should be protected by the First Amendment. When he arrived on campus, he proudly showed it to a professor, who, Redish said, dismissed the rookie law student's argument as ridiculous. The Supreme Court came around to Redish's view twenty-two years later, in 1989.

For his senior Harvard Law thesis Redish picked yet another

First Amendment subject, which he had begun to think about as an undergraduate at the University of Pennsylvania. He had worked as a research assistant there for a professor who was a devotee of Alexander Meiklejohn, a famed philosopher and educator. What intrigued Redish was that Meiklejohn, who was not trained as a lawyer, believed that if free speech was all about enabling self-government in a democracy, then the overriding value of the First Amendment was not only that you could express any view you wanted to, but also that you and everyone else in a democracy were free to hear or read and consider the broadest possible range of everyone else's views in order to make the best self-government decisions.

Accordingly, once the free flow of ideas focused on the *consumer* of ideas more than about who got to express them, why should the government, under the First Amendment, be allowed to restrict those ideas based on who the speaker is, even if it is a corporation? Self-government is about more than politics, Redish reasoned. It is also about making decisions in a free market about what kind of cars to buy, for example, or about what measures to take to protect one's health—information most likely to be conveyed by businesses. A commercial speaker's motive might be to make money, but why did that matter? Selfishness cannot be a valid disqualifier when it comes to free speech. Your motive may be to make money or otherwise advance yourself if you hand out a leaflet in front of a bookstore demanding your money back for this book, or if you walk a picket line seeking higher wages for you and your co-workers, or if you launch a web page demanding an end to a public policy that is hurting a member of your family. So what? Listeners should be free to hear from you, while perhaps taking their assessment of your motives into account.

"The Supreme Court," Redish said in one of a series of conversations, "had routinely cast aside the idea of corporate free speech. It just didn't make any sense to me."

When Redish's Harvard professor read the first draft of his senior thesis—arguing, in spite of all Supreme Court doctrine, that corporations should have the same free speech right as people because their arguments, too, contributed to the public dialogue—he told Redish he thought he was crazy. This was 1969, a time when corporations, which were being pilloried by Ralph Nader, Rachel Carson, and others, were not typically grouped with anti-war demonstrators as First

Amendment warriors. Still, recalled Redish, the Harvard professor "gave me an A. He thought I had guts."

While working the following year in a prestigious federal appeals court clerkship, Redish turned his Harvard thesis into a law review article. He hoped to get it published in a top law journal. The most prestigious ones turned him down. *The Yale Law Journal*, he recalled, rejected it with a "condescending letter," saying, "We don't think this argument deserves the attention you gave it."

That may have been partly because Redish's draft had dissed Yale Law professor Thomas Emerson, a legend among civil liberties and civil rights lawyers. Among other milestones, Emerson had won the landmark Supreme Court case striking down prohibitions on the sale of contraceptives and establishing for the first time the right to privacy that would end up banning restrictions on abortion or same-sex relations. In his revered 1963 text, "Toward a General Theory of the First Amendment," Emerson had dispensed in a footnote with the idea that commercial speech deserved First Amendment protection, writing, "The problem of differentiating between commercial and other communication has not in practice proved to be a serious one."

Redish's article, which was published by the law review of the George Washington University Law School in 1971, attacked Emerson frontally in the third paragraph as a "leading expounder of First Amendment theory" whose dismissal of commercial speech as not worthy of protection because it fell into a different category of expression amounted to an "analytical attempt [that] does little more than assume the ultimate conclusion." Redish spent the next forty-three pages explaining how an intellectually honest analysis would acknowledge that "it is important to perceive that information and ideas which are traditionally accorded substantial First Amendment protection may, on occasion, be disseminated in commercial form by those with commercial motives. . . . If the courts are to do justice to the concerns of free speech, they must delve beyond . . . preconceived prejudices that have existed in this area."

Redish reminded readers that the most celebrated First Amendment protection case of all—*The New York Times v. Sullivan* libel case—was about an ad (the ultimate in commercial speech) that had been published by a corporate defendant in this case, the *Times*, whom the Supreme Court decided to protect. Redish argued that the fact

that the ad involved an attack on an elected official and was, therefore, political in nature, did not mean that other types of commercial
speech—pitching a product, for example, or taking sides in a controversy that affected a company's business—did not also deserve protection. Listeners or readers could benefit from all types of information
to perform all kinds of acts of self-government, including making
decisions about what products to buy.

During his 1970–71 stint clerking, Redish worked on another article
that echoed the theme that the First Amendment was as much about
listeners as speakers. This time, he extended the idea to a different
context: campaign spending. Writing in the November issue of the
New York University Law Review at a time when Congress was debating
tightening restrictions on campaign spending, Redish conceded that
the growing dominance of television had forced candidates to raise
increasingly large sums to compete effectively. The amount spent on
broadcast advertising in the presidential elections had skyrocketed
from $9 million in 1956 to $40 million in 1968. (In 2016, TV and
radio spending would be about $845 million, largely as a result of the
legal scholarship that Redish was pioneering.)

"For those who lack the good fortune to possess a good fortune," he wrote in the 1971 article, "but who nevertheless aspire to
public office, the only alternative to political obscurity increasingly
appears to be a somewhat unseemly reliance on large contributors.
The obvious danger, of course, is that elected representatives will
become overly susceptible to the influence of those who pay their
bills." Nonetheless, Redish asserted, laws limiting the rights of a candidate or her supporters to spend money to speak to the voters did not
pass constitutional muster because they would cause the same listener
deprivation that he had outlined in urging that commercial speech
deserved First Amendment protection. "Once it is recognized that a
significant purpose of the first amendment is to ensure that the public
will be provided with information necessary to the performance of
its self-governing function," he wrote, "it follows that information
disseminated in the course of an election campaign must rank high in
terms of first amendment values."

As for the unfairness of one candidate being able to defeat an opponent simply by outspending him, Redish had an answer that was similarly built on the listeners' rights argument:

> It is generally argued that a wealthy candidate should not be permitted to "buy an election" with his finances and that legislated limits on campaign spending are therefore necessary. The reasoning . . . seems to be that, when one candidate's financial resources are limited, the only equitable solution is to require the wealthier candidate to reduce his spending. . . . In other words, if a portion of the voting public is to be generally unfamiliar with one candidate's views and record because of his financial inability to become well known, it is only fair that the public be almost as uninformed about the other candidate. Such reasoning presents at the very least a prima facie conflict with the First Amendment policy of encouraging as much communication in the political realm as possible.

BOOMERANG

The two prongs of Redish's listener-deprivation view of First Amendment protections—that both commercial speech, and speech financed through campaign spending, were parts of the marketplace of ideas that were vital for listeners in a democracy to have maximum access to—would ultimately come together in a series of Supreme Court decisions related to campaign finance laws. (As explained later, corporations would also use them to try to shield themselves from various types of regulation related to how they market and sell their products.)

The most famous, or infamous, of the political spending cases would be *Citizens United v. FEC*, in 2010. In that decision, the Supreme Court prohibited the Federal Election Commission from enforcing any restriction on corporate political spending that did not involve direct contributions to a candidate's campaign, and instead was directed at ostensibly independent political action committees and other outside groups supporting a candidate or issue.

In the circles Redish runs in, *Citizens United* is a reviled case. "I am a liberal Democrat," Redish groused over dinner one night, losing what is his usual affability. "I've even served as a precinct captain. But

I'm now regarded as something of a pariah. I love Rachel Maddow," he added, referring to the liberal MSNBC prime-time host. "I think she's great, but when I hear her ranting about *Citizens United* because it lets corporations speak, it drives me crazy. Here she is sitting there using the reach and resources of a giant corporation, Comcast"—the owner of NBC and MSNBC—"to push her views. What hypocrisy! Let's remember, *Citizens United* was about a corporation making a documentary attacking Hillary Clinton. The Court said they had a right to do that."

Redish is right about that, just as he and others on his side of the argument are right to point out that people on the left never dispute the right of unions to speak or to fund political campaigns. However, he did not mention that instead of finding for Citizens United—a conservatively oriented corporation formed in part to make these kind of political attack movies—on the narrow grounds that, like MSNBC, it was engaging in political speech as part of its corporate purpose, the Court veered off with a far broader ruling that there could be no limits on how much any corporation of any kind could spend through independent organizations formed to support or oppose candidates.

The first case leading to *Citizens United* had come in 1976, shortly after Redish's articles had begun percolating through academia. Campaign finance restrictions had been signed into law by President Nixon in 1972, and were then made more stringent following the Watergate scandal. In the 1976 case, *Buckley v. Valeo*, the Supreme Court ruled that individual contributions made directly to candidates could, indeed, be limited, because of the possibility of corruption posed by such a direct connection between a donor and a candidate. However, the justices declared that the First Amendment prohibited any limits on what the candidate himself could spend, or on the total amount the campaign could spend, or on how much independent groups could spend to support a candidate. Redish's NYU article was cited by the Court in its opinion.

The *Buckley* decision did not overturn long-standing prohibitions on corporate contributions made directly to candidates, nor did it strike down a $5,000 limit on how much a corporation could contribute to an independent group. (The latter is the limit that would be overturned in *Citizens United*). The Court's rationale in the *Buckley* case echoed Redish's argument that campaign money was necessary to give voters the information they needed. In effect money was speech, and speakers had a right to be heard and listeners had a right to hear them:

> A restriction on the amount of money a person or group can spend on political communication during a campaign necessarily reduces the quantity of expression by restricting the number of issues discussed, the depth of their exploration, and the size of the audience reached. This is because virtually every means of communicating ideas in today's mass society requires the expenditure of money.

The case's title bore the name of James Buckley, a wealthy conservative New York senator running for reelection. Other plaintiffs included Senator Eugene McCarthy, the liberal Democrat whose insurgent presidential candidacy had helped unseat Lyndon Johnson in 1968. Early on, this was not the mostly right versus left battle that money in politics would ultimately become.

The first prong of Redish's listener deprivation argument—the one related to commercial speech—also percolated slowly through academic circles until it, too, hit the Supreme Court in 1976, just five months after the *Buckley* campaign finance decision.

Given the political tinge that would later be associated with the corporate free speech movement, it is ironic who the litigants were in the case of *Virginia State Board of Pharmacy v. Virginia Citizens Consumer Council.* Consumer activist Ralph Nader's Public Citizen Litigation Group represented a Virginia consumer rights organization that sued to invalidate a law prohibiting pharmacies from advertising their drug prices. Their claim was that consumers benefited from price advertising because it encouraged competition. The drugstores, whose trade association liked the protection from competition that the advertising restrictions facilitated, hadn't sued to assert their First Amendment right to advertise. That meant that the Supreme Court immediately had to face the issue of standing: Did these plaintiffs—drugstore customers, who were the *recipients* of information—have First Amendment rights, too? The Court ruled that they did.

Writing for the majority, Associate Justice Harry Blackmun declared that refusing to protect speech only because it was commercial was a "simplistic approach" that, as Redish had argued in 1971, deprived the listeners of their First Amendment rights. "As to the particular consumer's interest in the free flow of commercial information," Blackmun ruled, "that interest may be as keen, if not keener by far, than his interest in the day's most urgent political debate. Appellees' case in this respect is a convincing one. Those whom the suppression of prescription drug price information hits the hardest are the poor, the sick, and particularly the aged."

The Supreme Court thus extended the First Amendment in a way that opened the door for money to enter politics as never before. Nader's suit would be followed by a steady succession of cases giving corporations the right to speak and ultimately the right to spend hundreds of millions of dollars to influence political debate and put favored candidates into office—and even, as we will see, block government regulations, including those aimed at protecting the sick from being targets of improper marketing of drugs that had life-threatening side effects.

"Talk about boomerangs," Ralph Nader told me in 2017. "That case was the biggest boomerang of all time."

NO MORE "APPEASEMENT"

Nader also played a key role in fomenting a boomerang effect of far broader dimensions, causing the new, expanded use of the First Amendment to upend the balance of power in America between those at the top and everyone else.

Nader had risen to prominence in 1965, with the publication that year of his attack on the automobile industry, *Unsafe at Any Speed*, which focused on General Motors. He then achieved star status because of media reaction to GM's clumsy attempts to smear him by hiring private investigators to look into his personal life. His reach had since expanded on multiple fronts. Donors contributed millions of dollars to support Nader's Raiders—teams of students coming out of college and law school organized to do research and issue reports (with headline-grabbing press releases) on all varieties of alleged business abuses, which the Raiders' legal teams then brought suits to stop. The assault on corporate America was starting to sting.

There were attacks from other groups seeking reforms aimed at protecting the environment, ending job discrimination against women and minorities, curbing the military industrial complex, and protecting employees against unsafe or unhealthy workplaces. Even President Richard Nixon, elected in 1968, seemed sympathetic. By 1972, he had signed or would soon sign laws establishing price controls, the Equal Employment Opportunity Commission, the Environmental Protection Agency, and the Occupational Health and Safety Administration.

In response, businesses, which had previously restricted their Washington activities to paying dues to relatively docile trade associations, began to open their own Washington lobbying offices and to push for those trade associations, particularly the U.S. Chamber of Commerce, to match the activist tactics that Nader and others were deploying so successfully against them. In August 1971, a manifesto that became their rallying cry and battle plan was written at the behest of the Chamber by an otherwise soft-spoken Richmond, Virginia, lawyer named Lewis Powell, Jr. Although originally intended to be a confidential memo for Chamber executives, it was soon photocopied and mailed from one corporate boardroom to another, reaching and rousing an audience far beyond its intended recipients.

Powell, then a month from his sixty-fourth birthday, was a senior partner at Virginia's richest law firm. He was the kind of business leader who was also a civic leader, serving on the local school board and making sure his firm did pro bono work. In this memo, however, Powell was taking the advice of Milton Friedman, whom he quoted, in arguing that business could no longer afford to worry about "externalities." It was time to focus on the bottom line. It was time to fight for capitalism.

In addition to having held multiple leadership positions at the American Bar Association, Powell had a blue-chip roster of corporate clients, including the tobacco companies that then dominated industry in the South. In the wake of a 1964 report from the U.S. surgeon general linking tobacco to lung cancer and other diseases, they had been under constant attack. The first law requiring warning labels on cigarette packs had sailed through Congress and been signed by the president. Powell had been on the front lines trying to fight off tobacco regulation and demanding equal time whenever his clients' products were impugned.

His uncharacteristically fiery thirty-four-page Chamber of Commerce memo reads today like notes taken during a panic attack. Powell, who had always been a gentlemanly, non-confrontational elder statesman of his community, his profession, and his country, was now suddenly confronting the kaleidoscope of 1960s movements and people that threatened everything he thought was right with the world. His memo offers a time-capsule-like picture of the business community's angry sense of victimization, and explains the determined, multi-pronged "We're not gonna take it anymore" counterattack that would follow.

"No thoughtful person can question that the American economic system is under broad attack," Powell began. "We are not dealing with episodic or isolated attacks from a relatively few extremists or even from the minority socialist cadre." Rather, Powell wrote, the assault was coming from "perfectly respectable elements of society: from the college campus, the pulpit, the media, the intellectual and literary journals, the arts and sciences, and from politicians." Although only a minority of those in these various groups participated in the attacks, Powell explained, they are often "the most articulate, the most vocal, the most prolific"—a problem exacerbated by all the uncritical attention the media were lavishing on them. Exhibit A was Nader, whom Powell called "the single most effective antagonist of American business, who—thanks largely to the media—has become a legend in his own time and an idol of millions of Americans."

Powell expressed scorn for the way that big business, particularly the media industry through its news coverage, "tolerates, if not participates in its own destruction." He made the same argument, even more angrily, about "the campuses from which much of the criticism emanates," which he noted were supported by "contributions from . . . funds controlled or generated by American business," and whose largest donors and trustees "overwhelmingly are composed of men and women who are leaders in the system." He singled out Charles Reich, a professor at Yale Law School, whose 1970 book, *The Greening of America*, was still sitting on best-seller lists and had made him a campus hero. Powell described Reich's book as "a frontal assault . . . on our government, our system of justice and the free enterprise system," and quoted a newspaper columnist reporting that Yale was graduating "young men who despise the American political and economic system. . . . They live, not by rational discussion, but by mindless slogans."

Powell didn't stop at this grim survey of the American landscape. Most of his memo was a lawyerly, point-by-point battle plan for an overdue counterattack. It began with the kind of part-scolding and part–pep talk a coach might give a losing team at halftime: "The painfully sad truth is that business, including the boards of directors and the top executives of corporations great and small and business organizations at all levels, often have responded—if at all—by appeasement, ineptitude and ignoring the problem. . . . The time has come—indeed, it is long overdue—for the wisdom, ingenuity, and resources of American business to be marshaled against those who would destroy it." Effort and money were needed on all fronts, he explained. Business leaders had to invest in lobbying and even spend time making their case in Washington personally. Writers had to be recruited to balance out the "leftist" arguments that dominated scholarly journals and editorial pages. Speakers bureaus had to be organized so that defenders of the American system could appear on campus to correct the leftist imbalance.

Powell was careful to emphasize that he believed in academic freedom. Business leader-donors could not and should not financially pressure universities to get left-leaning faculty fired or biased textbooks scrapped. Rather, the Chamber or other organizations should organize panels to review the balance of views presented by campus speakers or even by faculty, or the fairness of textbooks, and then not be shy about making their findings known and pushing for change. Similarly, panels needed to be hired to monitor the media and complain about unfair coverage.

The most important aspect of Powell's memo was his urging that these efforts not be scattershot one-offs. The Chamber of Commerce had to be reorganized and revitalized to create units aimed at implementing each aspect of the plan. New organizations, such as think tanks and even law firms, should be funded to do the same.

Critics of the efforts that followed Powell's call to action would later argue that he was advocating that business use money to pressure the press and academic institutions and unduly influence scholarly journals. Some of that happened, but what Powell actually wrote was nothing more—and nothing less—than that big business should begin to use the First Amendment. They should fight speech with speech. In fact, Powell even urged businesses to spend at least 10 percent of their advertising budgets on messages meant to defend the American economic system. In effect, he was advocating that big business use the First Amendment rights that Martin Redish just months before, in his still largely unnoticed law review article, had argued that they had.

Two months after Powell wrote his memo, he was appointed to the Supreme Court by President Nixon, where he came to be considered a relatively moderate member of the conservative side of the bench. (He wrote an impassioned concurring opinion, for example, supporting the right of undocumented immigrant children to be educated in public schools.)

Seven years later, in 1978, Associate Justice Powell cast the pivotal vote and wrote the decision in a 5–4 Supreme Court ruling that advanced corporate speech rights far beyond what the Virginia pharmacy advertising case had held. He declared unconstitutional a Massachusetts law prohibiting a corporation (the First National Bank of Boston) from spending to advertise on exactly the broad public policy issues (in this case an income tax referendum) that private lawyer Powell had urged businesses in his Chamber memo to devote a portion of their ad budgets to. The briefs taking the bank's side emphasized the value of the First Amendment in protecting informed debate, regardless of who the speaker was.

"The Constitution often protects interests broader than those of the party seeking their vindication," Powell wrote in agreement. "The First Amendment, in particular, serves significant societal interests. The proper question, therefore, is not whether corporations 'have' First Amendment rights and, if so, whether they are coextensive with those of natural persons. Instead, the question must be whether [the law prohibiting the bank's ads] abridges expression that the First Amendment was meant to protect. We hold that it does."

The dissent written by then–Associate Justice William Rehnquist, the court's leading conservative, focused on the undue influence that corporations might exert if allowed to finance political advertising:

"A State grants to a business corporation the blessings of potentially perpetual life and limited liability to enhance its efficiency as an economic entity. It might reasonably be concluded that those properties, so beneficial in the economic sphere, pose special dangers in the political sphere." Rehnquist also invoked an 1819 decision that had defined the limited role of corporations: "A corporation is an artificial being, invisible, intangible, and existing only in contemplation of law. Being the mere creature of law, it possesses only those properties which the charter of creation confers upon it, either expressly, or as incidental to its very existence."

THE MARCH ON WASHINGTON

Some of the legal work that successfully overturned the Massachusetts law was done by the Pacific Legal Foundation, a group formed by a team of California conservatives who were inspired by Powell's memo. Ralph Nader no longer had a monopoly on "public interest" law firms. Pacific Legal and then the Washington Legal Foundation, both funded by donations from corporations and wealthy individuals, sprang up beginning in the early 1970s. They were followed by others, including a large group of all-star lawyers organized under the umbrella of the Chamber of Commerce. They called themselves public interest law firms, too, although the press routinely used adjectives like "conservative" or "right-wing" to describe them.

Alongside the lawyers were policy wonks recruited into new think tanks, like the Heritage Foundation, or to the expanded ranks of the American Enterprise Institute, which had started modestly in 1938. Now there would be new scholarship presenting the conservative side of issues such as union rights, free trade, environmental regulation, and consumer protection laws. Trade organizations, lobbyists, and sympathetic politicians now had their own studies and reports to quote. As Jane Mayer documented in her book *Dark Money*, the think tanks were typically funded by wealthy conservatives including Richard Mellon Scaife, the heir to an oil, banking, and aluminum fortune, and beer magnate Joseph Coors.

These efforts were supplemented by an explosion in Washington of lobbyists and political fund-raising groups, called political action committees, or PACs, meant to supply the money that would give lobbyists the clout they needed.

The first PAC had been created by a labor union, the Congress of Industrial Organizations, or CIO, in 1943 to support President Franklin Roosevelt after the Republican Party picked up large numbers of House and Senate seats in the 1942 off-year election. With the support of conservative, mostly Southern Democrats, the Republicans redoubled their efforts to roll back FDR's New Deal. Reacting to a wartime coal miners' strike, the new Congress passed a law (over Roosevelt's veto) allowing the president to seize industries important to the war effort in the event of a strike. The same law included a provision barring unions from contributing directly to federal candidates. The CIO's PAC, organized and run by Sidney Hillman, the celebrated textile workers leader and a CIO cofounder, was a clever way to sidestep the new law. Shop stewards would solicit contributions to the ostensibly independent PAC at the same time that they collected the workers' union dues. The PAC could then contribute to its favored candidates. The new organization, Hillman announced in a fiery speech to a union conference in Philadelphia, was needed to fight "isolationist Republicans and their reactionary blood brothers in the Democratic Party" who are "venting their hatred on President Roosevelt" and who wanted to "destroy labor unions." Through the 1950s and 1960s there was far more political money in union PACs than in business-oriented PACs.

That changed dramatically in the 1970s. If the 1971 Powell memo was a battle plan, what galvanized the business community to put the plan into high gear was another union initiative, also in 1971. That year, unions—which had initially championed free trade—began to realize that global competition was costing them jobs and leverage. Employers could outsource manufacturing work abroad, or threaten to if unions didn't reduce their wage demands. Leaders of major unions became so concerned that they persuaded Indiana senator Vance Hartke and Massachusetts congressman James Burke, both Democrats, to introduce a sweeping bill that would eviscerate free trade and, in fact, block the emerging global aspirations of the country's leading businesses.

The proposed Burke-Hartke Act provided that U.S. taxes would be paid on any profits corporations made overseas (even if they were also taxed overseas). It also set quotas on all imports of goods that competed with goods made in the U.S. Finally, it allowed the president to restrict U.S. corporations from investing in factories or even companies overseas if doing so would threaten American jobs. America's major corporations—which today produce and sell so much around the world that half or more of the investment, employment, and revenue of the typical Fortune 500 company happens abroad—would have been forced to stay home.

It was a dramatic overreach, the product of the unions' sudden realization of the dangers of trade and of the iron grip they still had on the Democratic Party. And it produced a backlash that ultimately helped accelerate the demise of unions because it shocked the business community into overdrive. For the two years that Burke-Hartke was pending in Congress, corporate America feared that with the economy lagging and President Nixon running for reelection, he might be forced to sign the law if it made it through Congress, which was controlled by Democrats. Although the national press paid modest attention to the debate, businesses viewed the bill as an existential threat at a time when world markets were opening up. Blocking it was the corporate world's highest priority. Ultimately, they unleashed enough lobbying power, backed by think-tank-generated scholar-advocates and white papers, to get the bill killed without a vote in 1973. They now saw clearly how all that First Amendment–protected speech and lobbying could protect them.

The Powell wake-up call and Burke-Hartke fire drill produced an unprecedented redirection of business resources to Washington. According to lobbying historian Lee Drutman, the Chamber of Commerce, which had had 36,000 members in 1967, had 80,000 by 1974 and would have 160,000 by 1980. The National Federation of Independent Business, which focused on smaller enterprises, grew from 300 members in 1970 to 600,000 by 1979. The Business Roundtable, composed of the chief executives of the nation's largest corporations, was organized in 1972 and quickly became a muscular elite, whose members would lobby Congress and the executive branch one-on-one.

It added up to what political scientists Jacob Hacker and Paul Pierson called "a domestic version of Shock and Awe. The number of corporations with public affairs offices in Washington grew from

100 in 1968 to over 500 in 1978. In 1971, only 175 firms had registered lobbyists in Washington, but by 1982, nearly 2,500 did." By
2016, approximately 1,400 companies would have their own Washington offices, and the total number of corporations and trade associations represented by the city's 11,000 registered lobbyists (more
than twenty for every member of the House and Senate) would be
over 7,700. By then they would be spending $3.1 billion annually on
their registered lobbyists, and maybe as much as double that if the
Washington lawyers and consultants who were paid to influence Congress and the executive branch but did not register under the loosely
enforced lobbying rules were also counted. The spending was actually
higher, $3.5 billion, in 2009 and 2010 when consequential legislation,
such as the Affordable Care Act (Obamacare) and the Dodd-Frank
financial reform bill, was being debated.

All of that lobbying was more directly protected by the First
Amendment than Martin Redish's attenuated use of it to block restrictions on corporate speech or campaign giving. The First Amendment
explicitly protects the right "to petition the Government for a redress
of grievances." Thousands of knowledge workers were now climbing
into the top one percent by being hired to do that petitioning.

PAC money grew as fast as the lobbying brigades. In 1971, there
were 300 PACs associated with business interests. In 1980 there were
1,369. As of 2017, there were 2,353. With campaign spending now
skyrocketing because of the need to fund expensive advertising buys,
Democrats began to depend on these business PACs, too, *which meant
they, too, had to pay attention to what business wanted.* It was a shift exacerbated by the declining fortunes of unions and their ability to fund
the traditionally union-friendly party's candidates. In the early 1970s,
unions contributed more to congressional PACs than businesses did.
By the mid-1970s, the business PACs had caught up, and in 1980,
business PAC contributions outnumbered those of union PACs by
about two to one, a trend that would continue to accelerate. Moreover, declines in union strength and membership undermined their
traditional role in bringing out the Democratic vote on Election Day.

As a result, the 1976 election of Democrat Jimmy Carter and
the Democrats' continued control of Congress failed to produce the
kinds of policy gains for the Democrats that were expected following the post-Watergate rout of the Republicans. Carter's push for
new consumer protection and product safety laws was blocked in

Congress. A proposal to make the National Labor Relations Board enforcement process more friendly to unions—which were beginning to lose organizing battles because of employers' increasingly aggressive and often unlawful resistance—also failed. Despite there being sixty-one Democrats in the Senate and many moderate Republicans, the labor law reform bill could not muster the sixty votes necessary to break a filibuster. Carter's plan to change the tax code in favor of the middle class at the expense of the rich ended up being changed in Congress by lobbyists so that it did exactly the opposite: Capital gains tax rates were cut, other loopholes were preserved or expanded, and Social Security payroll taxes, which affect the non-rich disproportionately, were raised. In every case the Democrats' agenda was blocked by wavering Democrats in Congress, who were the recipients of business PAC donations.

One law—passed in 2003, and surviving in its current form to this day, despite the damage done to taxpayers and to consumers—best illustrates the soaring influence of big business, even on Democrats. For years, the pharmaceutical industry had fought off efforts by Democrats to have drugs added to Medicare's coverage in order to protect the elderly from increasingly high prices. The industry feared that if Medicare had to pay for drugs, there would be a provision in the legislation allowing Medicare, which under the new law would become by far the largest customer for all types of drugs, to use its buying power to negotiate prices. That would drive down the cost for Medicare. The lower prices were likely to flow through to private insurers, too. By 2003, however, the industry was so sure of the clout of its PACs and lobbyists that it thought it could get a Medicare coverage law passed that would *prohibit* Medicare from negotiating. So, it switched gears and pushed for drug coverage, along with a clause outlawing price negotiations. The industry won on both counts. It got millions of new paying customers, courtesy of Medicare, but Medicare was required to pay whatever the industry demonstrated was the average price it was charging everyone else—which, if the drug had a patent and, therefore, had monopoly status, was literally whatever its manufacturer decided to charge.

The provision prohibiting negotiations was agreed to not just by Republicans, but by some leading Democrats, including Montana senator Max Baucus. Baucus would later become the Senate Finance Committee chairman who helped write Obamacare—which, in return for the drug industry's support (including using its PAC money to run ads supporting the law), also did not include a provision backed by liberal Democrats to unshackle Medicare and allow the agency to negotiate prices. From 2003 to 2010, Baucus was the leading recipient of campaign contributions from the health care industry, much of it from PACs associated with the pharmaceutical sector. On the other side of the aisle, Billy Tauzin, the Louisiana Republican who steered the Medicare-drugs bill through Congress, resigned soon thereafter and took a $2-million-a-year job as the industry's lead lobbyist.

The drug makers' absolute power has remained undiminished, and the industry has continued to enjoy by far the highest profit margins of any industry sector.* Although President Trump frequently attacked drug companies for "rip-off" prices on the campaign trail and in his first year in the White House, none of his or the congressional Republicans' proposals to relieve Americans from high health insurance premiums that Republicans charged were caused by Obamacare included anything related to controlling what is actually the most obvious factor in rising insurance premiums: skyrocketing drug prices. In the first six months of the Trump administration, the pharmaceutical industry spent $145 million on lobbying. *The New York Times*, citing a Kaiser Health News analysis, reported that during the same period, the industry "gave $4.5 million to congressional campaigns, including six-figure donations" to the three Republicans up for reelection who could allow or block any congressional votes on drug pricing: the speaker of the House, the chairman of the House Energy and Commerce Committee, and the chairman of the Senate Finance Committee.

In 1985, Thomas Edsall, then a reporter for *The Washington Post*, wrote a book documenting how, despite what he called "adverse cir-

---

* A 2017 report by the Government Accountability Office found that profit margins for the twenty-five largest drug companies in 2015 were approximately 50 percent higher than those of the twenty-five largest companies in the seemingly higher-margin software industry and triple those of the 500 largest non-software or non-drug companies. Importantly, although the drug companies always justify their high prices by citing their high costs for research and development, their profit margin takes into account what they spend on R & D.

cumstances," such as Watergate and corporate scandals associated with President Nixon's fund-raising, business interests in Washington remained dominant through the Carter years and thereafter. The book's title and subtitle said it all: *The New Politics of Inequality: A Quiet Transfer of Power Has Taken Place in the Nation's Capital.* Surprisingly, at least in retrospect, Edsall's compelling, richly reported wake-up call was largely ignored. Sales were modest, Edsall recalled. *The New York Times Book Review* gave it a two-sentence mention in a "New and Noteworthy" roundup nearly two months after it was published.

Reform efforts on multiple fronts during the terms of the next two Democratic presidents, Bill Clinton and Barack Obama, were generally unsuccessful, too. Even in the two years of his term when his party controlled Congress, Clinton failed to get a health care reform bill out of congressional committees, had an infrastructure proposal reduced to less than was spent during the George H. W. Bush administration, and had to scrap plans for a carbon tax. Of course, his efforts were blocked still more completely once the Republicans took over the House and then the Senate. During the two years of the Obama administration when Democrats controlled Congress, Obama did get Obamacare passed, but only after having to eliminate plans, at the behest of some of the Democrats whose votes he needed, to include a liberal "public option" for health insurance, and only after he had to scrap most initiatives directed at controlling health care prices in return for getting the health care lobby's support.

From 1970 to 2010, spending per person on health care in the United States increased (in inflation-adjusted 2013 dollars) nearly 420 percent, from $1,742 to $8,400. Profits and executive salaries in the health care industry—including at supposedly non-profit tax-exempt hospitals—increased at the same pace. In theory, this should have been a hot political issue, drawing broad support for action. Health care was now squeezing workers with escalating out-of-pocket costs, even as their wages had been almost completely frozen over the same period. Employers were facing skyrocketing insurance premiums for their workforces, costs that were not borne by their foreign competitors. Taxpayers were seeing that Medicare and Medicaid were demanding a lion's share of federal and state budgets. Yet because the health care interests had plowed enough of their profits into what had become the largest lobbying arsenal of any American industry, none of the controls that prevail in every other country on prices for products that people usually have little choice but to buy ever made it out of a congressional committee.

I had a front-row seat in 2010 (when the Democrats controlled the White House and both houses of Congress) watching a shock-and-awe display of lobby power by another industry. That June, I camped out at the Capitol to write a cover story for *Time* magazine about the lobbying accompanying another Obama initiative—the Dodd-Frank financial reform law. The *Time* article's title: "The Best Laws Money Can Buy."

"We have three lawyers total working on this," the legislative director for the Consumer Federation of America, an organization representing 280 non-profits, said. "They [the financial services industry] can have three people working on a paragraph." The imbalance could be measured not just in bodies but also in the unending flow of alternative-language proposals and "white papers" that the lobbyists churned out. One was a glossy "study" full of color graphs and charts, written by consultants on behalf of a group representing private equity funds, defending the "carried interest" tax loophole. The seemingly authoritative graphs and heavily footnoted text purported to explain how taxing those who run these funds at the same rates that everyone else pays on their earned income would be disastrous for the economy, killing millions of jobs and driving away trillions of investment dollars. The purpose of such voluminous, jargon-filled gibberish, explained one lobbyist who chuckled when I questioned the backup for one of the footnotes, was to give members of Congress who wanted to side with deep-pocketed groups like the private equity funds some ostensible scholarship to point to in justifying their votes. The *Time* article concluded that, given the billions at stake, spending millions on well-connected lobbyists and their white papers was "the best bargain in Washington," even in the Obama years.

Almost since the founding of the country, ascendant conservative policies had been pushed back by liberal initiatives, only to be pushed back in the other direction by conservatives, who were then pushed back again by the liberals. In the 1970s, the cycle mostly ended. Now the historic American pendulum was frozen in place—by money's new dominance.

With the new knowledge economy thriving, the number of lawyers in Washington tripled from 1973 to 1983. As we have seen, many of the new troops were lobbyists working Capitol Hill and the White House. Thousands more did lobbying of a different sort: They were charged with defending corporate interests at dozens of regulatory agencies. Their work, as much as anything else, helped freeze the pendulum by grinding the gears of agencies that once would have been instruments of reform that addressed abuses of laissez-faire capitalism. Here again, the supporting actor is another core American value: the country's preference for the rule of law over the arbitrary rule of men—which can only be achieved by another unassailable virtue: due process.

In 1946, Congress was concerned about the power of the regulatory agencies established in the Teddy Roosevelt and Franklin Roosevelt reform eras. The agencies had been created to set rules in areas such as fair commerce (the Federal Trade Commission), labor organizing (the National Labor Relations Board), the stock market (the Securities and Exchange Commission), and the use of the airwaves for radio and television broadcasts (the Federal Communications Commission). Led by commissioners or board members appointed by the president and approved by the Senate, they were empowered to write detailed regulations consistent with the general rules that Congress embedded in the statutes establishing their agencies. Depending on the agency, they could also levy fines and make other enforcement decisions if the rules were broken. However, by 1946, many in Congress believed that unelected bureaucrats at the agencies had too much unchecked authority.

The Administrative Procedure Act of 1946 was designed to correct that. Instead of agency officials issuing a new rule by fiat, they were now required to go through an elaborate process, including holding hearings, drafting proposed rules, seeking comments on the proposed rules after publishing them in the Federal Register, responding to the comments, and then, when publishing the final rule, fully explaining its basis, including how they had considered all of the input gathered in the hearings or from the comments. Lawyers for the businesses involved could now be hired to pack the hearings, write thousands of pages of comments, schedule endless meetings, and otherwise try to fight off or water down the proposed regulations every step of the way. Moreover, the act made all decisions, including whether the agency had followed the required process in making decisions, subject to judicial review, giving the lawyers another forum to fight everything all over again.

It was all about guaranteeing due process, a movement that gained steam in the late 1960s as legal academics—led by Yale law professor (and Lewis Powell target) Charles Reich—began to argue that any agency action affecting someone's property rights required that it be carried out only under elaborate, airtight rules. From just 1969 to 1979, the Federal Register, which publishes all the rules, quintupled in page length, from 15,000 to 75,000 pages.

In the hands of thousands of newly hired Washington lawyers, due process became a process that either ended in nothing happening or produced rules that were comically complicated and so long that they offered thousands of ways for a regulated company's lawyers to find something to contest if a client was accused of a violation.

Instead of empowering the Occupational Safety and Health Administration, OSHA, to write a simple rule saying that workplace railings on staircases had to be high enough and sturdy enough to prevent accidents, and then allowing the agency to enforce violations, the lawyers demanded to know how exactly high and how sturdy the railings had to be and exactly why. Simply allowing agency inspectors to use common sense would violate due process. Instead of a rule saying that workers had to be given adequate, sanitary toilet facilities, due process demanded hearings and detailed rules defining "adequate," defining "sanitary," and even defining the specifications for toilet seats. If a rule required employers to provide life vests for construction workers at sites where they might fall into deep water, what exactly did "provide" mean? (Readers interested in a rumination on that question can go to docket number 88-1847 on the OSHA website.)

If the detailed rule was not to industry's liking, lawyers were at the ready to appeal the decision to the federal appeals court. In 1979, the appellate judges invalidated for lack of sufficient specificity the Federal Trade Commission's rules requiring the Katharine Gibbs secretarial school and other vocational schools to provide certain disclosures to students and offer refunds to them in situations where the disclosures were not adequate. A trail of cases requiring regulatory agencies to build still more voluminous records quickly followed. A 1980 Supreme Court decision about benzene required OSHA to do the same.

The first OSHA rulemaking to regulate hazardous chemicals in the workplace—about vinyl chloride—took about a year to complete and, with accompanying comments, was ten pages long when published in 1974. That seems like more than enough due process. A rule about methylene chloride took three years to write and was 126 pages when published in 1997. A rule about silica took nineteen years to write and was 604 pages when published in 2016. "We had a team of people working full time for years just responding to all of the industry's comments," recalled David Michaels, who ran OSHA when the silica rule was finally issued. The delays had real consequences. OSHA estimated, as part of the record prepared for rulemaking, that the rule would prevent 579 to 796 deaths a year once it cleared the rulemaking process.

Other proposed rules have been pending more than twenty years. "The delays mean money to these companies," said Michaels. His favorite example involved internal memos produced during litigation involving the tobacco industry, in which its lawyers wrote that they could delay a rule on indoor smoke in workplaces by three years just by submitting hundreds of comments to the proposed rule, which would all have to be read and responded to.

Although according to the Government Accountability Office two new chemicals are introduced into the workplace every day, OSHA has only been able to issue new rules regulating thirty chemicals since its founding in 1970. Only three have been finished in the nineteen years since the beginning of 1997. During eleven of those nineteen years, Democrats controlled the executive branch and presumably would have generally been more inclined than Republicans to write rules.

The rationale behind the Administrative Procedure Act's rulemaking regime was that bureaucrats at the various regulatory agencies should be due process umpires, not experts delegated to figure out the right rules. If a new rule might be needed, or if others on the enforcement side of the agency thought a rule had been broken, they would hear all the arguments on both sides and then issue decisions, based, in theory, only on those arguments. The conceit was that the evidence and arguments proffered by the lawyers on both sides dictated the text of the rules or the outcome of any enforcement action. But with lawyers on the business side swarming the process, outgunning any lawyers representing consumers or employees, the system was tilted toward the regulated.

As journalist John Judis wrote in his 2001 book, *The Paradox of American Democracy*,

> To restrict governmental intervention, in the determination of claims, to the position of an umpire deciding the merits upon the basis of the record as established by the parties, presumes the existence of an equality in the way of the respective power of the litigants to get at the facts. . . . In some spheres, the absence of equal economic power generally is so prevalent that the umpire theory of administering law is almost certain to fail. . . . By making government a passive arbiter in the contest among interest groups, it favored those groups who could command the greatest financial resources on behalf of their cause.

The due process, umpire theory of American governance involved a broader assumption about American democracy that was as old as the republic—and was starting to fall apart in the 1970s, too. It was based on the parallel idea that competing interests in any policy dispute would fight it out and ultimately, led by cooler heads on each side, reach some kind of middle ground that would produce the best and fairest result. This notion—generally called pluralism, meaning different and often opposing groups coexist and produce a common good—was celebrated by leading political science academics in the late 1960s and early 1970s, even as it was beginning to break down. It was the product of the prior decade, when interests representing two sides of an issue (unless the issue was civil rights or poverty) generally had equal power. Unions and management fought hard but ultimately compromised, as did Republicans and Democrats. Civic or religious groups were also players, and joined the fray on issues they cared about.

However, pluralism depends on a relative balance of power. With unions and civic groups generally in decline and the business community galvanized as never before, the balance was lost.

TRIPLE DIALING FOR DOLLARS

Congressman Jones said he was proud of the discipline that keeps him dialing for dollars four or five hours a day, even if he has to stick to the discipline of that "I don't give a shit" Post-it note. As he sprinted across the street and then up the steps of the Capitol so that he could vote on the floor of the House, however, he conceded the obvious: "I don't get to spend as much time with the people I represent. I try. I try to take their calls, and I try to go see them all over the district every weekend. But there's no denying that spending twenty hours a week on the phone with rich people is not what I came here to do."

The most common question he gets from former business associates whom he is constantly hitting up for money is, he said, " 'Why are you doing this? It's so demeaning.' Well, I still get a thrill when I walk up these steps, although it is starting to take a toll."

The toll finally became too much for a former colleague, Steve Israel. A Democrat who represented a relatively competitive Long Island district, Israel retired in 2016. He immediately began speaking out about the money grind, writing in a *New York Times* op-ed column that "I'll be leaving Congress at the end of this term . . . liberated from a fund-raising regime that's never been more dangerous to our democracy." Attending 1,600 fund-raisers over sixteen years organized by his own campaigns, and more put together by PACs, he wrote, was like "panhandling with hors d'oeuvres." Logging 4,200 hours begging on the phone was equally demeaning. Israel said he went to Congress with "dreams of feeding the poor and bringing world peace." They were shattered on the first day of freshman orientation when he was told he would have to raise $10,000 a week, every week, to keep his job.

As Israel gained seniority in the House, he got so good at fund-raising that he was chosen by his Democratic colleagues to run the Democratic Congressional Campaign Committee, giving him the job of raising money across the country for incumbents and for newcomers. "The most demoralizing thing," he recalled, "was telling a prospect with a great résumé and great intentions that if he jumped in he'd have to spend every morning and afternoon during the week raising money. Forget going to train stations to shake hands. We lost a lot of good people who didn't want to sign up to do that."

Today, Israel explained a year after his retirement, the $10,000 a week that was his initial goal "is coins in a cushion. You need forty thousand to be safe."

Israel and members on both sides of the aisle, including Congressman Jones, said that the preoccupation with money became an absolute obsession in 2010 after *Citizens United* and a case that quickly followed and was based on the *Citizens United* finding that corruption was not a risk if the money was spent by independent groups. That second case allowed PACs to become super PACS that could raise unlimited contributions from individuals and corporations to spend unlimited amounts on their own, ostensibly "independent" campaigns in support of a candidate. If, as Justice Anthony Kennedy ruled in *Citizens United*, an independent committee could, by definition, never corrupt a politician, then no limits on contributions to them or by them could be justified.

Independent committees boosting candidates on both sides have since made a mockery of Kennedy's confidence. They are typically run by former aides to the candidate or even relatives, and often have their offices in the same building where the candidate's campaign is run. Candidates even appear at their fund-raising events.

Candidates certainly know who the big PAC donors are, and are promiscuously grateful for their help. Top donors to "independent" super PACs supporting Donald Trump got positions on his transition team and in his cabinet. In fact, it is almost embarrassing even to argue whether they wield great influence over the people they elect, except that Justice Kennedy has made this alternate reality the law of the land and a turning point in the corruption of American democracy.

"Before *Citizens United*," Israel explained, "you at least had a good view of what the opponent would spend and what you would need to spend. Now, you're flying blind, because in the last two or three weeks some super PAC could come in with $20 million and wipe you out. You always have to keep raising money, just in case."

Super PACs raised $1.8 billion in the 2016 election cycle, as people such as Robert Mercer on the right and Tom Steyer on the left became the most important political power players most Americans had never heard of. That does not count at least $250 million in "dark money" raised by tax-exempt entities that did not call themselves political action committees, but made their own independent expenditures without even having to reveal donors because they instead declared that they were social welfare or educational organizations. All of that is apart from the $1.46 billion that the 2016 presidential candidates raised directly, and the $1.03 billion that candidates for the House and $668 million that candidates for the Senate raised, and the millions more that lobbyists bundled for them via conventional PACs, which are formed to give money directly to candidates.

It is a frenzy that has generated its own gallows humor. Arizona representative Kyrsten Sinema is celebrated in the halls of Congress, said Israel, for her "triple dialing. . . . She has staffers get three people on three phones at once for hours on end so she wastes no time between calls. She's a legend."* Although Sinema, a moderate Democrat, won by only 4 percent when first elected in 2012, she won by 21 percent in 2016. Yet she raised $4.4 million, or $42,000 a week, for that election. (The surplus in her campaign coffers on Election Day 2016 ended up being applied to a statewide 2018 campaign for the Senate that she announced in late 2017.)

As we will see, gerrymandering results in only forty-five to fifty House seats being truly contested in a general election, yet "most members try to raise as much as they can," Israel said, not because they are spooked by super PACs that could attack them in a general election but because they want to build a protective wall in their mostly gerrymandered districts to ward off a primary challenge. Also, as a result of reforms that eliminated seniority as the criterion for gaining important committee chairs or other leadership jobs, these positions are now based on the votes of members from the aspiring congressman's party. "The people who are safe raise the money so they can give it to other members," Israel explained. "That way they accumulate IOUs that they cash in when they go after leadership spots."

---

* A spokesperson said that while it is true that Congresswoman Sinema is "an efficient fund-raiser," "it is not true that she triple dials."

I had my own experience with how a leading Democratic congressman, who had not faced a serious reelection challenge in more than a decade, nonetheless chased money relentlessly. In 2008, I retained a lobbyist to get me in to see a longtime congressional committee chairman who had oversight associated with a business I was trying to start. The lobbyist was able to set up the meeting because his firm regularly ran fund-raisers for the chairman. It was a huge deal, I was told, to get in to see "The Chairman." But he fell asleep two minutes into the meeting. As I left, an aide who had kept the conversation with me going while the boss nodded off assured me that it had been a "great meeting. . . . I think The Chairman was quite impressed." Before I made it to the elevator I had an email on my BlackBerry from the staffer asking that I attend a fund-raiser that week. Over the next year, I got regular calls from The Chairman himself seeking money.

After Congressman Jones had come back from voting and had dialed for another hour, he went off to an Italian restaurant near Capitol Hill. The eatery had four private rooms upstairs, and because this was the last week of a quarter—when members go into high gear to raise cash in time for the quarterly fund-raising reports they would soon file—all four were reserved for cocktail party fund-raisers. Twenty-one people, who had paid $2,000 each, were at Jones's event. All were lobbyists, either working for lobbying firms or directly for the Washington office of mid-sized or large corporations. All but three represented businesses (or in one case a union) that had some connection to the committees or subcommittees Jones served on. All but two said they were going to at least three such events that night. One said she hoped to hit six. Each got a few minutes or more to chat with Jones.

They were petitioning the government just the way the First Amendment had promised, only the founders could not have anticipated this was how they would have to do it. Jones is not corrupt, nor were his benefactor-guests. For them this was business as usual. Nothing was hidden. Nobody seemed embarrassed to be there, or even that a reporter was among them.

That is what is so striking about the hold that money now has on politics. No one is proud of it. Most detest it. The politicians like Jones would rather be doing policy, and the cocktail partygoers would rather be home instead of shuffling around to a half dozen joyless events. But they do it, and have become so inured to it, that they don't seem to see the disconnect between this money-for-access ritual and democracy.

The culture is such that the Washington-based *Politico* group of digital newsletters has one called *Politico Influence* that is a scorecard of sorts for lobbyists. To outsiders it might read like a gotcha tip sheet. To the insiders, it is a chance to be acknowledged for their insider influence, and even advertise it.

Here are some sample items that ran at about the time Jones spent that day dialing for dollars and taking checks from lobbyists later that evening:

- Former Rep. Ander Crenshaw (R-Fla.), who retired last year, is headed to King & Spalding as senior counsel. He'll "focus on counseling clients on the impact of regulatory and legislative changes in the financial, defense and health care industries," according to a statement from the firm. Crenshaw served as chairman of the House Appropriations Committee's financial services subcommittee.

- Will Smith, the House Appropriations Committee's Republican staff director, is leaving the Hill to join Cornerstone Government Affairs as a senior vice president. Smith, a native Kentuckian, is a former chief of staff to Rep. Hal Rogers (R-Ky.), who stepped down as chairman of the House Appropriations Committee last month. "Will has been my right hand in the halls of Congress for nearly two decades, and I cannot imagine a more thoughtful adviser, a more capable strategist, or a more loyal friend," Rogers said in a statement.

- Former Sen. David Vitter (R-La.) this week joined Mercury LLC, whose clients range from corporate titans like Visa and NBCUniversal to the governments of Nigeria and Qatar. Vitter, whose title will be co-chairman, gives the firm a veteran lawmaker with deep relationships with top members of the Trump administration, including Attorney General–designate Jeff Sessions. . . . Vin Weber, a Mercury partner and a former congressman himself, called Vitter the firm's "top choice among retiring members of Congress. . . ." Mercury had been working to recruit Vitter since he announced he'd retire from Congress, Weber said. That may have given the firm an advantage over other lobbying shops that reached out to Vitter only after Donald Trump's victory. "When Donald Trump won the presidency, David Vitter became an even hotter commodity," Weber said. Vitter is forbidden from lobbying his former colleagues for two years under the "cooling-off period" mandated by legislation that Vitter himself worked to pass. . . . But the ban doesn't apply to the executive branch. "I can lobby the administration immediately," Vitter said. "That's really significant given President Trump's win."

- Also heading to Mercury: Al Simpson, who spent the past six years as chief of staff for Rep. Mick Mulvaney (R-S.C.), whom Trump tapped to be his Office of Management and Budget director. Simpson expects to engage Mulvaney on infrastructure, tax, and defense issues.

- TRUMP'S MASON TO H&K: Scott Mason, the Trump campaign's congressional liaison and a former in-house lobbyist for home improvement retailer Lowe's, is joining Holland & Knight. "I was very flattered in the wake of Election Day to receive a number of phone calls, and somewhat surprised to be candid," Mason said. "The president is going to need some people on the outside to help push his agenda as well."

  "Scott brings not just knowledge of people and relationships in the incoming Trump administration, but also he was there when no one in this town was supporting Trump," Holland & Knight partner Kathryn Lehman said. "In politics you remember who was part of the band of brothers and sisters when you started and the world was against you."

Then there was this routine item from *Politico's Power Briefing* newsletter: "CHEVRON gave $250,000 to the Congressional Leadership Fund, the House GOP super PAC, per recently released campaign records."

In 2014, the American Political Science Association's journal, *Perspectives on Politics,* studied how the preferences of the public, as expressed in public opinion polls, on 1,779 issues that were debated by Congress between 1981 and 2002 matched up with how Congress had decided those issues. The authors found that "organized interest groups" and "economic elites" so dominated the outcomes that even when 80 percent of the public wanted a change, they got it only 43 percent of the time. "Not only do ordinary citizens not have *uniquely* substantial power over policy decisions; they have little or no independent influence on policy at all," the authors concluded. "When the preferences of economic elites and the stands of organized interest groups are controlled for, the preferences of the average American appear to have only a minuscule, near-zero, statistically non-significant impact upon public policy."

They were describing a democracy that had become an oligarchy.

And that was from 1981 to 2002, when the role of money in politics had increased rapidly since the 1960s but was nothing near what it had become by the time Congressman Jones was working the phones in 2017.

A few weeks after that night on the lobbyists' cocktail party fund-raising circuit, I asked Martin Redish if there was anything the country should do about the way money, through lobbyists and campaign contributions, has come to dominate politics. "No, because the cure will always be worse than the disease," he answered quickly.

I told him about having watched the congressman cramped over the phone begging for money. Did he really think the Founding Fathers had in mind that those occupying the legislatures they were creating would spend more than half their workdays that way? "Well maybe if he did a better job talking to his constituents he wouldn't have to raise all that money," Redish said.

I asked how the congressman would defend himself against a super PAC swooping in at the last minute with a wave of ads and mailings that distort his record. "If he's a good congressman and is out there conveying that, people will believe him," Redish said. "Besides, money is often the only way for challengers to overcome all the advantages the incumbent has. Why is it that the only advantage we try to correct for—the only thing we try to equalize—is money? What about a candidate who's a celebrity, or who's better, like Trump, at getting news coverage? Why is it that the only thing we attack is the First Amendment?"

The obvious answer is that, unlike fame or good press, unlimited political money—including corporate money, which for Redish is synonymous with First Amendment–protected speech—is the "advantage" that corrupts policymaking. It is not a matter of equalizing the candidates' resources, but of removing the potential for undue influence over whoever wins.

ISSUE ONE

Polls continually show that most Americans are disgusted at how money has corrupted politics. Like Jones, most politicians are demoralized by the system, too. Almost everyone, however, seems resigned to accept it as the unchangeable new normal of American democracy, something, like bad weather, to complain about but live with.

There are exceptions. On the tenth floor of a modest, messy office on Fourteenth Street in Washington, a block from the infamous K Street collection of buildings known as the capital of lobbying, a group of twenty mostly young staffers crunch numbers, scan data from campaign finance records and the reports lobbyists are required to file, make the connections, tally the totals, and otherwise add to what is already an enormous stockpile of information and reports. All of it is then posted to an easily searchable website, fittingly called OpenSecrets, that lays bare the dark world of Washington money.*

Using OpenSecrets, you could find out in minutes how much ExxonMobil contributed in the last five or ten years to members of Congress holding a hearing on oil company tax breaks. You could learn how much the hospital, drug, and medical device industries gave to members of the Senate Finance Committee, and the Senate Committee on Health, Education, Labor, and Pensions, which write health care laws and oversee the Department of Health and Human Services and the Food and Drug Administration. You could identify

---

* Most of the numbers you have read above about political money come from OpenSecrets.

the leading funeral industry lobbyist, or how much the private prison industry contributed to politicians, including President Trump, who want the government to keep funding private jails and immigration holding cells.

The website is run by a non-profit called the Center for Responsive Politics, or CRP. Founded in 1983 by two recently retired senators (one a Democrat, the other a Republican), the original goal, explained executive director Sheila Krumholz, was to conduct research and produce papers aimed at suggesting ways to make Congress more effective. Early topics included dry, good-government issues like making the budgeting process more businesslike. Gradually, the role of campaign money became the overriding issue.

The staff of four was expanded to include investigative journalists, said Krumholz, who started as executive assistant to the founder in 1989, following her graduation from the University of Minnesota. She became research director eight years later and executive director ten years after that.

The evolving mission, she said, was to "develop systems to find conflicts—to link PAC money, for example, to the committees that members serve on."

In 1990, the staff wrote *Follow the Money*, a handbook to guide journalists in using publicly available but often obscure data to find these conflicts. The book, and CRP's staff, became resources for reporters.

The rise of the Internet in the mid-1990s allowed CRP to put its data and pointers on how to use it online at OpenSecrets.org. As CRP launched the OpenSecrets website and continued to develop its database and search engine, troves of information about the intersection of politics and money became instantly available to everyone. "The web revolutionized what we were able to do and the impact," Krumholz recalled. Suddenly, campaign fund-raising reports filed with the Federal Election Commission and posted by the commission online could be grabbed, sliced, diced, and analyzed by the growing CRP staff, as could quarterly reports that lobbyists are required to file with Congress listing their clients, what issues they had lobbied on, and how much they were paid. There are also articles written by the staff —and overseen by Viveca Novak, a former *Time* and *Wall Street Journal* reporter—highlighting trends and emerging issues that can be found digging through it all.

Funding had increased from just over a million dollars a year at the start, mostly from individual donors and foundations, to $2.5 million in 2017. That is an amazing leveraging of relatively little money to open up the billion-dollar world of lobbying and campaign contributions. Just one run-of-the-mill PAC, organized by Chevron, raised 50 percent more in the 2016 election cycle than CRP's budget.

The Internet may have crippled the business model for most of journalism, particularly newspapers and magazines, but it has allowed OpenSecrets to give journalists an important new accountability tool. OpenSecrets is now routinely cited in news stories about lobbying or campaign finance. And, as political money and the rise of Donald Trump have become increasingly hot topics, CRP has started getting hundreds of small donations from the public. "We keep adding to what we do," Krumholz said two months after Trump took office. "We now have a unit putting together data on conflicts of interest in the Trump administration." That involves not just mining the data, but manually matching different kinds of financial records, such as Trump appointees' disclosure filings, with issues the appointees might be working on or budget items they might supervise.

Another piece of detective work is aimed at shining light on "dark money"—the $250 million that poured into the 2016 election cycle from tax-exempt groups that the Internal Revenue Service allows to self-designate as "social welfare" organizations, thereby freeing them of having to disclose donors. (The rule was originally established to protect donors to groups like the NAACP from reprisal during the civil rights confrontations of the 1960s.) Krumholz has a full-time staffer who tries to trace who is behind the dark money organizations. Do its incorporation papers list the same address as the office of a law firm that has worked for a major corporation? Is someone named on the organization's IRS form as a board member also on the board of a super PAC (which has to list its donors)?

The exhilaration in CRP's offices is palpable. The money detectives love to talk about their work. Yet are they really changing anything, or just allowing reporters and their audiences to reconfirm what they already know and seem resigned to?

"You're grinding out all this great stuff, but no one seems to care. Don't you ever feel frustrated?" Krumholz was asked.

"Sure, it's totally frustrating that the FEC [Federal Election Commission] does nothing about how supposedly independent groups coordinate with candidates," she said, "or about how the IRS doesn't touch the dark money groups that are so political. But am I down on what we do? No, not really. Because we need to be here building the record so that when the opportunity arises, when people of good faith on both sides of the aisle decide that enough is enough, we will have armed them. . . . The system has careened off the tracks, and everybody knows it. But I'm impassioned, not discouraged."

Krumholz and her team do, indeed, supply the tools of transparency that the press needs. Yet it is difficult to think of Congressman Jones dialing for dollars, or lobbyists, checks in hand, ducking in and out of fund-raisers without concluding that the press should be using those tools much more aggressively.

Perhaps every time C-Span or any other cable news outlet carries a congressional hearing, next to the name of the congressman or senator displayed on the screen there should be a number listing how much money he or she has taken from donors (individuals, PACs, or lobbyists) associated with the industry or industries affected by the hearing. If the hearing is about regulating airlines and Congressman Smith has received $500,000 in the most recent election cycle from airline industry interests, it would say: "Smith (D) Illinois—$500,000." Newspapers covering hearings or statements from politicians could put the same information in parentheses the first time his or her name is mentioned.

Would this be embarrassing because it would imply that these politicians are being bought? Absolutely. Would it unfairly imply that they are all corrupt? Yes, it would. That, though, might move the uncorrupt to fix the system. More important, this kind of constant—indeed annoying, even infuriating—reminder might move the rest of the country to demand that it be fixed.

But how can it be fixed?

Four blocks from Krumholz's Washington office is the headquarters of Issue One, another good-government non-profit that is also focused on political money. Issue One is about organizing a nonpartisan political movement to get the fixes that Krumholz's data crunchers make clear that Americans need. The group's name is itself a profound statement about the overriding importance of somehow stopping money from completely overrunning American democracy.

It is derived, said Bill Bradley—the former New Jersey Democratic senator, who co-chairs its blue-chip board of advisers—"from the reality that this issue has to come before everything else. If we don't fix this, there is no way to fix the tax code, or income inequality, or climate change, or health care, or anything else."

Issue One executive director Nick Penniman explained that he had come to the same conclusion when he left a journalism career to merge two smaller non-profits into Issue One in 2014. "I saw that all the issues I was writing about could be traced back to some policy dysfunction, which could always be traced back to money."

Although Penniman, then forty-four, had a left-leaning background (he ran investigative projects for *The Huffington Post*, worked with veteran public television broadcaster Bill Moyers, and was an editor at the liberal *American Prospect*), he has pushed Issue One in a determinedly bipartisan direction. In fact, he has worked hardest at converting Republicans, especially conservative Republicans, to the cause.

Penniman's website and the materials distributed to donors by Issue One—which raised about $2.5 million in 2017 and was hoping to raise a million dollars more in 2018—are adorned with pie charts demonstrating how fed up both Republicans and Democrats are: Polls show that 72 percent of Americans, including 66 percent of Republicans, favored government-financed, small-donor campaign finance systems. Eighty percent of Republicans opposed *Citizens United*.* Eighty-five percent of Americans wanted to "see fundamental change" in the campaign finance system. Ninety-one percent of 2016 Republican Iowa caucus goers agreed that they were "mad as hell" about money in politics.

Accordingly, the roster of 179 politicians among Issue One's advisers and supporters (which also includes dozens of prominent business and non-profit leaders) was bipartisan, including Republicans like former Pennsylvania governor and Homeland Security secretary Tom Ridge and former senator Alan Simpson, as well as Democrats like Bradley and former Senate majority leader Tom Daschle. However, with a few exceptions, the Republicans and Democrats all have

---

* Caveat: Most Americans do not actually know that *Citizens United* was only about corporate political spending; they see the case as synonymous with unlimited political spending of all kinds, including by individuals.

"former" in front of their names. Most of those who are still out there fund-raising don't want to look hypocritical or, as Jones explained, get out in front on an issue that they don't think is going anywhere.

Those involved in Issue One vehemently reject that sense of futility. "Here's why I'm hopeful," said Penniman. "The alcoholic can't take much more. His liver can't process it. Members are sick and tired of spending five hours a day begging. And super PACs are scaring everyone, because it means that with *Citizens United* it's all now been nuclearized. They're realizing that their own money-raising efforts can be wiped out instantly by some super PAC that swoops in. . . . And, if they care about policy, which a lot of them do, they realize the chance for doing anything meaningful is pretty much gone." Pointing to a list of congressmen and senators from both parties who have cited the money race as their reason for quitting, Penniman added, "The level of disgust among the elite is so high that nobody can stand it. It's gotten so bad that it's got to get better."

A lunch Issue One held for about two dozen prospective donors in New York in late 2016 seemed at first look like another group of do-gooders, albeit with many all-stars in business as well as politics among them, hoping to throw relatively modest amounts of money at an activity that was more about hand-wringing than change. From Bradley's introductory remarks through Penniman's presentation, however, it was much more about practical, step-by-step solutions to work around *Citizens United*, rather than about rehashing the problem.

Penniman described a bipartisan coalition that he and his staff of fourteen were working to assemble on Capitol Hill to support a bill to revamp the Federal Election Commission. Instead of the perpetually deadlocked panel of three Democrats and three Republicans (appointed on the say-so of Senate Majority Leader Mitch McConnell, a die-hard reform foe), a blue-ribbon group of judges would appoint five non-partisan members. The commission might then at least monitor independent committees and discipline those that most blatantly coordinate with the campaigns they are supporting. "It won't be a sweeping solution, but it'll be a step," Penniman said. Another measure would combat dark money by requiring that any tax-exempt "social welfare" group that engages in any political activity disclose its donors.

More ambitious measures that Issue One was promoting included a bill to finance $200 tax credits that every taxpayer could allocate to a federal candidate or divide among several. They were also pushing a proposal to prohibit lobbyists from donating to candidates whose committees they lobby. "We've had seventy meetings with congressional offices in the last three months," Penniman said in mid-2017. "And we're rounding up support from disgusted conservative Republicans, as well as Democrats."

Penniman intrigued the lunch group by pointing out that these proposals had been enacted in some form in states and cities across the country. Although his organization leaves state and local lobbying to other groups promoting non-federal campaign finance reform while it lobbies in Washington, at the donor lunch Penniman touted these local breakthroughs as signs of progress that they hoped to get Washington to notice and adopt.

- South Carolina passed a law prohibiting lobbyists from giving anything to members of the legislature or holding fund-raisers for them. There was no reason, Penniman said, that Congress couldn't be embarrassed into adopting something similar.

- In Connecticut, lobbyists cannot contribute more than $100 to candidates or hold fund-raisers for them. The law was passed with overwhelming bipartisan support.

- New York City, Portland, Oregon, and other municipalities had public financing systems in place, under which candidates who volunteered to limit their spending and the dollar amount of contributions would in turn receive money to match smaller donations. It didn't eliminate the lopsided funding that a rich or richly financed candidate would have, but it did ease some of the effects of inequality by setting a floor of sorts; candidates of modest means could at least count on enough money to fund a campaign if they could attract enough small donors.

- Other cities and even some states, including Connecticut and Minnesota, have successful and popular laws in place to allow public funding of campaigns if candidates agree not to raise money privately and demonstrate enough support beforehand by raising a required number of small contributions. Polls showed that 80 percent of Connecticut residents supported their state's "Citizens' Election Program." It is similar to the system that candidate Obama abandoned in 2008 because he thought, correctly, that he could raise more money on his own than the money to be allocated under the federal law. Under *Buckley, Citizens United,* and other cases, this system cannot be forced on candidates, but no court decision had said a system cannot be sufficiently funded to entice more of them. However, as with other plans, like the matching grants or giving citizens vouchers to make donations, the potential abuse stemming from independent groups, which may or may not actually be independent, would not be eliminated.

- Washington State has a law requiring fast and full disclosure on a state website of campaign donations, including a special page to highlight donations of more than $1,000 coming just days before Election Day that would otherwise not become public until after the voting. Widgets were embedded in the website making it easy for media organizations to create instantly updateable graphs and other illustrations using the data.

- California has enacted tough rules aimed at making independent funding organizations truly independent by outlawing anything—such as involvement in the independent group by a member of the candidate's family or even a former staffer—that smacks of coordination.

However, what was not mentioned by Penniman or any of his colleagues at the lunch was that in 2016 five states had tried and failed, either at the ballot box or in the legislature, to pass highly publicized similar campaign finance reforms.

Although Bill Bradley strongly supported Issue One's work, he has long favored a more radical solution aimed at the elephant in the room that almost everyone engaged in the issue is trying to work around: the Constitution and the First Amendment. There may now be broad

agreement that Justice Anthony Kennedy's reasoning in his majority opinion in *Citizens United*—that impinging on the First Amendment could not be justified because there was no risk of corruption
in letting corporations spend unlimited amounts to fund independent
committees set up to support candidates—was an exercise in wishful
thinking then and has become pure fantasy now. However, that interpretation of the First Amendment is now the law of the land and is
unlikely to be overturned anytime soon.

In 1996, Bradley introduced a resolution in the Senate to amend
the Constitution that would give Congress "the power to set limits on
expenditures made by, in support of, or in opposition to the nomination or election of any person to Federal office," as well as "the power
to set limits on contributions by individuals or entities by, in support
of, or in opposition to the nomination or election of any person to
Federal office." In other words, there would be no more First Amendment right for a candidate or even an independent group supporting a federal candidate to spend unlimited amounts, and there would
be no First Amendment right for any person or corporation to contribute unlimited amounts to support or oppose a federal candidate.
Of course, Congress would have set the limits that the amendment
would authorize, but in a world in which Bradley's proposed amendment got the necessary two-thirds majority to get through Congress,
setting those limits would seem a foregone conclusion.

However, Americans do not live in that world, at least not yet.
Bradley's amendment did not even get a Senate vote until 2014, when
it failed to pass.

Penniman said he thinks the constitutional amendment idea is
"a waste of time; in fact, it has a suppressive effect because it's so
unrealistic that it discourages donors. Some guy with money will hear
that pitch and figure, 'That's not gonna happen; I'll give my money
to a homeless shelter.'" It is also, he argued, "a way for people to talk
about it without getting anything done."

However, as the polling numbers in Penniman's own handouts
suggest, this could be one aspect of America's breakdown where the
possibility of radical change may be the most likely—either through
a public revolt that shakes Congress into action, or even through the
other avenue available for constitutional amendments: a convention
calling for one by two thirds of the states. Most Americans already

know that this really is issue number one. How long can it be before their anger builds to the point where they do something about it and follow those, like the Issue One supporters, now in place to lead them to make it happen?

Even Bradley's amendment would not touch the money-tainted activity more explicitly protected than campaign financing by the First Amendment: lobbying, or, as the Constitution describes it, petitioning "the Government for a redress of grievances." Nor should anyone want to outlaw lobbying, or try to regulate which kinds of people can do it for what kinds of motives with how many resources. A private prison industry trade association seeking to block criminal justice reform, or a group of doctors specializing in pain relief organized and sponsored by opioid manufacturers hoping to block restrictions on painkiller prescriptions (yes, both lobbies exist), should have the same rights as a coalition seeking better health care for homeless veterans.

Congress, however, could do what states like South Carolina have done and restrict contributions or fund-raising by lobbyists. The courts have consistently ruled, at least so far, that the anti-corruption benefits of laws like that outweigh the loss coming from any rights taken away from a lobbyist, just as they have ruled for the same reason that requiring lobbyists to register and provide reports on fees collected is constitutional. Besides, if an amendment like Bradley's ever passed, the flow and the impact of all that political money, including from lobbyists, would be severely diminished.

There would still be an imbalance of power. Those with the most money could continue to hire the most lobbyists (and the most expensive lobbyists) to plead their cases, and members of Congress and staffers with even the best intentions frequently have to rely on lobbyists because they don't have the time or knowledge necessary to understand an issue fully.

There are two ways to correct much of that. First, Congress could create a non-partisan professional policy office to advise members on the most important issues being debated. The model would be the Congressional Budget Office, which writes briefing papers and publishes forecasts related to the fiscal effects of major pending legislation. The CBO has a well-paid professional staff of about 230 that costs about $48 million annually. Creating a similar team to provide unbiased input into decisions relating to the programs of a $4-trillion-a-year government seems logical. Second, the current policy staffs working for the members and their committees could be made more professional. The congressional aides who actually work on policy are paid far less than the lobbyists, causing most to jump to the lobbying side once they get significant experience.

For now, though, the playing field remains lopsided. Those who have the most have been largely allowed to get the most in Washington.

Making Markets Efficient— and Marginalizing Those Left Behind

The growing imbalance of power in Washington created by First Amendment–enabled political money has been accompanied and accelerated by the declining power of unions and the working class generally. As those at the top in the knowledge economy used their muscle in Washington to solidify their gains, the people who make things were marginalized—and then stiff-armed by their government. It began as another chapter in the story of American progress.

In 1962, John F. Kennedy—who had narrowly defeated Richard Nixon, thanks in part to overwhelming support from America's unions—summoned the country to embrace the new frontier of free trade and globalization, declaring, "A more liberal trade policy will in general benefit our most efficient and expanding industries— industries which have demonstrated their advantage over other world producers by exporting on the average twice as much of their products as we import—industries which have done this while paying the highest wages in our country."

Kennedy's optimism was understandable. Fewer than twenty years after America had helped save the world in World War II, the American economic engine, which had powered the buildup of factories making weapons, ships, fighter planes, and other war supplies, had been repurposed and refortified by the troops who had come home. Now these factories were supplying American consumers eager and able to spend in the post-war boom as they took new jobs and moved into new homes. With Europe and Asia still recovering from a war that had been fought on their soil and had decimated their infrastructures, American products truly were the best and were produced with unequaled efficiency. The numbers told the story: America had a trade surplus in 1961—$5.1 billion more came in from exports than the richest country in the world spent on imports. Growing those foreign markets still more by making new free trade deals, especially with the emerging, post-war European Common Market, was obviously a good idea.

America's top labor leader agreed. "Times have changed, the world has changed, and this country's trade policy must be changed to meet these new conditions," George Meany, the president of the 13.5-million-member AFL-CIO, told a hearing of the House Ways and Means Committee considering Kennedy's trade proposal. The week before, Labor Secretary Arthur Goldberg, the future Supreme Court justice who had been a revered union lawyer, told the same committee that the U.S. would forgo four million new jobs if it didn't liberalize its trade laws. Legislation authorizing what became the Kennedy Round of trade talks breezed through Congress with overwhelming majorities in the House and Senate. Few members of Congress or their constituents anticipated the calamitous impact that this action would have on untold millions of American workers and their pursuit of the American Dream.

Even as he was cheering free trade in 1962, Meany could see that progress of a different sort—technological innovation, or automation—was a threat to labor. The Taft-Hartley Act of 1947, which created union-free manufacturing options for companies that moved facilities to the now-air-conditioned South, posed a second threat. In fact, Meany and other labor leaders were so convinced of America's enduring superiority when it came to making things that they saw trade as a way to enlarge markets generally, thereby mitigating the damage of these two domestic threats. "The miracle of productivity has built a market for American goods around the world," Meany told the House committee.

It would take nearly a decade for the threat of globalization—in the form of jobs outsourced to lower-wage countries—to join automation and industry's fight against unionization in the South as a force that would cripple workers' power at the bargaining table and decimate the working class. Meantime, the fight they faced was at home.

MANAGEMENT FIGHTS BACK

Diminishing the power of unions was on industry's priority list well before Lewis Powell's 1971 wake-up call. Manufacturers didn't need a memo demonizing Ralph Nader or Charles Reich to tell them they had, from their perspective, a problem—albeit one that had resulted in unprecedented prosperity for people who did physical work.

The end of World War II brought an end to the promise many unions had made not to strike during wartime, accompanied by a post-war boom in demand for the products the workers made. Thanks to the New Deal's National Labor Relations Act, which established a breakthrough menu of protections for union organizing and collective bargaining, this gave workers and their union leaders unprecedented power. They used it aggressively. In 1946, there were strikes involving more than five million workers, many of them prolonged standoffs.

Taft-Hartley was passed to recalibrate the balance of power. It survived a veto by President Harry Truman, in part with the votes of Democrats, particularly those from the South. The new law strengthened a 1943 law prohibiting union political contributions, which had not achieved much other than giving unions the idea to invent the first independent political action committees. These union PACS were similarly unaffected by Taft-Hartley. Union members would continue to be asked by shop stewards to donate to the PACs apart from the dues they paid. More important was a provision prohibiting unions from organizing picket lines except at sites where the workers were actually striking, blocking a strategy unions had used to leverage the impact of a work stoppage at any particular unit. Secondary boycotts, another key instrument of union leverage that involved pressuring another company to stop doing business with the employer that the union was on strike against, were similarly declared an "unfair labor practice."

Still more important, employers—and any consultants or lawyers they hired—were freed to advocate in the workplace, including at mandatory staff meetings, against unionization, unless that advocacy included threats or reprisal against workers who supported the union. It was a seemingly fair provision, but one that, as we will see, opened the floodgates for a variety of employer abuses.

Moreover, under Taft-Hartley, states were allowed to pass "right-to-work" laws, prohibiting unions from demanding that employers require workers to join the union represented at the shop. This provision was particularly important to Southern members of Congress who knew that their states were hoping to attract business by promising a less union-friendly environment.

The Administrative Procedure Act, which had been passed in 1946, the year before Taft-Hartley, had begun to transform federal regulatory agencies, including the National Labor Relations Board, from decision makers into referees. They now had to observe strict procedures and go through elaborate hearing processes that could then be reviewed by the federal appellate courts. With Taft-Hartley now giving employers a new set of rights, the stage was set for management-union contests at the National Labor Relations Board.

Initially the effect was relatively mild. The unions had gained so much power by the late 1940s, and there was enough prosperity in America and enough of a spirit of non-aggression in the business community—at least relative to what would come later—that it took more than a decade before Taft-Hartley and the Administrative Procedure Act combined to turn the Labor Relations Board into a battlefield where those with the most resources, management, could win no matter how many whistles the referee blew.

Indeed, the 1950s and early 1960s had produced exactly the equilibrium between competing interests that the pluralists celebrated. Labor prospered, as did big business. So much so that it did not seem absurd when in 1953 the chairman of General Motors, who had been nominated by President Dwight Eisenhower to be secretary of defense, told a Senate committee during a confirmation hearing that he could not foresee any conflicts between his continued GM stockholdings and his loyalty to the country, because he had always thought that "what was good for the country was good for General Motors, and vice versa." GM and the other car companies had fought hard with the United Autoworkers Union, but they had always worked things out to their mutual benefit. Although the Standard & Poor's 500 stock index soared 180 percent from 1947 to 1960 in inflation-adjusted dollars, average family income, also adjusted for inflation, increased a healthy 39 percent.

That sense of shared progress began to change in the mid-1960s, when major employers suffered the first effects of competition from abroad. Because the South now had right-to-work laws and was eager to attract industry, manufacturers were rapidly shifting work there in an attempt to get their costs more in line with those of overseas competitors. They used the tools given to them by Taft-Hartley to furiously resist unions that were targeting the facilities in the South, while fighting harder than they ever had against unions at the plants that remained in the North.

In 1965, 42 percent of all companies had immediately acquiesced when a union filed a petition seeking to be recognized. In 1973 only 16 percent would. The rest fought back. In 1950, unions won 74 percent of all election contests to get certified at a workplace, yielding 754,000 new union members. In 1965, they won only 61 percent. In 1980, they won 48 percent, yielding just 175,000 new members. With companies shifting to non-union shops in the South or, later, laying off workers as jobs were automated or outsourced overseas, the dwindling number of new union members was more than offset by workers who went off the union rolls.

When Taft-Hartley was passed in 1947, about 37 percent of the entire private workforce in the U.S. was unionized. In 1960, it was still 32 percent. Then it began a downward slide that pushed unionization to 22 percent in 1980, and steadily lower after that. By 2016 it would be 6.4 percent. This was not an accident. In 1950 there were 4,472 charges of unfair labor practices against employers brought before the NLRB related to efforts to resist unionization. In 1980, there were 31,281 charges. Despite the escalating numbers, 39 percent were found to be substantiated in 1980 compared to 21 percent in 1958 (the earliest year for which substantiation percentages could be found).

Those are the statistics. What happened to the people behind them—the people whose livelihoods and dreams were at stake in these battles—is the more important story.

J.P. STEVENS AT THE BARRICADES

The company whose management and workers personified the labor-management battles that raged through the 1960s, 1970s, and 1980s was J.P. Stevens, which opened for business in 1813 as a small wool factory in Andover, Massachusetts. By 1963, Stevens was the country's second largest textile maker, employing 45,000 production workers—almost all of them at factories in the South. Family scion Robert Stevens, a grandson of the founder, ran the company from midtown Manhattan. He was determined to resist unionization, and to lead the fight he hired Whiteford Blakeney, a crusty partner at a Charlotte, North Carolina, law firm. Blakeney was backed up by a phalanx of Stevens's corporate lawyers in New York.

As the Stevens battle was nearing a crescendo in 1980, a Stevens executive told me that Blakeney's counseling with Robert Stevens, with other executives, and with the New York lawyers "were never point-by-point discussions of the law. . . . He basically told the company, You do what you think you have to do, and I'll hold off that damned labor board if they come after you." What Stevens and his team decided they had to do was fire or otherwise penalize any worker who supported unionization, which was a core violation of federal labor law. By 1980, the result was an unprecedented twenty-one court decisions, each written by increasingly angry federal judges, Republican and Democratic appointees alike, finding that Stevens had illegally fired hundreds of union-supporting workers, all the while concocting ever-more preposterous defenses.

The details of what was done to these workers are important. The losers in these battles were the first to fall as the American working class was marginalized. The NLRB consistently won in court fighting for these workers, but it didn't matter because the law didn't work to hold the lawbreakers accountable, and efforts to fix it were repeatedly blocked in Washington.

A 1967 decision of a three-judge federal appeals panel in New York, two of whom were Eisenhower appointees, illustrates the lawlessness that the J.P. Stevens lawyers defended and that their clients never had to answer for. In addition to Blakeney's firm, J.P. Stevens enlisted Paul, Weiss, Rifkind, Wharton & Garrison—one of New York's most elite meritocracies, generally known as a home of liberal, Democratic lawyers—to assist in this appeal. Were any of the firm's lawyers leery about defending Stevens given the firm's pedigree and Stevens's growing notoriety? "Not at all," the lead Paul, Weiss partner on the case told me. "All that stuff about twenty-one labor violations is just a numbers game. These people aren't worse than any other company."

The 1967 case involved seventy-one low-wage Stevens workers fired at twenty plants in North and South Carolina in 1963. "The triggering act was clearly the employee's advising [the Company] that he had joined the Union," the appeals court judges ruled, after reviewing the National Labor Relations Board's twelve-thousand-page record in the case. "The write-up or discharge, or both, followed as quickly as a pretext could be found. Frequently, it was found the same day. In many instances the write-ups would be the first ever received by the employee during a long course of employment."

Here is what the judges concluded had happened to William Aldridge, who had been fired in 1963 from his $1.90-an-hour job in Great Falls, North Carolina:

> The Company claimed that Aldridge was fired because he let the "laps" of cotton fibers, which are processed in the carding machines Aldridge tended, run out of several machines, causing damage to one of them. The [NLRB hearing] examiner did not believe the Company; he found instead that Aldridge was discharged because he had joined the Union. As support, the examiner pointed to the following evidence: Aldridge had been employed for nine years without once having received a derogatory write-up; less than three weeks before his discharge Aldridge had informed the Company of his Union membership; his name was posted on the bulletin board along with those of several others who had informed the Company they had joined; ever since then, his supervisors had more closely watched over him; Aldridge's immediate supervisor . . . did not testify to the nature or extent of the alleged damage to the machine; and two of the Company's witnesses could not point to any card tender having been fired for a similar offense, despite proof that it is not uncommon for laps to run out of a machine. . . .

Aldridge's name was posted on the Company bulletin board as a Union member about August 17, along with the names of six other employees. Within the next two days, three were discharged. Alarmed, two of the others went to their supervisors . . . to ask how to get out of the Union. [One supervisor] told them they would have "to prove" to him that they were no longer for the Union. These two employees were not discharged; eleven days later Aldridge was; within two more weeks the last of the seven was terminated. To describe this evidence as supporting a finding of discriminatory discharge of Aldridge is understatement.

Another firing, the judges ruled, illustrated "the flavor of . . . the Company's tactics in combating organizational activity and represents the frivolity of most of the Company's attack on the sufficiency of the evidence."

In that case, Stevens had targeted, among others, Jess Cudd and his son Donald. Jess had worked at the Whitmire, South Carolina, plant for more than fifty years, starting at age thirteen. He had last received a write-up for poor performance in 1948. Father and son were fired within days of expressing support for the union, just before Christmas—but not before a sympathetic manager suggested to Jess, the judges wrote, that to keep afloat financially he could adopt his son Donald's children, then "quit work and collect relief payments." That way, the manager explained, Don—who, unlike his father, was handing out union literature—could be "run off."

An NLRB lawyer involved in that case told me that "It was as if Whiteford [Blakeney, the Stevens lawyer] was going through the motions. Like he didn't believe the Labor Relations Act was legitimate. Like it was all a game."

For Stevens, it was a game worth playing. It took three years and ten months for the appeals resulting in the 1967 decision to run their course and for the workers to be reinstated. They only got back pay; under the law, no interest or other damages could be assessed. Other cases took longer. And, if the employees had found any other work during those intervening years, those earnings would be deducted from the back pay due them. Nor did the company pay any fines during seventeen years of similar stiff-arming for violating repeated NLRB and court orders to cease and desist.

Firings like these and others across the South had scared off Stevens workers enough so that when I got to a Stevens plant in

1980—by which time some angry judges had threatened to jail Stevens executives for contempt—the union had won just one organizing election over more than fifteen years, and the company was still refusing to agree to a contract at that plant. By then, the profit-and-loss statement for Stevens's obstruction, judged illegal in twenty-one cases, showed $1.3 million in back pay awards, plus approximately $3 million in legal fees—a total of $4.3 million invested to keep wages down for 34,000 workers over seventeen years. Just 25 cents per hour in union-won wage increases or fringe benefits would have cost the company $16 million in one year, or $277 million for those 17 years. The company had invested $4.3 million to obstruct the law and save $277 million. An excellent shareholder return.

Writing in the *Harvard Law Review* in 1983, Harvard Law professor Paul Weiler declared that "Contemporary American labor law more and more resembles an elegant tombstone for a dying institution. . . . A major factor in this decline has been the skyrocketing use of coercive and illegal tactics—discriminatory discharges in particular—by employers determined to prevent unionization of their employees."

Weiler used NLRB data to calculate that 10,000 employees were fired illegally for union activity in 1980, which added up to 5 percent of the 200,000 votes cast for unions that year in organizing elections. That meant, he wrote, that "the current odds are about one in twenty that a union supporter will be fired for exercising rights supposedly guaranteed by federal law a half century ago. The core of the legal structure must bear a major share of the blame for providing employers with the opportunity and the incentives to use these tactics," Weiler concluded.

In 1978, the unions had seemed on the verge of getting a reprieve from the way Taft-Hartley, the Administrative Procedure Act, and management's illegal resistance had combined to weaken them so severely. In the wake of the Watergate scandals, Democrats had been swept into power. They enjoyed large majorities in the House and Senate, and Jimmy Carter was in the White House. With fights like the Stevens union drive erupting across the country, at the top of the Democrats' agenda was a labor law reform bill that would have, among other provisions, speeded up elections once a majority of members expressed initial support for a union, imposed far stronger sanctions on employer violations, and required expedited review of

accusations of illegal firings. After six tries, proponents failed to get
the votes needed to override a Senate filibuster. Twenty Senate Democrats voted against overriding it. Lewis Powell's wake-up call and
the marshaling of business's resources that followed had prevailed.
Conservative-funded think tanks produced white papers giving labor
reform opponents the cover of weighty policy arguments. CEOs
themselves lobbied members of Congress. By 1978, contributions to
congressional candidates by business and trade association PACs—
which had lagged union PACs until 1975—exceeded funding from
union PACs by more than two to one.

This failure to enact measures aimed at correcting labor law
abuses ranks at the top of any list of events demonstrating that the
post-war equilibrium between the working class and management
had been destroyed. The pendulum had been frozen in place on management's side.

Through the 1980s, union-management battles became still more
lopsided, even in terms of giving unions the kinds of victories without
real relief that National Labor Relations Board decisions in their favor
meant. Under NLRB members appointed during the Richard Nixon
and Gerald Ford administrations, the board had decided in favor of
businesses 35 percent of the time. During the mid-1980s, appointees
in the Reagan administration decided for business more than two
thirds of the time. By the 1990s, the unions' taste for battle and the
resources available to them to make the fight had been so depleted
that efforts to win union recognition in elections were down to just
over a third of the number of organizing drives mounted in the 1970s.

In its early years, the Stevens fight rarely made national news. The
civil rights battles in the South, also against die-hard resisters, dominated the headlines. But by 1980, the Stevens fight had attracted
widespread news coverage, sparked by a union-led boycott of Stevens's consumer products (which included towels and sheets under
the Fieldcrest, Laura Ashley, Utica, and Ralph Lauren brands), and
by the blatancy of Stevens's defiance. In 1979, there was even a hit
movie about the confrontation, *Norma Rae*, for which Sally Field won
an Academy Award for her portrayal of a fired union organizer. That,
and belated judicial threats to jail Stevens executives for contempt of
multiple court orders, gradually tamed the company. Robert Stevens

replaced Blakeney as his lead lawyer, and the company began to allow union elections. The contests were still resisted by the company, but they were fair enough so that 17 percent of the company was unionized by the mid-1980s. Yet that tense peace didn't settle the worker-management standoff. Larger economic forces did.

In 1988, on the eve of its 175th anniversary, J.P. Stevens was sold off in pieces to a group that included its larger textile industry rival and two leveraged buyout firms. Business at Stevens had declined sharply because of international competition. Factories had been shut, and the workforce of 45,000 had been reduced to 23,000. The company adjusted successfully enough by selling off some units and upgrading its technology that the Stevens family was able to raise a line of credit to attempt a leveraged buyout of the public shareholders in order to maintain control. Their buyout offer quickly attracted outside raiders willing to pay more for the stock of a company that had shrunk but was still considered to have value. A bidding war pitting its larger textile rival and debt-financed raiders against each other ended with the competing bidders making a deal to split the assets. As *The Washington Post* put it, the company was "swept away by the wave of corporate takeovers and buyouts that have come to dominate American business in the 1980's."

The raiders' victory didn't last. As of 2016, the larger textile maker that had purchased the bulk of the Stevens operations in 1988 had gone through a 2003 bankruptcy stemming from foreign competition. It was then bought by corporate raider Carl Icahn. Most of its manufacturing is now done overseas, and what remains has been highly automated.

The industry as a whole shared the same fate. In 1973, there were 1,024,000 textile workers in the United States. In 2016, there were 112,000, and the average hourly wage for those left in American textile factories was 30 percent lower than it would have been if the low, non-union wages prevailing in 1975 (the year closest to 1973 for which there is wage data) had only kept up with inflation.

THE DYNAMICS OF MARGINALIZATION

The lasting meaning of the J.P. Stevens story is that it lays bare the sins of omission of a government so captured by big business that it failed to take the obvious steps, such as labor law fixes or job retraining, necessary to protect America's core rank-and-file workforce. The fight against unionization once manufacturing shifted south was the beginning of the end of the era of managers and owners sharing a reasonable portion of their wealth with their workers. Global competition later undermined the leverage of workers in thriving industries outside the South, too.

In some cases, such as the Big Three automakers, the wealth sharing in earlier decades was arguably so indulgent on both sides that labor and industry coasted along with so little attention to quality or consumer value that they created their own near-death spiral once global competition arrived. The result today is a relatively less well paid and sharply reduced auto industry workforce.

Other post-1960s advances in finance and commerce extending well beyond automation or trade also undercut workers. Franchising allowed fast food chains to avoid becoming the mass-employer bargaining targets like Stevens or GM because so many outlets were owned by individual franchisees who do not have to bargain as a group. In the new age of short-termism, outsourcing came into vogue, which encouraged the rise of firms offering temporary or even permanent contract workers. This has fundamentally changed the nature of the workforce and the career prospects for millions of Americans. Executives, who were now often focused on gathering funds for stock buybacks, were able to cut permanent payrolls and accompanying fringe benefits, and forgo the training required to move employees into more skilled positions. As a 2017 *New York Times* report pointed out, the once real prospect that an entry-level worker, even a janitor, could move up the ranks vanishes if those workers do not even work for the same company, and if those with additional skills can be hired laterally or brought in as needed from other outsourcing firms. At the same time the non-employee workers are often left in the dark about which hours or days they will be asked to work each week.

In the age of FedEx and then email, the U.S. Postal Service has shed 300,000 jobs since its peak employment in 1999, and would have lost more if politics and civil service laws didn't shield it from more efficiencies. The availability of cost-efficient natural gas and other changes in energy consumption and environmental regulations, in addition to technology advances, have eliminated 108,000 coal mining jobs since 1960. The number of jobs already lost in the retail sector from the surge in online shopping now far exceeds that number. Just a 20 percent drop in the country's more than fifteen million retail jobs in the next decade, which in the age of Amazon is highly likely, would sideline nearly four times the 784,000 people who worked in coal mines during the industry's peak year (1920) of employment.

An equally iconic American blue-collar occupation, truck driving, is also no longer a bedrock of the middle class. A combination of industry deregulation and law enforcement crackdowns against corruption in the truckers' Teamsters Union in the 1980s, both long overdue, created an environment where non-union trucking companies could compete so effectively that the Teamsters Union's division covering truckers and warehousemen declined from 450,000 members in 1978 to approximately 75,000 by 2017. In the 1960s and 1970s, the Teamsters Union was an engine of economic security and mobility. True, top leaders overpaid themselves and gave mob-connected trucking companies sweetheart wage deals, while siphoning off pension funds to finance the building of mob-run Las Vegas casinos. They left enough on the table, though, to boost their members into the middle class.

In 1977, I rode overnight with a tractor-trailer driver through Ohio while reporting for a book I was writing about the corruption-tarred union. He was grateful, he said, to be "making a good living, sending my kids through school, not owing any money on my house, and driving a good car." He also knew he had a decent pension to look forward to, even after the mob's take, and he was glad to have the cushioned seat and upgraded windshield wipers the union had won in the last contract. He was making 148 percent more per hour in 1977 than he had ten years earlier. He was, he told me, "living the Dream." By 2017, average truck driver wages had fallen about 60 percent since 1980 when adjusted for inflation, the once solid pensions had been drastically cut, and drivers faced the prospect of being replaced by self-driving trucks.

The bottom line is that along with the advantages management still enjoyed following the failure of labor law reforms proposed in 1978—and at the same time that buybacks, takeover fights, and other financial engineering were making rank-and-file payrolls tempting targets—globalization, automation, and other changes in the economy rightly regarded as progress have combined to marginalize unskilled or semi-skilled workers.

The trend was clear to anyone looking at the data showing this steady, relentless shift in workforce demand. The people in charge in America's boardrooms, however, were only looking at the bottom line—and they and their lobbyists were able to fend off efforts by anyone in Washington to protect workers or fund effective programs to retrain them to thrive in the new economy. Overall, the United States lost seven million of its 19.2 million manufacturing jobs from 1980 to 2015.

Trade has undeniably been an important cause of worker displacement, which should have been easy to anticipate. As Nobel laureate economist Joseph Stiglitz put it, "Add a few billion people into the market willing to work for much less than American workers will and what do you think will happen?" Yet even before what seems to be the coming onset of machines replacing workers en masse, automation has been a far more significant displacement factor than global trade. Depending on the economist, estimates of the share of American manufacturing jobs lost to trade varies from 10 percent to 20 percent. The rest were lost due to technology advances that replaced manual labor with machines or more efficient processes.

One study found that although the American steel industry lost 400,000 jobs between 1962 and 2005, it actually produced just as much steel. The job losses came largely from a technology breakthrough called the mini-mill, which required far fewer workers and much less space (and made the steel industry's growth rate in productivity per worker among the highest of any industry). This explains the shuttering of the large steel factories that dominated many cities and towns in the Midwest. Because workers have lost so much leverage as machines advanced, the wages of those who have kept their jobs have not increased in proportion to the increase in productivity per worker still employed and operating those machines.

Although it may be less obvious, automation, like trade, is a market force whose victims government has an obligation to help, particularly with the kind of training and retraining programs that every other developed economy deploys successfully. Automation is the product of government policy, such as a tax code that rightly encourages capital investment in job killers like the mini-mill. If a government's responsibility is to encourage a vibrant economy, part of that job is not only to use levers like the tax code to encourage innovation but also to do what it can to send citizens sidelined temporarily by innovation back into that economy.

Trade, however, is a far more obvious product of government policy, and, despite its second-place rank behind automation as a cause of job displacement, examining what America has done and not done about jobs shifted abroad provides a clear, grim picture of how Washington has abandoned the working class. Trade doesn't happen on its own. The government must allow products to come across its borders, and can slow or accelerate the flow with tariffs, quotas, and other measures. Even if it lets pretty much everything through with few limits, that, too, is a policy, especially if it is done in the face of other countries restricting products made by American workers, or if those countries give their businesses an unfair advantage by not imposing the equivalent wage, job safety, or environmental laws that the United States has chosen to impose.

Trade's negative side effects, therefore, have presented the clearest test for policymakers when it comes to helping Americans through upheavals in a dynamic economy. The victims of trade were undeniably the larger community's responsibility, because globalization was being pursued for the greater good of the larger community. If the American community, through its elected government, failed to respond to this most obvious responsibility—if it looked away, rather than reached out—what did that portend for how it would respond in the future to help workers displaced by all the other dynamics, especially technology advances, that are so obviously about to dominate the future?

CHAPTER 6

"Lip Service" for America's Workers

By 1970, George Meany and other labor leaders had figured out that their vision of American workers thriving by selling their superior products to eager customers around the world was an illusion. As early as 1967, when the U.S. trade surplus dropped to $4.1 billion from an all-time high of $7.1 billion three years before, Meany and others in the labor movement had begun to lobby Congress to do something about the globalization that they had so heartily supported in the Kennedy years. There were some holdouts, particularly the longshoremen's union, whose workers unloaded the ships bringing in the growing imports of textiles, footwear, machine tools, appliances, consumer electronics, cars, and other goods. However, by 1970—the year before the U.S. would fall into what would become a perpetual and growing trade *deficit*—the unions' position had jelled into outright opposition to the Kennedy Round of trade liberalization.

In May 1970, the AFL-CIO circulated a paper around Washington that read like a 2016 Donald Trump or Bernie Sanders speech. "The United States position on world trade deteriorated in the 1960's, with an adverse impact on American workers, communities, and industries," the union paper declared. Citing "managed [foreign] national economies with direct and indirect government barriers to imports and aid to exports," a "skyrocketing rise of investments by U.S. companies in foreign subsidiaries and the spread of U.S.-based multinational corporations," the union demanded that America's trade policy be reversed. If it wasn't, the AFL-CIO warned, those most victimized would be the "semi-skilled and unskilled production workers in an increasing number of industries and product lines," including "shoes, textiles, clothing, steel, ceramic tile, radios, tv, leather goods and others."

The change the unions demanded never happened. Their push a year later for the Burke-Hartke anti-trade bill that so galvanized the business community failed. Large numbers of Democrats and all Republicans rejected it amid big business's fierce lobbying campaign and because even trade skeptics feared that it went too far. However, one high-ranking Republican in the Nixon White House—a hardcore business establishment Republican named Peter Peterson—agreed with the unions that the damaging effects of trade were real and had to be dealt with. He told President Nixon exactly that in an exhaustive policy memo distributed by the president to his cabinet just eight months after the union had circulated its anti-trade manifesto.

In 1971, Peterson, a forty-four-year-old assistant to the president for international economic affairs, was already a superstar in American business circles. Born in Nebraska, Peterson worked his way through Northwestern University and the University of Chicago business school, then climbed quickly through Chicago's corporate suites. By the time he was forty-two, he had become chairman and chief executive of Bell & Howell, then a giant camera company. Peterson would later become Nixon's commerce secretary, then the chairman of Lehman Brothers, then the cofounder of Blackstone, the multibillion-dollar private equity fund. While amassing a fortune, Peterson also served as chairman of the Council on Foreign Relations and founded the Peter G. Peterson Foundation, an influential think tank focused on fiscal and economic issues.

Like all Republicans and a still large portion of Democrats, Peterson believed that free trade was highly desirable and inevitable. Like the labor leaders, however, Peterson saw that America's post-war hubris was blinding the country to the challenges of globalization. In the 133-page memo he prepared for Nixon in February 1971, titled "The United States in a Changing World Economy," he derided "our view that the international competitive superiority of the U.S. was an unalterable fact of life; that our competitive advantage was so great we could easily afford concessions here and there, in an ad hoc fashion, in the interest of maintaining flexible and friendly relations with our international partners and developing a prospering world market."

"I had read the union's memo," Peterson recalled in a 2017 interview. "And I certainly agreed with all the problems they described, though not their argument that we should retreat."

Much of Peterson's paper was devoted to how the United States should continue to pursue trade but also prepare to meet the challenges of the changing world economy by making broad adjustments in policies related to foreign exchange rates, the gold standard, and tariff negotiations. However, he also offered an unflinching view of the competitive challenges—and potential displacement of American workers—that would be the downside of globalization unless the country squarely faced the problem and prepared to retrain its workforce.

"I had seen what was happening in the camera industry with Bell & Howell and how the Japanese were starting to kill us," Peterson explained forty-six years later.

"Peterson saw a storm—a Cat 5 hurricane—coming. You read this 1971 memo, and you say, Wow, he warned us," said Edward Alden, a senior fellow at the Council on Foreign Relations, whose 2016 book, *Failure to Adjust*, documented America's failure to heed that warning.

Peterson's memo urged help for those likely to continue to be displaced by lower-paid labor abroad:

> As regards adjustments due to import competition . . . the burden may be [a] heavy one for a particular industry to bear. Furthermore, a program to build on America's strengths by enhancing international competitiveness cannot be indifferent to the fate of those industries, and especially those groups of workers who are not meeting the demands of a truly competitive world economy. It is unreasonable to say that a liberal trade policy is in the interest of the entire country and then allow particular industries, workers and communities to pay the whole price.

Importantly, Peterson's focus was not limited to workers victimized by trade. He also urged Nixon and his cabinet to prepare to deal with the larger group of workers whose education and training needed to be upgraded to meet the challenges, including automation, of the coming modern economy. "I believe," Peterson wrote to Nixon, "we may be approaching a decade in which fundamental reorientation will be necessary to provide the career education, upgrading, and conversion of old to needed skills in the labor force of the '70's."

"I thought training and retraining was our biggest challenge," Peterson recalled. "But Nixon and everyone else just paid lip service to it. Nothing really happened.

The Nixon administration was not the first to pay that kind of lip service to the idea of training American workers to be more competitive. It started in the Kennedy years.

When Kennedy proposed global trade liberalization in 1962, he tacked on a program called Trade Adjustment Assistance, or TAA. He justified it with the same argument to Congress that Peterson would make nine years later about not forcing a small group to pay the cost of a beneficial change in national policy. "When considerations of national policy make it desirable to avoid higher tariffs, those injured by that competition should not be required to bear the full brunt of the impact," Kennedy urged. "Rather, the burden of economic adjustment should be borne in part by the Federal Government."

The Kennedy program offered displaced workers payments of up to 65 percent of their prior wages for up to sixty-five weeks while they remained unemployed—in essence, an expanded program of unemployment insurance; enrollment in training and education programs to develop "higher and different skills"; and funds to help the worker and his or her family relocate to a different community where jobs might be available.

It seemed like a reasonable accommodation. Nonetheless the program faced strong opposition in Congress. Conservatives argued that the free market mandated free trade, but that the government should not interfere in the market to provide for its victims. L. Mendel Rivers, a Democratic congressman from South Carolina, attacked the Kennedy plan in a home-state newspaper column, arguing, "Such adjustment assistance would mean Federal subsidy. More subsidy would mean greater Federal control and ultimately higher taxes for such subsidies. . . . The only logical conclusion I can draw from the present trade bill is that socialization of industry must be the inevitable result if we embark on this avenue."

Others opposed TAA because the subsidies would give special treatment for those affected by trade liberalization. It was a position that might logically have led to the kind of overall job-training initiatives that would be advocated fruitlessly by Peterson in 1971. Instead, those making the argument used it as a rationale to block all subsidies. "Particularly objectionable is the treatment accorded workers dis-employed by imports under the bill," said Prescott Bush, a Republican senator from Connecticut (and father and grandfather of the future presidents Bush). "The group will be afforded special doles, special training and special expense money not accorded to that 5.8 percent of the work force who are unemployed for other reasons. Why discriminate between the unemployed? This seems unnecessarily harsh and cruel to the 4 million persons unemployed for other reasons beyond their control."

In the end, with labor's backing, Kennedy overcame the hard-hearted opposition and TAA became law. It didn't matter. The program helped almost no one get the "higher and different skills" Kennedy promised, or get jobs paying anything approaching the ones they had lost.

Trade Adjustment Assistance is a metaphor for how most politicians—and much of journalism, or at least journalism on the two coasts—neglected what was happening for five decades to working-class Americans until the years immediately leading up to the 2016 election, when frustrations boiled over into a political force that could not go unnoticed. Some attention was paid in Washington to the debate and passage of the bill. How it was implemented outside the Beltway over the next fifty-plus years, however, was then largely ignored. A search of the archives of major print news outlets from 1962 through 2015 yields just two substantive articles about how TAA was working. Or not working.

During the first six years of TAA, beginning in 1963, the federal commission set up to implement the law approved no company whose workers applied for its benefits, and not a single worker received assistance. The law required that companies prove that trade, and trade alone, was what caused the workers to lose their jobs. Applications were rejected because competition might also have been a factor. In other cases, because the companies manufactured components but not the final products for industries that had shifted assembly overseas, they, too, were rejected.

Even as the standards were eased and workers were accepted, TAA proved mostly a source of extended unemployment insurance—and a useful political shield for Democrats who could claim they were making the government spend about a billion dollars a year to help displaced workers.

The requirement that workers first had to complete a high school equivalency degree and then had to enroll full-time for a year or more—typically in community colleges or vocational schools—to receive their subsidized job training was impractical for most of those who were eligible. They needed to replace their incomes with another full-time job quickly, even if at lower pay. Many workers, especially older ones, were not receptive to the prospect of jobs, such as health aides, far afield from their factory work. Nor did they like the idea of uprooting their families to seek work in another part of the country. Beyond that, programs often overlapped, were confusing, and poorly run. A 1980 report by the GAO, or General Accounting Office (its name was changed to the Government Accountability Office in 2005) found that three quarters of the workers at companies that managed to qualify for the program never used it.

Henry County is in southwestern Virginia near the North Carolina border. A 2001 GAO study found that six thousand jobs—representing about a third of all households in the county—were lost there over five years beginning in 1993. However, less than 20 percent of the eligible workers enrolled in training, and most of those dropped out because they could not complete remedial classes and occupational training before their income support expired.

A series of similar studies over two decades struck the same chord. Some conveyed how TAA was such a neglected consolation prize for those who opposed globalization that officials managing the programs around the country typically didn't bother to collect data on its results. Others zeroed in on whatever data there was to report that the program rarely resulted in the few who enrolled ending up with jobs remotely equivalent to the jobs they had lost. The most exhaustive study, in which an independent policy research firm pored through nine years of TAA records and compared participants to eligible non-participants, concluded, "Overall, participation in TAA . . . had a negative effect on total income during the four-year follow-up period."

The TAA eligibility requirements were marred by bureaucratic inconsistency, which further alienated those the program was intended to help. A random search through a 2012 database of eligibility appeals made that clear. Workers for a solar panel maker that had moved production from York, Pennsylvania, to China had been ruled ineligible because the panels that they had made in Pennsylvania had been sold overseas; therefore, *domestic* sales had not declined, as required. The conservative Cato Institute, one of the influential think tanks funded by conservatives in the 1970s, complained in a white paper that "The very existence of trade adjustment assistance perpetuates the myth that freeing trade creates special 'victims' who deserve special programs simply because of the reason for their unemployment." The Reagan and George W. Bush administrations ran their own studies concluding TAA was wholly ineffective, but congressional Democrats were always able to keep it alive.

Other less partisan think tanks, including the Peter G. Peterson Foundation, have continued to push back, acknowledging that TAA does not work, but urging that job training be reformed and given much more funding. The more practical, or jaded, view was summed up by Texas Republican senator Phil Gramm when TAA came up for renewal, with increased funding, in 2002: "Socialist governments all over the planet are trying to stop doing this kind of thing, and now we're doing it. Having said that, I'm very much for the [trade] bill. The $12 billion we'll be spending over 10 years [on Trade Adjustment Assistance] is tribute we have to pay to get the bill. Over those 10 years, we'll have $13 trillion in exports, so the $12 billion is nine one-hundredths of one percent of that. Is it robbery? Is it tribute? Yes. But is it worth it? Yes."

"I tried relentlessly to make TAA into something real, and to expand it to retrain workers displaced for all reasons, including automation," recalled Robert Reich, who served as President Clinton's labor secretary and, as such, oversaw the TAA program. In 1994, Reich persuaded Clinton to propose a $13 billion radical upgrade and complete overhaul of federal job training programs, including TAA.

"But the business people in the administration—[Treasury Secretary Robert] Rubin and [then–deputy secretary Lawrence] Summers—were more worried about the debt, so we never fought for it. And then when the Republicans took the House after '94, it became impossible. The Republicans didn't believe in it, or didn't care. . . . And some of the unions were worried that workers would be retrained into non-union jobs. It's America's great unfinished business."

"Bob Reich was absolutely right about all of this, but we couldn't have gotten it through Congress, even before '94," Rubin said in a 2017 interview.

Compared to how other developed countries face these challenges, it is, indeed, unfinished business. Job training—preparing people to participate productively in the economy—is considered an obvious and fundamental responsibility in every country that America competes with globally. It is as much a part of what government does as K–12 education. In Germany, 60 percent of young people are in apprenticeship programs, funded in large part through government grants and tax incentives. In the United States, 5 percent participate in programs that are much less rigorous.

"It's hard to find an issue where America is more of an outlier than job training," said Alden, the author of *Failure to Adjust.* "We spend less on job training than any other developed country. Denmark spends twenty times more as a percentage of GDP than we do. France spends ten times as much and Germany spend five times as much."

"A HUNDRED-TO-NOTHING DEAL FOR AMERICA"

By the time Senator Gramm complained about TAA in 2002, political positions on trade had divided into three camps. Almost all Republicans were for it, because trade generally helped businesses, particularly the larger business interests that made up the Republicans' donor base. National Democrats—Presidents Carter and Clinton, and most Democratic congressional leaders—also favored it for the same reasons Kennedy and Johnson before them had: Trade was seen as benefiting the country as a whole, as well as their big business donors, even if it hurt discrete segments of workers. Like their national leaders,

Democrats from states like New York or California, whose constituents and donors benefited from global finance and exports, especially in the technology sector, supported trade, too. In the third camp were other Democrats, who represented high proportions of constituents who worked, or had worked, in manufacturing. Their opposition to trade had intensified as imports increased and job losses mounted.

The fact that trade prevailed—and, more important, that TAA never was made an effective way for displaced workers to be redirected back into the middle class—illustrated the political and economic realities of the age. As with lobbying over labor law reform, lobbying for or against trade or for or against effective job training was an unfair fight, pitting the business community against weakened labor leaders and the occasional congressman, mayor, or county commissioner worried about his or her community being hollowed out by jobs moved overseas. Real trade adjustment assistance—indeed, automation adjustment assistance, too, and any other adjustment assistance needed to de-marginalize the working class—was the victim of this imbalance of power. Despite all the rhetoric beginning in the Kennedy years, adjustment assistance was, indeed, nothing more than the petty cash "tribute" Senator Gramm said it was.

As the twenty-first century began, automation and trade accelerated the displacement of workers. A turning point came with the admission of China into the World Trade Organization in May 2000, which had been promoted by President Clinton. The Cato Institute, founded and funded by wealthy conservatives in 1977, published a white paper promising that "The economic benefits . . . to the United States are clear. As the U.S. market is already largely open to Chinese imports, it is primarily U.S. exporters who will benefit." The president of the US-China Business Council seconded the notion, promising, "Opening China's markets to U.S. products and services under this agreement is the biggest single step we can take to reduce America's growing trade deficit with China."

Clinton agreed, releasing a letter from a coalition of business leaders declaring that opening trade to China would "increase U.S. jobs and reduce our trade deficit." At a press conference, Clinton added, "This is a hundred-to-nothing deal for America when it comes to the economic consequences."

Clinton was right about how lopsided the deal was. He just got his winners and losers mixed up. From 2000 to 2009, the U.S. trade deficit with China nearly tripled, ballooning from $83 billion to $227 billion, accounting for 76 percent of the country's non-petroleum, worldwide U.S. trade deficit. Over the same period, the U.S. lost 5.6 million manufacturing jobs, including 627,000 in computer and electronic products, industries for which the trade deficit with China grew to $109.6 billion by 2010. Executives and shareholders at large multinational companies thrived by going global, but their American blue-collar workers lost out. Or in the case of booming technology companies like Apple, which arranged from the start to produce most of its newer products overseas, they never got hired in the first place.

By 2016 the trade deficit with China was $347 billion. Much of the gap stemmed not just from China's low-wage competition but also from the country's failure to live up to promises to liberalize regulations on foreign imports, ownership, and investment, and to curtail state subsidies of industries (such as solar power) that had enabled them to compete unfairly abroad. Continuing regulations on the use of foreign-owned technology and, for many years, currency manipulation also put the country's thumb on the scale of fair free trade.

As already noted, one side effect of the enormous Chinese trade deficit was its role in the debt crisis and financial collapse of 2008–9. Because the Chinese were accumulating so much cash and needed a safe place to invest it, they dramatically increased demand for U.S. Treasury bonds. That pushed interest rates in the United States down to unprecedented lows, which contributed to easy money being available to finance even the riskiest mortgages and, with them, the mortgage-backed securities and their derivatives that eventually drove the economy into the abyss.

The North American Free Trade Agreement, or NAFTA, negotiated by President George H. W. Bush and pushed through Congress by President Clinton in 1993, had produced similar, though smaller, deficits, despite promises to the contrary. The American Enterprise Institute produced a data-filled paper promising that by 1995 the U.S. would enjoy a $7 billion–$9 billion trade *surplus* with Mexico. In 1995 the U.S. had a $15.8 billion *deficit*. By 2016, it had grown to $64.3 billion. In part, this was because lobbyists pushed Republicans and some Democrats in Congress to force Clinton to abandon union-backed protections that they had attempted to include in the agreement that would have eased differences in wages and environmental regulations between Mexico and the U.S.

In 2014, Beth Macy, a reporter for the *Roanoke* (Virginia) *Times* and the daughter of a factory worker, published *Factory Man*, documenting the struggles of a family-owned furniture maker in Bassett, Virginia, to fight off competition from China following the country's admission into the World Trade Organization. Macy's powerful narrative attached the faces of a proud but decimated community to what had been an abstract issue for much of the country. The book also attracted national press attention to a reality that the more progressive wing of the Democratic Party had been screaming about for years.

Macy did not hide her contempt for TAA and its failure to help the workers in Bassett, which is in one of the counties, Henry, that the 2001 GAO audit used to illustrate the program's failures. "The only government program designed to ease them into new work," she wrote, "was an outdated Trade Adjustment Assistance (TAA) run by people who looked down their noses at the displaced. (My personal favorite exchange, from a TAA training session I attended: 'We're not gonna pay for you to be in school and find out you're in Myrtle Beach,' a presenter said, stressing strict school attendance. 'Who here has money for a vacation?' said the laid-off worker sitting next to me. 'I'm worried about losing my house.')" Macy also noted that more laid-off workers got themselves onto Social Security's program for the disabled, by claiming ailments, than enrolled in TAA. In fact, sharply rising enrollment in the disability program has been recorded across the United States in the last two decades, a barometer of the disaffection, frustration, or lack of initiative that parallels a broader national trend of lower labor force participation—meaning fewer adults, especially white males, are even trying to find work.

In 1960, Henry County voted 59 percent to 41 percent for the creator of TAA, John F. Kennedy. In 2016, the county went 63 percent to 34 percent for Donald Trump.

Macy's book was a best seller and earned rave reviews, many of which suggested she had uncovered and powerfully conveyed an important story hiding in plain sight, or at least in plain sight where *she* lived. "I find myself deeply sympathetic to Macy's essential point," wrote *New York Times* columnist Joe Nocera in 2014, "which is that globalization inflicts a great deal of suffering on millions of people, something the news media should do a better job of acknowledging and the government should do a better job of mitigating."

Throughout President Obama's presidency, he acknowledged TAA's failure and tried to reform and expand it, but Republicans consistently rejected any changes or additional funding. Congressional Democrats, having grown cynical about global trade, failed to take up a fight that they would have lost anyway once Republicans gained control of the House in 2010. In 2015, most congressional Democrats were so opposed to Obama's push for the Trans-Pacific Partnership trade pact, or TPP, that they joined a successful Republican effort to reject the additional TAA assistance that Obama had proposed to accompany it. Many dismissed it as a fig leaf to cover up the damage TPP would inflict on American workers. One Democrat, Lloyd Doggett of Texas, referred to it as "burial insurance, because it delivers limited help after a job is dead and buried."

There is, of course, another side to trade, the macro side that focuses on the overall greater good that has undeniably come to the American and global economies from allocating the production of goods to those that produce them most efficiently and by making those goods available to buyers in more markets. That perspective was expressed in a 2016 speech by FedEx founder and CEO Fred Smith. "History shows that trade made easy, affordable and fast—political obstacles notwithstanding—always begets more trade, more jobs, more prosperity," he said, using, among other examples, these data points:

> From less than $50 billion in total trade in 1966, the U.S. now imports and exports over $4 trillion annually in goods and services. Container ships have grown from carrying a few hundred boxes on each trip to the new Triple-E behemoths that transport over 18,000 containers called TEUs, or 20-foot-equivalent units. The cost is 1/500th of the shipping rates per pound of the early 1960s. The profusion of agricultural products from the "Green Revolution" . . . combined with ever more efficient shipping, has resulted in mas-

sive amounts of grain traded around the world, something unimaginable to farmers 50 years ago.

For consumers that has meant a steady decline in the cost of most products. Before free trade, the average family spent 6 percent of its annual budget on clothing, compared to 3 percent in 2017. Most cars, food, appliances, electronics, and furniture now also cost less in inflation-adjusted dollars. According to *The Economist*, "Consumer prices for televisions, adjusted for quality, fell more than 90% in the 15 years after China joined the World Trade Organization."

"Yes, trade has cut costs and spread jobs and wealth around the world and taken millions of people out of poverty," said Joseph Stiglitz, the Nobel laureate who served as the chairman of President Clinton's Council of Economic Advisers, and who supported Robert Reich's unsuccessful efforts to get the Clinton administration to fight harder for expanded job training. "But we live in the United States, and we have done nothing to take care of the people here who paid the price for all that."

The failure of TAA to ameliorate the damage to some of a policy, free trade, that produces benefits for others and undeniably makes sense for the country and the world is part of the larger story of how the country has failed to help members of the community—whether displaced by a Chinese worker, a robot, a software program, or a mini-mill in a domestic steel factory—stay in the middle class. Conservatives did not believe in that kind of help. And by the mid-1970s, the businesses that benefited from the new technological and global efficiency had pooled their resources to gain the political clout to resist unions and have their way in Washington. They could avoid paying for what Peterson had warned Richard Nixon was the "fundamental reorientation . . . necessary to provide the career education, upgrading, and conversion of old to needed skills." Whether it was a matter of ideology, short-termism, simple selfishness, or all three, they used their power to force the American community to look the other way and ignore what was happening to those left out of the knowledge economy.

The result was exactly as Peterson predicted in 1971. Writing forty-three years later in his best-selling book about economic inequality, *Capital in the Twenty-First Century*, Thomas Piketty would describe what happened this way:

It is obvious that lack of adequate investment in training can exclude entire social groups from the benefits of economic growth. Growth can harm some groups while benefiting others (witness the recent displacement of workers in the more advanced economies by workers in China). In short, the principal force for convergence [Piketty's term for a narrowing of the gap between the rich and everyone else]—the diffusion of knowledge—is only partly natural and spontaneous. It also depends in large part on educational policies, access to training and to the acquisition of appropriate skills.

LEARNING THE CODE

The failure of TAA is inexcusable because it was not inevitable. Training or retraining working-class people to thrive in the modern economy is not impossible. In Queens, New York, even an amateur is proving that it can be done.

In May 2017, a group of thirty-four men and women who had worked in unskilled jobs paying an average of $18,000 a year sat at laptops undergoing the "fundamental reorientation" envisioned by Peterson. They were enrolled in a program run by a non-profit called Coalition for Queens* that puts TAA's billion-dollar-a-year efforts to shame. At what was once a zipper factory in what had become a once-again-booming section of Queens across the East River from Manhattan, a group that included a waitress, a part-time cab driver, a messenger, and a Foot Locker sales clerk were learning how to code for web development. Two other groups of about thirty-five each met at night and on weekends at the zipper factory to learn IOS or Android coding.

The students will spend twenty-five to forty-six hours a week in class (depending on the class) and dozens of hours more completing assignments at home, for ten months. The classes start with the absolute basics, taking baristas and sales clerks quickly into their new world. A class that I sat in on during the sixth day of one of the Fall

---

* The author joined the board of the organization in 2016, when its name was Coalition for Queens. Its name is in the process of being changed, probably to Tech Equality, as this goes to press.

2017 programs buzzed with enthusiasm as the instructor, bounding around the room in sneakers and jeans, put students through drills making sure they had mastered the vocabulary—"bits" versus "bytes," "variables," "values," "arrays."

"How many bits would you need to accommodate the value 28,232?" The answer, 15, was instantly provided from near the back of one of the zipper factory's converted classrooms by a man who looked like a Pittsburgh Steelers lineman and worked part-time as a nightclub bouncer. Next came exercises in the simplest code writing, done on the laptops Coalition for Queens provided. Every day, the instructor and a program manager monitor each aspiring coder's assignments to see who might be falling behind.

The sixth and seventh months are devoted to intense teamwork. Students work in small groups to create software programs aimed at solving problems or producing new sources of digital entertainment or information. They then demonstrate their inventions to an assembly of other students, faculty, alumni, and friends of the program. A panel of judges drawn from tech start-up luminaries rates the projects. The last three months involve additional class work, plus career preparation, which includes interviewing skills and what the program calls "job readiness training."

Jukay Hsu, who runs the program, knows nothing about coding. A Harvard graduate who earned a Bronze Star serving as an Army captain in Iraq, Hsu was twenty-seven when he founded the non-profit, which he called the Coalition for Queens, in 2011. His goal was to help establish the New York borough where he was raised (after being born in Taiwan) as a high-tech business incubator that might match the revitalization going on in neighboring Brooklyn. He promoted meetups for aspiring tech entrepreneurs, organized informal hackathons and training programs, and sponsored speakers programs. By 2012, he recalled, "I could see that the most productive opportunity was to focus on using technology to boost the 64 percent of New Yorkers who lack college degrees and are the poor and the working poor into the middle class." He also was inspired by his military experience, where, he says, "some of the smartest, hardest-working people I've ever met were soldiers who didn't graduate from college."

Through a network of high school and college friends and others he had met through various local civic and business organizations,

Hsu recruited a handful of managers and volunteer coding teachers. The first training program started in 2013, with twenty-one students. After graduation, most got jobs at relatively small tech start-ups, while others were hired by more established companies including BuzzFeed and Condé Nast. By the time the second class was launched, in 2014, Hsu and a team of about half a dozen full-time managers had raised $1.6 million (up from about $350,000 in the prior year) from a growing list of prestige donors. There were fifty-one graduates the following June, and the list of blue-chip tech companies that hired them was growing. The next year Hsu replaced volunteers with paid teachers, and hired program directors to supervise them, as well as a job placement professional.

The eighty-eight recruits who began the course in September 2016 and graduated in June 2017 ended up in jobs averaging $85,000 a year at companies that included Uber, Blue Apron, Pinterest, Google, BuzzFeed and JPMorgan Chase. They were 52 percent female and 60 percent African American or Hispanic.

Fifty-two percent lacked college degrees, a number that increased to 55 percent in the class entering in September 2017, when the program expanded to four classes and 144 students (who, like those recruited the year before, were earning about the same $18,000 average income from the jobs they had when they applied).

Because the Coalition for Queens was increasingly able to boast so many success stories, it received approximately $4 million in funding in 2017 from a glittering array of New York charities, including the Robin Hood Foundation, the New York Community Trust, the Rockefeller Foundation, and the charity arms of Google, Blackstone, and the Hearst Corporation.

In 2017, Hsu, having realized that his success in training unskilled workers to participate in the new economy could have broad ramifications, began making plans to change the organization's name, probably to Tech Equality. At the same time, he created an ingenious business model that made expanding the program more realistic, while also making it more than another hot charity. Beginning with members of the class graduating that June, those who were placed in jobs paying more than $50,000—which was most of them—had to agree to pay the organization 12 percent of their earnings for the following two years. It was not a student loan that could trap those who did not graduate or get good jobs; they would owe nothing and would have paid nothing, because the program charges no tuition and, in fact, even helps pay the subway and bus fares of the poorest students. Yet based on its students' past success, it was likely that most graduates would end up with more than $50,000 starting salaries, thereby offering a path for the organization to solicit philanthropies and others on the idea of "investing" rather than donating.

The new pitch to some donors, called "18-85 Job Outcomes Bonds," was Hsu's way to tap into the trend of major foundations looking for ways to make their gifts self-sustaining. (The "18-85" was meant to deliver the message about the program's record of raising incomes, from $18,000 to $85,000.) Instead of donating, a foundation could invest in a bond to advance the $25,000 per student it costs to run the program. The bond would pay the investor an annual dividend of 6.6 percent, with the dividends funded by the student paybacks. (At 12 percent of the then-average $85,000 starting salary, the payback over two years would be about $20,000.) Ultimately, as the program expanded and costs per student were reduced (or the payback was extended for three years), the 12 percent paybacks might finance most or all of the program through these "18-85" bonds, without much need for outright gifts, and the capital invested by the donors into the bonds could either be returned or used for expansion, as could any outright gifts. By the end of 2017, Hsu had drafted plans to expand what he might now call Tech Equality and his 18-85 bonds beyond Queens. There is certainly a broad need and widespread interest; in 2017, the Queens operation attracted 1,550 applicants for 144 places.

Other private non-profits offer training in a broader mix of job categories to people who would otherwise flounder in the American economy. Year Up, founded in 2000 in Boston by Gerald Chertavian, the head of a software development company, now operates in twenty locations across the United States and has trained 18,000 students for technology-related jobs that are more modest than the Coalition for Queens's focus on higher-paying coding jobs but that nonetheless propel their students into the middle class. Year Up's programs target eighteen- to twenty-four-year-olds in urban areas who are high school graduates or have high school equivalency degrees, including some enrolled in community colleges.

They are given six months of intense training and mentoring in the technical skills, such as hardware repair or help desk operations, and in the communications skills that employers would expect for those filling these entry-level, middle-skill jobs. Each student signs a contract committing to tough standards of conduct and participation. They get 200 points at the beginning and then lose points for any transgressions, such as being late or disrespectful, or failing to complete homework on time. Twenty-five percent typically lose the 200 points and are then removed.

Year Up pairs the 75 percent who complete their training with local corporations, which are recruited by Year Up's eighty-five experienced corporate salespeople. The companies agree to hire the enrollees for six months as interns, with the expectation that they will then be offered full-time jobs. The mentoring continues through that second six months. In 2017, 85 percent of the 2,000 Year Up students who completed the program were either employed or had enrolled in college. Their average starting wage was $18.00 an hour.

Year Up has been growing at a rate of about 25 percent a year, and plans to expand to 10,000 students a year by 2022. Founder and CEO Chertavian presides over a budget of more than $100 million annually. About half comes from contributions; the other half comes from the corporate employers, who pay for the training dispensed to students whom they have agreed to take on as interns.

Year Up's chief operating officer is Garrett Moran, who until 2013 had the same title at Blackstone, the giant private equity firm. He may have changed what he wants to get out of a job, but he had not changed what he puts into it. "I had an itch for a long time to do something beneficial for others," Moran said. "It feels great, but there's a lot that has to be done. I'm sitting here dealing with spreadsheets all over my desk just like I used to at Blackstone, and I'm sixty-three and am taking the same vacation time I did twenty years ago."

Moran believes that Year Up works because it focuses "totally on outcomes. . . . Government programs pay community colleges, vocational schools, or their own programs to train, not to produce outcomes," he explained. "Focusing on outcomes is what the government should be doing. That takes real cohesion and leadership and intense attention to detail, to getting the right people to do it, and then bringing employers into the process by getting them to help design the programs they need for the workforces they need."

. . .

Estimates vary widely of the exact number, but there is little doubt that there are hundreds of thousands of openings in the United States for coders and those with related technology skills that are going unfilled for lack of trained workers. No matter how much Coalition for Queens/Tech Equality or Year Up expand, they could never fill all of them. Nor could they be filled if dozens of other organizations could replicate their success—which far exceeds the results of less rigorous for-profit vocational schools and less focused community college training programs. This is a job that the government, which still spends a billion dollars a year on training programs that mostly don't work, has to tackle—by making its own programs effective and by funding the growth of more non-profits like Coalition for Queens/Tech Equality and Year Up.

Instead, in 2017 President Trump proposed cutting job training programs by 36 percent. Although with his daughter Ivanka he touted a new push for apprenticeship programs through an executive order, the order was only a directive to his Department of Labor to encourage such programs. No new funds were allocated.

The federal government should also provide tax credits or other inducements to corporations to offer retraining programs for workers about to lose their jobs because of automation. When unions were strong, they were sometimes able to negotiate that help into their contracts. After Ford announced plans to close an assembly plant near San Jose, California, in 1983, workers received what could have become a model retraining and transitional income support program. It didn't help everyone, but more than 80 percent of the workers got new jobs, including 25 percent in the blossoming tech industry in neighboring Silicon Valley. Again, job training and retraining is not rocket science, but it does require resources and intense effort by smart people.

The lack of programs that prepare young Americans who would otherwise only have a high school education as they enter the job market is one of the primary causes of the country's economic angst and the marginalization of the middle class. Studies done by economists repeatedly find a steady decline over the last five decades in the starting incomes of young high school graduates and in their career prospects thereafter in an economy that demands skills beyond a high school diploma. As *The New York Times* reported in 2017, when adjusted for inflation, "in 1967, the median income at age 25 was $33,300; in 1983, it was $29,000. In 2011 . . . [it] was less than $25,000." As a result, the *Times* concluded, incomes for these workers as they advanced from these lower starting points were also lower: "In 1973, the inflation-adjusted median income of [all] men working full time was $54,030. In 2016, it was $51,640."

In December 2016, *Bloomberg Businessweek* published a telling report on the openings for skilled labor jobs—auto glass installers, for example, and workers who could operate new technology-enabled machinery, such as robots—that were going unfilled for lack of qualified applicants. In mid-2017, unemployment was down to 4.3 percent. However, that measured only the portion of those sixteen or older "participating" in the job market, meaning they were working or looking for work. By 2017, this job participation rate had fallen to 62.7 percent. Through the 1990s, by which time women had entered the workforce at rates equivalent to modern levels, the participation rate had been 66–67 percent. The steep decline—more than ten million people—came more from males over sixteen but not yet sixty-five than it did from the increasing number of retirees. The prime members of the nation's workforce demographic had stopped participating because, although there were a record six million job openings going unfilled, they had given up hope of finding jobs that they were qualified to do.

The crisis of the working class, then, is not a matter of not enough good jobs. It is about not enough people being able to fill them because they have not been properly trained. The results at Coalition for Queens/Tech Equality and Year Up prove that, as does what is happening at Baruch College.

New technology does eliminate old jobs, but as with the invention of the car, which idled drivers of horse-drawn carriages, technology also creates new jobs. Cars and trucks may soon drive themselves, but someone will have to program them, repair them, and monitor them, while others will find work in industries that might not have been created yet, or in growing sectors like home health care. That will only happen if they get the training they need.

Yet President Trump has continually tried to cut already inadequate job-training programs, while federal and state support for public colleges and universities, like Baruch, which also offer paths into the modern economy, has continued to be slashed. Nor have enough two-year community colleges received the necessary funding—or the long-overdue reorientation to make them more vocationally oriented rather than pale versions of four-year programs. America continues to fail at the basic responsibility that every other developed country takes for granted: underpinning the economy with the training necessary for its workers and the country as a whole to prosper.

In 2016, four economists at the National Bureau of Economic Research studying data on election results in districts most affected by global trade found "strong evidence that congressional districts exposed to larger increases in import competition disproportionately removed moderate representatives from office in the 2000s." Frustration from trade policies had apparently left many voters feeling victimized enough to look to less mainstream political leaders for help.

That voters would seek more alternatives when they believe incumbent officeholders are not being responsive to their needs is hardly surprising, nor is it surprising that some politicians would seek to exploit that frustration by taking extreme positions. Moreover, foreign trade and its benefits and consequences was only one of many issues—including civil rights, union rights, welfare, taxes, health care, the Vietnam War, and the myriad battles of the culture wars—that began to divide America in the last decades of the twentieth century. What was different, however, was how so many of America's leaders—not just outliers on the fringes, but most of them, or at least most of them on the Republican side of the aisle along with many Democrats—responded to those divides. They sought to capitalize on those divisions rather than bridge them. Their idea of winning became making sure the other side didn't win. In the process, as with job training, they paralyzed the government's ability to provide for the common good. How did the character and problem-solving capacity of American politics deteriorate so fundamentally?

CHAPTER 7

Dysfunctional Democracy

The checks and balances that the Founding Fathers wrote into the Constitution have always been considered a masterstroke of ensuring the capacity of a democracy to govern decisively while preserving the input and rights of those who do not enjoy majority support. However, that system depends on people of good will on opposite sides of an issue compromising so that something can get done. If checks and balances instead become tools for one side to refuse to yield any ground to the other, the result is a dysfunctional government. The Republicans' unanimous, virulent opposition to the Affordable Care Act, or Obamacare, from the day President Obama took office offers a vivid example.

The proposal Obama and Democrats in Congress put together in 2009 was not something Republicans should logically have been resisting. In fact, it was easy to imagine that Obama had decided to back Republicans into a corner by daring them to take yes for an answer. For Obama was pushing a more conservative version of health care reform than what Richard Nixon had proposed in 1972, or what Republican governor Mitt Romney had implemented in Massachusetts in 2006.

Health care reform in America has always been about two issues: the high cost of health care compared to other countries that produce as good or better results, and the fact that, unlike most other countries, large numbers of American families did not have protection against those costs through insurance or some other mechanism (such as government-provided health care). Just as Romney had done, and Nixon had proposed, Obamacare attempted little to deal with the first problem. As explained earlier, to the dismay of many Democrats in the House and Senate, there would be no interference with the only-in-America profits of drug companies, medical device makers, or hospitals by controlling what they could charge. Instead, in order to buy the support of the players in the industry, Obama opted to subsidize Americans who could not otherwise afford health insurance so that they could become paying customers in the same overpriced system. The same providers making exorbitant profits would keep making those profits, but their customer base would be enlarged by millions more patients able to pay for their products and services with government-subsidized insurance.

In choosing this route, Obama discarded Democratic orthodoxy going back to the New Deal era that, as with Medicare for seniors, called for the government to squeeze costs by becoming the single payer that would insure all Americans and use its buying power to negotiate lower prices. Although Democrats enjoyed majorities in the House and Senate when Obamacare was being drafted, the health care lobby, by far the most well funded in Washington, had leaned on enough Democrats on Capitol Hill to make these traditional liberal proposals non-starters. So, Obama deferred the fight over costs and profits in order at least to get expanded access. Like Romney and Nixon, whose proposal failed because Democrats thought it was too much of a gift to the industry, he chose a plan that the industry would support.

True, there would be a provision aimed at making the insurance pool big enough to keep costs lower than they would be if people only bought insurance when they got sick. Everyone would have to buy insurance (with subsidies where necessary), or pay a penalty. However, that big government mandate had first been suggested by the conservative Heritage Foundation think tank in 1989 under the banner of a classic *conservative* principle: "individual responsibility." Romneycare had included the same mandate.

Nonetheless, although their usual allies in the pharmaceutical and most other medical industry sectors either supported or did not oppose it, Republicans attacked Obamacare when it was proposed and just as relentlessly in the years after it was passed with only Democratic votes (except for one Republican House member) in the House and Senate. They called it a government takeover of health care, when, in fact, it was a classic Republican/business lobbyists' solution that was exactly the opposite: The government was fortifying the private market by subsidizing millions of new paying customers for the still-private health care system. (Which is why the stocks of most companies in every industry sector—insurance, drugs, device makers, for-profit hospitals—began a steady climb from the day the law was passed.)

Although some Senate Republicans had initially strung along the Democrats, purporting to be interested in negotiating a bill that would be acceptable to them before walking away from the table months later, the ultimate, strictly partisan result had been preordained on the night Obama was inaugurated. That evening, Republican pollster and strategist Frank Luntz, who had helped then–House speaker hopeful Newt Gingrich fashion the 1994 "Contract with America" platform to oppose Bill Clinton, invited prominent Republicans to a dinner in a private room at a restaurant a few blocks from the inaugural balls. Luntz's guests included ten Republicans each from the House and Senate, along with about a dozen Republican strategists, including Gingrich, and lobbyists. The topic: how to block the incoming president from day one.

"The goal was to talk about what we could do about Obama, and health care was probably number one on the list," Luntz recalled. Referring to the handful of Republican senators who were initially inclined to negotiate with the Democrats to address the growing problem of so many Americans not having access to care, Luntz said, "The sense was that we'd let them play along, but then come up with the arguments and polling that would get them to drop out." The overriding goal, Luntz explained, was that "we couldn't let Obama have a victory."

Luntz and others did, indeed, produce the arguments, in the form of the pungent turns of phrase that had become a Luntz specialty since he had coined "death tax" to demonize the inheritance tax. Obamacare's "government takeover of health care" would "put some bureaucrat between you and your doctor," Republicans said. These messages, along with completely fictional claims that the law would establish "death panels" to decide which elderly people were so hopelessly ill that they should be cut off from Medicare, were seized upon by the Tea Party groups that sprang up in the spring and summer of 2009 and made blocking Obamacare their battle cry. At no time did the Republicans offer an alternative to Obamacare, no doubt because Obamacare had always been *their* alternative—which foretold the embarrassment they would suffer seven years later when they seized control of Congress and the White House and still could not agree on an alternative.

How and why had this happened? Why was the highest priority for one political party, beginning on Inauguration Day, making sure the president from the other party did not have a victory, even if his victory was rooted in their policy? And why did the Democrats, still indignant about how Republicans stiff-armed Obama at every turn, make their party's highest priority in the Trump years seem, despite some occasional rhetoric to the contrary, the same goal of thwarting this president? (Yes, Trump was such an outlier that blocking him seems more defensible, but would the Democrats have wanted a Ted Cruz or even a Jeb Bush to have big victories and glorious White House signing ceremonies?)

Clearly, much had changed in Washington and among the electorate since the great policy initiatives of the 1950s and 1960s had passed with broad bipartisan support—Eisenhower's interstate highway system, Kennedy's nuclear test ban treaty, Johnson's civil rights laws and Medicare and Medicaid.

The bipartisan breakdown over Obamacare was anything but an outlier. Checks and balances had been weaponized.

In the midst of the financial crisis, the Republicans had refused to back Obama's 2009 stimulus plan to help the economy recover, even though it was loaded with tax cuts to lure them. The country's skyrocketing debt, which virtually everyone agreed was unsustainable, also produced no agreements on a solution. In 2010, a plan to address the deficit was hammered out by a bipartisan commission chaired by Bill Clinton's former chief of staff Erskine Bowles and former Wyoming Republican senator Alan Simpson. Although eleven of eighteen members of the commission supported the plan, it went up in smoke when the additional three members from either party necessary to ratify it and send it to Congress for an up-or-down vote failed to support it.

Obama refused to take a position on the compromise plan. Simpson told me soon thereafter that Obama had been "gutless" in refusing to "offend his base" by backing the deal. White House officials at the time explained that Obama feared that supporting the compromise would only reinforce Republican opposition to it. It is difficult to tell which explanation presents a more embarrassing picture of Washington dysfunction.

The failure of this and other efforts at compromise resulted in the Budget Control Act of 2011, which appointed yet another bipartisan committee, this time consisting of members of Congress, to negotiate yet another compromise. This time, a supposed fail-safe was included. If they failed to find common ground, a doomsday, set-in-stone percentage of funds would be automatically deducted from almost every agency's budget. Republicans would never allow these kinds of butcher-blade cuts to be made to their favorite expense categories, such as defense. Democrats would not want the same to happen to their favorite domestic programs. The fail-safe failed. No agreement was reached, and the government was then hobbled by formulaic cuts being made across the board without regard to which programs were more important or more cost-effective.

Then, of course, there is the modern proliferation of Senate filibusters, the rule that allows minorities in the Senate to block a vote unless sixty members agree to proceed. Obstructionist Southern senators used it to block civil rights legislation in the 1960s, and pro-business interests used it to block labor law reform in 1978. Other than that, however, it was rarely deployed.

As with the Bill of Rights and the constitutional requirement that only super-majorities could amend the Constitution, the rationale behind the filibuster (which is a Senate rule, not a constitutional requirement) was consistent with the role the founders envisioned for the Senate as being a moderating force on democracy and on the impulses of the majority. It was meant to force the politicians to forge a broader national consensus. As with the Constitution's other checks and balances, however, this kind of restraint on impulsive action would turn into a straitjacket if those on either side were motivated to avoid consensus and block everything.

Filibusters exploded during the George W. Bush years, when Democrats used them to block judicial nominations and other actions, starting with an appellate court appointee in 2003. From then on, through the Obama years, when Republicans seized the weapon, filibusters became routine. By 2013, Democrats in the Senate were so frustrated by Republicans using filibusters to block so many Obama administration nominations for executive appointees, ambassadors, and judges that then–Senate Majority Leader Harry Reid invoked the so-called nuclear option. Needing only a majority vote (available just from the Democrats), he changed the Senate rules to allow non–Supreme Court nominations to be exempt from the filibuster. In 2017, the Republicans, having gained control of the Senate in 2014, returned the favor and upped the ante by changing the rules to allow Trump Supreme Court nominee Neil Gorsuch to be confirmed with just a majority vote.

This has not eliminated the Senate gridlock problem because legislation, unlike presidential appointments, can still be filibustered, unless the Republicans change that rule, too. Although the lack of bipartisan support can still block important bills because the filibuster is still in place for legislation, even if it were eliminated, legislation aimed at addressing important issues would still lack the bipartisan support it used to enjoy. Therefore, any significant laws that manage to pass with only the votes of one party would be perpetually hobbled by replays of the original fight to pass it and the prospect of repeal when the other party took over. That, of course, is what happened to Obamacare, which became law with only one Republican vote. Because it continued to be so bitterly attacked by Republicans, even the traditionally routine process of cleaning up the most uncontroversial hiccups discovered in a statute after it is passed—such as simple typographical errors—could never be done. Nor would the Republicans consider substantive but incremental steps to improve the law, as both parties had repeatedly done in prior decades to fix major legislation. In fact, long after Obamacare became the law of the land, Republican House Speaker John Boehner often continued referring to it as a "bill," as if it was still being debated.

The House does not have filibusters, but it has become increasingly partisan, and often even bitterly divided by factions within the Republican Party, especially since the Republicans created what came to be called the Hastert Rule when they took over the House in 1995. The rule stipulated that a majority of Republicans had to support a bill before the Republican speaker would allow it to go to the floor for a vote. The rule was named for Dennis Hastert, a Republican from Illinois who became speaker in 1999, but it was actually initiated by Newt Gingrich, the fiery partisan who had preceded Hastert in 1995.

In practice, the Hastert Rule meant that if, for example, the Senate had passed a bill that 45 percent of House Republicans and 80 percent of House Democrats were prepared to vote for, it would still never be considered despite commanding an obvious majority of House votes—a fate that befell a widely supported comprehensive border security and immigration reform law passed with bipartisan support in the Senate in 2013.

"With the Hastert Rule, you become speaker of your party, not the country," said Ray LaHood, a former Republican congressman from Illinois who served as President Obama's first transportation secretary and was a top aide to Bob Michel, the Republican House minority leader during the Reagan presidency and the first two Clinton years. LaHood was being polite. What he was really saying—what the reality is—is that Republicans decided to break American democracy by resisting any notion of reaching common ground for the common good. They have insisted on winning, even if pandering to donors and potential primary voters by holding out for an unachievable win means that their country loses.

The best evidence is how Congress has dealt with its bedrock responsibility: writing and passing an annual budget for the federal government to operate. Since 1994, Congress has failed to pass a single comprehensive budget. Instead, an unending series of deadlines have been met with last-minute agreements to extend whatever the prior year's spending was for an agency, or with temporary piecemeal appropriations. Hovered over by squadrons of lobbyists, the agreements are typically lumped together at midnight into hundreds of incomprehensible pages for the people's representatives in Washington to approve the next morning. No middle schooler would get away with producing a book report this way, a sentiment widely shared across the country, where Congress routinely receives approval ratings in low double digits and sometimes even single digits.

A law passed in November 2015 to fund the Department of

Transportation's budget for highway maintenance and construction illustrates the dysfunction. Highways were originally financed by a federal gasoline tax, the revenue from which went into a trust account to assure a steady flow of funds. In 1993, however, Congress stopped a decades-long progression of increases in the gas tax, always supported by Democrats and Republicans alike, meant to keep up with consistent increases in traffic, or at least keep up with inflation. Since then, a variety of stopgap gimmicks have been found just as the trust fund was about to run out of money, meaning highway maintenance and construction projects would have abruptly stopped. In 2014, for example, Congress rejiggered the accounting method that large corporations with pension funds could use. That temporarily lowered what they had to contribute to pension funds, but as a result increased their profits, at least on paper. That in turn increased their expected corporate income tax payments. What does that have to do with highways? Those expected new tax revenues were slid over at the last minute into the highway trust fund account.

In 2015, a new gimmick had to be found, again with only days to spare before the highway money ran out. First, some petty cash was discovered to extend the drop-dead date two months. Then, in December, a $300 billion appropriation was cobbled together that in theory would keep the highway trust fund alive for five years. That in turn depended on a series of short-term, speculative maneuvers— the sale of oil from a strategic petroleum reserve, hiring private collection agencies to go after tax evaders, getting the Federal Reserve Bank to kick in $19 billion from a rainy-day fund. Together, they were unlikely to add up to $300 billion and did not provide long-term security to the trust fund, but it was a way to appear to be resolving the crisis. Moreover, as I will detail later, the $300 billion over five years is a fraction of what the United States needs to maintain and rebuild a decaying infrastructure that was once the world's best, but that ranked sixteenth internationally by 2016.

"We have people in office now who don't believe in compromise and, I have to admit, on the Republican side don't even believe in government," said LaHood. "When I got to Washington, everyone at least believed in transportation infrastructure. It was routine. Reagan raised the gas tax, but Clinton couldn't do it after the Republicans took the House in 1994 and Newt [Gingrich] became speaker. And Obama refused to even try."

REFORMS THAT BOOMERANG

Many, including LaHood as well as former Republican leader Bob Michel, believed that government dysfunction started with the ascendance of Gingrich, a take-no-prisoners partisan who became speaker in 1995 and was a thorn in Michel's side for several years before that. Actually, it started earlier, and it involves First Amendment professor Martin Redish and the lawyers, fund-raisers, and others who followed him and enabled money to dominate politics. It also involves those who, through their corruption and abuses of power in the 1960s and 1970s, created an environment that cried out for reform, as well as those who demanded reform but ended up undermining democracy in their drive to fix it.

America was founded as a representative democracy, meaning that intermediaries at various levels—federal, state, local—charged with determining the common good would be a check on the direct and often impulsive will of the people. Over the last fifty years the roll of those intermediaries has been steadily eroded, in large part because they abused their power. In the wake of the 1968 presidential elections the large anti-war wing of the Democratic Party was enraged that Hubert Humphrey had won their nomination at the chaotic Democratic convention in Chicago without running in a single primary. In 1970, a party commission chaired by South Dakota Democratic senator George McGovern (who would become his party's 1972 presidential nominee) pushed through rules that virtually eliminated the role of state and local party bosses in picking the presidential standard bearer.

The reformers had hoped to have party caucuses in each of the states become the dominant forum for choosing a nominee. The old guard, fearing that liberal activists would dominate the caucuses, won a compromise that resulted in a mix of caucuses and statewide primaries, beginning in 1972. The Nixon Republicans, who had little fear that the president would be challenged for renomination, chose to adopt the same reforms.

From then on and to ever-increasing degrees, candidates running in caucuses or primaries have usually tried to appeal to their party's most liberal (in the case of Democrats) or conservative (in the case of Republicans) voters, because these voters were the motivated base most likely to turn out to vote in a primary or caucus. Unless a candidate had the luxury of being able to think ahead to the general election, he or she had little incentive to appeal to the moderates, who have continued through decades of increasing polarization among officeholders to constitute the largest core of American voters, and who party "bosses," worried about broadening their power base, would have been more likely to be sensitive to when deciding on nominees. As the same reforms spread down to state and local primaries for members of the Senate or Congress, or for local executive or legislative offices, these candidates also had to run in primaries and steer their positions and loyalties further right or left.

Meantime, because part of the Watergate scandal involved the president's campaign taking suitcases full of cash from secret donors (who were in some cases trying to influence Nixon administration decisions, such as whether to prosecute anti-trust cases), campaign finance laws were tightened. As explained earlier, the Supreme Court struck down limits on how much a candidate for president or the House or Senate could contribute to his own campaign, how much the campaign could spend overall, or how much ostensibly independent groups could spend to help a candidate. However, the Court did allow limits on direct campaign contributions to candidates by individuals to continue and allowed limits on how much individuals or groups could contribute to political parties to finance campaigns.

The combination of these reforms in the nominating process and in what the courts allowed and rejected in considering campaign finance limits meant that candidates were no longer able to rely on party bosses to choose them, or hope that the party or direct mega-donations from individuals would finance them. However, they could spend unlimited amounts, as could their opponents. So they had to become free-agent fund-raisers, raising their profiles in the hope of attracting limited amounts from as many people as they could solicit, while also hoping to attract unlimited funds from independent groups that usually had a strongly conservative or strongly liberal (for the Democrats) agenda.

As a result, when the winners got to Congress, they were not beholden to the party or its leaders. Instead they had to keep their donors happy and pay attention to the less mainstream issues that their donors cared about or pursue the narrow issues that had impelled them to buck party bosses and run in the first place.

For example, Tom DeLay had come to Congress in 1985 obsessed by what he believed were the Gestapo-like tactics of the Richard Nixon–created Environmental Protection Agency and by the harm inflicted by Rachel Carson, the darling of the environmental movement. DeLay had run a small exterminating business in Texas and was outraged when the EPA banned Mirex, a pesticide that was later found to be not as uniformly menacing as the EPA had initially ruled. He came to Washington determined to eliminate regulations, like the Mirex ban, that he believed were crushing small businesses. DeLay soon became an ultraconservative fund-raising machine, raking in millions for himself and other like-minded Republicans from business PACs organized by K Street lobbyists. All the while, DeLay fumed at Republican leader Bob Michel's centrist approach until he helped Gingrich force him out. (DeLay described Michel in his autobiography, aptly titled *No Retreat, No Surrender,* as the "epitome of what was wrong with the Republicans.")

Post-Watergate changes meant to reform how House committees were organized also backfired. For decades, committee chairmen (always men) had iron grips on legislation related to their panel's jurisdiction. They alone could decide whether to hold hearings or a vote. They could unilaterally dispense favors, which made the men running the appropriations committees and subcommittees virtual kings. They were put in their chairs by virtue of their seniority, meaning those who stayed in the institution the longest got the power. The post-Watergate liberal Democrats who swept into power in the 1970s were determined to change that; and, given the 1960s legacy of autocratic Southern committee bosses blocking civil rights legislation, they had vivid recent history to motivate them. They also were more driven by the Vietnam War and the civil rights struggles than by issues like union rights and controlling big business abuses, which had cemented the New Deal Democratic coalition. This meant that their assumption of power and the priorities they pursued—which by the 1970s included affirmative action and drives to integrate public schools by busing students to distant schools—were likely to alienate crucial working-class elements of the coalition.

As highlighted in an article in *The Atlantic* in 2016, an important casualty of their agenda was Wright Patman of Texas, a populist when it came to banking and anti-trust laws who had been against civil rights legislation and for the Vietnam War. Patman was deposed as chairman of the House Banking Committee when the reformers overturned the seniority system by requiring committee chairs to be elected by the full Democratic caucus. Ardent old-school Democrats like Patman could have been important voices opposing what would become the banking industry's growing power and abuses.

Combining these shifts away from autocratic power with a world in which money was becoming the increasingly dominant force in Washington produced a pivotal unintended consequence. From the 1980s on, with seniority no longer relevant, congressmen like DeLay—who could raise the most money and dispense it to other members in return for their loyalty—would get the leadership positions and the committee and subcommittee chairs. When they did, they were free agents not likely to worry about the broader needs of the national party or the country. They were more accountable to those who gave them money than to the party establishment. For the same reasons, members who didn't get chairmanships or other leadership positions would also be relative free agents, because the chairs and leaders depended on their votes to stay in their chairs, while they depended on outside interests to finance *their* campaigns.

Committee chairs and the speaker and his top deputies could still punish or reward members with various favors, but beginning in 2006, a series of other reforms weakened and then removed completely the most important tool in that arsenal: earmarks, which were special appropriations added at the behest of individual congressmen to fund pet projects in their districts. By 2011, following headlines about the minority of such projects that were clearly the products of corruption or other abuses (such as the infamous Alaska "Bridge to Nowhere"), earmarks had effectively been banned altogether. No longer could they be dispensed to win a pivotal vote on a larger, more important bill. As all of this played out, groups and coalitions, such as the conservative Freedom Caucus, that were almost completely independent of the leadership coalesced, based on relatively extreme ideology or their commitments to narrow special interests.

In 2013, conservative members of the House, at the urging of the Senate's most promiscuous free agent, Texas Republican Ted Cruz, shut down the government. Ignoring their own party leaders, they refused to agree on a deal to extend the budget even temporar-

The equalizer: Yale College Admissions Dean R. Inslee "Inky" Clark, in 1965. He discarded the "old boy" network in favor of admitting applicants (including the author) on their merits and regardless of their ability to pay. The meritocracy revolution was a breakthrough for equality but had unintended consequences.

Yale Law professor Daniel Markovits, addressing the school's 2015 graduating class. The meritocracy Clark launched forty-eight years earlier, he told them, had morphed into a new, "more entrenched" aristocracy that they were about to join.

Economic diversity czar: As president of Amherst College from 2003 to 2011, Tony Marx led a successful campaign to make his school much more of an engine of economic mobility than Yale and other elite colleges.

Students at New York's Baruch College riding the escalator, literally and figuratively, to more income equality.

As a wunderkind economics professor in the 1970s, Michael Jensen (now an emeritus professor at Harvard Business School) created the intellectual underpinning for corporate America to binge on the new meritocrats' legal and financial "innovations"—which boosted short-term profits but exacerbated income inequality and undermined the country's economic vitality.

$2.00

THE AMERICAN LAWYER

FEBRUARY 1979
VOL. 1, NO. 1

Flom Firm Takes Over As Top Money Maker In '78

By Steven Brill

With lead partner Joseph H. Flom involved in 21 of the 22 major corporate takeover fights in 1978, New York's Skadden, Arps, Slate, Meagher & Flom far outpaced all other law firms in the country in earnings per partner for the year.

Average partner earnings at Skadden, Arps for 1978 exceeded $350,000. This is more than double the estimated $170,000 that knowledgeable sources say will be reported later this year in the new Price Waterhouse survey as the median income for partners at the largest New York firms. "The Skadden, Arps numbers are way out of line, even compared with the most successful Wall Street firms," a Price Waterhouse official explained. As one Skadden, Arps partner noted: "We dropped out of the Price Waterhouse survey in 1977 because it was irrelevant to us."

The firm's stunning 1978 performance becomes clear when earnings are broken down by partnership seniority:
• Nine third-tier partners at the firm, whose ages range from 38 to 42, made in excess of $450,000 each.

continued on page 12

Shunned by blue chip law firms because he did not fit the mold, corporate takeover pioneer Joseph Flom got the ultimate revenge. He invented guerrilla legal strategies that terrified their boardroom clients, accelerated the quest for short-term profits, and put him atop one of the world's most successful firms.

Martin Lipton, Flom's nemesis in the takeover wars. For four decades, he has warned against short-termism while building a law firm even more lucrative than Flom's.

This cartoon from *The New Yorker* hangs outside the office of the Aspen Institute's Judith Samuelson, who has galvanized a group of business heavyweights to fight short-termism and the gospel that shareholder profits should be a corporation's only goal.

"Yes, the planet got destroyed, but for a beautiful moment in time we created a lot of value for shareholders."

Super-banker Lewis Ranieri. His championing of "securitization" in the late 1970s allowed mortgage availability to expand exponentially, but separated mortgage lenders from the risks they were taking and ultimately led to the 2008 crash.

Like thousands of other meritocrats in the new "knowledge economy," Dennis Kelleher of Better Markets is a lobbyist. But despite his Wall Street pedigree, he lobbies to hold the bankers and financial engineers accountable.

Ralph Nader attacking corporate America in 1966 congressional testimony. Ten years later, he won a consumers' rights suit freeing pharmacists to advertise discounts on drug prices. He now concedes that this suit "boomeranged" into the legal doctrine that spawned the *Citizens United* decision allowing unlimited corporate political money.

Law professor and corporate free speech advocate Martin Redish. His 1969 attempt to stand out at Harvard Law School by writing a "courageous" student thesis became a blueprint for Nader's lawyers, but was then used for legal challenges to restrictions on commercial advertising and corporate campaign contributions.

Robert Post, the legal scholar who is fighting Redish and others who argue that the First Amendment prohibits regulation of commercial speech and political money. He's frustrated because he can't condense his argument into "good sound bites" the way his opponents can.

Nick Penniman, the founder of Issue One, has gained steady traction lately, making the case that campaign finance reform really is issue number one. Soon, a new scandal involving money and politics will "become the final gulp of alcohol that the liver rejects," he hopes.

CONFIDENTIAL MEMORANDUM

ATTACK ON AMERICAN FREE ENTERPRISE SYSTEM

TO: Mr. Eugene B. Sydnor, Jr.   DATE: August 23, 1971
         Chairman
         Education Committee
         U.S. Chamber of Commerce

FROM: Lewis F. Powell, Jr.

This memorandum is submitted at your request as a
basis for the discussion on August 24 with Mr. Booth and others
at the U.S. Chamber of Commerce. The purpose is to identify the
problem, and suggest possible avenues of action for further
consideration.

Dimensions of the Attack

No thoughtful person can question that the American
economic system is under broad attack.* This varies in scope,
intensity, in the techniques employed, and in the level of
visibility.

There always have been some who opposed the American
system, and preferred socialism or some form of statism

*Variously called: the "free enterprise system", "capitalism",
and the "profit system". The American political system of
democracy under the rule of law is also under attack, often by
the same individuals and organizations who seek to undermine
the enterprise system.

The Powell manifesto: As a private lawyer and pillar of the legal
establishment, future Supreme Court Associate Justice Lewis Powell wrote
a 1971 memo urging big business to fight back against Nader and other
reformers that became the call to arms that helped tip the balance of power
by money and lobbyists pouring into Washington.

Congresswoman Kyrsten Sinema, Democrat of Arizona, is reputed to juggle three phones at a time when dialing for campaign dollars. Her colleagues, though less efficient, spend an average of five hours a day begging for money.

Political money detective: Sheila Krumholz's OpenSecrets.org tracks the funds that lobbyists and their clients pour into politics, documenting connections between money and policy so ubiquitous that her website has become a guide to the corruption of American democracy.

Compromiser: Bob Michel, the Republican House Minority leader in the 1980s, was disdained by Newt Gingrich for working with the Democrats. "I think [Gingrich] thought I was a bit of a jerk . . . He only wanted to fight, go after people," Michel recalled.

Polarizer: Freshman Congressman Gingrich, in 1979. The future Speaker took advantage of the newly invented C-Span to launch the modern era of attack politics.

The Bipartisan Policy Center's 10th Anniversary Dinner in 2017 brought together politicians from both parties who like and respect one another— and who have become a kind of shadow Congress, hammering out sensible policy compromises that the real Congress continues to avoid. *Seated, from left:* former Senator Bob Dole, former Vice President Joe Biden, and former Senators George Mitchell and Tom Daschle. *Standing:* BPC president Jason Grumet.

Former basketball great and New Jersey Senator Bill Bradley. American politicians don't play for team America the way his teammates played for the Knicks, he says. "They're representing interests, not the people as a whole."

Private equity billionaire Peter Peterson. As a forty-four-year-old Nixon aide in 1971, he warned that growing global trade and automation required massive investments in job training. However, he recalled, "Nixon and everyone else just paid lip service to it."

Technology as a divider: The launch of Matt Drudge's website in 1995, along with the start of Fox News, then the coming of other outlets on the left, and then the spread of social media as a prime news source polarized a country already heading in that direction.

In 2000, Bill Clinton said opening trade to China was "a hundred-to-nothing deal for America when it comes to the economic consequences." He was right about the lopsided deal, but got the winner and loser mixed up.

Sally Field in the 1979 movie *Norma Rae*, which chronicled the war on unions that raged throughout the South, in which management's defiance of New Deal labor laws ultimately carried the day.

Job training done right: Jukay Hsu's small Queens, New York–based job training non-profit turns waitresses and bar bouncers into software coders. They join the program earning an average of $18,000 and leave with jobs averaging $85,000. If only the government's billion-dollar-a-year training programs were that good.

Protected: Sharon Helman, who ran a veterans hospital in Phoenix, where, in 2014, records were found to have been doctored to cover up long waiting lists. A tortured reading of civil service law protected her from responsibility.

JPMorgan Chase CEO Jamie Dimon complained about how complicated and profit-threatening the Dodd-Frank Act was. But his lobbyists worked overtime to complicate the law's rules, and seven years after the law was passed, his bank was bigger and more profitable than ever.

Max Stier of the Partnership for Public Service: "Policy making is the sugar high in Washington, but implementation and government effectiveness have no constituency, except for me, I guess," says the dogged champion of civil service and other management reforms.

The corporate moat: As attorney general in the Obama administration, Eric Holder conceded that because America's top executives presided over such large organizations, it might be impossible to prove them personally responsible for criminal wrongdoing.

Johnson & Johnson's Alex Gorsky. A division he ran pled guilty to illegally marketing a powerful drug, but no one was held personally responsible, and he was promoted to CEO.

The arbitration moat: Beginning in the 1990s, a consortium of corporate lawyers plotted a legal strategy that forced consumers, such as those cheated by banking giant Wells Fargo, into arbitration and barred them from bringing class actions or otherwise seeking justice in America's courts.

TEXT OF THE FEDERAL INCOME TAX LAW OF 1913.

Being Section II of an Act to Reduce Tariff Duties and to Provide Revenue for the Government, and for Other Purposes, Approved, October 3, 1913.

Section A. Subdivision 1.

1   That there shall be levied, assessed, collected and paid
2 annually upon the entire net income arising or accruing
3 from all sources in the preceding calendar year to every citi-
4 zen of the United States, whether residing at home or abroad
5 and to every person residing in the United States, though not
6 a citizen thereof, a tax of 1 per centum per annum upon such
7 income, except as hereinafter provided; and a like tax shall
8 be assessed, levied, collected and paid annually upon the entire
9 net income from all property owned and of every business,
10 trade or profession carried on in the United States by persons
11 residing elsewhere.

Subdivision 2.

1   In addition to the income tax provided under this sec-
2 tion (herein referred to as the normal income tax) there
3 shall be levied, assessed and collected upon the net income
4 of every individual an additional income tax (herein re-
5 ferred to as the additional tax) of 1 per centum per annum
6 upon the amount by which the total net income exceeds $20,-
7 000 and does not exceed $50,000, and 2 per centum per an-
8 num upon the amount by which the total net income exceeds
9 $50,000 and does not exceed $75,000, 3 per centum per an-
10 num upon the amount by which the total net income exceeds
11 $75,000 and does not exceed $100,000, 4 per centum per
12 annum upon the amount by which the total net income ex-
13 ceeds $100,000 and does not exceed $250,000, 5 per centum

The tax moat: As first written in 1913, the income tax code was twenty-seven pages long. It now runs twenty-five hundred pages and has become a catalog of special interest loopholes, with still more added in the Republicans' 2018 tax "reform" bill.

THE YALE LAW JOURNAL

| VOLUME 73 | APRIL 1964 | NUMBER 5 |

THE NEW PROPERTY

CHARLES A. REICH*

THE institution called property guards the troubled boundary between individual man and the state. It is not the only guardian; many other institutions, laws, and practices serve as well. But in a society that chiefly values material well-being, the power to control a particular portion of that well-being is the very foundation of individuality.

One of the most important developments in the United States during the past decade has been the emergence of government as a major source of wealth. Government is a gigantic syphon. It draws in revenue and power, and pours forth wealth: money, benefits, services, contracts, franchises, and licenses. Government has always had this function. But while in early times it was minor, today's distribution of largess is on a vast, imperial scale.

The valuables dispensed by government take many forms, but they all share one characteristic. They are steadily taking the place of traditional forms of wealth — forms which are held as private property. Social insurance substitutes for savings; a government contract replaces a businessman's customers and goodwill. The wealth of more and more Americans depends upon a relationship to government. Increasingly, Americans live on government largess — allocated by government on its own terms, and held by recipients subject to conditions which express "the public interest."

The growth of government largess, accompanied by a distinctive system of law, is having profound consequences. It affects the underpinnings of individualism and independence. It influences the workings of the Bill of Rights. It has an impact on the power of private interests, in their relation to each other and to government. It is helping to create a new society.

This article is an attempt to explore these changes. It begins with an examination of the nature of government largess. Second, it reviews the system of law, substantive and procedural, that has emerged. Third, it examines some of the consequences, to the individual, to private interests, and to society. Fourth, it considers the functions of property and their relationship to "the public interest." Finally, it turns to the future of individualism in the new society that is coming. The object is to present an overview — a way of looking at many seemingly unrelated problems. Inevitably, such an effort must be incomplete and tentative. But it is long past time that we began looking at the transformation taking place around us.

*Associate Professor of Law, Yale University.

Charles Reich's seminal 1964 article launched a much-needed upgrade in the due process rights of everyday citizens. Then it morphed into a weapon deployed by swarms of lawyers and lobbyists. One result: a 604-page OSHA rule governing the use of the chemical silica in the workplace that took nineteen years of "due process" to write.

Top left: A voice for accountability: Federal judge Jed Rakoff refers to the big banks as recidivists because of the multiple corporate criminal plea agreements they have negotiated, and is sharply critical of how the system works to protect their CEOs from personal responsibility.

Top right: A staid corporate lawyer who became disgusted with legalese and bureaucracy, Philip Howard wrote *The Death of Common Sense* and became a champion of stripping away abuses of due process that blocked infrastructure projects and made regulations hopelessly complicated.

Right: Champion and innovator for the most unprotected: Former Robert F. Kennedy aide Peter Edelman's plan to revamp America's employment infrastructure could bring the poor and middle class together and help both groups while revitalizing the entire economy.

Collapse of the I-35W Mississippi River Bridge in Minneapolis in 2007. Emblematic of America's neglected infrastructure and, more generally, the country's paralyzed government, the bridge had been reported to have been rotting away since it was inspected in 1991. It had been built in the 1960s' heyday of America's infrastructure investment.

ily unless President Obama eliminated all funding for Obamacare. It was an obviously ridiculous demand, but they held out for nearly two weeks before popular disgust forced party leaders to break the Hastert Rule and join with Democrats to override them.

In a brilliant 2016 essay, also in *The Atlantic*, Jonathan Rauch called the effect of these reforms "chaos syndrome":

> Chaos syndrome is a chronic decline in the political system's capacity for self-organization. It begins with the weakening of the institutions and brokers—political parties, career politicians, and congressional leaders and committees—that have historically held politicians accountable to one another and prevented everyone in the system from pursuing naked self-interest all the time. As these intermediaries' influence fades, politicians, activists, and voters all become more individualistic and unaccountable. The system atomizes. Chaos becomes the new normal—both in campaigns and in the government itself.

GERRYMANDERING

An effort to bring more minorities to Congress was another reform that boomeranged.

The Voting Rights Act of 1965 outlawed election rules that had the effect of discriminating against African Americans. The most blatant examples were poll taxes and literacy tests, which had long suppressed the minority vote in the South. Another, more subtle tactic involved the shaping of congressional and state legislative districts in ways that diluted the votes of those African Americans who did manage to cast ballots. For example, Mississippi had blocked blacks from having much power in elections for county representative by replacing single member districts with county-wide elections. In those elections, all the voters in the county voted for all the candidates, and the group of candidates getting the most votes won. With that kind of arrangement, the votes of blacks in discrete districts with large concentrations of black voters who would have elected one of their own were overpowered by the majority white county-wide electorate.

Banning these county-wide elections, therefore, made sense. So did the Justice Department's early successes in getting the federal courts to outlaw the gerrymandering, or rejiggering, of the boundaries of congressional or state legislative districts in ways that divided up concentrations of African Americans so that they had no hope of electing their favored candidates.

In 1982, at the behest of civil rights groups and with the approval of the Reagan administration, Congress went further. The Voting Rights Act was amended so that *intent* to discriminate in drawing congressional or state legislative district lines was no longer required to overturn them. Rather, if the *result* was that minorities were denied proportional representation, that would be, the law said, "one circumstance that may be considered" in deciding whether the districts should be invalidated. By 1986, civil rights lawyers arguing in the Supreme Court had turned that "one circumstance that may be considered" into a near-guarantee of proportional representation. The Court ruled that if the evidence in a case demonstrated that whites voted as a bloc, which was largely then the case in the South, and if minorities also voted as a "cohesive" group, which was also largely the case, then the Voting Rights Act required that districts be drawn so that minority groups would be concentrated in enough districts to achieve their share of representation.

Four years later, that decision encouraging but not requiring proportional representation had been seized on by Republicans as a way to complete the shift of the white majority in the South to their party. It was the culmination of a process that had begun in the 1960s, when large numbers of white Southerners, disgusted by Lyndon Johnson's civil rights laws, shook off the Democrats' long-standing hold on them and turned to the party of Abraham Lincoln, by then represented by Richard Nixon. Since then, the only dynamic that had been standing in the way of Republicans achieving complete domination in the South had been African American voters, whose ballots in many districts could still swing the election to moderate white Democrats. Now, recalled Ben Ginsberg, the Republican Party's lead lawyer at the time, the Supreme Court decision "pushed us to agree to what you could call a devil's bargain" with civil rights leaders.

At an April 1990 meeting of the Southern Republican Leadership Conference, party officials announced that they would work with civil rights groups to create one or more all-black congressional districts in each state, which would leave all of the other districts almost completely white and all but certain to vote Republican. As a result, the South became almost completely polarized, divided between a few liberal minority congressional districts and the balance of conservative white districts, with the same split soon taking shape among the state legislatures. Except for these few black liberal Democrats, the South was almost completely conservative Republican.

Nationally, the end of white Democrats holding office in the South, who had needed to be relative moderates to win over whites and blacks in previously mixed districts, and their replacement by Republicans, who needed to toe a conservative line, was the decisive factor in polarizing the two parties. With these white Southern Democrats gerrymandered out of office, a large contingent of the moderate wing of the Democratic Party was gone. At the same time, the balance of power in the Republican Party shifted to the new conservative Southern bloc—people like Gingrich and DeLay—whose major concern at election time was the possibility that a primary opponent might try to challenge them from the right.

The newly drawn African American 12th District in North Carolina meandered diagonally up from the black neighborhoods of Charlotte, in the southern end of the state, through to the minority areas of Greensboro in the north, with boundaries sometimes literally no wider than the lanes of a highway. The results of redrawing the map this way were extraordinary. In 1988, eight of North Carolina's eleven congressional seats had been held by Democrats, all of them white. By 2017, only three Democrats occupied what by then were thirteen seats. Two were held by African Americans, while the third was held by a moderate representing the liberal-leaning enclave around the Raleigh-Durham university community. Civil rights advocates had won; they got two new seats. Republicans had won; they got nine seats compared to the three they had held. The Democratic Party lost: Democratic candidates got 44 percent of the overall vote, but ended up with 23 percent of the seats.

In Georgia, when Newt Gingrich won his seat in 1978, he was the only Republican in the ten-member delegation. The other nine were white Democrats. By 2017, nine of Georgia's now thirteen seats were occupied by Republicans. The other four were held by African American Democrats.

For the candidates involved it was a terrific arrangement. All were safe in the general election, running in a district certain to elect the candidate from their party. In North Carolina, no candidate won by less than 13 percent in 2016, and most won by more than 20 percent. The only threat was a primary challenge that might come if an incumbent was thought to be too moderate.

When the Republicans' 1990 deal with the civil rights groups was announced, Ginsberg, the lead Republican lawyer, told *The Washington Post* that his party would be using "truly space-age" computer software to redraw the congressional districts. That was 1990. In 2010, Ginsberg's notion of space-age software advanced to a new space age, and a new group of savvy Republicans—funded by a variety of super PACs—hatched plans to take gerrymandering to a new state of the art.

Gerrymandering dates to 1812, when a Boston newspaper coined the term to describe how Governor Elbridge Gerry was maneuvering the boundaries of state senate election districts to his advantage. It was used routinely; Barack Obama's original state senate district had been gerrymandered. But it was never done as broadly and rarely as blatantly as the 1990s process that produced the contorted all-white or all-black districts in the South. Yet even that paled against what happened beginning in 2010, which ended up giving Republicans impregnable majorities in state legislatures and then congressional delegations in battlefield Midwestern states, despite barely outscoring and sometimes even falling behind the asleep-at-the-wheel Democrats in raw votes.

As documented by David Daley in his book, *Ratf***ked*, Republican operatives, backed by *Citizens United*–enabled super PACs, began putting money into state legislative races in target states so that they could obtain majorities who would be deciding how congressional districts would be redrawn following the 2010 census. That done, they deployed armies of lobbyists, backed by a software program called Maptitude, to redraw the districts with stunning precision, down to particular streets and even households. The website of the company selling Maptitude promised "a complete set of mapping and spatial analysis functions, sophisticated geocoding, [and] tools for complex data manipulation." The data included not just how residents might have voted in the past, but variables like income, family status, and even consumption habits.

In the first congressional election, in 2012, reflecting the gerrymandering crew's work, an estimated 1.4 million more Americans cast their votes for Democratic congressional candidates than for their Republican opponents, yet the Republicans won a thirty-three-seat majority in the House. In Pennsylvania, for example, Democrats won 83,000 more congressional votes, but the state sent thirteen Republicans to the House and five Democrats.

The pattern has continued since, so much so that in 2017 a massive data analysis by the Associated Press revealed that four times as many of the 4,700 districts of state representatives up for reelection across the country were skewed in favor of Republicans than in favor of Democrats. The same AP report calculated that the Republicans had won an extra twenty-two seats in the U.S. Congress in 2016 because of gerrymandering, which meant that the GOP's twenty-four-seat majority when President Trump assumed office would otherwise have been a razor-thin two seats, and easy prey for the Democrats in 2018.

Gerrymandering has produced such disastrous results for the Democrats that when President Obama left office in 2017 he helped to organize a group to fight in state legislatures and the courts to rebalance the districts. Mapping districts fairly is not challenging—if that is the goal. In recent years, five states have established bipartisan or independent commissions to draw congressional district lines instead of allowing the dominant party in the legislature to choose their own voters. In those states, the proportional representation of Democrats and Republicans in the House of Representatives more closely reflects the states' Democrat-Republican statewide votes. In Washington State, for example, Republicans won four of ten House seats in 2016 and received 44.7 percent of the statewide votes for Congress that year. In a clear sign of public disgust for the blatantly unlevel playing field that gerrymandering enables, all but one of the state commissions formed to draw district lines were established by citizen ballot initiatives or referenda.

Nationally, efforts to fight gerrymandering in the courts have been frustrated by a divided Supreme Court. Conservative justices have ruled that while drawing district lines in a way that helps or disadvantages a *racial* group may be unconstitutional, gerrymandering to help one *political* party or the other is a political issue for legislators to decide and for courts to stay out of. Liberals on the Court have supported the challenges that argue that such extreme gerrymandering violates the constitutional guarantee of equal voting power and the First Amendment right of free association by discriminating against the members of a political party who are on the losing end of a gerrymandering scheme. The justice in the middle, Anthony Kennedy, has acknowledged that gerrymandering produces unfair results, but he has then thrown up his hands at the prospect of fashioning some kind of legal ruling that would rein it in, thereby in effect siding with the conservatives.

However, the High Court's hands-off stance was challenged anew in 2017 when the justices agreed to hear an appeal that fall from a lower federal court's decision to invalidate a 2011 Republican gerrymander of state assembly districts in Wisconsin that had produced perhaps the most lopsided results ever. Republicans had won sixty of ninety-nine assembly seats in 2012 even though the Democrats had won 51 percent of the statewide votes for assembly. Pre-trial discovery in the litigation challenging the system had produced voluminous documents and testimony demonstrating just how dark the science had become. After reviewing evidence revealing how the Republicans had used elaborate demographic and psychographic data to model the outcomes of different configurations of district lines and had then chosen the one that maximized the impact of likely Republican voters while diluting the impact of Democratic votes, two of the judges (one a Reagan appointee, the other a Carter appointee) on a three-judge federal appeals court panel ruled that district lines that the Republicans' software concocted violated the Democratic voters' constitutional rights by effectively disenfranchising many of them. "To say that the Constitution does not require proportional representation," the judges ruled, "is not to say that highly *dis*proportional representation may not be evidence of a discriminatory effect."

When the appeal of that decision was argued before the Supreme Court in October 2017, Justice Kennedy sharply questioned lawyers defending the Wisconsin redistricting plan, but as of March 2018 no ruling had been issued.

The consequence of recent gerrymandering is not only that one party has an unfair advantage. It also means that with districts overloaded with voters from one party or the other, officeholders in both parties have little incentive to appeal across party lines and move to the middle. It is as if compromise itself has been legislated out of American democracy.

NEWT

Beyond the broader dynamics—money overrunning Washington, gerrymandering's erosion of the influence of moderates, reforms neutering the power of political parties and of other intermediaries between the people and elected officials—the personal chemistry of politics also changed for the worse and contributed mightily to America's decline.

The quintessential twentieth-century novel of Washington political intrigue, *Advise and Consent*, is set in Washington in 1959. Although Allen Drury's masterpiece was about the behind-the-scenes horse trading, blackmailing, and sexual hijinks accompanying a fight over the Senate confirmation of a new secretary of state, what stands out nearly sixty years after it was published—because it is so different from the Washington of today—is that it is full of scenes where Democrats and Republicans have lunch together, drink together, drive to work together, spend evenings with their spouses together, and cut deals together. That is nothing like today's Washington.

Perhaps that is because, unlike prior decades of Democratic dominance, since 1994 the control of one house of the legislature or the other, as well as the White House, has been constantly up for grabs. That has created a permanent campaign, making the contestants unlikely to want to do anything to help the other side. Maybe it is because the constant need for money has forced politicians to be out fund-raising day and night, rather than spending time at lunch or dinner with colleagues on the other side. Besides, they now typically leave town by Thursday and do not come back until Monday night in order to press the flesh. Or perhaps the decline of camaraderie or even civility in Washington is because a different breed—ideologically motivated mavericks or ambitious strivers, focused mostly on themselves and their donors—has replaced the party stalwarts of old, who were loyal to Congress as an institution and who had moved up through the ranks based on their seniority. Whatever the reason, and it is probably a combination of all of these changes and more, politics has become uglier than the relative civility that prevailed in Allen Drury's Washington. The players on opposite sides and even many on the same team don't like each other, and they do little to hide it.

Some, mostly Republicans, date the beginning of the ugliness to the Democrats' fierce opposition to Robert Bork, a brilliant judge whom the Democrats attacked relentlessly as they blocked President Reagan's bid to appoint him to the Supreme Court in 1987. More observers, including many Republicans, date it to the rise of Newt Gingrich, whose ascendance began at about the same time as the Bork war.

In 1974, Gingrich was a restless history professor at West Georgia College. His first foray into politics had been working for liberal New York governor Nelson Rockefeller in 1968, when Rockefeller lost the Republican nomination to Richard Nixon. Gingrich got the Republican nomination in 1974 for a House district just outside Atlanta to oppose John Flynt, a longtime Democratic incumbent. He made headlines with what at the time were unusually sharp personal attacks on Flynt's integrity. Gingrich lost in a close election, then lost again in 1976, also by a tight margin. In the second contest he focused his attacks on what he called, accurately, Flynt's failure as chairman of a House ethics committee to go after members of Congress caught up in scandals.

In 1978, Gingrich finally won, beating state senator Virginia Shapard, who had replaced the retiring Flynt on the Democratic ticket. Gingrich attacked Shapard as a rich person "who doesn't understand how we live." His campaign also passed out a brochure proclaiming, "If you like welfare cheaters, you'll love Virginia Shapard," explaining that she had been a "welfare worker for five years" and that she and black state senator Julian Bond, a civil rights leader, had "fought together to kill" a bill aimed at curbing welfare fraud. (Shapard responded that she had supported a stronger bill.)

After the 1978 congressional elections, Norman Ornstein, a veteran political analyst, congressional expert, and author, helped the American Enterprise Institute organize a series of dinners for congressional freshmen. "Newt totally stood out," Ornstein recalled. "He was outspoken. Couldn't sit still. . . . He talked about taking back Congress from the Democrats, which hadn't happened in years. He talked about how corrupt everyone was. How this was a time to fight, not get along. His strategy," said Ornstein, "was to destroy the institution by showing how corrupt it was in order to come in and save it."

Gingrich soon latched on to a new tool to boost his profile. A few months after he took office in 1979, the House allowed the cable television industry to launch a public service channel, C-Span, to televise House proceedings. For years, members had gone to the floor of the House at night to give speeches that they could submit into the *Congressional Record* but that would be seen and heard only by the handful of staff or members who happened to be in the near-empty chamber. Now, Gingrich realized, he and his allies could give the same speeches to a nationwide television audience. Under the rules, the camera was fixed on the speaker so as not to reveal whether anyone else was in the chamber. No one would know that when Gingrich and his band of renegades attacked Democrats for being corrupt or even being soft on communism, the absence of argument back from the other side was not because they did not dispute the charges, but because Gingrich and the others were pretty much talking to themselves.

For years, the Democrats didn't pay much attention to the Gingrich and friends television show because, even though the Republicans frequently used sound bites of their best performances to promote themselves, C-Span's actual viewership was minimal. However, Gingrich's C-Span antics reached such a fever pitch in 1984 that Democratic speaker Thomas "Tip" O'Neill decided to reveal the Potemkin Village nature of the House "debate" by ordering the cameras to show the empty chamber. O'Neill then took the floor to accuse Gingrich of impugning the integrity of members of the House. The dramatic confrontation made headlines, with a video clip broadcast on the evening news.

All of this was happening at a time when President Reagan and O'Neill, a Massachusetts liberal, were famously cutting deals, with the help of Gingrich's putative House boss, Republican minority leader Bob Michel.

"Newt was different from anyone I'd known up here," Michel recalled. We spoke over lunch at the Capitol Hill Club, a social club for Republicans steps away from the Capitol. It was a few weeks before he died in 2017, at age ninety-three, amid obituaries that lauded him, as *Politico* put it, "the face of decency and public service."

"Newt had this bucket mop of hair all over the place, and he seemed to sneer at me when he talked," Michel remembered. "I think he thought I was a bit of a jerk. . . . He only wanted to fight, go after people." Michel recalled a fight over an anti-crime bill proposed by Reagan in 1984. Michel was working with O'Neill to forge a compromise to get it through the Democratic-controlled House. "Newt objected. I remember we were in the cloak room and he screamed at a bunch of us, 'No! We have to keep the issue alive!' We wanted a bill; he wanted an issue to keep him in the newspapers."

What animated Gingrich most was scandal. He organized a group of like-minded Republicans to launch a series of ethics charges against the Democrats on issues ranging from their use of the House bank to write checks on overdrawn accounts to abuse of the House post office. "The Democrats had been in control for forty years," Michel recalled, "so there had been a lot of abuses. Newt was more interested in that than anything else. It got him above the fold on the front page of the newspaper."

Arriving as he did in the years immediately following Watergate, when journalists, too, had come to see going after scandal as a ticket to career advancement, Gingrich found willing collaborators in the press, not to mention lots of ammunition because the Democrats, indeed, had turned the House into an ethical morass. After O'Neill retired, Gingrich was able to force his successor, Texas Democrat Jim Wright, out of the House in 1989 on charges that he had channeled money into his pocket from supporters by getting them to make bulk purchases of a book that had been ghostwritten for him. No speaker had ever been driven from the House on ethics charges, although after Gingrich became speaker he would become the first to be reprimanded by the House for ethics violations. In 1997, members would vote 395–28 to fine him $300,000 for using a phony tax-exempt organization, disguised as a political science course, to funnel money into his political activities.

There was also a substantive side to Gingrich, all of it related to taking a harder conservative line than even President Reagan espoused, and a far tougher stance than that of George H. W. Bush, who succeeded Reagan. That culminated in Gingrich becoming House Republican whip in 1989 and then pushing Michel out as Republican leader and would-be speaker in 1995. It came after Gingrich's ultraconservative "Contract with America" manifesto (the key provisions of which were never enacted) carried Republicans to a 1994 election sweep that gave them control of the House for the first time since 1955.

Gingrich's rejection of bipartisan compromise continued. He was a leader in the effort to impeach President Bill Clinton over the president's sex scandal, even as it turned out that he was having his own extramarital affair at the same time. Impasses between him and Clinton resulted in two government shutdowns, after which Gingrich seemed to relent enough to negotiate several deals with Clinton, including major welfare reform legislation.

TECHNOLOGY: THE GREAT UNITER
BECOMES THE GREAT DIVIDER

At the same time that Gingrich was fomenting the polarization and bitterness in Washington that became a dominant force in America's tailspin, breakthroughs in technology began to produce the tools that would further break the country apart.

In 1995, Matt Drudge, a twenty-nine-year-old Californian who had made a hobby of gathering gossip while working in a gift shop at CBS studios in Hollywood, took advantage of the increasingly popular Internet to create a website reflecting his personal interests. The *Drudge Report* mixed Hollywood gossip with opinion pieces reflecting Drudge's conservative outlook, and, beginning in 1996, occasional political scoops. As the Internet became more widely used, Drudge picked up a following. Then in January 1998 he became an overnight media megaforce, when a group of anti-Clinton activists, frustrated that their months-long effort to get information about Monica Lewinsky's affair with Clinton published in *Newsweek* was stalled, leaked to Drudge that *Newsweek* was sitting on the scoop. Drudge's breathless report attracted millions, especially Clinton haters, as regular readers. It was the beginning of a new distribution channel for news, curated not by traditional journalism institutions but often by people or groups with strong points of view targeted at one side or the other of the political spectrum.

As early as 1988, Rush Limbaugh had stoked a right-wing audience with his syndicated radio show. With the rise of Drudge, it became possible for conservatives to consume a full menu of news that reinforced their worldview. He attracted millions and then tens of millions of website visitors to his scoops and, more important, to his headlined links to dozens of stories from around the world that put a highly conservative spin on the news. Before long, the left got its own versions of the same menu, with aggregators such as *The Huffington Post*.

Just as the Internet began to flourish, cable television, courtesy of parallel advances in digital technology, was able to send dozens, then hundreds, of separate channels to cable boxes in every living room. With the capacity for fifty or a hundred channels instead of fifteen or twenty, television offerings could be targeted to more specific interests. Niche channels for everything from sports to cooking to history to courtroom trials began to proliferate. In 1996, media mogul Rupert Murdoch and Roger Ailes, a skilled television producer and veteran Republican media consultant, teamed up to target one of those niches, which turned out to be more than a niche.

Fox News—with hard-core conservative opinion at night, supplemented with ostensibly straight news during the day that nonetheless was more sympathetic to the conservative side than broadcast news or CNN—attracted a wide audience almost from the start. By the time of the Clinton impeachment imbroglio in 1998, MSNBC had seized the opposite flank, providing a liberal counter to Fox.

Beginning a decade later, social media intensified the process of splitting Americans into separate corners. They could sign up for news alerts and other emailed bulletins from the websites they agreed with, or short-circuit the whole process by relying on Facebook news feeds and tweets provided by friends and others whose point of view they shared. That often led to relying on news and facts that produced a one-sided spin, as well as being exposed to what came to be called "fake news" that had been piped into news feeds by interests (such as hackers working for Russia) deliberately trying to deceive readers. *BuzzFeed News*, after conducting an analysis of web traffic and engagement following the 2016 American election, found that "the top-performing fake election news stories on Facebook generated more engagement than the top stories from major news outlets, such as the *New York Times*, *Washington Post*, *Huffington Post*, NBC News, and others."

The invention of radio had united the country by allowing everyone to share the same experience. They could listen together to an FDR fireside chat or an Edward R. Murrow report from London as the bombs fell. With the coming of television, they could watch together as Murrow took on Joseph McCarthy, as John Kennedy, Jr., saluted his father's coffin, as Walter Cronkite reported on the Vietnam War, or as Neil Armstrong walked on the moon. By 1970, the three major television broadcast networks had grown to command at least 75 percent of all American eyeballs. That these and a few print outlets had a near-monopoly a half century ago on presenting the news had its own severe problems; David Halberstam wrote a compelling book about that in 1979, *The Powers That Be*. The modern digital breakthrough in democratizing news, however, has allowed people to yield to the temptation to see what they want to see and shut out the other side. Today, most Americans, indeed, most people around the world, observe events through self-chosen prisms.

It has been a core cause of the polarization that has hamstrung America and rendered the country unable to address its fundamental challenges. It becomes so much harder to get people to argue civilly with their opposites, much less find middle ground, if the news they consume doesn't allow both sides to start with the same set of basic facts. In 2017, one poll reported that 89 percent of Republicans believed President Trump was more trustworthy than CNN, while 91 percent of Democrats believed the opposite. A 2016 survey found that two thirds of those who supported President Trump believed Barack Obama is a Muslim, and 59 percent believed he was not born in the United States. An earlier third poll had found that half of all Democrats believed that the George W. Bush administration was "very likely" or "somewhat likely" to have been complicit in the September 11 terrorist attacks.

It makes for a perfect vicious cycle. Political money and political reforms aimed at eroding the power of parties turns politicians into free agents focused on building their own profiles and campaign coffers; gerrymandering and the avid agenda interests of donors push the free agents, operating now in an embittered political environment, to the more extreme ends of the spectrum; and the media environment reinforces all of that. The result: Checks and balances metastasize into paralysis, and the country's major issues—income inequality, education, job training, the tax code, infrastructure, the deficit, health care—continue to go unaddressed.

There is another, parallel element in the mix, also powered by advances in digital technology, that reinforces the paralysis. With advertising and messaging platforms such as Facebook and Google that can target voters with exquisite granularity, the politicians' own marketing tools have become as polarizing as the media.

In March 2017, Chuck Todd, the host of NBC's *Meet the Press*, took time out from one Sunday morning's usual panel discussions to offer a mini-essay about the problem, which was obviously bothering the lifelong political junkie. "The misuse of big data is destroying the American political system," Todd declared. "Campaigns traditionally aim to win the middle, and if you won the middle, you won the election. Now campaigns are using or abusing big data to identify and mobilize like-minded voters, rather than using it to make arguments that change minds.

"How bad has this polarization gotten in the last twenty years?" Todd asked. "In 1994 there was a good deal of ideological overlap between the two parties. Thirty-six percent of Republican voters were more liberal than the typical Democrat, and thirty percent of Democrats were more conservative than the typical Republican. Today, [that is] no longer the case. In 2014, just eight percent of Republicans, [and] six percent of Democrats, were more liberal or conservative than the members of the opposite party. . . .

"A complete hollowing out of the political center," Todd concluded, "coincided with the advent of micro-targeting in 2004, then advanced by team Obama, and now, of course, everybody uses it. . . . The electorate and politicians alike used to be conditioned to know that the middle mattered. That's why big deals in Washington were bipartisan."

THE BIPARTISANS

One evening in March 2017, a group of Washington's elite gathered in a ballroom over drinks and dinner to reaffirm their determination that polarization was not a permanent fact of life, that something had to be done and could be done about it. Twelve hundred self-labeled "partisans," evenly split between Republicans and Democrats, convened six blocks from the Capitol to celebrate the ten-year anniversary of a non-profit think tank called the Bipartisan Policy Center. Founded by four icons of the good old days of bipartisanship—former Republican Senate majority leaders Bob Dole and Howard Baker, and former Democratic majority leaders George Mitchell and Tom Daschle—the BPC attracts $20 million a year from foundations and individual donors drawn to its mission as a polarization resistance movement and its reputation for producing quality bipartisan policy solutions.

"We didn't need to exist thirty years ago, and it's unfortunate that we do exist," said BPC president Jason Grumet.

The founders and the five honorees at the dinner—former vice president Joe Biden, two Republican legislators, and two Democratic lawmakers—gave speeches about how much they respected each other, how much they appreciated that those on the other side were patriots, too, and even how much they liked each other.

Three weeks after the dinner, Grumet, a Harvard-trained lawyer who directed a national commission on energy policy before joining BPC as its founding president in 2007, said that "despite the political climate, or maybe because of it," he was "as serious about this work today as I was ten years ago, maybe more so." Grumet and a staff of one hundred highly credentialed policy wonks, along with a group of distinguished former officeholders, have built a kind of shadow Congress that negotiates among themselves and produces a steady stream of policy papers aimed at solutions to the issues that have paralyzed the real Congress. For any current officeholder who cares, their work could be a blueprint for reviving the country on multiple fronts.

Daschle and former Republican Senate majority leader (and physician) Bill Frist, working with Democratic and Republican staff experts, had produced a sensible set of fixes for Obamacare. BPC had an infrastructure plan ready to go, as well as proposals for reforming the federal budgeting process, for streamlining government regulations, and for fixes to NAFTA. "Everyone should agree with them," Grumet said. "NAFTA is twenty-three years old and stuff like the IP [intellectual property] provisions certainly needs fixing." The organization had "decisive input over many long days," Grumet recalled, in shaping the 2013 immigration reform bill that passed the Senate in a bipartisan vote. It is an issue the team had kept working on despite the refusal of the Republican House to consider the bill.

"We're not non-partisan," Grumet emphasized. "We're partisans. Non-partisanship is quaint BS. That's not the world we live in, or will ever live in. The best ideas come out of partisan debates. We argue with each other. We do research, and debate what we find. We have fights, and then we compromise based on basic principles and trust. Then we take positions—in our name, not in the individual writers' names. Our goal is to get people to think, If these guys can agree, why can't we agree?"

For now, however, the partisans with the power show few signs of being impressed. Like Sheila Krumholz's data on political money sitting on OpenSecrets.org, the work Grumet and his earnest team have done is only ammunition at the ready when policymakers are finally moved to use it. Only when they are will BPC's work and the way that they have persisted in keeping the flame burning not be wasted.

CHAPTER 8

Moat Nation

Those who have thrived in the post-1970s world of the new meritocracy, the casino economy, the marginalized middle class, and the dominance of political money are not interested in the Bipartisan Policy Center's solutions. They are more concerned about what the government can do *to* them than *for* them. A minimum wage law means that they have to pay more, not that they earn more. Campaign finance reform would limit their power rather than enhance it the way it would for average citizens. Affordable health care might cut into the profits of those at the top of the American health care economy, which is nearly one fifth of the country's overall economy. Tougher government regulation to protect consumers or to rein in Wall Street would constrain, not protect, them. For those at the absolute top, even fixing airports, highways, mass transit, power grids, or other infrastructure would soak up their tax dollars and reinforce confidence in a government that they would prefer to look incompetent, while doing little to enhance lives that are backstopped by private aircraft, home power generators, and limousines. For them, the evaporation of public trust in the federal government, which peaked at 77 percent in 1964 and was hovering at or below 20 percent five decades later, was an opportunity, not a problem.

Conservatives have always preached self-reliance while liberals favored an activist government that assures the common good. However, this is a new, wider, and more dangerous divide—between those at the top, who enjoy unprecedented power, and everyone else. For those at the top, the common good is no longer good for them.

A few years ago, a private equity mogul shared what he said was his secret to success. "I always look for companies that have an unfair advantage," he explained. "I look for companies that have a moat protecting them." A congenitally self-satisfied type, he seemed proud to have discovered and perfected this playbook, although actually he was only parroting Warren Buffett. What Buffett had meant was that he was attracted to companies that had such good products with such great reputations, predominant market shares, and good managements that competitors would have a hard time getting across the moat to attack it. However, the man I was talking with brought up his moat theory because he wanted to know whether a company he was investing in that I had founded, which was creating a system by which people could pay to be prescreened and get expedited access through airport security, was hiring the right lobbyists to make sure various airports didn't do business with any newcomers that might try to compete with us. That was the kind of unfair advantage, or moat, he was looking for—protection from the marketplace and the consequences of my company not performing well enough to win on the merits.

Similarly, what investors and businesses of all kinds began to seek in the wake of the 1971 call to arms triggered by events like Lewis Powell's memo and the Burke-Hartke anti-trade proposal was protection of all kinds. Because of the money they could spend on financial engineers, lawyers, and lobbyists, they were able to get that protection. Since then, America has increasingly become a Moat Nation, producing a parade of unfair advantages for those with the resources to deploy the knowledge workers to build and fortify their moats while contributing to the overall decline of the country.

These moats matter. By blocking accountability for irresponsible conduct that undermines the common good and by creating the overall sense among the vast majority that the deck is stacked against them, they have sabotaged the idea of a United States of America. They are the metaphorical, as well as the physical, opposite of bridges.

More often than not, the lawyers and lobbyists, who became Washington's leading growth industry in the 1970s, have been paid to keep a good thing going for their clients by protecting them from anything that might threaten how they do business. It usually works because they and their clients have a single-minded interest that makes them willing to devote more time, and certainly more money, for white papers and campaign donations, than the other side will—because the other side is usually the more amorphous public interest. That is why that study we noted earlier found that even when overwhelming majorities of the public questioned in polls prefer a public policy change, they get it less than half the time.

Drug companies have been able to fight off price controls that prevail in all other developed countries and that overwhelming majorities of Americans favor. As we have seen, the version of health care "reform" that could make it out of Congress in 2010, Obamacare, was a law that produced government-subsidized profit increases for all the players in the industry. The health care lobby, by far the most heavily financed of any American industry sector, protected their clients' moats, despite what should have been overwhelming public interest in breaching it.

In ways that most Americans do not appreciate, because the effects are indirect, the failure to control health care costs has done as much to hurt the middle class as anything else in the last fifty years, including the decline of private sector unions. Most people have a sense that middle-class wages, relative to inflation, have remained nearly frozen. What is not as widely appreciated is that the *cost* to employers of hiring workers has risen by at least 30 percent in inflation-adjusted dollars because their health insurance costs per employee have increased by more than 300 percent. Had health care costs merely kept pace with inflation, employers could have had that much more to pay their workers in wages. (Whether in the new world of decimated unions they would have decided to pay it is another question.)

At the same time, the share of out-of-pocket costs for workers who had insurance has increased rapidly, erasing the benefit of whatever minimal cash raises they might have gotten. From 1980 to 2016, personal, out-of-pocket spending for health care (in deductibles and co-pays for costs covered by insurance, and in employees' shares of premiums for employer-provided health insurance) grew 460 percent. The percentage of workers who were no longer offered insurance (at least until the passage of Obamacare) either because employers decided they could not afford it or because they shifted to outsourced, contract workers to avoid the cost, also increased. That cut further into workers' disposable income.

Moat fortification is why big businesses in all industries—telecommunications, beer, hospital systems, cereals and canned foods, media—have consistently been able to consolidate since the 1970s. Using the raiding and merger tactics and the financial engineering created by Joseph Flom and the investment bankers, and given almost complete freedom beginning in the 1980s, when President Reagan loosened anti-trust enforcement, they have steadily concentrated their power and protected themselves from the consumer account-ability that comes with the competition that anti-trust laws passed at the beginning of the twentieth century were meant to ensure. The result, according to multiple studies, is the ultimate unfair advantage: less competition and, with it, the ability to cut service and product offerings while extracting higher prices from consumers. At the same time, their concentrated buying power forced suppliers to cut their prices, which put an additional squeeze on the wages these suppliers could pay their workers.

Anti-trust laws still require that these mergers run a gauntlet of regulatory review. However, it is a process that big businesses and their lawyers—who often had jobs earlier in their careers on the other side of the table, working for the government—have mastered. Their law firms prepare or commission from credentialed experts (often from academia) voluminous studies expounding elaborate economic theories demonstrating that the merger will be good for everyone. At the same time, political and media consultants are retained to drum up support from different interest groups.

In 2017, news reports of the grotesque dragging of a passenger off a United Airlines flight, watched worldwide courtesy of a passenger's smartphone video, were quickly followed by calls for a boycott of the airline, which had overbooked its seats as part of a routine, customer-unfriendly practice aimed at maximizing revenue. Those stories were soon followed by reports quoting business analysts and consumer group representatives pointing out that a boycott of United was unlikely. The airline industry had been allowed to consolidate so tightly through mergers, blessed by anti-trust regulators in Demo-cratic and Republican administrations alike, that customers often had little or no choice but to fly United on most routes, no matter how high its prices, how cramped its seating, or how likely it might be to abuse its captive passengers. In fact, in its first quarterly financial filing following the debacle, United reported a boost in profits and passengers compared to the corresponding quarter in 2016.

Even supposedly non-profit hospitals have taken advantage of lax anti-trust enforcement. If you think your local hospital's prices are too high or its services inadequate, there is often nothing you or your insurance company can do about it. Across the country, hospitals have been allowed to merge with abandon—and to buy up the practices of local doctors, who then must refer all their patients to the new parent company. In New Haven, Connecticut, the Yale New Haven Health System, with the help of a 2,500-lawyer international law firm, has been allowed to merge and buy its way into owning just about everything related to health care in that city and in the surrounding area stretching all the way down to Greenwich, in southern Connecticut. When hospitals merge, they always promise that the transaction will cut costs and improve quality by consolidating overlapping facilities and luring the best talent. Yet every time, including at Yale New Haven, subsequent studies show that prices go up faster than inflation and faster than the higher rate of overall health care inflation, while quality does not improve. The reason is obvious: Would you want to be the executive at an insurance company hoping to sell health insurance in New Haven who has to negotiate prices with the only provider in town? If you don't have Yale New Haven in your network, you have no hospital and few doctors to offer to customers. Yale New Haven, which is a tax-exempt non-profit, reported $3.8 billion in revenue in 2016 and cash flow of more than $300 million.

In 2016, President Obama's Council of Economic Advisers issued a report that, while listing various administration efforts to encourage competition, was an indictment of the government's record in controlling concentration over the prior two decades, including Obama's eight years. "Consumers and workers would benefit from additional policy actions by the government to promote competition within a variety of industries," the report concluded. "Recent indicators suggest that many industries may be becoming more concentrated, that new firm entry is declining, and that some firms are generating returns that are greatly in excess of historical standards. In addition, the dollar volume of merger and acquisition activity is at record levels." The significance of the White House report's conclusion that "new firm entry" had declined was underscored in a September 20, 2017, analysis by *The New York Times*'s Ben Casselman, who found that the number of businesses launched each year as a percentage of all operating businesses had been declining significantly since 1980. He cited economists who attributed the trend to "the rising power of the biggest corporations, which they argue is stifling entrepreneurship by making it easier for incumbent businesses to swat away challengers—or else to swallow them before they become a serious threat." The result, he wrote, was a less dynamic economy and "anemic wage growth" because employment opportunities had become so concentrated among large employers. "Start-ups," Casselman added, "are key drivers of job creation and innovation, and have historically been a ladder into the middle class for less-educated workers and immigrants."

Then there is the American income tax code, which was regarded as unusually complex at twenty-seven pages when first passed in 1913. It is now thousands of pages long, and has become a catalogue of moats, called tax preferences. It was created and then protected by specialist lawyers and accountants in a wealth protection industry whose rise roughly parallels the beginning of the rise of business lobbying (and the fall of private sector unions) in the 1970s. Since then, the American tax code, originally conceived as a way to balance the burden fairly among the have-nots, the haves, and the have-a-lots, has become a blueprint for protecting the wealthy with tax rates 20 percent to 40 percent lower than the international norm for developed countries and with loopholes that can make even those rates meaningless. Overall, by 2017, Americans paid a lower share of the gross domestic product in all taxes—federal, state, and local—than all thirty-five countries in the Organisation for Economic Co-operation and Development except for Ireland, Chile, and Mexico.

In 1970, the income tax rate for the highest earners was 70 percent. By 2017—at the same time that Social Security taxes, sales taxes, and other fees proportionately hitting lower earners the hardest had increased—the rate on the highest earners had fallen to 39.6 percent and was about to fall to 37 percent as a result of the Republican-driven tax cut legislation passed in December 2017. Even that rate was mostly irrelevant. Beyond offering the wealthy a basket of offsetting tax deductions, the tax code allowed earnings for those at the top, who typically accumulate their wealth through investments or stock grants, to be taxed on those earnings at a capital gains rate. That rate had always been lower than earned income rates, and has kept getting lower, beginning with the lobbyists' reversal of Jimmy Carter's tax reform proposal in 1978. Those who can often be found at the absolute top of the earnings scale—people who manage hedge funds and private equity and venture funds—enjoy a loophole that allows the money they make by investing money for others (their "carried interest") to be taxed as capital gains, not earned income, even though they get the money for their work, not as a return on money they have invested.

Despite that carried interest loophole (which came from a little noticed but ardently lobbied IRS decision in 1993), Americans who have focused on such issues have been conditioned to believe that capital gains deserve favorable treatment. The rationale is that policymakers want to encourage investment and account for the fact that returns on those investments may occur over longer periods, during which inflation may have reduced the real value of any paper profit. It is a reasonable argument, but it is worth noting that at the dawn of the income tax in the early twentieth century, amid debates about how the system should operate, no less a conservative capitalist than financier, industrialist, and Republican treasury secretary Andrew Mellon proposed in a book he wrote in 1924 that capital gains should be taxed at rates *higher* than earned income. Mellon's argument was that income from labor should get the more favorable treatment because it "is uncertain and limited in duration; sickness or death destroys it; and old age diminishes it."

Even reduced capital gains rates have frequently been rendered little more than hypothetical for the wealthiest Americans because additional loopholes and credits available to them can reduce their taxable earnings still more, often to zero. Since the 1960s, those in the real estate business, including President Trump, have become the world champions at securing these breaks.

A bipartisan tax reform law, pushed in 1986 by President Reagan and by Democrats led by then-Senator Bill Bradley, cut back on the most blatant loopholes. However, many were gradually clawed back by the lobbyists in the years that followed, while new ones were added. None were removed (and some were added) by the Republicans when they pushed through their "tax reform" package in late 2017, which reformed nothing, made the tax code longer and still more complicated, and cut taxes mostly for corporations and the country's wealthiest families.

Some moats have consequences that are more than financial. In 2015, federal law enforcement officials considered banning a certain type of best-selling bullet that could be loaded into semi-automatic assault weapons and had been specially manufactured to penetrate protective armor, including the bulletproof vests worn by police officers. They proposed a regulation to include them under a law that already banned many types of armor-piercing bullets. It seemed a logical, unassailable way to protect police while not infringing on hunting. (Even assuming a hunter would use an assault rifle, deer or ducks are not likely to be wearing vests.) The Obama administration had to scrap the idea, however, after the manufacturers of the armor-piercing bullets—the leading one of which was owned by a giant private equity firm called Cerberus—activated the powerful gun lobby, which is largely funded by the gun industry and backed by millions of gun enthusiasts. Letters and phone calls poured into Congress, which in turn demanded that the regulators stand down, or face a law or litigation that would erase the regulation. The police were not protected, but Cerberus, whose gun company makes the semi-automatic assault weapon used in the Sandy Hook school massacre, was.

WALL STREET MOATS

That America had become Moat Nation became most obvious following the Great Recession—beginning with how those at the top took advantage of their most protective moat of all: the fact that the sheer mass and interconnectedness of the big banks and other non-bank players like AIG dictated that the government could not allow them to fail. Years of lobbying had eliminated the guardrails of regulations restricting the spread of their activities and the risks that they could take. So they now had to be bailed out of all those disastrous gambles in mortgage-backed securities, credit default swaps, and synthetic credit default swaps because, in the wake of the collapse of Lehman Brothers, it was clear that letting another big bank go under would take them all down in a calamity no responsible official wanted to allow. Hundreds of billions of taxpayer dollars were allocated to save them, even as individual mortgage holders were thrown out of their homes because they couldn't or wouldn't write checks to cover the ballooning payments due on homes suddenly worth less than the money they owed because of the collapse of the housing market.

When the Obama administration arrived in 2009, there was broad sentiment on both sides of the aisle, at least rhetorically, that these rescued financial institutions now had to be reined in. That way, the country would never again be whipsawed into having to bail out the Wall Street gamblers because they were, in a phrase that had quickly become a cliché, "too big to fail." The 2010 Dodd-Frank Wall Street Reform and Consumer Protection Act, named for Democratic co-sponsors Senator Chris Dodd of Connecticut and Congressman Barney Frank of Massachusetts, was supposed to create that protection.

The usual imbalance of passion and resources between special interests and the public that so often blocks change in Washington can occasionally be erased when the population at large is focused and angry. Allowing the sale of bullets that can go through police officers' protective vests may not be an issue that rises to that level, but millions being thrown out of their homes and jobs, while the bankers who caused the disaster got bailed out, was. That made the passage of some kind of financial reform law with real teeth inevitable, especially with Democrats holding majorities in both houses of Congress during the first two years of Obama's presidency. The question was how big the bite would be. That was the war the lobbyists fought until July 2010, when Dodd-Frank was finally passed. It was also the war they continued to fight in the years after.

We have already seen how lopsided the Dodd-Frank lobbying troop count was in favor of business interests. Another demonstration of that imbalance is that since 1989, the forty-three members of the joint House-Senate committee that negotiated the final language of Dodd-Frank in 2010 had received $112 million from donors associated with the affected industries. "You can say that lobbyists on the Hill are like lawyers in the courtroom and that the advocacy system produces the best result," David Arkush, the director of the Ralph

Nader–associated group Congress Watch said at the time. "But in court you don't have the lawyers and clients donating to the jury."

The 1914 law establishing the Federal Trade Commission, with its sweeping regulations of commerce and anti-trust protections, was eight pages. The 1935 Social Security Act, which also dealt with unemployment compensation, child welfare services, and a complex allotment to states for aid to dependent children, was twenty-one pages. At 848 pages, Dodd-Frank was unintelligibly complex to almost anyone except the congressional staff members and the lawyer-lobbyists, many of whom were former staff members. The lobbyist ranks were so well stocked that a half dozen of them representing the banks could be down-in-the-weeds experts on any given paragraph or page.

Their job was to cajole staffers and members of Congress to tweak each of those paragraphs, adding qualifiers to weaken them, or at least make them vague enough so that the regulations that would later have to be written to implement them could become a new lobbying battlefield. In fact, because they knew that the political climate made blocking the law impossible, their primary lobbying goal—and victory—as the law was being written was to make sure they could fight on in the years after the law passed and the attention paid to it had faded. Some provisions in the bill settled issues decisively, and sometimes not in the industry's favor. Barney Frank and other Democrats were able to establish a Consumer Financial Protection Bureau that had real power, including independence from Congress when it came to funding. More often than not, however, the reformers got what they wanted directionally, but the industry succeeded in having the details punted to multiple regulatory agencies, including the SEC, Federal Reserve, Federal Deposit Insurance Corporation, and Comptroller of the Currency, which were instructed by the statute to write 243 regulations and conduct sixty-seven studies.

About a week after the final text of the law emerged from that joint House-Senate committee, one of the lobbyists working on the bill for JPMorgan Chase told me, "You think this is the end, right? No, it's halftime. The real work for us starts now, with the regs. With the press gone and the [C-Span] cameras [that televised the joint committee deliberations] gone, now we go to work."

A bedrock goal of the Obama administration and Dodd-Frank's congressional sponsors, of course, had been to eliminate the risk of

banks being too big to fail. From the beginning, the lobbyists succeeded in blocking the obvious solution: No banks were broken into
smaller entities. In fact, by 2016 the share of all banking assets (in
essence their market share) held by the top five banks was slightly
higher than it was the day Dodd-Frank passed. Each had grown bigger in revenue, profit, and their grip on the economy.

Another idea was to restore the New Deal's Glass-Steagall Act.
Glass-Steagall had prohibited government-backstopped chartered
banks from engaging in the riskier activities, such as making markets
in and trading derivatives, that had enriched the investment banks,
which did not have government guarantees behind them. It was the
repeal of Glass-Steagall in 1999 that allowed chartered banks like
JPMorgan, Citigroup, and Bank of America to join Goldman Sachs,
Lehman Brothers, Morgan Stanley, and other investment banks in the
mortgage-backed securities and credit default swaps markets. When
the crash came in 2008, the absence of Glass-Steagall allowed investment banks like Goldman and Morgan Stanley to become chartered
banks themselves, overnight, so that they could receive Treasury bailouts after Lehman collapsed.

However, instead of breaking up the dominant banks or forcing a new Glass-Steagall Act on them, Dodd-Frank imposed several narrower rules intended to limit the risks the banks could take.
The most controversial, dubbed the Volcker Rule, was proposed by
Paul Volcker, a former Federal Reserve Board chairman. Under the
Volcker Rule, chartered banks would not be allowed to engage in
trading derivatives for their own accounts at their own risk. Nor
would they be able to invest in high-risk vehicles like hedge funds.
These were exactly the types of activities that had required that they
be bailed out.

Banks were horrified by the prospect of the Volcker Rule, because
these were the gambles that had fueled the increases in their profits in the run-up to the Great Recession. They argued that they had
learned from their mistakes and that tying their hands by prohibiting
these activities would kill their profits. Other rules being put in place
under Dodd-Frank, they maintained, such as requiring banks to keep
more capital on hand as a cushion, would protect them from failing.
The lobbyists succeeded in getting several pivotal exceptions added
to the original draft of the Volcker Rule that became law when Dodd-

Frank was passed. They would have years to unwind the investments they had already made, for example.

However, as that JPMorgan Chase lobbyist had promised, it was after the bill passed that he and the other 3,658 lobbyists—who filed reports disclosing that they were paid $483 million working for the financial industry that year—really went to work. With the lobbyists' encouragement, Dodd-Frank had provided that five agencies would jointly draft the regulations implementing the Volcker Rule. That made sense given that each had jurisdiction over some of the entities that would be regulated, but the lobbyists knew that this assured not only that they would get five bites out of the apple in pleading their cases, but also that the rule writing would be prolonged as the five agency staffs fought among themselves.

The first draft of the regulations to implement the Volcker Rule was seven pages long. When the regulations were finally promulgated in December 2013—following meetings with lobbyists that averaged seven per workday over the three and a half years from the day the law was signed until the regulations were issued—it was 27 pages, supplemented with 245 pages full of heavily lobbied exceptions and clarifications. JPMorgan Chase CEO Jamie Dimon and other bankers, whose troops had pushed to inject all those exceptions and clarifications, now had a new complaint: They mocked the Volcker Rule's length and attacked it for being too complicated. Since the final promulgation of the rule's regulations, the lobbying has continued unabated, and deadlines to implement some key provisions, even with all the exceptions, have been extended into 2019, or nine years after Dodd-Frank was passed.

The banks argued, and still do, that the Volcker Rule—as well as the safety measure requiring banks to be less leveraged and to keep more capital sitting in reserve in order to provide more of a firewall against a potential failure—would drastically reduce their profits. Yet in 2016, the banking industry would report its largest profits ever—a total of $171 billion for the country's 6,000 banks. That was far higher than the go-go years running up to the 2008–9 crash. JPMorgan Chase earned a record $24.7 billion, 60 percent more than its pre-crash high of $15.3 billion in 2007, although in his annual letter to shareholders in 2017 Dimon would still be complaining about Dodd-Frank. The bottom lines associated with the 22,000 pages of rules promulgated by 2017 to implement Dodd-Frank were that banks that had been too big to fail became bigger and achieved record profits.

Seven years after Dodd-Frank became law in 2010, the lobbyists had so bottled up the process that approximately a quarter of the required rules related to other provisions, including some of the most important ones, were still tied up in unfinished drafts. Others had only recently been completed but had not yet been implemented— and they were unlikely ever to be implemented (at least until after the next presidential election) because the Trump administration, which opposed Dodd-Frank and promised to scale it back, had frozen the rule-making process and begun promulgating new rules to roll back the old ones.

One important Dodd-Frank provision had to do with what was called "clawbacks." A key factor in driving the economy almost over the cliff had been that executives were eager to maximize their annual bonuses by taking risks that might show a paper profit in the short term but end up being catastrophic money losers. By the time Dodd-Frank was being debated, tens of millions of dollars in bonuses paid to AIG executives for the profits supposedly coming from their sale of all those credit default swap insurance policies, which later exploded and required a massive bailout, had become exhibit A for why this was necessary. Thousands of other executives, salespeople, and traders at the major banks had similarly benefited. The clawback rule was supposed to guard against that by requiring public companies to defer full payments on bonuses long enough so that they could be adjusted downward or eliminated, and some bonuses already paid could be recaptured, if it turned out that the profits were illusory, or that the executive had engaged in reckless risk taking or other misconduct that had ended up hurting the business.

By the time President Trump took office, the clawback rule, which was supposed to be co-drafted by six agencies, had still not been written, and the drafts that were pending had been watered down following heavy lobbying so that the clawback period was not long enough to identify the kinds of illusory profits that had prevailed in the run-up to the crash. The language had also been changed to make the withholding or recapture of bonuses only something that the company's board had to "consider."

The continued lack of a clawback rule generated front-page

attention in 2016 when the giant Wells Fargo bank agreed to pay a $185 million fine after it was found to have opened a million and a half bank accounts and 565,000 credit card accounts for customers who had never asked for them.* The phony accounts were the result of pressure put on the bank's tellers and salespeople to cross-sell additional services to customers who already had accounts at the bank. Wells Fargo had long touted its market-leading cross-selling prowess as the key to the bank's brand strength, superior culture, and growth prospects. The cross-selling metrics it regularly produced for stock analysts had boosted the stock and, with it, the bonuses paid to top executives.

Stories about customers complaining about being charged for the phony accounts had first appeared in the *Los Angeles Times* in 2013. Even earlier than that, the bank had also received complaints to its internal whistle-blower hot line from staffers reporting the pressure to open the phony accounts. After the $185 million settlement was announced, it was revealed the bank's chief executive (who had received the 2015 "CEO of the Year" award from the Morningstar stock analysis firm) and the executive in charge of the bank's retail businesses had received tens of millions of dollars in performance-related bonuses from the bank's board *after* the whistle-blower calls and the 2013 revelations in the *Times* articles.† Yet neither the executives nor the board had done anything to curb the fraudulent cross-selling or the metrics that were touted to shareholders and stock analysts. It was only then that fifteen Democratic members of the Senate—citing the Wells Fargo scandal and noting that the bank's 2015 proxy statement had trumpeted its success in cross-selling to justify the bonuses—wrote to the half dozen agencies that were supposed to have written the Dodd-Frank clawback rule six years earlier and demanded, fruitlessly, that it be completed. In the end, the Wells Fargo board, which had forced the executive in charge of retail to give back about half of her bonuses a few months earlier, fired the CEO and demanded a clawback from him, too. It did so only because it was

---

* A subsequent investigation completed in 2017 found that the fraud had begun in 2009 and actually included an additional 1.4 million unrequested bank accounts.

† The exact amount is not known because the time periods related to when the bonuses were earned by the two executives remain unclear.

embarrassed by all the publicity, not because it had to. By mid-2017, the financial regulatory agencies, now controlled by Trump appointees, had shelved the effort to write the clawback rule.

Even when the rules implementing Dodd-Frank finally got written, the lobbyists' work was not done. As happened with many of the tax loopholes that were eliminated by the 1986 Reagan tax reform law but then were gradually restored, when the right opportunity presented itself, setbacks could be reversed. In December 2014, four and a half years after Dodd-Frank was passed, the banks got a key provision of the Volcker Rule significantly softened by inserting 819 words, mostly drafted by lobbyists for Citigroup (according to *The New York Times*), into a 1,600-page, $1.1 trillion spending bill that had nothing to do with banking regulation. The amendment was cosponsored by two House Democrats who had received significant campaign funding from Wall Street.

The rules that survive depend, of course, on regulators enforcing them. In both the Obama administration and the Trump administration there has not been a single enforcement action taken against any institution for violating any aspect of the Volcker Rule. In theory, that could mean that no financial institution is speculating for its own account at all anymore. More likely, it is evidence that the rules are still too vague to be enforced and that those who are supposed to enforce them are choosing to interpret them the way the banks want them to.

This kind of moat maintenance was able to succeed in undermining a law passed in the wake of a calamity that had frightened and outraged much of the country. That is when maintaining the moats is the hardest. The more typical and easier cases are when the protection gained may have been equally unfair but the visibility and accompanying passion on the other side was muted.

CLOSING OFF THE COURTS

After Wells Fargo's practices became public thanks to the *Los Angeles Times*, a California plaintiffs' lawyer gathered a group of the bank's customers to bring a class-action suit to recover costs they may have been charged for the unrequested accounts opened in their names, or from damage done to their credit ratings from unpaid bills related to those charges. The case seemed ideally suited for a class action. These kinds of suits had been allowed by American courts in some form or another since the early nineteenth century. They allow many people suffering relatively small damage from one defendant charged with committing the same alleged act against each of them to band together and hire a lawyer on behalf of the group. Although it would not be worth it for each of them to sue individually, the legal expense of pursuing the case could be divided among them. Class actions also spare the courts the burden of multiple cases litigating the same set of facts.

The lawyers can earn a contingent fee if they win, typically ranging from 15 percent to 30 percent of the total awarded to the hundreds or thousands of plaintiffs, depending on what the judge approves. It would be their reward for risking their time to vindicate the rights of the class and for bringing suits that might deter defendants from selling defective cars or cheating bank customers.

In 1966, changes to federal court rules made class actions easier to prosecute and much easier for lawyers to gather large groups into the class. At a time when sensitivity to product safety, consumer rights, and the rights of bank customers to non-discriminatory credit and full disclosure of loan terms was on the rise, these 1966 reforms aimed at democratizing the civil legal system and giving plaintiffs' lawyers an incentive to bring these kinds of cases made sense. They still do.

Class actions also opened the floodgates to abuse. Dubious or frivolous suits could be filed, opening corporations to attack by opportunistic lawyers acting ostensibly on behalf of thousands of shareholders or hundreds of thousands of customers. Avoiding the risk of bad publicity, even for a baseless claim, and potential damage awards from juries in the millions or billions of dollars was worth the cost of settling with the plaintiffs' lawyer for a fraction of the claim. It became common, for example, for a lawyer to bring a shareholders' class action against a company whose stock had suddenly dipped a point or two, claiming hundreds of millions in damages for the shareholders. Settlements would then be paid—ironically, by the company owned by those shareholders—with the lawyers' shares far exceeding the few dollars distributed to each of their thousands of ostensible clients. Or a lawyer could allege that a bank's overdraft charges had not been disclosed properly and sue on behalf of its five million customers. The bank might settle for a few million dollars, with a third of it going to the lawyer, but only a few dollars going to each of her clients.

As with the unions' initial deployment of PACs or their sponsorship of the trade-killing Burke-Hartke bill, the plaintiffs' lawyers' aggressive and often coercive use of class actions eventually provoked a shock-and-awe response from the corporate law community. Reform laws were passed in many states, as was a federal law, in 1995, curbing shareholder class actions by erecting higher barriers of proof before they could proceed. Another law, in 2005, made it easier for class actions to be moved to federal courts from state courts, where plaintiffs' lawyers' abuses were more common.

The most important move was made by the potential defendants themselves. Beginning with a 1999 meeting at the New York office of a Washington-based law firm founded by Democratic stalwart and former Jimmy Carter White House counsel Lloyd Cutler, a blue-chip consortium of lawyers representing multiple banks and other large consumer-facing companies planned a counterattack. Their strategy was to insert clauses into the boilerplate contracts people signed for cell phone service, credit cards, bank accounts, and other services requiring that any disputes between the customer and the company would have to be settled in a private arbitration hearing, not in the courts. Most important, by signing the boilerplate contracts containing these clauses, the customer was giving up his or her right not only to sue, but also to participate in any kind of class action, even a class action arbitration proceeding.

Although some companies had pioneered the clauses a few years earlier, the consortium's work began to make them an industry standard. By 2008, they were included in the vast majority of consumer contracts and even in employment agreements workers signed with large employers. Democrats in Congress tried and failed three times between 2007 and 2011 to pass laws making these clauses unenforceable in governing these kinds of disputes.

In 2016, Wells Fargo had exactly that kind of arbitration clause buried in the pages of small print that its customers acknowledged and agreed to in writing when opening an account—or by checking a box online. The plaintiffs' lawyers bringing the class action against Wells Fargo argued that these clauses could not possibly apply because their suit was about the setting up of bank accounts that their clients had not agreed to and had never signed up for. That, in fact, was the point of the suit.

Wells Fargo was represented by Los Angeles–based Munger, Tolles & Olson, among the nation's most successful and meritocratic law firms (and one of whose lawyers was in the Yale Law School 2015 graduating class that Professor Markovits had addressed). The Munger, Tolles lawyers argued that the arbitration clause the customers had agreed to when opening their *original* accounts—not the second, fictionally "cross-sold" bank account or the credit card account that they never knew about—had a clause stating that the arbitration clause would apply to "any dispute relating in any way to your accounts and services." Based on that language, a federal court judge ruled that because the dispute over the fraudulent accounts had "some relationship to their banking with Wells Fargo," including allegations that "employees at Wells Fargo used information connected to their legitimate accounts to open new, unauthorized accounts," they had to go to arbitration, and that the arbitration clause's prohibition on plaintiffs teaming up to hire one lawyer for a class arbitration would also prevail. To add insult to injury, the judge buttressed that reasoning by adding that the same Wells Fargo arbitration clause required that even disputes about whether the arbitration clause applied had to be decided by an arbitrator.[*]

How could it be that a clause keeping consumers out of court, or from bringing class actions even in arbitration, embedded in the pages of small print that everyone routinely agrees to online (for Amazon accounts, for example), or when they rent a car or sign up for a credit card or bank account is actually enforceable? Consumers do not knowingly agree to that, because they almost never read those

---

[*] After Wells Fargo's practice of setting up phony accounts became a public relations disaster amid the 2017 congressional hearings, the company's reliance on the arbitration clause became an additional public relations nightmare. Thus, in 2017 Wells Fargo agreed to establish a $142 million settlement fund to settle other class action suits brought on behalf of customers claiming damages related to the fraudulent accounts. However, the company has never disavowed its defense that the arbitration clauses were enforceable, and the bank's new chief executive refused in congressional testimony in September 2017 to promise not to use arbitration clauses in the future.

pages of legalese. Besides, what choice do they have if every online retailer, credit card company, student loan processor, area nursing home or medical clinic, and car rental, ride-sharing, cell phone, and cable service has the same clause? What choice do they have if they are asked to sign an arbitration clause on the first day of a new job that prohibits them from bringing a suit based on violations of anti-discrimination laws that once were viewed as bedrocks of civil rights protections? Doesn't enforcement of such clauses run counter to the idea that the civil courts are supposed to be open to all, therefore making arbitration agreements like these invalid under an old doctrine making contracts against public policy unenforceable?

In 1925, Congress passed the Federal Arbitration Act, which required courts across the country to recognize and defer to arbitration clauses. However, the language of the act referred to such clauses being enforceable in "any maritime transaction or a contract evidencing a transaction involving commerce." The debate in Congress when the law was being considered clearly indicated that Congress was concerned that arbitration clauses negotiated at arm's length by two business parties, such as shippers, were being reneged on after the fact by one of them, who hoped to wear the other side down by engaging in a long, expensive battle in court. Given that context, state and federal judges had often refused to enforce the relatively few arbitration clauses they were asked to rule on before the 1990s that instead involved a consumer or employee in a dispute with a large company that had drafted and insisted on the clause.

These and other legal questions are what that consortium of corporate lawyers wrestled with at that 1999 meeting. Their goal, according to two lawyers who were there, was to bring a series of cases that would get the courts to establish a new, far broader meaning for the old Federal Arbitration Act. They faced multiple hurdles, beginning with the precedent of those earlier cases, where the clauses had been frowned on by judges who did not welcome ceding their turf to private tribunals and were skeptical of arbitrations that were far from the ones involving maritime transactions that Congress seemed to be trying to protect in passing the 1925 law. Also, the little data available from the generally secret arbitration panels indicated that they were likely to be stacked against the plaintiffs. The corporate defendants—who, according to the arbitration clauses, got to pick the ostensibly neutral referees or at least share in the selection process—were likely to pick those who had established records of being friendly to their side so that they might get chosen again. The plaintiffs, on the other hand, were one-time customers.

Despite all those hurdles, in 2011, lawyers who were part of the consortium persuaded the Supreme Court to strike down a California law that would have invalidated an arbitration clause written into an AT&T cell phone service contract. A lower federal court had upheld the state law on the ground that the arbitration clause enabled the company to escape any realistic chance of accountability if it had cheated consumers out of small amounts individually that could add up to hundreds of millions of dollars when aggregated in a class action. However, the Supreme Court reversed the lower court decision and ruled that even if the arbitration clause was unfair, "States cannot require a procedure that is inconsistent with the [Federal Arbitration Act], even if it is desirable for unrelated reasons."

In 2013, in another suit brought by the group, the Supreme Court all but wiped out any hope that class actions could survive arbitration clauses. A California restaurant owner had tried to file a class action anti-trust suit alleging that American Express's charges to merchants were unfairly high and an illegal use of the card's market power. Rejecting the argument that the credit company's boilerplate arbitration clause effectively eliminated the restaurant's ability to bring an anti-trust case that would involve legal fees that no single merchant could afford, Associate Justice Antonin Scalia ruled that "the antitrust laws do not guarantee an affordable procedural path to the vindication of every claim." Joining in Scalia's 5–3 majority decision was Chief Justice John Roberts, who as a Washington lawyer had represented clients in other cases seeking to protect arbitration clauses from judicial interference.

As was highlighted when Fox TV anchor Gretchen Carlson sued the then-CEO of the company, Roger Ailes, for sexual harassment in 2016, most employment contracts used by large corporations by then also had arbitration clauses similarly designed to put the dispute into a more friendly venue, keep it secret, and prevent it from becoming a class action.

It is difficult to overstate the degree to which the ubiquity of arbitration clauses has un-leveled the playing field by protecting corporate defendants who abuse their relationship with consumers or workers—and how this in turn has eaten away at the legitimacy of the American government. Every time an average American feels cheated or abused and discovers that he or she is bound by one of these clauses marks another moment when someone realizes that the system has failed—that moats have been dug even around America's treasured courthouses to protect those with power. I spent a good portion of my early career writing and editing articles about abusive plaintiffs' lawyers, particularly those who try to shake down corporations with frivolous class actions. Some of the businesses I have run have been the victim of frivolous suits, forced to incur painful legal fees to win cases that should never have been brought. However, there has to be a balance between curbing these abuses—with fines or even awards of attorneys' fees to defendants who are victimized—and eliminating the chance that average citizens can get civil justice. Instead, the corporate bar has been able to take advantage of the overreaching of many plaintiffs' lawyers to convince judges and legislatures to allow exactly that kind of wholesale locking of the courthouse doors.

Even American servicemen and -women fighting overseas have been unable to escape the damage. Following frequent instances of unfair treatment, two federal laws were passed during the war in Iraq to protect service members dealing with lenders, including one that required that debt collection court proceedings and similar efforts be suspended while a serviceman is overseas. However, in 2012 a judge ruled that because the laws did not specifically outlaw arbitration clauses in service members' loans, an Army National Guard sergeant could not bring a suit, let alone a class action, after an auto loan lender whose contract had included an arbitration clause had repossessed his family's Kia while he was fighting in Iraq.

Nursing home patients claiming to have suffered substandard care have also been unable to sue or bring class actions. In 2016, a federal judge, citing once again the arguments that the consortium successfully made in the Supreme Court, enjoined an Obama administration regulation from being enforced that would have prohibited nursing homes receiving Medicare or Medicaid funds from enforcing arbitration clauses. The Trump administration decided not to appeal.

The Dodd-Frank financial reform law presented the Trump White House and Republicans in Congress with their greatest challenge in defending arbitration clauses from the Obama administration's attempts to curb them. In July 2017, the Consumer Financial Protection Bureau—the agency set up under Dodd-Frank that was given broad independent powers—promulgated a rule prohibiting banks, credit card issuers, and other finance companies under its jurisdiction from embedding clauses in future consumer contracts forbidding class actions. The agency had issued a draft of the rule in mid-2016 following a long study-and-comment period culminating in a 728-page report that revealed how anti-arbitration clauses had all but eliminated the ability of credit card customers and other banking clients to redress deceptive practices. Although consumer rights groups and Democrats in Congress had made outlawing arbitration clauses an issue with strong populist appeal, lobbyists for the banking industry and the Chamber of Commerce fought back. Arguing that the government should not enrich greedy trial lawyers by interfering in contracts agreed to by private parties to forgo the courts in favor of arbitration, they quickly got the Republican-dominated House to pass a law repealing the regulation. In the Senate, where Republicans held only 52 of 100 seats, getting a majority to override the consumer protection agency's rule and once again allow forced arbitration seemed less likely.

By September 2017, tampering with the rule became still more politically difficult after Equifax, a leading credit rating agency, was revealed to have exposed the personal and financial records of nearly half of all Americans to hackers. After Equifax responded that to offset any damage the hack might have caused, it would provide free identity theft protection to anyone who wanted to sign up for it, there was an uproar when consumer groups complained that the company had slipped an arbitration clause governing any interaction the consumer had with Equifax into the small print of the document that consumers had to sign to get the free protection. The clause would have shielded the company from class actions related to its failure to protect the consumer's data. Equifax—and consumer arbitration clauses in general—were attacked by politicians on both sides of the aisle. The company abandoned attaching the clause to the identity theft protection agreements, and a flood of class action suits followed, seeking damages for the 145.5 million people whose private information had been compromised.

However, for foes of arbitration clauses the victory was short-lived. At 10:00 p.m. on the night of October 23, 2017, the Senate voted 50–50 to follow the House's lead and repeal the consumer protection bureau's prohibition on forced arbitration clauses, whereupon Vice President Mike Pence cast the tie-breaking vote in favor of the banks and other financial institutions. The law taking back the chance for a day in court for consumers cheated by credit card companies and banks, including servicemen and -women deployed overseas whose cars had been wrongfully repossessed, was the first significant legislative achievement for congressional Republicans and the Trump administration.

THE CORPORATE CRIME MOAT

In November 2016, the U.S. Department of Justice announced that JPMorgan Chase had agreed to pay $264.4 million in fines and criminal penalties for violating the Foreign Corrupt Practices Act, which prohibits American companies from bribing officials of a foreign government to get business. According to the settlement agreement, beginning in 2006 the bank's Asia subsidiary had systematically hired relatives of top Chinese government officials so that the officials, who controlled the process by which major government-owned enterprises launch stock offerings, would steer that lucrative business and other investment deals to the bank.

"The so-called Sons and Daughters Program was nothing more than bribery by another name," Leslie Caldwell, who ran the Justice Department's Criminal Division, announced in a press release. "Awarding prestigious employment opportunities to unqualified individuals in order to influence government officials is corruption, plain and simple. This case demonstrates the Criminal Division's commitment to uncovering corruption no matter the form of the scheme." It might have demonstrated a commitment to *uncovering* corruption, but holding actual people accountable for the corruption was another matter.

The press release referred to some of those involved as "senior bankers." An accompanying twenty-one-page statement of the facts, which both sides in the settlement had stipulated to, referred to "executives" and "senior bankers" having "institutionalized the practice of making hires for the purpose of winning business." A flood of internal emails subpoenaed by the investigators and quoted by the Justice Department in the statement of facts portrayed a practice that was common and, at least at the JPMorgan Asia unit, even a hot topic of office gossip. There was speculation that the "napping habit" of one of the Chinese princelings being transferred to the New York office would be "an eye opening experience for our New York colleagues." Another's skill with the office photocopier was described as surpassing anything she knew about investment banking. Promoting the daughter of a prominent official despite what an email called her "undeniable underperformance" was deemed necessary because the "deal is large enough [and] we are pregnant enough with this person, that we'd be crazy not to accommodate her father's wants."

Despite the juicy detail, neither the press release nor the supporting document included the name of a single person. Nor was anyone, let alone any of JPMorgan Chase's senior executives, charged. In fact, the papers referred mainly to the bank's Asia subsidiary, as if no one at the New York headquarters would have had any way of knowing what was going on in this key profit center, and even though some of the laughably incompetent hires were placed in the New York office.

Since 2010, JPMorgan had settled three other criminal cases by the time the Sons and Daughters deal was announced by paying hundreds of millions of dollars in fines and agreeing to clean up its act. The crimes involved helping to facilitate famed Ponzi-schemer Bernard Madoff's fraud, rigging bids on municipal bond offerings, and participating in an elaborate multibank conspiracy to defraud clients by fixing rates in a key $500-billion-a-day international exchange rate market. The bank had also paid fines and penalties (some of which were tax-deductible) of over $32.4 billion to resolve fifty-five Justice Department, SEC, and other enforcement proceedings alleging civil violations of various banking laws and regulations—including cheating credit card customers with fraudulent debt collection practices, manipulating electricity markets, illegally foreclosing on homes owned by people serving in the armed forces, and fraudulently selling toxic mortgage-backed securities in the run-up to the 2009 crash. In no case was a senior executive of the recidivist bank charged, nor has JPMorgan as a corporation ever had to plea to the kind of criminal charge that, under various banking laws and regulations, could result in the suspension or revocation of its banking licenses.

Most policymakers and prosecutors take the view that sidelining a giant bank or putting it out of business would cause too much collateral damage to employees, customers, other banks, and the economy as a whole. In 2013, that previously unspoken rationale was actually spoken when then–Attorney General Eric Holder told the Senate Judiciary Committee that he was "concerned that the size of some of these [financial] institutions becomes so large that it does become difficult for us to prosecute them when we are hit with indications that if you do prosecute, if you do bring a criminal charge, it will have a negative impact on the national economy, perhaps even the world economy."

In other words, if banks had to be bailed out because they were too big to fail, prosecuting them fully had to be avoided because they were also too big to jail. As with the bailout dilemma, that would seem like an argument for breaking up the giant banks. Instead, it has become, like too big to fail, yet another moat for America's most powerful businesses, allowing even recidivists like JPMorgan to escape effective accountability. Again, these kinds of moats eat away at the fabric of the American community, reminding average Americans that the basic rules of responsibility and accountability do not apply to those at the top.

The too-big-to-jail dilemma became more vivid in 2016 when a House of Representatives committee, following a three-year investigation, revealed in a report—titled "Too Big to Jail"—that English banking giant HSBC had been spared criminal prosecution in 2012 only after higher-ups in the Justice Department overrode the decision of the line prosecutors working the case. The prosecutors had wanted to charge the bank criminally for what they found was a prolonged practice of helping drug cartels launder money and allowing Iranian and Libyan entities linked to terrorism to evade sanctions.

When the HSBC non-prosecution deal had been announced in 2012, Oregon Democratic senator Jeff Merkley had charged that the Obama Justice Department's decision meant that "four years after the financial crisis, the Department appears to have firmly set the precedent that no bank, bank employee, or bank executive can be prosecuted." This follow-up investigation by the House Financial

Services Committee added voluminous detail to back that charge of a hands-off policy. A criminal indictment had been blocked, congressional investigators found, when higher-ups in the Justice Department expressed concerns in emails, memos, and phone calls about the potential fallout from bringing criminal charges against the bank. Although the prosecutors' frustrated internal emails described the unit of the bank as something akin to an organized crime operation, the final agreement only required that HSBC pay a $1.9 billion fine (which amounted to 14 percent of the year's profit) and enter into what is called a deferred prosecution agreement, which has become the fallback of choice for prosecutors going after big corporations. In return for no criminal prosecution, HSBC agreed to put new controls in place aimed at changing its behavior. The Justice Department also agreed not to prosecute any individual bankers. Nonetheless, the Justice Department press release announcing the deal proclaimed, "HSBC is being held accountable for stunning failures of oversight—and worse" that had made it the bank of choice for drug cartels and rogue nations.

Not a single HSBC employee was named in the announcement. Not prosecuting the corporation seemed at odds with that proclamation of accountability, but the even more troubling lapse was that once again no executives were held accountable.

Until 1909, no corporation in the United States was ever charged with a crime; only people working for corporations were. The prevailing legal doctrine had been that only actual people could have the guilty intent, called *mens rea*, necessary to be guilty of a crime. Corporations are paper entities, logos, or buildings—"artificial beings," as the Supreme Court put it in 1819—not people capable of making decisions. In the 1909 case, the High Court changed direction, ruling that because corporations had grown so big, they needed to be held accountable for acts committed by agents acting on their behalf. The ruling cleared the way for the New York Central Railroad Company, along with one of its salesmen, to be prosecuted for paying illegal rebates to a sugar company in return for its shipping business. "The Court will recognize that the greater part of interstate commerce is conducted by corporations, and it will not relieve them from punishment because at one time there was a doctrine that corporations could not commit crimes," the justices ruled.

The decision was seen as a breakthrough by reformers interested in making the justice system work more equitably. In many ways, it was. Why blame only a lowly employee for something he or she was pressured or forced to do by a big corporation? And why not be able at least to hold the corporation accountable if no person in the corporate labyrinth could be identified as the guilty party? Following Ralph Nader's crusade against unsafe cars in the 1960s, the prosecution of Ford for manslaughter after three teenagers died in the fiery crash of a Ford Pinto was hailed as a breakthrough in corporate accountability (although the company was acquitted because certain key evidence was ruled inadmissible). Other such corporate prosecutions have followed.

But in another unintended consequence, rather than be what the 1909 Supreme Court case envisioned—a way to hold *both* the corporation and the employees accountable—holding *only* the corporate entity responsible has become the default position. As with HSBC and the other banks, all of the focus was on whether to charge the corporation, and, if so, how high the fine should be. This typically allowed the people who run the corporations and preside over criminal behavior to be ignored.

Beyond being unfair and sending the message that the system is unfair, this undermines one of the core goals of criminal law: deterrence. An executive is far more likely to be deterred by the prospect of prison than by the threat that his corporation may have to plead guilty and his shareholders may have to pay a fine. Indeed, one of the abiding ironies of treating white-collar criminals so much more gingerly than those who commit street crimes is that the shame and life-changing nature of handcuffs and prison jumpsuits weigh so much more heavily on white-collar offenders than it may on street criminals, who might be less embarrassed or upended by a stint behind bars.

More important, shielding any significant group of people, especially the powerful, from accountability undermines the premise of a democratic society. America and any other democracy depends on its citizens adhering to some level of responsibility for the greater good, which obviously includes obeying the law. That in turn depends on those citizens assuming that they will be accountable if they are irresponsible. If the powerful don't feel the pull of accountability, they will continue to behave irresponsibly, and do more damage to the common good. Conversely, if one group of people, especially the powerful, is perceived by everyone else not to be accountable for their irresponsibility, then everyone else will feel less of an obligation to be responsible for the greater good and resist being accountable, too. This is what has happened in America. The system's glue has deteriorated almost completely. People have become cynical about the obligations of responsibility and resistant to the consequences of accountability because they see that those at the top aren't accountable. They have lost confidence in their government's capacity to deliver basic fairness. So they are looking out for themselves, reinforcing resentment and polarization as they focus on their narrow interests.

In 2016, *The Wall Street Journal* tallied all the charges brought against the big banks—including JPMorgan Chase, Citigroup, Bank of America, Morgan Stanley, Wells Fargo, and Goldman Sachs—for the fraud associated with the Great Recession. It was arguably the most destructive corporate misconduct ever—the sale of trillions of dollars' worth of securities tied to mortgages that were destined to go bust, and that subsequent investigations revealed the bankers either knew were likely to go bad, or knew enough to know that they should not pause from counting their bonus money to take the trouble to find out. (Remember the traders' favorite phrase: IBGYBG—"I'll be gone, you'll be gone.") The *Journal* found that in 81 percent of 156 criminal and civil cases brought against ten big Wall Street firms, no individuals were charged or even named in the suits. And of only forty-seven employees charged in the other 19 percent of the cases, only one was a corporate officer, who was charged in a civil case seeking a fine, which he settled. Only one employee, a lower-level executive at UBS Group, was cited as being charged criminally, and he was convicted in a bid-rigging case not directly associated with the crash. In all, the banks ended up paying $110 billion in fines to settle civil charges related to the crash that they caused. None of the corporations pled guilty to a crime associated with the crash.

When the federal commission investigating the causes of the crash completed its work in 2011, it sent a series of "referrals" to the Department of Justice outlining possible criminal conduct it had found at fourteen major financial institutions. The boxes of documents amassed during the inquiry, which the National Archives released for public inspection in 2016, could have provided a road map for prosecutions. One alleged "potential fraud" at Citigroup implicated the bank's CEO, Charles Prince, as well as former treasury secretary Robert Rubin, the chairman of the Citi board's executive committee. The referral cited "statements to the market [meaning stock analysts] in 2007 that the company had only $13 billion in subprime exposure when, in fact, the company ultimately disclosed $55 billion in subprime exposure." The referral further asserted, "It is clear that . . . Chuck Prince, and Robert Rubin . . . knew this information . . . no later than September 9, 2007," which was a month before they had made those statements to the market. Neither Rubin nor Prince was prosecuted (or even named in civil suits), nor were any executives at the other thirteen Wall Street firms named in the commission's referrals to the Justice Department.

"If they ever sent a referral to Justice, I was completely unaware of it," Rubin told me in 2017, adding, "Chuck [Prince] and I had no idea these [mortgage-backed securities] were anything but triple A, because that's what the ratings agencies said. This was just never something on our radar."

Prosecutors involved in these cases defend their record with two arguments. First, conduct that is negligent, stupid, reckless, or greedy is often not criminal (although knowingly hiding the disastrous results of that negligence, stupidity, recklessness, or greed in required financial disclosures would be). Second, proving beyond a reasonable doubt—with documents or credible testimony—that a top executive in a giant company actually knew about wrongdoing going on in an office a few floors below him or at an outpost on the other side of the world is difficult. How could it be proved that they knew their traders were selling mortgage-backed securities or credit default swaps that the traders knew were shaky?

As with Rubin's explanation, executives like Jamie Dimon of JPMorgan Chase can plausibly claim not to have had direct knowledge of, much less have participated in, the hiring of the Chinese princelings, the rigging of exchange rates in London, or anything else related to the four criminal pleas or non-prosecution agreements and fifty-five civil enforcement settlements that have taken place since he became CEO. All of that conduct may have contributed to profits, which determined his compensation. He and his top lieutenants may have pressured employees with sales or profit targets that were so high that the bankers and traders decided they had to break the law to reach them. They may even have suspected wrongdoing, but preferred not to probe. (Did any senior executive at JPMorgan Chase wonder why the Asian unit was hiring all of these offspring of top Chinese officials?) But that didn't prove guilt beyond a reasonable doubt.

As then–Attorney General Holder put it in a 2014 speech, "In some instances, it is simply not possible to establish knowledge of a particular scheme on the part of a high-ranking executive who is far removed from a firm's day-to-day operations." What he was conceding was that those at the top of large companies, who benefit most from the company's profits, cannot be held responsible for wrongdoing carried out in pursuit of those profits. "Too big to manage" had joined "too big to fail" and "too big to jail" in a trifecta of corporate moats. The benefits of corporate misconduct flow up, but responsibility and accountability get trapped in the CEO's personal moat: the company's massive organization chart.

Consider how differently the lawyers of the new meritocracy spun the rights and obligations of corporations when their goal was to free their corporate clients to finance their favorite political candidates or, as we shall see, evade regulations governing how they market their products. For those situations, they succeeded, courtesy of Martin Redish, in creating a legal doctrine that corporations had the same First Amendment rights as people. Yet when it comes to holding the *people* who run the most powerful corporations responsible for their misconduct, their lawyers have been able to get the legal system to treat their clients as if they were inseparable from their corporations and, therefore, could not be held responsible as if they were people.

Although there have been a handful of successful prosecutions of top executives in the last decade, much of what seems to have been the most obvious illegal conduct related to the 2008 crash went unpunished. The best example may be Angelo Mozilo, whose aggressive marketing of subprime mortgages at Countrywide Financial was detailed earlier. We saw how Mozilo was at the front of one of the major pipelines providing trillions of dollars' worth of what he conceded in internal emails were "toxic" mortgages to homeowners, and then selling them off in bundles as securities. In that sense, he was one of the bosses who began the daisy chain that ultimately took the economy down, causing so much hardship for so many Americans. It is clear from the emails and his testimony before the post-crash investigating commission that Mozilo set his company's loan policies. It seems equally clear from his emails that when he assured shareholders and the buyers of those mortgage-backed securities in SEC filings that his company's "loan quality remains extremely high," he did not always believe it.

In 2009, the SEC sued Mozilo in a luridly detailed fifty-two-page civil complaint alleging fraud associated with some $1.5 trillion in mortgages and mortgage-backed securities sales. Also included were charges of insider trading for exercising stock options and then selling the stock at a $139 million profit at a time when, the SEC charged, he knew his company's mortgages were on thin ice. The $139 million was on top of $200 million Mozilo had already taken in salary and stock-based bonuses from 2002 to 2005. Yet in 2010, the SEC allowed Mozilo to settle for $67.5 million in civil fines and penalties. In 2014, Bank of America, which had purchased Countrywide, agreed to pay a $16.6 billion civil settlement related to Countrywide's fraud. Mozilo, the man at the center of it all, was never prosecuted criminally.

A high-ranking Justice Department lawyer who assumed office after the Mozilo SEC settlement recalled initially being mystified by the failure to prosecute him. Soon it became apparent to the lawyer that there was a predisposition among most federal prosecutors in cases like these to seek big-dollar fines or guilty pleas by the corporation instead of going after individuals. Convicting people was just so much harder.

There was a subtle cultural dynamic at work, this Justice Department official concluded. The highly credentialed lawyers defending the targets were likely to be able to persuade their colleagues on the other side to pursue the easier path of getting a big headline by negotiating a big fine precisely because they *were* colleagues: They typically had gone to the same top law schools and often changed sides during their careers. Federal white-collar prosecutors went off to blue-chip law firms, and those from the corporate defense side did stints of public service in prestigious prosecutors' offices. It wasn't a matter of corruption. It was about a common mind-set. Rather than go through all the warfare and risk all the hurdles of overcoming reasonable doubt to put some banker in jail, it was much easier and more natural for the two sides to have long, even tough, negotiations over money and then come up with a deal that was a win for both: The defense lawyers protected the client from real accountability, while the prosecutors vindicated justice by winning billions for the taxpayers.

THE DRUG MAKERS' CORPORATE PLEA-BARGAINING MOAT

Another arena where that kind of cultural explanation has been in play in the last decade has to do with pharmaceutical companies reaping tens of billions in profits by aiming the marketing of their powerful prescription drugs at categories of patients the Food and Drug Administration (FDA) had told the companies not to market to. By 2016, eight of the nine major drug makers had paid billions of dollars over the prior decade for violating a criminal statute prohibiting what is called off-label marketing—promoting drugs for uses not approved by the FDA. Federal officials at the Department of Health and Human Services, the FDA, and the Justice Department in both the George W. Bush and Obama administrations regarded these violations as major white-collar crimes that endangered or even killed thousands of people. Yet while the corporations all pled guilty and paid large fines, no executives at the companies were prosecuted.

The FDA labeling regulations were seen as important steps in advancing public safety when the law establishing them was enacted in 1962. In the wake of scandals involving thalidomide—an antidote for nausea for pregnant women that caused them to produce deformed babies—President Kennedy signed a law beefing up the FDA and giving the agency the broad power it has today to vet and approve drugs. The laborious series of tests and clinical trials required under the new law would culminate in a drug being allowed to be marketed with an FDA-approved label, a dense document that tells doctors what a drug is supposed to be used for, what possible side effects to be aware of, and what the appropriate doses are.

The stringent process was pushed in the 1960s by Senator Estes Kefauver, a Tennessee Democrat. Kefauver was concerned about tight labeling and the need to police off-label sales. Once a drug was approved for any initial purpose, he argued, "the sky would be the limit and extreme claims of any kind could be made" about the safety and effectiveness of selling that drug for other uses. Because the FDA had not vetted it for those additional uses, off-label promotion would undermine the balance of benefits versus risks that the new law required the FDA to weigh. A drug might be worth the risk of significant side effects if it helped alleviate a schizophrenic's hallucinations or urge to commit suicide. It might not be worth the risk if it was used to treat a restless nursing home patient or a toddler acting up in kindergarten.

The FDA, however, has no authority to regulate how doctors practice, including what drugs they prescribe. A physician who believes that a drug approved by the regulators for one purpose can be useful for another purpose is free to prescribe it for the other, off-label purpose. That flexibility and encouragement to innovate has often been beneficial; aspirin was found to be useful in reducing the risk of heart attacks or strokes, and many drugs developed to attack one kind of cancer have been found to work on other strains. However, if drug companies were not required to get a labeling change from the FDA before marketing a product more widely, they would have little incentive to undertake the clinical studies necessary to test the safety of the drug when deployed for those new uses. Why test whether a drug approved only for adults is safe for children if you can market it to children anyway?

Over the years, the FDA had navigated this issue with rules dictating that doctors, researchers, or other objective parties could write articles in medical journals noting that an off-label use had been productive, but if the authors were paid or the research had been sponsored by the drug company whose product was being blessed, that sponsorship had to be disclosed. Moreover, no article or study touting an off-label use could be marketed proactively to doctors or others who didn't ask for the material. It could only be published in medical journals where doctors who were interested might find it.

In the 1990s drug companies began running roughshod over those rules. A prime example, which was the subject of a 2015 series I

wrote for *The Huffington Post*, was Johnson & Johnson's off-label promotion of the powerful anti-psychotic drug Risperdal to children and
the elderly. Although the FDA had repeatedly rejected Johnson &
Johnson's efforts to get Risperdal approved for children, the company
engaged in a broad multi-year campaign to pay prominent pediatric
psychiatrists to hold conferences praising the drug's efficacy in helping children with behavior disorders or attention deficits. A separate
nationwide salesforce was deployed to distribute sales materials and
samples to pediatricians, aimed at encouraging them to prescribe the
drug for their young patients. Child-friendly Risperdal-labeled pop-
corn packages and Legos with the Risperdal logo were given to the
pediatricians' nurses during these sales calls for distribution in the
waiting room, creating the sense for parents and kids alike that this
powerful anti-psychotic was a routine, and fun, part of children's lives.

An elder care sales unit was set up to target the elderly—the other
population that had specifically been walled off by the FDA because
Risperdal was thought to risk strokes, diabetes, and other side effects
in that group. Companies providing pharmacy services to nursing
homes were offered special rebate plans.

Pre-trial discovery in suits subsequently brought against Johnson
& Johnson revealed evidence that at the same time that these off-label
marketing campaigns flourished, Johnson & Johnson had altered or
covered up research indicating what the FDA had feared: that the
drug caused young boys to grow large breasts and that the elderly
faced increased risks of strokes, diabetes, and other ailments. Nonetheless, by 2001, seven years after Risperdal had been approved by
the FDA only for severe psychotic disorders in non-elderly adults,
two thirds of all prescriptions were going for off-label uses, typically
to alleviate anxiety or even sleeplessness in elderly nursing home
patients and to control attention deficit disorder and other behavioral issues in children as young as three years old. Despite evidence
accumulated in the subsequent litigation, when the FDA began asking about the prescription data and about sales materials it had seen
that were clearly aimed at doctors treating children and the elderly,
the company insisted that it was doing no proactive marketing, just
responding to demand.

In a deposition conducted in 2012 as part of one of thousands
of suits later brought on behalf of the young boys who had grown

large breasts, Johnson & Johnson CEO Alex Gorsky was shown cop-
ies of his company's business plan for the year 2000 that called sales of
Risperdal into the children's market a "Key Base Business Goal and
Objective." He was asked how he could have pursued that goal legally
if Risperdal was not allowed to be marketed to doctors treating children. "Well, my interpretation of that is," he answered, "[that] this is
in fact a marketing plan, not a selling plan. As a marketing plan, its
intent is to cover a wide range of activities regarding the development
as well as the promotion of Risperdal." Everything Johnson & Johnson had done had been "appropriate," Gorsky insisted.

From 2013 through 2017, those answers did not cut it with juries,
who awarded millions of dollars in damages to families of boys who
were deformed after taking Risperdal. Thousands of similar suits
were settled during that period, adding up to more than $800 million
in legal fees and civil suit payouts. Nor did the company's denials fly
with the government, which in November 2013 cut a deal with Johnson & Johnson in which the company paid $2.2 billion in fines and
penalties and pled guilty to one criminal count of selling Risperdal
off-label. The company had "recklessly put at risk the health of some
of the most vulnerable members of our society—including young
children, the elderly and the disabled," Attorney General Holder
declared at a press conference.

Profit from Risperdal sales in the United States totaled approximately $18 billion, at least half of which was probably derived from
off-label sales to children and the elderly. If $3 billion ends up being
spent to deal with all of the remaining litigation, a high-end estimate,
and with about $3 billion already paid out in verdicts, settlements,
and legal fees, that would add up to Johnson & Johnson having spent
$6 billion to clean up after all of the alleged illegal conduct. That
means the company will still have cleared $3 billion from its off-
label sales. The worst possible result of the company's lawbreaking—
getting caught red-handed and being buried in lawsuits that end up
with terrible verdicts or settlements—was still highly profitable. The
American justice system had been transformed by those who operate
it into a system that rewarded one of America's largest and best known
companies for breaking the law and risking the health and even the
lives of the country's children and elderly. It is difficult to imagine a
moat more destructive to the country.

On the last trading day before the $2.2 billion settlement with the Justice Department was announced, Johnson & Johnson stock closed at $93.37. A week after the announcement, it closed at $94.29. A year later, as thousands of Risperdal personal injury suits were pending, it would be at $108.62. It kept rising through 2017, despite hundreds of pending Risperdal suits, as well as litigation related to other allegedly defective or dangerous J&J products, including its iconic talcum powder.

On the regular calls with Wall Street analysts who follow Johnson & Johnson stock, a question about these suits almost never came up. "This is a company with $19 billion a year in profit, even with those lawsuits," one analyst explained to me. "If they pay out a billion or two a year, we don't really care."

The arena, then, to hold such companies accountable would seem to be applying the criminal law to those responsible. Again, Johnson & Johnson was one of nine major drug companies that were prosecuted for the same dangerous and criminal behavior. Beyond the fact that because of its popular consumer products (baby powder, Listerine, Band-Aids, Visine) it is an American business icon, what was especially intriguing about Johnson & Johnson's case was that the chief executive when its federal criminal case was settled, Alex Gorsky, had been the Risperdal sales manager and then head of the J&J division that included Risperdal during its explosive sales growth. Yet like the other drug companies' top executives, he was untouched personally by the government's discovery of his company's criminal conduct. In fact, he was awarded a 48 percent raise in salary and bonus, to $25 million, in the year following the $2.2 billion plea bargain.

Here was one case, it seemed, where "too big to manage" should have been irrelevant; the current CEO had been in charge of selling the product at the center of the illicit marketing activity before he had moved up the ladder. Documents the government subpoenaed during its investigation placed Gorsky at meetings related to the conduct that the government prosecuted and showed him on email chains that discussed it. When, as Johnson & Johnson's CEO, Gorsky was asked in that 2012 deposition to explain the Risperdal business plan for the year 2000 that targeted children despite the FDA's prohibition on marketing to them, he was being asked to explain the business plan that he was in charge of.

So why wasn't Gorsky charged? Why instead was Johnson & Johnson allowed, like the other drug companies, to pay a fine and have the corporation (actually, only its drug subsidiary) plead guilty to one crime, a misdemeanor associated only with its marketing to the elderly?

In 2015, when I attempted to find the answers for *The Huffington Post*, the prosecutors who had worked on the Johnson & Johnson case seemed surprised by the question. As we sat in their conference room in Philadelphia, they looked at me blankly, as if I didn't understand that getting the $2.2 billion fine and the misdemeanor plea was a big victory, squeezed out over months of tense negotiations. One of the lawyers involved later said that the idea of prosecuting Gorsky had been mentioned casually by the prosecutors at the start of the negotiations, but that it was never brought up again as the talks continued, and that no one on either side had considered it a serious possibility. Instead, the bargaining was focused on the kinds of issues the lawyers now considered standard in the game: the amount of the fine, the conduct that would be specified and acknowledged and how it would be worded, and the terms and text of a long agreement that would spell out the controls and monitoring that the company would put in place to prevent future illegal marketing.

Johnson & Johnson wanted to admit only to marketing the drug illegally to the elderly, because the heirs of old people who might have been killed by the drug were unlikely to recover much if anything if they brought civil suits. (Even the best plaintiffs' lawyer would have trouble proving what caused an eighty-five-year-old's stroke, much less what the money damages to the family should be.) Young boys who had decades ahead of them of living with a deformity, on the other hand, were already plaintiffs in thousands of suits, so admitting to conduct that might have harmed them could have further undermined the company's already shaky defense in these cases. A compromise was struck: The government would cite both the elderly and the children as victims, but Johnson & Johnson would only admit to having marketed to the elderly illegally and settle the charges about the children without admitting or denying them. Another issue that had to be negotiated was what would be categorized as a criminal fine and what would be termed a civil penalty. Penalties can be tax-deductible if structured correctly, so moving the line $100 million or more one way or the other meant millions in corporate savings, which was well worth the time of the $1,000-an-hour lawyers.

To anyone outside the process—and certainly to the victims of the illegal conduct whose consequences are being bargained away—this kind of gamesmanship should be appalling because it undermines the core values of responsibility and accountability on which America and its legal system depend. Yet lawyers on both sides of this high-stakes, white-collar plea bargaining have come to love the game. It advances everyone's career, even if it doesn't advance justice.

Like friends engaged in a fierce tennis match, there's a collegiality binding both sides. Zane Memeger was the U.S. attorney in Philadelphia when the Johnson & Johnson deal was negotiated. An affable lawyer with a sterling résumé, Memeger was part of the club. He had won awards as a government prosecutor before becoming a partner and white-collar crime specialist at one of Philadelphia's largest corporate firms. He had then been appointed U.S. attorney by President Obama in 2010, allowing him to catch the tail end of the office's high-profile off-label marketing cases. In 2017, he was back at his old firm doing white-collar defense work. The page on the firm's website describing Memeger's recent client service listed "assisted a foreign-based pharmaceutical company resolve criminal and civil allegations of off label marketing," and "assisted a major medical device company resolve criminal and civil allegations of Anti-Kickback Statute."

Johnson & Johnson's Gorsky has remained one of America's most admired CEOs, running one of America's most admired companies, according to polls of business leaders. He regularly receives the awards and appointments to prestige panels that go with that stature, including the Presidential Medal of Honor board of directors and the IBM board of directors. Just ten months after negotiating the corporate plea bargain related to criminal conduct that the attorney general said had recklessly endangered "young children, the elderly and the disabled," Gorsky, a graduate of the University of Pennsylvania's Wharton business school, would be toasted at a dinner of the school's New York alumni society, where he was given the Joseph Wharton Leadership Award. Six days after that, at a Washington gala he would be honored as the "Humanitarian of the Year" by CADCA, the Community Anti-Drug Coalitions of America.

BIG BUSINESS'S FIRST AMENDMENT MOAT

As the Johnson & Johnson lawyers were finishing their negotiation with the Philadelphia prosecutors, the J&J board asked them about a possible defense that had been bubbling under the surface for more than a decade and that now seemed to be emerging into something useful. The board members had started grousing that they should dig in and fight using the argument that the First Amendment allowed them to do the marketing they were being prosecuted for. In Washington, lawyers at the Justice Department as well as the Department of Health and Human Services, more so than their Philadelphia colleagues, saw that as potentially more than a bluff. They had already been brushed back in the federal courts by exactly that First Amendment claim.

By 2013, Martin Redish's idea that corporations, too, had free speech rights had been spilling over from court challenges to limits on corporate-financed political speech to challenges related to the basic ways government regulated commerce—restrictions on billboards, limits on cigarette advertising, disclosure standards for financial advisers, prohibitions on gun dealers setting up sales booths at county fairs. The courts—and Redish's Harvard Law School thesis theory—had come a long way since Ralph Nader's lawyers had persuaded the Supreme Court to throw out that Virginia law prohibiting drugstores from advertising their prices. With the ascent of more conservative judges to the courts, including the Supreme Court, the emphasis on commercial speech benefiting the rights of the listener (the reasoning in the Virginia case) had gradually been supplemented by a more radical, libertarian deregulatory rationale. Absent some overriding danger allowing the government to interfere, which libertarians rarely find, corporations, like people, ought to be free to speak, the libertarians argued.

In 2011, the Supreme Court handed down a decision that would have been startling thirty-five years before, when its ruling providing a First Amendment right for drugstores to advertise their prices seemed to have been a victory for the consumer rights movement. The court overturned a Vermont statute that prohibited the sale and use of data that revealed the prescribing practices of individual doctors unless the doctors gave permission for their data to be sold. The data was collected and sold by a company that supplied it to drug companies so that they could target the doctors for sales calls. It was a decision that placed more emphasis on the data corporation's right to "speak," and how it was being discriminated against because it was a commercial operation, than it did on the rights of the other commercial operation in the relationship—the drug company—to "listen" to the speech. Moreover, by categorizing the sale of the data as speech, the court was moving toward categorizing most of what corporations do to transact business—write contracts, sell information about stocks, label its products, collect and distribute data, produce advertisements—as speech that could not be restricted absent some overriding danger.

A variety of other decisions in the last two decades have taken the same approach. They include a challenge to a District of Columbia law requiring that tour guides be licensed (shouldn't anyone have a free speech right to give visitors a tour?), and a case overturning the government's right to require graphic depictions of the dangers of tobacco on cigarette packages (based on long-standing legal doctrine, rooted in a case forbidding students from being required to salute the flag, that the First Amendment's free speech protections also included the right *not* to speak). In most of these cases, organizations such as the Washington Legal Foundation or the Pacific Legal Foundation, founded in the 1970s by conservative donors and now financed in large part by business interests seeking freedom from regulation, brought or assisted in the litigation.

Not all the cases had gone in the same direction. A federal law requiring "factual and non-controversial" country-of-origin information on meat labels was upheld, for example. But amid the volume of all these challenges, the trend was clear. In perhaps the most radical commercial speech decision yet, a majority opinion written in 2015 by Supreme Court associate justice Clarence Thomas, a libertarian-minded skeptic of restricting corporate speech, and joined in by, among others, liberal Justice Sonia Sotomayor, overturned a local ordinance in Arizona that imposed different rules for outdoor signs based on what they were advertising.

Signs promoting or directing people to events being held by non-profit organizations, or signs pointing to a church parking lot, did not require permits under the Gilbert, Arizona, town ordinance. The same kinds of signs related to commercial events, or even directing motorists where to park at commercial facilities, did have to apply for permits. Thomas's opinion went beyond ruling that such discrimination was unconstitutional; he declared that *all* laws that discriminate on the basis of the content of speech are "presumptively unconstitutional" and therefore must be thrown out unless they pass a burdensome "strict scrutiny" test showing that the state has a "compelling interest" in the law rather than simply a rational interest.

In a concurring opinion, Justice Elena Kagan found that the ordinance could have been overturned because it so obviously discriminated based on no logical rationale. However, she argued, Thomas's sweeping holding went too far. The town's sign restrictions were so irrational that they didn't even pass a "laugh test," she declared, but as a result of Thomas's far more sweeping decision on behalf of the Court's majority, regulations relating to all kinds of signage would now be mired in the courts, because:

> courts would have to determine that a town has a compelling interest in informing passersby where George Washington slept. And likewise, courts would have to find that a town has no other way to prevent hidden-driveway mishaps than by specially treating hidden-driveway signs. (Well-placed speed bumps? Lower speed limits? Or how about just a ban on hidden driveways?) The consequence . . . is that our communities will find themselves in an unenviable bind: They will have to either repeal the exemptions that allow for helpful signs on streets and sidewalks, or else lift their sign restrictions altogether and resign themselves to the resulting clutter.

Lower courts have since relied on the Supreme Court's decision in this case to overturn laws restricting panhandling and "robo" telemarketing calls. A broad cross section of lawyers believes it could put all kinds of other regulations—SEC laws governing what stockbrokers can say to clients, for example, or rules about how cigarettes can be advertised—in jeopardy, too.

Martin Redish told me he regards decisions like the signage case, or challenges to tobacco advertising, as "breakthroughs for freedom and a blow against hypocrisy. . . . If you don't like cigarettes, ban them; don't restrict what people can know about a legal product." Similarly, he wants to force a binary choice when it comes to drug marketing, rather than allow the old regime that gave doctors the flexibility to try off-label prescriptions while not encouraging drug companies to flood the market with sales pitches for non-approved uses. "If the government doesn't like off-label use," he said, "then they should have the guts to ban doctors from doing it, period. They won't because they know it helps millions of people." It can also kill them.

While other lawyers on his side have fought cases like those involving the Gilbert sign ordinance, Redish has been churning out scholarly articles. In 2016, an academic study declared him the thirteenth most cited legal scholar of all time. Redish has also pursued commercial speech frontiers that are, in a word, more commercial than fights over street signs. Working for the prominent Chicago law firm Sidley Austin, he has produced white papers making the case against laws aimed at curbing childhood obesity by prohibiting the advertising of sugary cereals on television shows targeted at children. (His paper argued that adults may be watching the programs with their kids and have a right to see the ads.) He also authored a law review article in early 2017 making the case that scientific claims by those selling a product should not be unlawful if they turn out to be false if the person making the claims cannot be shown to have known they were false or to have been reckless about ascertaining whether they were false. The article is weak on defining knowing falsity or recklessness when it comes to drug companies making what turn out to be false or even dangerous claims about their products, although its reasoning parallels legal doctrine in libel cases that requires that on issues of public concern a plaintiff must prove that a speaker knew what he was saying was false or that he spoke with reckless disregard for its truth or falsity.

Some of Redish's most prominent work has been the academic backup he has provided for a coalition cofounded by Sidley lawyers on behalf of drug industry clients aimed at overturning the kind of marketing restrictions that Johnson & Johnson paid $2.2 billion in fines for violating. As the J&J board members knew when they complained about having to pay the fine, the fight had been brewing for more than fifteen years. It started with a 1997 suit filed in federal court in Washington by the conservative Washington Legal Foundation—with financing from the drug companies, the foundation's chief lawyer conceded—challenging the FDA guidelines for when and how information related to off-label uses of a drug could be disseminated to doctors.

The core of the argument tracked Redish's original listener's rights doctrine: The drug companies wanted to provide factual information to doctors about the potentially valuable off-label uses of a drug. Doctors, who are certainly professionally equipped to evaluate the information, should have the opportunity to receive it without having to ask for it proactively, they argued. Patients deserve the benefit of having their doctors receive and weigh as much information as possible.

The FDA replied that this was a path back to the thalidomide disaster. Once a drug company got a product approved for one narrow category or disease or patient, it could, as J&J was doing when this case was filed, expand its market exponentially without going through years of a multi-stage clinical testing and approval process that was far more rigorous than having a doctor, who might be being paid by the drug company, try the drug on a few dozen patients and report his results (or not report them if the results were negative).

In 1998, the FDA had survived the Washington Legal Foundation's legal challenge with a procedural maneuver. The agency then spent more than a decade sidestepping litigation or threats of litigation brought in Washington and other courts where Republican appointees dominated the bench. Then in August 2012, the Second Circuit Court of Appeals—the New York–based court that is a rung below the Supreme Court—had thrown out the conviction of a drug company's salesman for selling drugs off-label, ruling that his pitches were protected by the First Amendment. Three years later, a federal district court judge in Manhattan (who was appointed by President Obama), citing that appellate court decision, ruled that a drug company could provide truthful promotional materials about its cholesterol drug to doctors who might want to use it for patients whose cholesterol levels were below the extremely high level for which the FDA had limited its approved use. Fearing a loss, the government did not appeal.

The drug company's lawyer in that case was Floyd Abrams, the famed First Amendment litigator who had represented *The New York Times* in the 1971 case prohibiting the Nixon administration from blocking the publication of the Pentagon Papers.* Abrams had also

---

* Abrams has represented me or companies that I have run in several First Amendment suits.

filed a friend-of-the-court brief opposing corporate campaign spending limits in *Citizens United*, and had represented cigarette makers in fighting off more stringent disclosure notices on their packaging. When Standard & Poor's was sued beginning in 2009 by investors and the government for the conflict-filled favorable credit ratings it consistently gave to banks selling toxic mortgage-backed securities, Abrams used, among other defenses, a claim that bond ratings were "opinions" protected by the First Amendment. The cases were ultimately settled, with S&P paying more than $1.3 billion to the federal and state governments and to private parties.

As they had in Abrams's cholesterol drug case, in the last years of the Obama administration, Justice Department and FDA lawyers held back on pushing the drug labeling issue, despite their adamant view that the court's liberation of the drug companies threatened the regime of drug testing and labeling begun in the 1960s. They were hoping to get relief in the form of a newly aligned Supreme Court after the 2016 election brought Democrat Hillary Clinton to the White House.

Through the summer and fall of 2016, the FDA had engaged in a holding action of sorts, by declaring that in light of recent court decisions a loosening of some of its restrictions, as it had done with the cholesterol drug, was being considered. The agency even scheduled a two-day hearing at its Maryland headquarters, which began the morning after Election Day, to solicit comments from industry representatives and from those who opposed the industry's push for a freer rein.

Then–FDA commissioner Robert Califf, who opened the session, was non-committal, saying only that "The issues related to . . . communications about unapproved uses are numerous and complex." By then it was clear to the industry lawyers that with the Trump era dawning, Califf didn't matter. With a Scalia-like libertarian replacement likely on the way to the Supreme Court, freedom from the FDA's restrictions seemed a foregone conclusion.

Although lawyers who represent clients before the FDA are typically measured in expressing any disagreement with their all-powerful regulators, by mid-morning the gloves were off.

"In failing to address or even mention First or Fifth Amendment requirements, the hearing notice itself suggests that the agency does not appreciate or may be unwilling to accept the limits imposed by the Constitution," Kellie Combs, a lawyer representing a coalition of drug and device makers called the Medical Information Working Group, told Califf and other FDA senior officials assembled in the auditorium. "Rather than asking how to conform agency regulations to constitutional requirements, the notice starts from the premise that the FDA has the authority to determine for itself what truthful, non-misleading speech is valuable . . . and what speech it will prevent. That is not how the Constitution works."

The man who took FDA commissioner Califf's job in the Trump administration—Scott Gottlieb, a doctor and entrepreneur, who had been a Resident Fellow at the American Enterprise Institute—had long opposed the off-label promotion restrictions and the way the government had forced the drug makers to pay billions of dollars in settlements for violating them. In 2012, he had written in an American Enterprise Institute white paper that "A fear of investigation has put many drug makers on the extreme defensive. . . . In highly specialized fields in which communication concerns truthful, non-misleading scientific material, physicians should be trusted to properly weigh a wide variety of information."

Until the post-election 2016 FDA hearing, drug industry lawyers had been careful to assure skeptics that their clients only wanted the freedom to communicate that kind of truthful or non-misleading, data-heavy information (such as the results of studies) to doctors and to the insurance companies and pharmacy benefit managers that need the information to decide whether a drug should be covered on an insurance claim. However, information directed only at doctors or other professionals is not a limit that Redish and other lawyers working for the drug companies have ever conceded in claiming their First Amendment rights. At that November 9 hearing, with the Trump administration now about to take over, the industry apparently felt free to be unabashed about that. Coleen Klasmeier, another lawyer representing the Medical Information Working Group, who had co-authored white papers with Redish, said that information about the off-label uses of drugs should also be allowed to be given to consumers through the kinds of ads that Americans (unlike citizens of most other countries) now see on television and in magazines: "If it's truthful, then the Constitution is agnostic as to audience," she declared.

Even truthful is not necessarily a requirement. Referring to the article he had recently written on the subject, Redish reminded me a few months after the hearing that he believed that if his clients' *opinion* is that a drug may be safe and effective for an off-label use, they should be allowed to communicate it—a position that would track exactly the hard-line view of Gorsky and some of his fellow Johnson & Johnson board members before the lawyers convinced them to settle.

Moreover, Redish took the view that even if the FDA does not believe the drug is effective or safe, the company's expression of a contrary opinion would be constitutionally protected as long as the statement is made in good faith and does not include any incorrect facts. "If the First Amendment means anything, it prohibits government from suppressing one side of a political debate because it fears that the public might be convinced to make 'the wrong' choice," he wrote in a 2011 article coauthored with Klasmeier.

At the post-election FDA hearing where Klasmeier spoke, Joshua Sharfstein, a former FDA principal deputy commissioner in the Obama administration, reminded his former colleagues of the thalidomide era that preceded the current rules, and pleaded for caution. "Off-label promotion," he argued, "reduces the incentives for research to know what really works. If companies can get products sold without ever doing the definitive studies, everybody loses. And having people argue or having judges determine what in the gray area can be said or not said is just so much worse than having the evidence that really should be guiding patient care. . . . There are major risks to public health in an ahistorical, ideological view of the First Amendment."

As of the end of 2017, the FDA had not yet formally reversed off-label promotion regulations, but the consensus in the industry and among industry lawyers was that the enforcement efforts that had been an FDA and Justice Department priority in the prior two decades of Democratic and Republican administrations had ended and that rules promulgating a formal rollback were in the works. The First Amendment now seemed on the verge of giving drug companies the "sky's the limit" freedom that Senator Kefauver worried about more than fifty years ago.

In a 2016 law review article looking across the landscape of these developments, legal scholar Amanda Shanor concluded that because nearly everything associated with commerce involves speech, a continuation of the trend "would presumptively preclude regulation of fraud, malpractice, business licensing, drug warning labels, consumer and environmental spill disclosures. . . . This argument calls on the First Amendment, long cited as the mainstay of democracy, to undo self-government."

Even now lawyers representing big business have been able over the last fifty years to turn a constitutional right meant to level the playing field by giving every citizen an equal right to speak into a moat that gives their clients freedom from regulations meant to protect those citizens. As Shanor points out, they have succeeded with the help of conservative judges who once claimed to be adamantly against judicial interference, but who have blazed a path for the courts to interfere in, and subvert, the most basic governmental functions. It may be the most hypocrisy-laced aspect of America's tailspin.

FIRST AMENDMENT MOAT BUSTERS

In 2017, Shanor was a Yale Law School graduate who had stayed on to complete a PhD. Her mentor was the school's then-dean, Robert Post, who has led a group of increasingly frustrated First Amendment scholars determined to rebut Redish, Abrams, and the growing number of judges who have ruled that speech should be protected, no matter who is speaking or whether the speech is advancing purely commercial interests or infecting the election process. To Post and his confreres, those on the other side have hijacked the First Amendment much the way conservatives during the New Deal hijacked the guarantee of due process to get the courts, briefly, to overturn commercial regulations in areas such as minimum wage laws on the theory that they were violations of the right to engage in commercial contracts.

Like every legal academic who knows Post and his work, Redish acknowledged that "he's a towering intellect and a terrific person." But a breath later he dismissed Post and his allies as "hypocritical liberals who claim to care about intellectual consistency until it gets in the way of the result they want."

"This probably drives Robert crazy," Shanor said, "but people like

Redish have a simple, compelling, alluring argument that judges like [swing-vote Supreme Court associate justice Anthony] Kennedy like: Speech is speech. Why not just treat everything the same and give everything strict scrutiny?"—meaning that the courts would have to apply the Constitution's most stringent test to every restriction of any kind on commercial speech. "That's absurd," she continued. "We use speech for so many purposes and in so many contexts that it makes no sense to have one rule to cover writing a contract, advertising, student speech, tax returns, or speech in the military."

Couldn't the courts just apply the strict scrutiny rule to all of that and decide accordingly?

"You really want the courts judging everything on the same basis?" she said. "You want them deciding that some disclosure line on a tax return isn't truly necessary and therefore is unconstitutional, compelled speech, but that another line is okay? Then, you have the courts truly managing the government."

"I'm not a sound-bite kind of person," Post said. "I've been working on this for years. It's complicated and I want to get it right. As I work it through, I publish more and more of it." However, Post, like Shanor, has generally confined himself to dry books and academic journals, in which he tries to explain the nuanced intellectual underpinnings of his counter-theory in what may seem to laymen like exactly the contorted, convoluted reasoning that Redish accuses him of.

Boiled down to its basics, Post's argument is that everything may involve words, and, therefore, speech, but the only speech the Founding Fathers meant to protect was speech having to do with what Post calls "public discourse." Speech for other purposes is not protected and may be regulated in the normal course of governing. For example, a doctor who gives a patient the wrong advice can be sued for malpractice, but the same doctor who writes an op-ed piece suggesting that patients generally should take the same advice is engaging in protected public discourse, not transacting with a patient. The challenge is how to define "public discourse" in a crisp, intellectually consistent way when the context is more complicated. Is a drug company's marketing to thousands of doctors or millions of patients, urging its product to be used off-label, public discourse? No, Post would argue, because the purpose of the speech is transactional—to get doctors to prescribe or patients to buy, not to advance a general debate about the efficacy of the drug.

"If you go back to the idea that commercial speech was supposed to be for the benefit of the listener, and not to vindicate some libertarian idea that began springing up in the seventies that everyone, even corporations, should be free to say anything," Shanor added, "then you can make the argument that not allowing a drug company to market beyond a drug's approved use will incent them to conduct more clinical trials [to get the drug approved for new uses], which provides more information to the listener—in this case the doctors or the patients." Post pointed out that many, probably a near-majority, of federal judges (some of whom he has trained) still share this view. He is confident, he said, that more will when they agree, as Shanor concluded, that seeing all speech as protected speech will lead to a government that cannot govern. However, "for now," he said in a moment that bared the soft-spoken professor's frustration and fear of how the bench might be stacked in the Trump era, "We're fucked. It's totally clear."

THE WALL STREET MOAT BUSTER

Dennis Kelleher's K Street office, full of video monitors and framed newspaper clips commemorating his firm's exploits, looks like the home of a typical K Street lobbyist. The boss looks the part, too. A former congressional staffer and partner at Skadden Arps (the firm propelled to the top by takeover lawyer Joe Flom), Kelleher wears bespoke shirts and elegantly tailored suits. And he can talk in only-in-Washington acronyms like the best of insiders. Kelleher *is* a lobbyist—but he lobbies against many of the other lobbyists through a non-profit organization called Better Markets, of which he is the president.

Born into a family in central Massachusetts that, he said, lived in a housing project and was on food stamps "for a while," Kelleher went to Skadden Arps after graduating from Harvard Law School in 1987, having spent four years in the Air Force before that. He became a partner in 1996, handling merger deals out of the firm's Boston office. He took a year off to work for Senator Edward Kennedy, returned to the firm, and then went back to Capitol Hill in 2004, holding down a series of increasingly senior staff positions.

Kelleher is not modest about his stature or his sense of self-sacrifice. He left Skadden Arps, he said, speaking with a heavy New England accent, "because too many brilliant people spend their time making rich people richer. I didn't think the world needed another one. . . . I had seen the perversion of the legal profession up close. It's unbelievable how amoral and nihilistic it has become. No matter what your client wants to do, you figure out how to do it. . . . Most people who make it never look back. I did."

In the wake of the crash, Kelleher worked for Democrats on Capitol Hill who were pushing to make Dodd-Frank as tough as possible. "It failed in a lot of ways," he said, "but Dodd-Frank was the best that the political process could produce at that time under the circumstances, which is saying something." Once Dodd-Frank was passed, Kelleher began thinking about what to do next. "I was on a first-name basis with senators," he said. "I was offered millions to be a lobbyist, but I wanted to do something for the world. . . . I've never seen a U-Haul attached to a hearse."

During the Dodd-Frank deliberations Kelleher had met Michael Masters, a successful hedge fund manager from Atlanta who had embarked on a crusade of sorts, testifying in Congress that the financial markets needed to be cleaned up. "Mike was looking for someone to give money to so he could start some kind of group to work on that and then could go home," Kelleher recalled. "We hit it off, but I told him I was a big institutions guy—Skadden, the Air Force, Congress—not a start-up guy. But he promised me $3 million a year for five years so we could pay people more than the usual non-profit, and I became a start-up guy."

Since then, Kelleher and a staff of eighteen at Better Markets, including some drawn from the ranks of congressional aides who would have been likely recruits for more conventional lobby shops, have become a constant if unusual presence at hearings and in the offices of the agencies that write rules like the ones that followed the passage of Dodd-Frank. "We're the only game in town, when it comes to this stuff," Kelleher said, "so we have to be all over the place, and we are."

Kelleher has also become a go-to source for reporters looking for the other side of the story told by the financial community when it complains about regulations, or pushes to water them down. He has learned to be quick with irresistible quotes. The Trump administration is "government by Goldman Sachs." Some of the Democratic-oriented political groups and think tanks are filled with people "who feel good when they go to sleep at night but don't accomplish anything" and "are the same back-scratching Democrats who preach moderation while they take money to do events with people like [Goldman CEO Lloyd] Blankfein."

When the government settled with Goldman Sachs for $5.1 billion for its involvement in selling the toxic mortgage-backed securities and other dubious financial instruments that caused the crash, Kelleher pointed at tax credits and deductions hidden in the deal, telling a *New York Times* reporter that the government had "grossly inflated the settlement amount for P.R. purposes to mislead the public, while in the fine print enabling Goldman Sachs to pay 50 to 75 percent less. The problem all along, with all of these settlements—and this one highlights it even more—is that they are carefully crafted more to conceal than reveal to the American public what really happened here—and what the so-called penalty is."

Kelleher's indignant turns of phrase are backed by substance. Better Markets churns out obsessively detailed rulemaking submissions to regulators (pointing out gaps in drafts of the clawback rules, for example). A flow of white papers and bulletins for policymakers and the press can be counted on to rebut the Wall Street line with credible collections of facts and arguments putting the banks' claims in context. The big banks may argue that the repeal of Glass-Steagall did not cause the crash, a Better Markets bulletin acknowledged, because the precipitating event leading up to the crash had to do with worthless mortgages peddled by firms like Countrywide and passed on to the banks for them to trade. However, it was also true, Better Markets explained, that Glass-Steagall allowed the banks to engage in that trading and to be "supersized," which is what made their failure inevitable and their bailouts necessary.

As for the banks' repeated claim that Dodd-Frank's risk-avoidance regulations hamstrung them so that they could not reinvigorate the economy by lending more to businesses, Better Markets distributed data showing that lending has been going up in recent years, and that the reason there has not been even more of it is that smaller businesses still haven't recovered from the crash to be creditworthy enough to qualify for loans. "They're complaining about a problem that they caused," Kelleher claimed. "This is the industry's favorite and most effective club with elected officials: deregulate or we can't lend and there won't be economic growth or jobs. They make up numbers to argue that they want to be free of regulation, not because they care about revenues, profits or, God forbid, bonuses. No, they only care about economic growth and jobs. So please, please, please lighten the regulations for the sake of your voters, neighbors, and all Americans!"

With the Trump election, Kelleher—who had already gotten Masters, his Atlanta hedge fund patron, to renew his funding pledge, at the same time that he began attracting other donors—began what he calls "a holding action, to try to stave off whatever we could." Now Better Markets would become the side trying to block change.

Immediately upon taking office, the Trump administration moved to reverse a rule promulgated by the Obama administration that would have given brokers a "fiduciary duty" to make investment recommendations that are best for the clients, rather than recommendations that might steer them into investments in which the firm that the brokers work for has a vested interest. Realizing that postponing or reversing a rule already written required the same kind of rulemaking process that the original rule required, Kelleher and his staff helped form a coalition of sympathetic groups, such as labor unions and consumer rights activists, to mount the kind of legal blocking action that those on the other side usually deploy. Now they were the ones submitting hundreds of comments into the rulemaking process, which they knew the agency charged with eliminating the rule would have to respond to, in writing. They were the ones insisting on meeting with agency officials who had been ordered to kill the rule, and they were the ones suing to block the reversal because the agency hadn't jumped through all of the due process hoops. "We know the same blocking tricks they do," Kelleher told me. "It's our turn to use them."

Kelleher and his allies gummed up the works enough to force the Trump administration to allow the first stage of the fiduciary duty rule to go into effect in June 2017 because they could not push through a new rule in time to delay the original rule's June start date. Officials at the Trump Department of Labor continued with plans to reverse the Obama administration rule that went into effect and proposed an eighteen-month delay of implementation of a second stage of the rule, scheduled to take effect in 2018. However, if they did proceed with the delay or tried to reverse the rule with a new rule, they faced a court challenge from Kelleher's group claiming that the facts established in the Obama administration's rule-making proceedings clearly justified the need for the fiduciary rule and that delaying or reversing it was an abuse of discretion. "We're gonna educate them on the Administrative Procedure Act," Kelleher explained.

As noted, another organization set up to hold Wall Street accountable was established under Dodd-Frank itself: the federal Consumer Financial Protection Bureau. By the end of the Obama administration, the CFPB had collected nearly $12 billion on behalf of consumers cheated with deceptive advertising, fraudulent charges, and other malfeasance by banks and credit card companies. Because people like Kelleher and Dodd-Frank co-sponsor Barney Frank and their allies in the House and Senate successfully pushed to give the agency independent funding, it was initially able to ward off efforts by the Republican Congress and the Trump administration to neuter it.

As described earlier, during the first year of the Trump administration, a rule that had been drafted in the last year of President Obama's term became the CFPB's most significant industry-wide achievement. It prohibited banks, credit card companies, and any other financial institutions from using arbitration clauses that preclude class actions. Yet despite the growing reach and unpopularity of forced arbitration clauses, exacerbated, as we have seen, by the way Wells Fargo and Equifax tried to use the clauses against aggrieved consumers, the Republican-controlled Congress voted in October 2017 to repeal the CFPB rule. President Trump promptly signed the bill, although he did so quietly with none of the Trump White House's usual fanfare. The following month he installed his budget director, Mick Mulvaney, as the CFPB's acting director after Obama appointee Richard Cordray resigned. As a congressman, Mulvaney had been a staunch opponent of Dodd-Frank generally, and of the CFPB in particular, having called the bureau a "sick joke." He quickly announced plans to reverse many CFPB regulations that Trump had said placed a "stranglehold" on the nation's financial system, including rules protecting the kinds of workers who were the core of Trump's 2016 political base from usurious interest rates and undisclosed penalties charged by payday lenders.

THE ANTI-MOAT JUDGE

In cases involving Wall Street, judges routinely approve settlements allowing corporate executives to evade personal responsibility and the corporations to pay fines but admit nothing. One New York federal district court judge—Jed Rakoff—is an exception.

In 2011, Rakoff, a Bill Clinton appointee who was a white-collar criminal defense lawyer for two Wall Street firms as well as a federal prosecutor, rejected a $285 million settlement agreed to by the SEC and Citigroup. The giant bank had been charged by the SEC with fraud for both its sale of mortgage-backed securities and for buying credit default swaps on the same securities—meaning it was betting against its own clients that the securities would default, something many of the other banks settling cases and paying big fines had also been accused of.

The SEC-Citigroup deal, called a consent decree, required Citigroup to pay the money and agree not to commit any such misconduct in the future.

However, the bank was not required to admit guilt. Federal law, as interpreted by prior court decisions, requires that a judge presiding over this kind of case must decide that any consent decree settlement is "fair, reasonable, adequate, and in the public interest" before approving it. In practice, judges rarely question settlements. They assume, with little independent inquiry, that if both sides had good lawyers and negotiated at arm's length, the deal must be fair. Rakoff made no such assumption. Declaring that the SEC had "a duty, inherent in its statutory mission, to see that the truth emerges," he ruled that he could not tell what the government was getting from the settlement "other than a quick headline." The $285 million, he ruled, was "pocket change" for Citigroup, which he repeatedly referred to as a "recidivist." Rakoff also pointed out that the facts alleged in the SEC complaint had indicated that Citigroup had "a knowing and fraudulent intent," yet the bank had only been charged in the complaint with "negligence," and the only individual named as culpable by the SEC (which can only bring civil suits, not criminal indictments) had been a mid-level manager.

Complaining about Citigroup having been allowed not to admit even to those charges, the judge declared that he had no information about the "proven or admitted facts upon which to exercise even a modest degree of independent judgment." He called plea agreements like this, in which the defendant admits nothing, the "S.E.C.'s long-standing policy—hallowed by history, but not by reason." He refused to approve the deal.

Three and a half years later, in 2014, the federal Second Circuit Court of Appeals restored that hallowed ground, ruling that Rakoff's rejection of the SEC-Citi deal was an abuse of his discretion. It was a strange and closely watched appeal. On the same side were the former adversaries, the SEC and Citigroup; on the other side was a pro bono lawyer whom Judge Rakoff got to argue for him. The Chamber of Commerce and trade associations representing the drug and banking industries, among others, filed briefs in support of the effort by Citigroup and the SEC lawmen to keep Rakoff from upsetting their deal. Dennis Kelleher of Better Markets, along with a lawyer representing the far-left activist group Occupy Wall Street, filed briefs supporting Rakoff.

Tweaking the language established in prior cases, the three appellate judges (one appointed by Bill Clinton, two appointed by Barack Obama) declared that Rakoff could only apply a public interest standard if the record clearly showed that the public interest would be "disserved." Otherwise, law enforcement agencies like the SEC were free to make the deals that they decide are appropriate. "It is an abuse of discretion to require, as [Rakoff] did here, that the S.E.C. establish the 'truth' of the allegations against a settling party as a condition for approving the consent decrees," the judges ruled. "Trials are primarily about truth. Consent decrees are primarily about pragmatism."

"It's so much easier for the law enforcement people to do these deals," Rakoff told me, "but it's not much of a deterrent."

Rakoff may have lost in the appellate court, but after his refusal to go along with the traditional "neither admit nor deny" system stirred controversy in business and legal circles (and made him a hero of sorts in anti–Wall Street circles), the SEC announced that in "egregious cases" it would no longer allow settlements where the defendant doesn't concede guilt.

These consent decrees are only about civil cases. Rakoff had even stronger feelings about how business leaders escape criminal prosecution. Writing in *The New York Review of Books* in 2014, he charged that

federal prosecutors, who failed to prosecute a single senior banker
for the multiple frauds leading up to the 2008–9 crash, had "offered
one or another excuse for not criminally prosecuting them—excuses
that, on inspection, appear unconvincing." The prosecutors' thought
process, he wrote, was, "You don't go after the companies, at least not
criminally, because they are too big to jail; and you don't go after the
individuals, because that would involve the kind of years-long investigations that you no longer have the experience or the resources to
pursue."

Rakoff said that he was sympathetic to the challenge of convicting executives sitting atop a large organization because, with few
exceptions, the law requires proof beyond a reasonable doubt of
guilty intent before the state can imprison someone, as it should. He
added, however, that there is a doctrine of "willful blindness" that can
be applied to situations where the boss's guilty intent is proven by
the fact that he deliberately blocked himself from knowledge about
wrongdoing that he must have suspected was going on. The conduct
of bankers in the years leading up to the crash is arguably one such
situation, he said.

Rakoff said that when he was head of the business and securities
fraud unit in the Manhattan U.S. Attorney's Office in the 1970s, there
was a strict policy against prosecuting corporations instead of people.
The policy was generally followed by federal prosecutors across the
country through the 1990s. As a result, unlike what happened after
the 2008–9 crash, some eight hundred executives, including kingpin
Charles Keating, went to prison in the wake of the collapse of savings
and loan banks in the 1980s and 1990s.

"The idea was that you treated it like a mafia or drug kingpin
case," Rakoff recalled. "You start with people at the bottom and get
them to flip until you work your way up as high as you can." The
challenge, he added, was that "going after people like this could take
two or three years. And some of my [assistant U.S. attorneys] didn't
like that, because it took so long and you never knew if you would end
up with something until after you had put a lot of time into it." The
process began to change, the judge explained, "when defense lawyers
convinced prosecutors that they could make a quicker case with less
hassle by going after the corporation. Getting a big fine would be
pretty much a sure thing, and it would look great on [the prosecutor's]

résumé. Every firm wants to hire someone who got a billion-dollar fine." The defense lawyers, Rakoff added, "perfected this completely reasonable argument that you could have more impact on society by going after the corporation and getting them to agree in a settlement to clean up their conduct. It was reasonable, but it was BS; so many of them became recidivists."

If executives cannot be jailed when their guilty intent cannot be proven, or even when their blindness cannot be established as willful, securities laws or banking regulations should be changed to require that the top executives of any public company at least pay with their careers and their wallets. For example, if the company they run is found guilty of three civil violations or two criminal violations within any ten-year period, the law could require that they must be fired by the board with no severance paid and all stock options and vested stock surrendered.

This would make sense for two reasons: First, if the CEO cannot manage well enough to keep his company from breaking the law, the board should get a new, more competent (or more honest) CEO. Second, if officials are worried about prosecuting a corporation criminally because it is too big to fail and if there is not enough proof to convict the CEO, firing the CEO seems to be a way to ensure accountability without risking collateral damage. Certainly, a corporation that is so big that the CEO cannot be held directly responsible for any misdeeds must be big enough to find another CEO.

"The SEC already has that model for brokerages," Rakoff explained. "You can lose your license to run a brokerage house for failure to supervise. But don't hold your breath waiting for Congress to pass a law like that applying to bank executives or others in big boardrooms."

Another way to hold executives responsible would be to have them pay some or all of the fines that enforcement officials now extract from the corporations—and, therefore, from the shareholders who had nothing to do with the illegal conduct. True, the shareholders might have benefited from the resulting profits, but the top executives are likely to have benefited more in performance-based bonuses. The best way to achieve this might be not only to finish writing the long-overdue clawback regulations contemplated under Dodd-Frank, but to make them tougher by changing the statute to require that a certain percentage of any civil or criminal fines paid by the corporation, perhaps 20 percent, must be drawn from any performance-based compensation paid to corporate officers during the time that the misconduct took place. To make the board of directors more vigilant, some of their compensation paid out during that time could be clawed back, too.

"Sure, that would make sense," Rakoff said. "But it's really a cultural problem. No one is accountable for anything."

Some companies that have had run-ins with the law deliberately shield those in charge from responsibility for fines the shareholders have to pay. In July 2017, *The New York Times*'s Gretchen Morgenson reported that McKesson Corporation, a giant pharmaceuticals wholesaler, had been fined $163 million for two different violations of its duty to report suspicious sales activity related to opioids and other controlled substances—violations that were allegedly linked to the opioid abuse epidemic that had spread across the country. However, the company's board had specifically excluded the cost of the fines when calculating the company's annual profits in order to determine its CEO's bonus. A McKesson spokesperson told the *Times* that the practice was common to the industry. "This helps investors compare financial results to those of other companies in the same industry and provides information about our operating performance and comparison of past and future financial results," she said, the implication being that the cost of illegal activity is not a relevant measure of operating performance. In the years from McKesson's first settlement, in 2008, through the second settlement in 2017, CEO John Hammergren had received $682 million in salary, bonuses, grants of stock, and cashed-in stock options. Two months later, Morgenson reported that top executives at Equifax—the credit reporting and data company that allowed the records of 143 million Americans to be exposed to hackers—were protected by a similar policy against counting fines or litigation costs against profits when calculating management performance bonuses.

People like Kelleher of Better Markets, Judge Rakoff, and Professor Post are working in different spheres to breach the moats. Changing regulations and laws, however, is ultimately about politics. And politics has become all about money, which is what those protected by the moats have in abundance and are determined to protect by building ever-stronger moats. Until there is enough broad-based disgust at this undermining of democracy, so that people like the increasing numbers of prestige names supporting campaign finance and lobbying reform groups like Issue One can lead a rational version of a populist revolt against the overwhelming influence of political money, the moats will only be strengthened.

The coming of the Trump administration featured the ultimate in moat fortification. As we have seen, Americans have been divided into two groups: the vast majority who count on government to provide for the common good, and the minority who don't need the government for anything and even view the government as something they often need to be protected from. One of the most breathtaking outrages of the Trump presidency is that those in the latter group were brought to Washington to run the government. As CEOs, financial engineers, lawyers, and lobbyists, they had spent their lives building moats to shield themselves and their way of doing business from the country's instruments of accountability—the courts; the tax code; laws promoting competitive, honest markets, clean air and water, and safe, fair workplaces; and the cabinet departments and regulatory agencies that are supposed to implement those laws. Yet they are the people whom President Trump chose to set the policies, propose the laws, staff those agencies, and sit on the courts. "Because of Trump's tweets, the crazy things he does, and the crises he ignites, we're not paying attention to what he's doing to the day-to-day functions of the country," Kelleher warned. "He has spread all these termites throughout the departments and agencies who are eating away at all aspects of our government, day and night. They don't believe in the laws they have sworn an oath to enforce."

Lobbyists for the for-profit universities whose abuse of student loan programs had cost families and the federal treasury billions were put in charge by President Trump of dismantling regulations aimed at curbing those abuses. Lobbyists and executives from the nursing home industry and other health care sectors went to work at the Department of Health and Human Services, where, among other actions, they reversed the Obama administration initiative, described earlier, to prohibit nursing homes from using forced arbitration clauses to block suits, including class actions brought by patients and their families alleging negligent or abusive care. Bankers and their lobbyists were put in charge of scaling back Dodd-Frank. Energy company executives and lobbyists were sent to the Environmental Protection Agency, where the new boss was the former Oklahoma state attorney general who had sued the EPA on behalf of oil companies. The job of enforcing job safety regulations for President Trump's beloved coal miners remained unfilled for the first nine months of his administration, and the man nominated to fill it faced congressional opposition because he had been the chief executive of a mining company with a record of repeated clashes with the mine safety agency he was now slated to run. The new White House counsel had been the leading Washington lawyer fighting campaign finance regulations.

We all seek moats, even if most of us never get the impregnable ones described here. We all want income security. We all want to keep our families well fed and safe, and to protect their access to education, to opportunity, to health care. The difference is that, unlike those who want to be protected from the government, most Americans need government for some of that protection. Whether they are wounded veterans, commuters driving over pothole-filled roads, cancer sufferers living in poverty, parents of children in public schools, workers depending on a fair wage and safe workplace, or consumers trying to figure out which credit card or cell phone service to sign up for, they look to the officials they vote into office to help them. They may be proud and independent, but they depend on the common goods a government is supposed to provide. That is the purpose of government, and a country whose government fails to fulfill that responsibility, let alone puts people in charge who want to abrogate it, is on its way to becoming a failed state.

We have already seen that Washington cannot even produce a budget, let alone produce the kinds of laws and programs aimed at addressing broad policy challenges that marked the 1950s, 1960s, and early 1970s. Worse than that, government has now become unable to fulfill even its core functions. That is the subject to which we now turn.

CHAPTER 9

Why Nothing Works

Protecting national security is one government function that works. America may have made terrible foreign policy decisions when it comes to choosing to go to war, and the Pentagon overspends scandalously on national defense because of a bureaucratic and industry-dominated procurement process, but Washington does not neglect the job of keeping the country secure. It does so for the same reason Americans are willing to pay their local governments to maintain traffic lights. We are all willing to stop at red lights even if it is inconvenient because we know that if everybody does, it will prevent crashes at intersections. Similarly, everyone benefits from a strong national defense apparatus. Both are classic common goods.

Another example: Jury duty in New York City was traditionally a miserable experience. The clerks were rude, holding rooms were dirty and uncomfortable, and the waits were interminable. In 1996, the chief judge of the New York State courts initiated a series of jury duty reforms aimed at making the system fairer by limiting the possibility that citizens could get out of serving by claiming they were too important or too busy. The most radical reform was the elimination of automatic occupational exemptions for all professions, including lawyers.

Immediately, the judge started getting complaints from friends or from lawyers who accosted her at bar meetings about the shabby

holding rooms and the chaotic process. Jury duty had become something everyone, rich and poor, depended on the government to operate. So it got fixed. The accommodations were upgraded, the staff
became solicitous, and a telephone (and later online) alert service was
added to keep prospective jurors from showing up on days when they
would not be needed.

Other than traffic lights, protection from missiles raining down,
or maybe getting or renewing passports and driver's licenses (although
there are paid services available to expedite those hassles), it is now
difficult to think of other government functions that touch everyone
equally. For pretty much everything else, those at the top have moats
to protect them from the government not working. As a result, the less
effective the government gets, the more unfair the country becomes.

Inadequate public education can be sidestepped by those who can
afford private schools, or who live in wealthier communities that have
effective, responsive public schools, well funded by property taxes.
Access to affordable health care is available to those with employer-
provided insurance who can supplement any insurance gaps out of
their own wallets.

Because of the elimination of the draft in 1973, which was President Nixon's way to ease popular pressure to end the Vietnam War,
the country as a whole is not touched by even the most drastic act of
government: going to war. Even when there was a draft during the
earlier years of the Vietnam War, deferments for college students and
often easy-to-get medical excuses enabled most better-off families to
avoid the sacrifice.

"The difference between us and the World War II generation
that came to Congress, is that they were all in the foxhole together, so
they tended to think about the country as a whole," said Bill Bradley,
who offered this explanation during a discussion about his frustrations serving in the Senate that veered off into a conversation about
how his Senate years compared with his time playing basketball with
the far more diverse yet more team-minded New York Knicks. "No
one in Washington thinks that way anymore," he continued. "They're
representing interests, not the people as a whole. They don't worry
about government, per se, whether it's basic operations or solving big,
long-term problems like climate or campaign finance."

It should be no surprise, then, that the failure of Trade Adjustment Assistance programs in places like Henry County, Virginia, was ignored. Another example of the country's non-foxhole mentality is how the government cares for the minority of today's Americans who actually did serve in the foxhole—veterans of the country's more recent wars. In 2014, the poor performance of the Veterans Administration became a national scandal. News organizations, beginning with CNN, reported that veterans were waiting months or longer to get the care they needed, and that the problem was being covered up by managers at VA hospitals who were distorting patient appointment and waiting list data to make their performance look better.

The problem had actually existed for at least two decades before the headlines forced the public and officials in Washington to pay attention, at least temporarily. In 1998, the General Accounting Office began issuing a series of reports, using the veterans agency as its case study, that highlighted how the federal government's performance ratings of civil service workers, especially managers, was a sham. Since 1994, the first year covered by the initial 1998 GAO report, all 477 Veterans Administration health care facility managers had been rated "fully successful." The same was true for personnel across the government, where 99.9 percent of senior managers were declared "fully successful." The GAO noted, however, that VA officials at headquarters conceded that there were "poor performance" issues among at least 10 percent of those managing health care facilities. Despite multiple GAO reports that followed in subsequent years and repeated calls to make the ratings system meaningful, by 2016 the GAO reported that 99.6 percent were rated either fully successful or fell into two new, higher categories: "exceeds fully successful" or "outstanding." Every manager involved in the VA waiting list scandal had received one of those high ratings.

Going back fifteen years before the issue hit the headlines, through Democratic and Republican administrations alike, GAO and congressional hearings had highlighted the backlog of veterans being kept waiting months at a time to see a doctor. A 2010 report had scathingly attacked a VA program that had attempted to solve the problem. "After spending an estimated $127 million over 9 years on its outpatient scheduling system project, VA has not implemented any of the planned system's capabilities and is essentially starting over," the government's auditors told Congress. "Of the total amount, $62 million was expended for, among other things, project planning, management support, a development environment, and equipment. In addition, the department paid an estimated $65 million to the contractor selected to develop the replacement scheduling application. However, the application software had a large number of defects that VA and the contractor could not resolve. As a result, the department . . . determined that the system could not be deployed." In the eyes of those responsible, the people running the VA health service were "fully successful." It was what they were supposed to be running that was a failure.

That split between those who are in control and those who depend on them defines much of what America has become, from members of Congress being reelected in safely gerrymandered districts while their constituents see Congress as a failure, to bankers succeeding in getting bailed out and keeping their bonuses while their mortgage customers lose their homes. It constitutes a failure of the American system to ensure the two elements of any viable community: everyone's responsibility for contributing to the common good even as they seek to advance themselves, and the government's capacity to hold those accountable who are irresponsible. America's tailspin came because all of the dynamics we have identified—meritocracy, financial engineering, political money, due process, democratic reforms of the political process, polarization—contributed in their own way to the erosion of responsibility and accountability.

THE PUBLIC EMPLOYMENT MOAT

The best way to understand why a government service works or doesn't work in a democracy is to look at who worries about it. While all Americans might instinctively appreciate what soldiers do and have done for the country, the quality of their health care is not something that touches most Americans directly the way the prior generation was touched by those who came home from World War II, or even the way jury duty now touches most New Yorkers. While some members of Congress, including veterans and those serving on the relevant committees, might care sincerely, this is not one of those special interests with big-money lobbies that will get almost everyone's attention on Capitol Hill. So, beyond the patients and their families, who are a relatively small group with modest resources, the field is mostly left to those directly involved—those who work in the system, or who, like that failed supplier of patient appointment software, sell into the system.

Most who work in the VA's massive health care system are no doubt dedicated to what they do. Certainly, the caregivers are, as demonstrated by the fact that the quality of care at the VA is almost universally regarded as excellent. If what was revealed from the multiple investigations that followed the 2014 waiting list revelations is any indication, the problem had to do with those who manage the care. That stems from a civil service system that has been overwhelmed by a web of due process restrictions that, as with those "fully successful" ratings, holds few accountable for poor performance. (Most of the managers at the hospitals with the doctored waiting lists had consistently received thousands of dollars in performance bonuses.) In other words, the civil servants have a moat, too.

As with much of what now ails America, protecting government workers with a civil service system began as sensible reform. Since the Revolution, hiring and firing federal workers had been corrupted by politics and cronyism. What had been an unspoken practice was institutionalized by the populist president Andrew Jackson, who openly championed what became known as the spoils system in 1829.

Following the assassination of President James Garfield in 1881 by a former government worker apparently enraged at being the victim of the spoils system, a growing movement for change produced the Civil Service Reform Act of 1883. The law required that workers be hired on the merits after competing in qualifying tests. Initially, only about one in ten jobs were covered, but coverage grew rapidly. A series of statutes and court decisions gradually expanded the hiring protections to include limits on firing workers, too.

A reform, initiated by President Carter in 1978, applied more rules to the hiring and firing process through a new Office of Personnel Management and a Merit Systems Protection Board, set up to adjudicate claims of unfair personnel practices. The law also added a "senior executive service" category intended to select and encourage the best workers, and attempted, with no success, to improve the rigor of performance reviews across all job categories.

At the same time, the legal reform movement sparked by Yale Law professor Charles Reich—whose book *The Greening of America* had been attacked so harshly by Lewis Powell—was catching on in the courts. Reich's push to expand the scope of legal rights to protect those at the grass roots from what he viewed as arbitrary government action had begun with what became a celebrated essay in *The Yale Law Journal* in 1964, called "The New Property." He argued that just as government could not take away someone's land without due process, it was time that government benefits and programs also be treated as a form of property that could not be taken away without due process. It was not that people had a right to get these benefits, but that once they had the benefits, they could not be taken back without a good reason vetted by a fair process. Among those benefits, in addition to welfare, was government employment.

In 1985, the firing of a school security guard in Cleveland, who had falsely stated on his employment application that he had never been convicted of a felony, was overturned by the Supreme Court. The Court ruled 8–1 that he was entitled to "oral or written notice of the charges against him, an explanation of the employer's evidence, and an opportunity to present his side of the story." (When he got that opportunity following the court's ruling, he was still fired.)

By 2016, all of that due process reform had morphed into this: Sharon Helman, a longtime senior executive service VA manager who was in charge of the Phoenix veterans hospital whose waiting lists were at the center of the 2014 scandal, was declared by an administrative law judge at the Merit Systems Protection Board not to be responsible for the phony record-keeping on her watch. The judge found that it was clear from the evidence that Helman's hospital was not in compliance with the agency's record-keeping rules, and that even if, as Helman claimed, she did not know about that, she should have known and done something about it. Nonetheless, the judge ruled that the charge that had been brought against her for "lack of oversight" did not "expressly set forth any particular actions or inactions by the appellant which could constitute misconduct by her." Put simply, due process required that the charge against her should have specified what kind of oversight she should have exercised.

As if to rub in the semantic nonsense that due process had become and through which, Helman—who was paid $169,000 a year, plus a

$9,000 performance bonus—was being allowed to avoid accountability, the judge added that if the wording in the charge against Helman used to justify her firing had included "a line to the effect of 'and you did not attempt to bring it in to compliance' or perhaps 'you allowed that state of affairs to persist,'" the charge would have "set forth something the appellant did or failed to do."

Luckily for the taxpayers, Helman was held liable for another kind of misconduct that was discovered after investigators descended on her hospital following the headlines over the wait list scandal. It turned out that in addition to her management lapses, Helman had also accepted tens of thousands of dollars in gifts—including tickets to a Beyoncé concert and a trip to Disneyland—from a consultant seeking business from the hospital for his clients. She ultimately pled guilty to a felony charge for that.

That Helman was not held accountable for how she performed in overseeing her hospital's waiting lists was not surprising. A long line of due process jurisprudence, complete with casebooks, legal treatises, and specialist law firms, has sprung up around the civil service rules. Reading through the burgeoning case law involving the rare federal or local civil servant who actually gets removed in a given year for any reason other than agency-wide layoffs is a journey through a series of decisions eviscerating accountability in the name of the kind of due process precision that Helman's judge found lacking in the charges brought against her.

One of the cases frequently cited by lawyers to get employees reinstated involved a supervisor at a post office in Oklahoma. He was fired for leaving work one night without securing hundreds of thousands of dollars' worth of packages. He had never been given instructions that were explicit enough, the Merit Systems Protection Board ruled. That case was later cited as precedent for a decision involving two regional supervisors at the General Services Administration. They were dismissed in the wake of a 2012 scandal involving their roles in a Las Vegas regional "conference" for employees that cost $823,000 and featured an array of extravagances, commemorative gifts, and team-building exercises that included a clown and a mind-reader. The two were reinstated because, the merit board ruled, "A supervisor cannot be held responsible for the improprieties of subordinate employees unless he actually directed or had knowledge of and acquiesced in the misconduct." In other words, a supervisor who fails to supervise is not responsible.

Although a minuscule portion (less than half of one percent) of the country's millions of federal, state, and local civil servants get fired for performance-based reasons in any year, there are enough who do, and who, as explained, file appeals, that several law firms have developed a specialty in getting them reinstated. When I googled "Merit Systems Protection Board" to get some initial background on the agency, the first ad that popped up was for Tully Rinckey, a seventy-four-lawyer firm with offices in Washington, D.C., New York, Texas, and California that specializes in serving government employees.

"We're the largest federal employees' firm in the country," said Cheri Cannon, the managing partner of the firm's Washington office, who had served as chief counsel of the Merit Systems Protection Board. "We have hundreds of cases at any one time, and one way people find out about us is when they use Google to look for information about how the Merit Systems Protection board works." Although the firm accepts retainers at rates far lower than its corporate law firm neighbors, "we generally make that up," Canon explained, "because the law requires that the government pays our fees if we win. And if we settle, which is most of the time, they usually pay the fees, too."

Cannon offered a perspective on civil service protection that should not be ignored: "Supervisors can be irrational, and with the new bosses in the Trump administration especially, they're under pressure to do erratic things and fire people without observing the legal process. We hold them accountable. . . . Our clients are people who want to do public service, and they are willing to take a financial hit to do that. It's not unreasonable that they get some extra job security in return. So, yes, it should be a property right, because you're asking people to sacrifice for the greater good."

It typically takes nine months to a year and a half to fire a federal employee for misconduct and longer for simple but prolonged incompetence, depending on how many of the different appeals routes the employee and his lawyer pursue. It can take longer if the worker claims to have been discriminated against because of a disability or race or gender, or because he or she is a whistle-blower being fired for accusing the boss of wrongdoing. Of course, there are real cases of unfair termination of whistle-blowers and real cases of discrimination, but the process of determining which cases are real has been in a state of atrophy for decades.

In large part because of the headlines over the 2014 waiting list scandal, in June 2017, President Trump signed a law supported by overwhelming bipartisan majorities in the House and Senate cutting back the civil service protections of those at the VA, like Helman, categorized as senior executives. Those in the upper ranks would no longer have the right to appeal dismissals to the Merit Systems Protection Board. The decisions of the secretary of veterans affairs would be final in terms of the executive branch. However, the secretary's decision could still be appealed to the federal Court of Appeals. Also, the change only applied to the Department of Veterans Affairs; and even there, rank-and-file workers kept their protections, although their deadline to appeal to the protection board was shortened and some of the evidentiary obstacles were scaled back.

In local governments, especially in major cities, the situation may be worse. In 2009, writing for *The New Yorker*, I discovered the Rubber Room. Actually, there were seven Rubber Rooms. They housed six hundred K–12 teachers who had been adjudged by the city's Department of Education as too incompetent (or, in some cases, too dangerous because of criminal charges lodged against them) to be allowed in a classroom. Instead, they reported to special centers rented for them in office buildings scattered around the city and watched over by attendance monitors. Some lounged in beach chairs they had brought in. Others traded stock. Some slept next to alarm clocks they had set to wake them at 3:15 so that they could leave on time, because the required hours in the Rubber Rooms mimicked the school day. Under provisions of New York's civil service laws and their union contracts, all remained on the payroll, awaiting arbitration hearings, run by arbitrators who had to be approved by their union. It took two to five years in the Rubber Room before the clogged arbitration calendar allowed for a teacher's case to be heard, and the arbitrators, whose reappointments each year have to be approved by the teachers union, typically favored fines or suspensions rather than dismissal for even the most egregious cases.

One hearing that I watched involved a fifth-grade Brooklyn

teacher. Her five-thousand-page transcript for a hearing that ended up stretching over forty-five hearing days revealed that she had failed to correct student work, prepare lesson plans, or fill out report cards. The morning I sat in on the hearing, her union-paid lawyer contested whether there was any proof that the teacher had ever possessed the instruction manual that told her to do all of these basic tasks.

This teacher was part of a rare group—one of only 1.8 percent of teachers rated unsatisfactory by New York City school principals—in a school system where a large majority of the children were consistently found to be performing below grade level in reading and math. That was up from one percent since Michael Bloomberg had become mayor in 2002 and tried to make teachers in the city's failing school system more accountable by penetrating the protections, including that arbitration process, long embedded in the teachers union contract. After the Rubber Rooms were publicized, New York City eliminated them. Instead, the incompetent teachers were allowed to stay home, report to offices at individual schools, or in many cases return to classrooms.

Protecting teachers and other municipal workers with tenure and other job security measures had been another much-needed reform that blossomed in the 1960s. In 1962, a rare male teacher in New York named Albert Shanker had become so angry about how teachers were treated—among other indignities, he was ordered by his abusive principal to spend his lunch hour catching student shoplifters at a nearby grocery store—and how underpaid they were that he organized a union. Teachers soon began to get paid something closer to what they were worth, and working conditions were improved. By the 1980s the hold that teachers in New York and elsewhere had on their school systems had become too much of a good thing. They, too, now had a moat. In the context of a discussion about responsive, accountable government, it is worth noting that the United States spends more per capita on public K–12 education than most other developed countries, yet its student achievement scores rank well below the countries long considered America's rivals. It is equally important to note that public education can largely be ignored by those at the top, who can send their children to private schools, or who live in the well-to-do communities where they can force the school system to be more accountable.

About ten years ago an education reform movement began to challenge the power of teachers unions across the country. The reform-ers, who were concerned that the poorest children most in need of high-performing public schools were being victimized the most by the failing schools, wanted to scrap the system of lockstep compen-sation based on seniority that the unions had won in the contracts and instead reward teachers based on performance. They argued that those who were not serving children should be retrained or moved out of the classroom if they could not do the job.

In most big cities unions are a major political force, especially in low-turnout primaries for usually dominant Democratic candidates, where they have the incentive to show up in force and contribute decisive amounts of money. That is what makes public employee unions so different from those in the private sector: They typically have a major role in electing the boss who will sit on the other side of the negotiating table. That is how they have been able to build their moat.

In recent years the teachers unions have been willing to ally with those on the other side of the political spectrum to shield themselves from accountability still more. In 2009, a program called "Common Core" was pushed by Republican governors and the education reform movement and also encouraged by President Obama. The governors wanted states to agree to a common set of high standards, so that chil-dren throughout the country would have the same enhanced goals, and school systems would be measured by how well they advanced their students toward achieving them. In order to measure progress in that achievement, however, the students would have to be tested regularly. The teachers unions had long objected to tests of student progress, because they could be linked not just to a school system or a school, but also to how well individual teachers advanced the children for whom they were responsible. Fighting back, they charged that Common Core was encouraging government to harass children by forcing them to take standardized tests.

Initially, the Republican governors—backed by a minority of Democrats, including Obama, who were willing to buck the union—fought back, protesting, correctly, that this was a voluntary pro-gram organized by governors, not a Washington mandate. As the Tea Party sprang up, however, the union was able to convince these ultra-anti-Washington conservatives that, like Obamacare, Common Core—which, again, was created and implemented by the National

Governors Association—was another Washington assault on freedom. Except for Florida's Jeb Bush, Republican governors who had promoted Common Core switched to the other side. Business leaders, such as then–Exxon CEO and future secretary of state Rex Tillerson, who had made Common Core a leading element of their seemingly non-controversial drive to get the country to prepare its children to compete with the rest of the world, also retreated.

Public employee unions typically work in monopoly industries. Except for publicly financed charter schools—which operate outside union contract restrictions and which teachers unions have fiercely resisted—teachers, firemen, transit workers, and police cannot have their jobs endangered or their wages and benefits reduced by competition, or by the boss threatening to move production south or out of the country. Even automation is not much of a threat, yet. This explains why, even as private sector unions dissipated rapidly, teachers union leader Shanker and his colleagues across the country made rapid progress from their start in the 1960s. In 1960, about 10 percent of all union members worked in the public sector. In 2017, 50 percent did.

However, the twin advantages public employees have had—helping to elect their own bosses and being protected by a monopoly market for their services—have not given them economic security. In municipalities and states across the country, the job protection, benefits, and pensions that they have won, which exceed what most workers in the private sector now receive, have begun to evaporate in a wave of draconian cutbacks and even bankruptcies as their state and municipal employers face the reality of pensions having to support longer life spans, skyrocketing health benefit costs, stagnant or shrinking local tax bases, and declining federal aid formulas. They still may not be accountable for their job performance, but they are facing a fiscal reckoning.

IGNORING THE TALENT DROUGHT

Whatever the restraints that public employee unions or the civil service system create for dealing with poor performers, the bigger problem is hiring talented employees and rewarding them sufficiently so that they stay in their jobs. Not ensuring that America's children sit in front of high-quality teachers is the most inexcusable example of the nation's failure in this regard. Childhood education is the springboard for everything else a country should care about—economic opportunity, civic engagement, and the general prospect that the next generation will lead fulfilling lives. Yet the United States does not make public education the priority that every other developed country does. Attracting, training, and retaining the three million men and women whom America depends on to educate most of its children is the overriding problem, and it is only partly explained by union-forced lockstep compensation systems that blunt incentives and deaden morale by treating the worst and best teachers the same. The rest is explained by lack of commitment from those who have the power, primarily because they do not rely on underperforming public schools to educate their own children. Union work rules, mismanagement, and dated traditions like the nine-month school year (based on the old agrarian economy) result in the United States spending more per capita for public education than any other country. However, the pay for high-quality teachers is too low, no matter how compensation is rejiggered, and the priority and recognition given to these custodians of the country's children pale in comparison to the importance of their work.

With that in mind, the issue of rank-and-file public employee accountability in all job settings needs to be put in context, because those who see government as something they want to be protected from rather than something that serves the greater good are too often able to seize the issue to discredit all government workers as being bureaucratic, slothful, uncaring. I have spent hours in the bowels of those supposedly slothful government bureaucracies—public school systems locally and the federal Homeland Security, Education, Justice, and Defense departments and the agency running Medicare. What I have seen overwhelmingly, whether in public school classrooms or at the huge complex near Baltimore, where dedicated civil servants process more than three million Medicare claims a day with stunning efficiency, are people who care about what they do, care about their country, and certainly spend their days caring more for the common good than what we might expect to see on a Wall Street trading floor. As with so much else about America's tailspin over the last five decades, there has been a failure to achieve the right balance because there are forces arrayed on each side who seek an imbalance. On one side are union leaders and mediocre workers who live off of a lockstep system paralyzed by due process. On the other side are those who do not value the work of public servants and don't want to pay adequately for it. Both sides have largely been allowed to have their way, producing the worst possible outcome for the two groups in the middle: the talented, dedicated public workers stuck in a system that does not reward them and the citizens who depend on their work.

The bigger issue, then, is not the performance of the rank and file. It is about how the country has neglected the basics of managing them by acquiescing to civil service rules and lockstep union contracts and underpaying the vast majority of performers. Those who want to do their jobs well have been betrayed and their work has been undermined. Part of the fix requires developing systems to evaluate and reward workers fairly but unflinchingly, rather than shielding them behind an elaborate due process gauntlet that gives managers an excuse to do nothing. The more important part is attracting the right people, and managing and rewarding them effectively. It is a problem that has been festering in Washington for decades—the kind of long-term, quietly snowballing crisis, like climate change and the nation's deteriorating infrastructure, that bipartisan national leadership stopped addressing decades ago.

In 2000, Paul Light, a government operations scholar and renowned New York University professor, described the crisis this way: "The federal government is losing the talent war. . . . Its personnel system is slow in hiring, almost useless in firing, overly permissive in promoting, out of touch with performance and penurious in training." In the nearly two decades since, Light has written white papers and testified in Congress countless times, sounding the same alarm. He has been echoed every few years by government commissions and presidential task forces and czars. (Remember Al Gore's "Reinventing Government" project?) Every year or two, the government has announced new programs to address the challenges—poor recruiting, unrealistic pay scales, low morale—documented by the commissions and task forces. However, little has changed, except in the wrong direction.

The most troubling indicator of the metastasizing government may be that, in 2017, 36 percent of the national workforce was thirty-four or younger, but only 17 percent of the civilian federal government workforce was. Worse, agencies with high percentages of workers nearing retirement age had even lower rates of younger employees, meaning that as the most experienced workers were nearing retirement, not enough of the next generation were in line to replace them. Overall, by 2017, there were three times as many civil servants over the age of sixty as there were workers under thirty.

Assuming young people thinking about government service can navigate the federal Office of Personnel Management hiring website, whose constant upgrades intended to make it jargon-free and consumer-friendly have been the subject of repeated ridicule, the problem they come up against is pay scales. The civil service system has fifteen pay categories, or "grades." Each is subdivided into ten "steps" based on seniority or experience. Despite repeated calls from reformers to modernize the system, it has not been changed significantly since 1949, leaving little to attract smart, ambitious people starting their careers because, as one GAO report put it, the system emphasizes "time in position, rather than performance."

Generally, starting tech workers can expect to make 30 percent to 50 percent less in the government than they will in the private sector, assuming they can be induced to consider what most would regard as an uncool civil service job. Agencies lucky enough to find cyber security specialists who want to answer the government's call for help have to work around a classification and pay system that obviously did not contemplate when it was set up seventy years ago that a star with one or two years of experience at a Silicon Valley firm should be a high-priority hire.

Moreover, the candidate and the supervisor who wants to hire him or her must survive a maze of application procedures and other hurdles (including contending with the near-automatic but often impractical preference that will be given to a veteran applying for the same job). Between posting the often opaque job description on the equally opaque website, culling through applicants, and surviving a chain of approvals and clearances, it takes an average of ninety days for someone to be hired. That may be more than anyone who has alternative offers in the private sector—where the average time from job opening to hire is twenty-three days—may be willing to endure. To outsiders, including the taxpayers who pay for this broken system and suffer under what it produces, these details are hardly top of mind. Yet they demonstrate how those officials whom the taxpayers rely on to make their government function have failed their country. Democrats and Republicans alike have allowed the United States government—the biggest, most important, hardest-to-run enterprise in the world—to rot away in a manner that no private enterprise could survive and no sentient leader of such an enterprise would tolerate.

After the Veterans Administration hospital scandal erupted, the Obama administration went on a caregiver hiring spree so that the waiting lists could be whittled down. Yet by the end of 2016, despite billions in new appropriations, the VA was unable to hire 9,000 of the 28,000 new doctors and nurses budgeted. Recruiting leaders to run VA facilities ran up against all of those antiquated hiring regulations. The doctor selected to be medical director of the Salt Lake City center, for example, turned down the job because he could only be offered $155,000 under government pay scale rules. He pointed out to those trying to hire him that the doctor with the same job at a nearby non-government hospital was being paid $700,000.

If other potential recruits in priority areas, such as cyber security or fixing the VA's customer service IT systems, do consider government service, it is likely to involve working for the private contractors that ring the Beltway doing outsourced work for the government at exorbitant rates that are typically based on how many hours of staff time it takes to do the job. The contractors' performance has been so bad, yet so expensive, that the same Paul Light who attacked the government's hiring and firing system in 2000 has written that the government also "lacks any system at all for managing the government's vast, hidden workforce of contractors and consultants who work side-by-side with civil servants."

THRIVING IN THE SWAMP

Those contractors have thrived, powered by a network of lobbyists and former or future employees working at the agencies that give them contracts, and by members of Congress pushed by lobbyists to reward them and ignore their failures to produce on prior contracts.

They have been enabled by the failure of the public and its surrogates in the press to pay enough attention, and by the gridlock that prevents reform.

The biggest government buying machine of all—the Pentagon—has produced a bipartisan series of disasters over the last four decades, with escalating price tags. The continuing money drain now occupies three thousand people at the Government Accountability Office, which audits spending and operations throughout government agencies and issues more than seven hundred reports and studies a year citing management blunders and calling for reform.

The most notorious fiasco is giant defense contractor Lockheed Martin's F-35 advanced stealth fighter. When procurement began under the George W. Bush administration in 2001, the program was budgeted at $233 billion for 2,866 planes. As of 2017, it was expected to cost $379 billion (63 percent more) for 2,457 (14 percent fewer) planes, or $154 million per plane. Maintenance and parts over the life cycle of the program will bring the total cost to more than a trillion dollars. Each of the helmets the pilots use on the F-35, with its array of miniature computer screens and projectors, costs $400,000.

Whether it is the F-35 or any other program, the goal for Pentagon managers is always the same, one GAO auditor explained: "Get a 'Go' decision. Their careers are tied to that—putting a great new product out in the field. So their incentives are always to, first, present an estimate that is low enough that it doesn't get pushed behind some other program; second, to present really cool, cutting-edge features; and, third, have little enough actual knowledge of what it will cost and whether the features are achievable that you're not deliberately deceiving anyone. Once you get the project under way, it then becomes hard to stop."

Frank Kendall, who served as the Pentagon's under secretary for acquisitions, technology, and logistics in the Obama administration, recalled that when he first reviewed the F-35 program, "I said, 'Who is running this, Lockheed Martin or us?' Once you begin production, it solidifies support, because you've spread the work out to lots of congressional districts. . . . Everybody's happy." (For the F-35, Lockheed Martin involved hundreds of subcontractors in forty-six states.)

Even when Pentagon procurement officials get the urge to economize, they are likely to be stymied by a Congress overrun with lobbyists for the contractors. "We got thousands of pages in so-called 'guidance' from Congress every year in the defense authorization bill," recalled Robert Gates, who served as defense secretary for Presidents George W. Bush and Barack Obama, and who made a mark by canceling thirty-six projects whose costs had run wildly over-budget. "They make it as hard as possible to save money." A GAO report in 2010 found that of the sixty-three largest Pentagon programs (all initiated before Obama took office), only thirteen were on budget and on schedule. The rest were over-budget by a cumulative $296 billion, an amount that would give nearly three million Americans a $100,000 college education, or rebuild the country's fifty largest airports.

Amid all those overruns, the contractors have thrived. The stocks of the contractors delivering the ten costliest programs enjoyed cumulative total returns that nearly tripled the performance of the S&P 500 index between 2002 and Election Day 2016. During 2016, the defense industry spent $128.8 million deploying 757 lobbyists in Washington, of whom 72 percent had previously worked in Congress or at a government agency on jobs related to the industry.

A favorite term to describe the Pentagon's contracting swamp is the "Iron Triangle," the three corners of which are acquisition bureaucrats at the Pentagon; the Beltway contractors and their lobbyists; and members of Congress and their staffs who listen to the lobbyists when funding has to be authorized (or increased when costs exceed the budget). "The reason the Iron Triangle always seems to win," said a veteran GAO auditor, "is that these people depend on each other and even may rotate from one place to another." As the auditor explained, "It's not really a matter of personal corruption; it's just an insidious culture that is corrupting." Those with the most at stake control the process and protect each other. Washington is not a swamp; it's a giant moat.

Other government agencies routinely overrun budgets and schedules with impunity, too, often to the benefit of the same defense contractors. Following the September 11 terrorist attacks, multiple programs—salivated over by Beltway firms that formed "capture teams" to reel in business—were launched with exuberant announcements, after which they quietly collapsed amid implementation delays, revised promises, and finally failure.

Two billion dollars was doled out to improve the Transportation

Security Administration's screening at airports of checked bags for bombs, but the new equipment yielded no discernible improvement. Another $1 billion was spent on a network of motion sensors and camera towers across just a fraction of the U.S. border with Mexico as the first step in what was to be a $5 billion program. When the government awarded the coveted contract to Boeing in 2006 (to replace a failed $2.5 billion program started in 2004), President Bush heralded it as "the most technologically advanced border project ever." Once deployed, the system's sensors set off alarms when wildlife moved around, and its cameras swayed in the wind and failed to provide visibility in areas where the land wasn't level. The program was euthanized in 2011, after which an Israeli firm was brought in under a new contract to provide a system that apparently works. When that new contract was solicited, Boeing went after it, taking ads in a Beltway trade journal touting its "Proven Experience" in border security technology. That Boeing asked for a do-over, and apparently thought it had a shot at getting it, is emblematic of a clubby ecosystem of Beltway contracting in which the big players seem unembarrassed by even the most glaring failures.

Still, the urgent environment in which these contracts are awarded—in response to the 9/11 attacks or, in the case of the F-35, a need to shore up defenses in a dangerous global environment—as well as the enormity of the programs, makes solving the problem more complicated than substituting good guys for bad guys. The Pentagon spent about $300 billion in the 2017 fiscal year on outside goods and services, and it was not all done with the cavalier disregard that the phrase "Iron Triangle" suggests. Most of it was done by the book—in fact, a massive set of books called the Defense Federal Acquisition Regulations System (or D-FARS in the acronym-plagued building).

D-FARS is a tribute to Charles Reich's "New Property" doctrine of the 1960s, in which the right not to be unfairly denied a government contract became the new property in question worthy of due process protection. D-FARS is so voluminous and spread among so many volumes and appendices that no one at the Pentagon could say how many thousands of pages it is. The big book is administered by *207,000* people who work in acquisitions and procurement. That is more than twice the number of police officers in America's ten largest cities combined and 12.5 percent more than the entire Marine Corps. A study by a

Defense Department advisory board in 2015 was convincingly critical of the Pentagon's bloated non-combat workforce, but it is also true these acquisitions and procurement troops are responsible for a portfolio of contracts and purchases that is multiples larger than any corresponding activity in the private sector or in any other government.

There is even a Defense Acquisition University at a fort in Virginia (and at twenty-five regional campuses) that offers hundreds of classes on topics including applied cost analysis, small business contracting, fraud awareness, making oral presentations, and "basic flow-charting." About 150,000 acquisition specialists take these courses every year. "The funny thing is that these are really good people," said a veteran GAO auditor. "They want to do the right thing, but their attitude is, We want the best weapons systems, regardless of the bottom line. And we do have the best weapons systems. . . . It's really a problem of culture. They see their job as winning at all costs and fighting off those who want to block them."

Beyond culture and the sheer enormity of the job, three factors make the process impossible to run like a conventional business.

First, there is the fact that it is the taxpayers' money at stake, which combined with constant pressures from lobbyists and Capitol Hill on behalf of favorite projects are what produce the paralyzing thousands of pages of rules. In theory, the rules are granular enough to preclude all discretion that might corrupt the fair result that due process is supposed to produce. In practice, they make little room for commonsense judgment, while enabling misguided, unsure, stubborn, or lobby-influenced procurement officials to justify any decision.

Second, there is the federal hiring problem, with all those category classifications and below-grade salaries. The members of the contractors' "capture teams" of salesmen and negotiators typically earn much more than those representing the taxpayers on the other side of the table. That produces a skills gap, or a desire to please, or both. "We need sharp-penciled negotiators with an incentive to cut costs, but we don't provide those incentives," former defense secretary Gates explained. "They'll go to work for a contractor someday, so they don't want to be perceived as a pain in the ass."

Third, when the Pentagon thinks of a new plane or weapons system that it needs, it has to ask the vendors to invent something that only the Pentagon (and perhaps allied forces) will want to buy, if it works. This means that the suppliers have the leverage and the justification to ask taxpayers to assume the risk of development. That involves the expensive front end of the process that undermines realistic budgeting, because, although the contractors are happy to submit lowball promises, no one can really tell how much time it will take to develop the new product. The contractor's incentive, of course, is to have it take longer and, therefore, cost more.

Juxtapose those challenges against a review of who in the American democracy cares about overcoming them. Taxpayers, having only seen an occasional headline about the ballooning cost of a project like the F-35, are generally numb to the problem. They assume Washington is a lost cause, a swamp full of the waste, fraud, and abuse that the opponents of the party in power like to talk about, and that the press occasionally uncovers. With the exception of people like Arizona Republican Senator John McCain, a war hero who has been relentlessly consistent about identifying and attacking Pentagon waste, most members of Congress often denounce Pentagon largesse as a general matter but are happy to have that waste flow into the districts they represent, or into the coffers of the companies on whom they depend for contributions.

Those who care the most about how the system works are those who operate it: the companies getting the contracts and the bureaucrats making the decisions. In fact, the only real accountability challenging the system typically comes when a segment of those who do care—the contractors that lose out on a deal—deploy their due process rights to protest a contract award.

This is another under-the-radar corner of due process litigation that has mushroomed in Washington. From 2008 to 2016, formal protests of bid awards each year increased 78 percent—to 2,789, or more than fifty per week. Although the protests, which are usually lodged with the GAO and sometimes in federal court, can delay a contract from proceeding for months or even a year or more, they have been sustained just 13 percent of the time. Yet they have become a routine way for a losing bidder to seek a do-over or, as is far more likely, to negotiate a settlement that gives the loser some portion of the work awarded to the winner.

All the work that goes into meeting the requirements of the contracting regulations—elaborate requests to the industry for information, then still more elaborate requests for proposals (called RFPs), then industry requests for the RFPs to be amended or clarified, then the bidding, then the decision anointing the winning bidder (based not just on price but on the promises made as to quality and timing), then the fending off of protests—typically causes the process to take years longer than it would in the private sector. Equally important, some of the best potential suppliers, particularly when it comes to high-tech contracts, are so turned off by the prospect of running this gauntlet that they don't bother to bid, leaving the field to the usual Beltway contractors. Too often the Beltway incumbents are better at working the process with their capture teams and lobbyists and writing proposals full of promises that check all the boxes than they are at delivering on those promises.

Perhaps the oddest and most destructive aspect of awarding a government contract is that the agency officials who will actually have to use whatever product or service is being bought have nothing to do with the decision. Beyond describing what they need, they are walled off from the choice of who gets selected. Rules aimed at ensuring the integrity of the buying decision (another aspect of due process) require that major contracts be handled by a wholly separate procurement staff. It is as if you were in charge of your company's marketing but could not participate in the selection of a new advertising agency, let alone meet the executives who will be working on your account.

THE HEALTHCARE.GOV FIASCO

The most vivid demonstration of all of these shortcomings in government procurement was the dramatic crash in 2013 of the website that the Obama administration built to launch the consumer health care insurance exchanges that were central to Obamacare. By the end of the first hour of the launch of the Obamacare e-commerce site on October 1, 2013, the system was down, and no one knew why. Because it had been built so incompetently, without the monitoring metrics that are standard for any e-commerce system, no one even knew how badly it was crippled. No competent manager had actually been put in charge of the implementation by the president. In fact, at least seven people—all with great policy and academic credentials and none with the necessary management or e-commerce experience—told me just before the launch that they were in charge.

The walled-off procurement officials had turned to the usual D.C.-area government contractors, none of whom had ever built an e-commerce system, let alone one as complicated as this one—which required descriptions, pricing plans, subsidy calculations, and instant identity verification to process millions of applications for dozens of different insurance offerings across hundreds of counties in thirty-six states. It was all paid for with "cost-plus" contracts, meaning the vendors charged for how long it took how many people to build the self-immolating product. In all, the government paid contractors more than $2 billion for the version of Healthcare.gov that launched on October 1, 2013.

When it crashed, a panicked Obama turned to friends in Silicon Valley for help. A rescue squad—coders and supervisors, including some former Obama campaign workers—parachuted into Washington to take over for the hapless Beltway contractors. By December 1—six weeks after the team had arrived—the site had been completely rebuilt, at a cost of a few million dollars, and was working well. The discarded, original e-commerce site had taken more than two years to build.

Obama told me he had "learned a lot of lessons" from the Obamacare crash, "and we've taken steps to apply those lessons across the government." The primary lesson involved a fresh look by the administration, from the chastened president on down, at how the government buys and uses technology.

One of the leaders of the Healthcare.gov rescue squad was Mikey Dickerson, a coding and systems wizard from Google whose title there was "site reliability engineer." Then thirty-four, Dickerson, who had a penchant for cartoonish T-shirts, had taken a leave from Google a year earlier to help the Obama 2012 campaign boost the capacity of its website and create what became its celebrated Election Day turnout software. Obama was so impressed with Dickerson's engineering and leadership that once the health care site was stabilized, he offered him a job in the White House. Dickerson was to run a new U.S. Digital Service office that would act as a flying squad of Silicon Valley engineers taking leaves from their jobs to work two years in the government tackling digital technology problems agency by agency.

Working out of a crowded government-owned townhouse just steps from the White House, Dickerson (still wearing T-shirts) and his team spent 2015 and 2016 rescuing a variety of consumer-facing government websites and processes from the clutches of the failures produced by the Beltway contracting culture. They opened doors for businesses started up by young techies to compete by sponsoring sessions in which companies had to have the actual people who would do the work if they won the contract participate in code-writing contests. Using the contest winners, plus their own talents, they fixed a benefits sign-up system at the VA's website, created a user-friendly scheduling app for the national parks, and modernized the Defense Department's travel system (which spends $8.7 billion a year and has 1,600 pages of rules). Another parallel, if less successful, tech services program was launched within the General Services Administration, the bureaucracy that does the government's centralized buying.

The last years of the Obama administration saw much more attention paid to these kinds of nuts-and-bolts management challenges. Obama and chief of staff Denis McDonough, as well as Jeffrey Zients, a seasoned management executive who recruited and supervised the Healthcare.gov rescue squad and who became head of Obama's National Economic Council, had been shocked by the Healthcare.gov debacle into realizing that bad management can trump lofty policy goals. Others who assumed top positions in the last years of the Obama administration were similarly oriented. Shaun Donovan, who became director of the Office of Management and Budget in 2014, doubled down on a number of initiatives, including getting agencies to share back-office financial and human resources services. He also forced turf-conscious agencies to boost the negotiating power of a government that purchases over $270 billion worth of basic goods and services annually by buying products ranging from laptops to double A batteries together rather than letting dozens of agencies negotiate on their own.

At the Pentagon, Ashton Carter, who was Obama's last defense secretary, had spent his career studying and running defense systems and procurement. He had begun tackling those issues as Obama's under secretary for acquisitions and procurement and then as deputy secretary before taking the top job. As secretary, he and his under secretary for acquisitions brought the F-35 largely back under control, and the number of major acquisitions significantly above budget and behind schedule had dropped precipitously.

Although Mikey Dickerson left when the Obama administration ended, the Trump administration allowed those whose two-year stints at the U.S. Digital Service had not expired to continue. However, the program was not ramped up, as had been planned, and by the end of 2017 it was unclear if and how it would continue. Although Trump's son-in-law and senior adviser, Jared Kushner, announced a White House office charged with bringing the private sector's technology innovations to the government, the office was thinly staffed and had not produced any changes at any agency. A president who abhors process in favor of impulsive transactions seemed unlikely to lead an administration determined to improve the basics of governing.

Still, even the Obama initiatives made only a slight dent in a government that had gone off the tracks through decades of inattention. The asylum was largely left to the inmates—civil servants who could not be fired and were recruited in a process unlikely to attract the best talent, and contractors who got paid regardless of performance. All of Shaun Donovan's push for government agencies to buy products jointly, for example, yielded announced savings of $3 billion over two years. That is a lot of money in most contexts, but it was less than five cents for every hundred dollars the government spends. Improving the Pentagon's travel expense controls was obviously a step forward, too. Fixing the process by which the next weapons or software system will be procured is another matter altogether. On the big stuff, the Beltway incumbents continued to be able to fight back.

THE LONELY LOBBY

All of these malfunctions are rooted in an increasingly lopsided misal-location of talented, motivated people over the last fifty years. We have seen that the rise of meritocracy provided new opportunities for those with the most talent and drive, but that they were attracted in large numbers to jobs as lawyers or financial engineers, where they could make the most money. To the extent that they are attracted to the public sector—because they are lured by high-profile work, because they want to affect policies that they believe in, or even because they envision lucrative careers afterward as lobbyists—they are far more likely to want to be involved in major policy debates rather than the low-profile work of making those policies happen. There are significant exceptions. The Peace Corps still has seven thousand volunteers, and there are thousands of talented, committed civil servants and congressional staffers. Nonetheless, it is generally true that the mission of serving in the trenches of government has faded.

Max Stier, the president and chief executive of the Washington-based Partnership for Public Service, is another of those exceptions. "Policy fights and policymaking is the sugar high in Washington," Stier likes to say, "but implementation and government effectiveness has no constituency. Except me, I guess."

Stier is implementation's only lobbyist. He joined the non-profit Partnership in 2001, at age thirty-five, when it was founded with a grant from corporate takeover mogul and hedge fund manager Samuel Heyman. A Stanford Law School graduate and former Supreme Court clerk and lawyer at a prestige Washington firm, Stier was, he said, "always attracted to government service since I was a kid volunteering in the Iowa caucuses before I could vote."

Heyman's grant to the Partnership was intended to fund fellowships to lure talented students coming out of top colleges to spend a year or two in public service. The Partnership still does that, but with additional grants from major foundations and individual donors Stier has expanded its work with a variety of programs costing about $18 million a year. They are all directed at addressing the unglamorous challenges of making government work. "We realized this was a much bigger problem than just getting some young talent," Stier explained. In 2017, Stier had 110 full-time employees, twenty-five interns, and another twenty part-timers who act as management "coaches" for government agencies. The coaching sessions touch about five thousand federal workers a year, he said.

The most intensive program trains about 450 managers annually in what Stier calls "leadership issues." Each coach runs a class for two or three dozen relatively senior civil servants, drawn from fifty agencies ranging from the CIA to the National Weather Service. They meet in seven three- or three-and-a-half-day sessions spread over ten months. One class I attended was a bit heavy on soft subjects, such as stopping to take "a deep breath" when change "may be scaring you," but other aspects provided the kind of practical pointers ("breaking a big problem into small steps") that made sense. Overall, the class seemed to give the heavily engaged participants the sense that their work is important and worth doing well, and that peers in other agencies face the same challenges that they do. During the Obama administration, Stier began convening higher-level meetings in which the deputy secretaries of all cabinet departments would discuss management issues. The deputies, who are responsible for the nuts-and-bolts management of their agencies, compared notes on topics like technology and human resources.

The lower-level coaching sessions continued into the Trump administration. However, the deputies' sessions were shelved, in part because through the first year of his administration Trump failed to appoint many of these key officials, and in part because few of those appointed were professional operations executives.

By fall 2017, Stier was sure that with Trump and the Republican Congress proposing broad cuts across most government agencies in budgets that had still not been resolved, the fees allocated to pay for his coaching programs were sure to be cut. "There is no specific line in any federal budget for training—for investing in the workforce," he explained. "So when agencies get cut or when budget deadlines are met only with stopgaps so that the agencies don't know how much they will have in three or six months, the first thing that goes is that kind of investment, which has no tangible short-term payoff."

Since 2003, the Partnership has conducted a detailed survey of employee satisfaction and engagement at every federal agency. The resulting annual rankings of the best and worst places to work in the government "are now part of the conversation from the day they get published," Stier said. "I used it as a key management benchmark," recalled Jeh Johnson, the Obama administration's secretary at the Department of Homeland Security from 2013 through 2016. DHS had long languished low in the rankings, but began to see moderate improvement after Johnson forced management changes across his department.

Stier's outreach to agency managers has also led to one-on-one engagements, in which he has acted as a troubleshooter and consultant. "I was having trouble dealing with apparent restrictions on some procurement issue we were trying to get through to increase hiring flexibility," recalled David Kappos, who headed the Patent and Trademark Office during the first four years of the Obama administration. "When I reached out to Max, he connected me with a procurement guru in the government who I had work with my procurement folks, and they were able to devise a solution that made a big difference in our hiring."

Kappos is one of the agency heads whom Stier points to as "a superstar—the kind of person you want running your government. He improved the agency's productivity immensely." Before Kappos arrived, the Patent and Trademark Office had ranked 172nd out of 200 in Stier's agency morale and engagement surveys. When he left, it ranked number one. In the job he had before coming to Washington—as IBM's chief intellectual property lawyer, running a staff of hundreds who at the time filed more patent applications than any other company in the world—Kappos had, he said, "always seen the work the agency did from 30,000 feet." When he got there he dove in, spending one of his first weekends reading the kind of patent applications and the offices' draft decisions on those applications that his new staff had to work through every day, looking for ways to improve the process. He walked the halls or parked himself in the middle of the cafeteria, chatting with workers who had never seen the boss before.

Kappos ended up convincing his bosses at the Department of Commerce and the White House to allow a seemingly counter-intuitive change to the work rules. He had decided to give the staff more time to read applications, which, he had figured out, would result in fewer time-consuming rewrites of decisions when the quality control staff reviewed the draft of the decision. "I used to have a poster of [hockey player] Wayne Gretzky in my office," Kappos recalled, "with the quote, 'You miss every shot that you don't take.' In government, there is a bias for inaction. You have to be willing to act."

Over Kappos's four years, the agency's backlog of patent applications dropped from thirty-five to twenty-nine months even as applications increased 24 percent. "Imagine being a government agency and telling a business that gives you money to process an application, 'Thanks, we'll get back to you in three years,'" Kappos recalled, adding, "I fired no one. I went from the agency being a dog to being the best without firing a single person."

By the time he left to become a partner at the Wall Street law firm Cravath, Swaine & Moore, Kappos's tenure was being written up as a Harvard Business School case study. "Dave is the kind of leader the government needs," said Stier. "He came up with a plan, and he hung on for four years to make it happen."

More needs to be done to follow the lead of schools like Amherst and Baruch Colleges in democratizing meritocracy. The other challenge is to restore in political leaders the necessary sense of responsibility and mission when they staff government agencies so that public service is attractive and rewarding to more people who, like Kappos, have won the meritocracy race. Our leaders need to get thousands of David Kapposes to jump into Washington's trenches and then give them the recognition they deserve that will encourage still more to join them.

Stier's Partnership is doing its part in that regard, too. Since 2002, it has sponsored the annual "Sammy" Awards, named after founder Sam Heyman, that spotlight the work of the outstanding civil servants who are already on the job. Presented at a gala that gets only a portion of the publicity (a write-up in *The Washington Post* and coverage in other local or trade media) that it deserves, each year the awards serve as a reminder that the majority of people who work for the government do it for the right reasons and are good at what they do, and that lots of them are unheralded superstars. The 2017 finalists included a team at the Environmental Protection Agency and the Department of Justice who uncovered Volkswagen's evasion of auto emission standards; a U.S. Agency for International Development team that led the effort to deliver food and water to victims of war-torn Syria and Iraq; a Veterans Affairs employee who designed a wheelchair that provides enhanced mobility and add-ons, such as robotic arms, for disabled veterans; a Justice Department lawyer who helped Albania write a constitution; and a NASA scientist who developed a new beacon system for small aircraft to use in the event of a crash.

Stier and his staff have produced research papers and lobbied on issues aimed at attracting more of this talent, such as civil service reform, improving the cyber-security workforce, and streamlining the antiquated vetting process for presidential appointees. Their success has been limited, though, mostly to fringe issues that are important but that illustrate just how hobbled the federal government has

become by laws that put managers in straitjackets. One law authorized the appointment of an internship coordinator at each agency.
Another enabled agencies to share their best job candidates, so that
a qualified person for whom there is not a spot at one office might
be recruited at another without starting the application process over.
That either of these minor, commonsense initiatives required an act
of Congress said much about what Stier is up against.

On bigger issues, Stier has made no progress. His white papers
and congressional testimony on the need for flexibility in government
hiring and firing were, like Professor Light's books and monographs,
praised in good-government policy circles but never acted on. His
arguments that Congress "violates its fiduciary duties" by having no
long-term budget, by not requiring the executive branch to "produce
real-time performance information," and by spending "80 percent of
the government's $90 billion annual information technology budget
maintaining antiquated equipment while refusing to spend to upgrade
it" have all gotten nowhere.

His complaint that "The GAO issues a report and then the agency
that gets attacked promises a plan to fix it, but the people in charge
are gone before the plan can be implemented" has always been met
with nods of agreement. Congress, however, has never considered
his follow-on idea that federal agencies ought to have non-political
deputy secretaries, or chief operating officers, who are appointed for
fixed five- or ten-year terms so that strategic plans can actually be
carried out.

"Yes, people like [Obama budget director Shaun] Donovan were
smart and did some good things," Stier explained. "And Ash Carter
was terrific about inviting in the digital services guys to fix some
stuff at the Pentagon, but these people come and go. They have a
shelf life of eighteen months, maybe two years. And then we start
all over. It takes real sustained leadership, like a Dave Kappos, that
lasts, that stays there and doesn't let the forces against change outlast
them."

The most substantive proposal that Stier got through Congress
was a bipartisan bill in 2010 to fund a robust presidential transition
office for both major party nominees leading up to the quadren-
nial election and for the winner after Election Day. Since then, the
Partnership has supplied consulting sessions, checklists, and other

guidance to the transition teams, and issued public reports on the progress incoming administrations were making in vetting and making appointments.

By 2016, Stier and his staff had dramatically professionalized the transition program. That only caused him and his staff heartache when, the day after the election, the incoming Trump administration fired the transition team, led by New Jersey governor and Trump supporter Chris Christie, that Stier had been working with since the summer. The new Trump team proceeded to ignore the Partnership's guidelines for vetting candidates and appointing them on a tight timetable aimed at making sure the leadership of the government was well staffed early on. Stier's subsequent public report cards and comments to the press on the Trump administration's transition failures and later shortfalls in selecting hundreds of senior appointees on time were polite, but unflinching.

Had the arrival of the freewheeling Trump administration that seemed to have no use for Stier and his work been a final straw after years of failing to achieve real reform? "Look, have we turned the ship around? Not yet," Stier said. His face seemed to flush a bit as he continued: "My kid complained the other day that he still couldn't play the violin even though he'd been practicing for two days. Well, yeah that's true, but you have to keep at it. . . . No one is going to tell me that the NRDC [Natural Resources Defense Council] ought to go away because the environment isn't perfect yet. Do I fold my tent and go home and cry? No way. Persistence is an underrated virtue." Stier was clearly disappointed that the new president and his team seemed unlikely to enable him to continue the progress, however slow it might have been, that he believed he had made over the last fifteen years. Yet, he said, "My focus is always on playing the cards I am dealt—on how we can do what's possible."

DROWNING THE BABY IN THE BATHTUB

Grover Norquist, the conservative founder and president of Americans for Tax Reform, was famously quoted during the debate over President Bush's proposed tax cuts in 2001 as telling National Public Radio, "I don't want to abolish government. I simply want to reduce it to the size where I can drag it into the bathroom and drown it in the bathtub."

Had Norquist fully realized his dream, he might not have had an audience to talk to via NPR, which is in part supported by federal funds. Yet much of his vision has now been realized when it comes to those areas of government that the one percent cares least about and has no desire to support. The converse is true, too: Except for the minority who are ideologically consistent, business interests defend rather than attack spending on farm subsidies that help agribusinesses, or tax breaks that fortify the oil industry, just as they supported the bank bailouts.

One especially indefensible example is what has happened to Social Security. The agency's operations have been starved by Congress. The math is obvious: From 2010 through 2016, the number of Social Security beneficiaries increased 12 percent. This had nothing to do with the program suddenly getting more generous or lax. It was because of the increasing number of baby boomers reaching Social Security age. During the same period, funding for Social Security's administrative services—answering phones, processing claims, handling appeals—dropped by 10 percent in inflation-adjusted dollars, forcing a hiring freeze as the number of people served continued to rise. Funding would have dropped still more had Republicans in Congress gotten all of the cuts they wanted.

As a result, even with the agency successfully moving many of its transactions online, by 2017 wait times at its local offices had increased 40 percent; one in six callers to the customer hotline got a busy signal; more than half of claimants seeking an appointment had to wait more than three weeks; and the average processing time for an appeal involving a claim for disability insurance had grown to 596 days. Disability insurance is a lifeline for many in the American community. In 2016, 1.1 million citizens seeking disability payments were on these waiting lists.

The cutbacks accelerated in 2017, after President Trump took office. In June 2017, the trade publication *Government Executive* reported that an internal agency memo had targeted 25 percent of its workforce with buyout incentives aimed at getting them to leave their jobs voluntarily before layoffs are implemented in 2018. The budget cutters' claims that the agency was inefficient may ring true in a country that sees headlines about federal employees junketing in Las Vegas. But Social Security, like Medicare*, is one of the government's truly efficient agencies. Just 1.5 percent of Social Security's outlays go to anything having to do with administrative costs.

The funding of the Internal Revenue Service is a stark example of starving a government agency that not only doesn't serve those at the top, but threatens them. Congress allocated $900 million less to the IRS in 2016 than in 2010—an 8 percent reduction in actual dollars and a 17 percent cut in inflation-adjusted dollars. In 2016, less than half of all taxpayers who called the IRS with questions were able to get through. Those higher up the income ladder, who can pay accountants and lawyers to deal with the IRS, were not bothered by that. In fact, they would have been glad to know that the reduced funding had forced a severe cutback in audits, resulting in an estimated $10 billion reduction in taxes collected, meaning that by cutting $900 million in expenses the government produced awful customer service and lost $10 billion in taxes owed. If anything, a sharp increase in IRS funding, including paying more to recruit the best accountants, lawyers, and law enforcement agents, would make sense and reap profits. The latest Treasury Department estimates are that over $450 billion in taxes goes unpaid every year and that every additional $1.00 invested in IRS tax enforcement beyond current levels would yield $4.00 in increased revenue. Those estimates were calculated before Republicans passed their tax legislation at the end of 2017; asking the understaffed IRS to explain, enforce, and write regulations for the enormously complicated and hastily drafted new law is certain to result in unprecedented chaos and still more lost revenue.

It is not difficult to understand why those who took over Washington beginning in the 1970s wanted to undermine the IRS and didn't worry much about the Social Security Administration's customer service. But what about infrastructure? Why has America been allowed to fall apart physically, too?

---

* Medicare spends less to process each claim than any publicly traded private sector insurance company, and consistently records a lower percentage of fraudulent claims paid, while receiving high ratings for customer service.

CHAPTER 10

Broken

On April 21, 2017, power outages almost simultaneously cut off electrical service to mass transit systems in New York City and San Francisco, and at Los Angeles International Airport. In the brief time before a terrorist attack was ruled out, this was breaking news, prompting email alerts and fevered bulletins scrawled across the bottoms of cable news screens. Once the blackouts were attributed to a coincidental sputtering of aging power lines or transformers, attention subsided. Americans were apparently unruffled by the idea that years of neglect that would cost billions of dollars to fix was the culprit. That their country was broken, physically, seemed to have become, like the weather, a fact of life.

As noted earlier, most people accept the idea of stopping at traffic lights because if everyone ignored them everyone would be endangered. It is equally obvious that traffic lights are a governmental function. If government doesn't install and maintain them, who will? In some instances, a block association could form a private organization and chip in for the traffic light on the block, but that would be the equivalent of government—people organizing for the common good. Also, the association members would be providing a free benefit for motorists who do not live on the block but benefit from the traffic light. So, having a broader-based government pay for it usually makes more sense. By the same token, no one else is going to build a highway, except the government (or perhaps a government agency that arranges for a private builder, who gets paid back with tolls). America's neglected infrastructure is, therefore, a metaphor for how American government has been so undermined by those in charge that it now fails to fulfill even its most obvious responsibilities. Every broken highway or rotting water main whose repair has been neglected, every power grid or mass transit system whose escalating needs have been ignored, is evidence of the country's failure to govern.

Three elements of the tailspin figure most prominently in this collapse. First, the rise of political money—which has produced public officials as selfish as their benefactors—has created an overwhelming anti-tax agenda that has precluded adequate infrastructure investments. Second, the forces of polarization, including political money, have robbed Washington of its capacity to produce bipartisan solutions to meet major needs, even the most obvious ones. Third, due process protections have been weaponized to block much of the building and rebuilding that any country must continually pursue to remain vital.

On an average day in America, there are 657 water main breaks across the country. None generate anything more than local news reports, if that. With 22 percent of the country's water mains over fifty years old, the gushers have become routine, as have the signal troubles and other mishaps plaguing the country's commuter trains and rail systems.

Crowded waiting areas, dirty bathrooms, and leaky ceilings at the nation's major airports, many of which are ranked in passenger surveys as among the world's worst, have also become routine. Flight delays are so much a staple of air travel that the airlines build them into their scheduled arrivals, so that they don't seem to be as bad as they are. Yet arrivals well after even the elongated flight time are still standard. A much heralded "next generation" air traffic control system—conceived in 2003 to replace a network designed in the 1950s and not upgraded since the 1970s—will be almost a generation overdue if, as last announced, it gets fully deployed between 2025 and 2030.

Congested, aging streets and highways, where potholes now cost Americans $8 million a day for repairs to tires and suspension systems, have pushed America's surface transportation system down to nineteenth in world rankings, four below Namibia. In 2016, FedEx had to replace tires on its trucks twice as frequently as it did in 1997. Thirty-nine percent of America's bridges are at least fifty years old and most have not been maintained in any way consistent with engineering standards. More than 56,000 were rated "structurally deficient" by the American Society of Civil Engineers in 2017. The engineers group, which issues a report card every year on the state of America's infrastructure, declared in 2017 that there was a $1.1 trillion gap between projected infrastructure spending over the next ten years and what is needed to be spent to repair, maintain, and improve the country's roads, highways, ports, waterways, dams, levees, schools, parks, water systems, sewer systems, power grid, airports, and bridges.

Over the last fifty years, the corrosion and decay have happened slowly but inexorably. One waterway project in crisis that few Americans had ever heard of until 2016, when *The New York Times* published a feature about it, "Choke Point of a Nation," involved the replacement, begun in 1998, of two locks on the Ohio River in southern Illinois. The locks are crucial to the American commercial supply chain because they enable cargo ships to move $22 billion worth of grain and other goods in and out of the middle of the country annually. Beginning about two decades ago, ships often experienced hours or even days of delays as the locks, built in 1929 and constantly on the verge of collapse, broke down.

American children go to class in public school buildings that are an average of forty-four years old. A 2014 Department of Education survey found that 53 percent of the buildings needed repairs and modernization, and that 31 percent were relying on the use of trailers or other temporary facilities to handle overcrowding. At home or in school, American children are increasingly in danger of drinking water from aging pipes that may be carrying lead or other contaminants. The engineers society estimated the projected ten-year spending gap for water and sewage systems to be $105 billion.

In 2007, an eight-lane bridge in Minneapolis that carried Interstate 35 across the Mississippi River collapsed during the evening rush hour, killing thirteen and injuring 145. Built in the 1960s, the bridge was part of that era's great American infrastructure boom, highlighted by President Eisenhower's earlier plan to build the interstate highway system, which included that bridge.

In 1991, federal inspectors found corrosion on the bridge, and labeled the bridge "structurally deficient," the designation that would be shared by 56,000 bridges in 2017. Annual inspections that followed until the bridge's 2007 collapse documented additional problems, including more corrosion, "stress cracking," and "fatigue." Just after the bridge collapsed in 2007, Minnesota governor Tim Pawlenty, a conservative Republican, said there had been plans to replace the bridge in 2020, although no funds were designated for the project.

Behind the collapse of that bridge, and the collapse of infrastructure generally, looms every dynamic behind the breakdown of America.

Fifty years before, America's leaders had rallied their country to seize the future by investing in it. From the mid-1950s to the early 1970s, Eisenhower's interstate highway program was accompanied by, among other projects, the construction of transit systems in Atlanta, San Francisco, and Washington, D.C.; the building of Dulles and Dallas–Fort Worth airports, the dramatic upgrading of Chicago's O'Hare Airport, and the conversion of New York's Idlewild Airport into a gleaming, multi-terminal international gateway, renamed for John F. Kennedy; the building of the world's longest suspension bridge at the time, the Verrazano; and the rise of the World Trade Center's twin towers.

By the mid-1970s, the party was over. Net federal spending for non-defense infrastructure projects—the amount spent *in excess* of the declining value of assets due to wear and tear—peaked in 1968 at $45 billion annually (in inflation-adjusted 2016 dollars). Except for a brief uptick powered by President Obama's 2009–10 economic stimulus spending package, it has headed straight down since, leveling out to about $10 billion in 2017, the lowest level since the interstate highway spending began in 1958. Ten billion dollars is the cost of sixty-four of the 2,457 F-35 fighters purchased by the government.

It is not as if the need to spend much more is not clear, and not only in terms of the potholes, bursting airports, or stalled trains that everyone can see and that are supposed to serve a population that has grown by more than 60 percent since 1970. White papers abound confirming the obvious—that roads, train tracks, and structures have finite useful lives, and need regular repair and eventual replacement. The same studies say that America will be home to 70 million more people by 2050, requiring thousands more schools, new sources of clean water and energy, and better roads and rail systems to move all those people and, according to the projections, haul twice the freight the country's infrastructure now handles.

The fiscal logic of these investments is equally clear. They more than pay for themselves—in the long term. By 2020, America's lagging infrastructure will cost millions of jobs and trillions in reduced gross domestic product. That is what happens when freight takes longer to deliver, when people are stalled in traffic or on trains, when trade groups move their conferences to countries with modern airports, or when businesses decide to set up shop in countries where their goods can be transported faster, where electricity and broadband service is more reliable, where workers can commute to work more easily, and where life generally has fewer hassles. This kind of international competition is not hypothetical. The United States ranked tenth in the world in overall infrastructure quality in 2017. It ranked fifteenth in percentage of gross domestic product being invested in infrastructure.

States and local governments have been unable to make up for the gap. In fact, they have added to it. Since the Great Recession and in the years that have followed, pressing needs to meet the demands of accelerating health care costs owed by states and cities for their shares of Medicaid payments and their premiums for government employees' health insurance, as well as the pension obligations negotiated by powerful public employee unions, have made infrastructure needs a priority that, by comparison, is never as urgent.

Ignoring maintenance and repairs has outsized costs even when, unlike the collapse of the bridge in Minneapolis, the result is not a catastrophe. When a bridge, road, or water system reaches a crisis point after years of neglect, the cost of repair is far more than would have been necessary had regular funds been allocated for maintenance all along. Washington, D.C., area residents know that the cost of neglect is more than dollars. In 2016 and 2017, they suffered through accidents, disruptions of service, and then prolonged suspensions of service because their Metro system, hailed as a breakthrough when it was launched in 1976, had been allowed to fall into total disrepair. New Yorkers in 2017 shared their pain, when officials finally had to initiate prolonged cutbacks and even suspensions of service because the tracks running in and out of the dilapidated Penn Station had been neglected for so long. While service in and out of that station was curtailed through the summer of 2017, more New Yorkers suffered through an escalating series of breakdowns on the city's subway system, which was 112 years old and carrying record numbers of passengers. Maintenance schedules on tracks and subway cars had been cut back so severely years before that New York governor Andrew Cuomo declared that the system was in "a state of emergency."

Every debate in America over government spending in recent years has been fought out in the context of an austerity refrain—that tough choices have to be made because resources are so limited. As we have seen in looking at Pentagon procurement, government spending should, of course, be more efficient; the waste is rampant and inexcusable. But one of the most amazing phenomena that has developed over the last fifty years is the broad acceptance of the nonsensical idea, spread by those at the top, that America cannot afford to invest in effective job training, housing assistance, infrastructure, or other basics of a functioning government. The truth is that America absolutely can afford those investments, but that those in power have decided not to maintain a tax system that could make the money available. The country's ongoing budget deficits, which provide the mathematical underpinning for the mantra that times are tough and that government has to keep cutting back, are in part the result of waste and of Washington's unwillingness to curb health care prices that are costing Medicare and Medicaid so much. However, as America's near-bottom rating among peer countries in taxes as a portion of GDP that we observed earlier demonstrates, budget deficits in the United States are also the result of a country that does not tax its people enough. Like a shabbily dressed rich man who has a fetish about not spending money on clothes, America's infrastructure isn't threadbare because the country is poor. It's threadbare because the country became cheap when it came to asking those with the most to spend something close to what citizens of other wealthy nations spend on common goods.

"In the fifties and sixties, rich people were okay with paying 70 or 90 percent taxes on the last dollars they made each year," said Gabe Klein, an entrepreneur and investor who became an infrastructure guru and advocate for public-private collaboration in infrastructure investments after serving as the transportation commissioner in Chicago and Washington. Klein was referring to the higher marginal tax rates that prevailed until they were lowered by President Reagan in 1982 to 50 percent, and then down to 28 percent by 1988. The marginal rate as of 2018, 37 percent, is still far below that of every other developed country, and, as explained, does not account for tax breaks and loopholes that reduce tax rates for the wealthy still more while keeping the actual rates the richest corporations pay inordinately low as well. The claims by proponents of income tax cuts that they stimulate the economy have never been borne out, nor have arguments that rate increases suppress the economy. Economic growth, for example, was higher in the 1990s, when President Clinton raised taxes, than it was in the 1980s, when President Reagan cut them.

Klein said that the same short-termism that he saw take hold in the business world has undermined the possibility for long-term investments for public infrastructure, too. "Politicians, like CEOs, only think short-term," he explained. "They're not going to raise taxes or spend money on something where the ribbon cutting may come five or ten years later, or for repairs to a bridge, a train track, or a water system that no one can see. They just don't think like that anymore, or at least not enough of them do."

As early as 1981, damage from the new failure to look ahead had started to become clear, at least to those who were watching. That year, two academics wrote *America in Ruins* for the Council of State Planning Agencies, which warned of the country's decaying infrastructure. Authors Pat Choate and Susan Walter were among the first to use the term "infrastructure" as shorthand for the bricks and mortar that allow a community to function efficiently. More studies followed, but infrastructure investment continued to lag.

With President Reagan having taken office proclaiming that government was the problem, not the solution, that should not have been a surprise. But at least he raised the gas tax, as did George H. W. Bush, in 1993. That Presidents Clinton, George W. Bush, and Obama could not summon the will or the support to raise the tax, which since the 1950s had been earmarked into a trust fund to build and maintain highways (and later mass transit), marked the end of infrastructure investment being considered a bipartisan bedrock of American public policy. It would now have to be debated like everything else, and debated in an environment of partisan gridlock and paralysis, where the prime goal of the party out of power is to prevent victories and signing ceremonies by the party in power.

The fiscal effect of freezing the tax was enormous because the tax was a set amount per gallon, 18.4 cents. As cars made dramatic gains in fuel efficiency, increasing the miles driven per gallon, the tax yield for cars driving the same distance (and, therefore, causing the same wear and tear on highways) was reduced. As drivers drove less to avoid paying higher gas prices, the yield per car declined further. The combination of these factors produced a drop from 2000 to 2013 in federal gas taxes from $55 billion to $32 billion in inflation-adjusted dollars. Meanwhile, the costs associated with highway construction and maintenance increased faster than inflation.

The newfound resistance to gasoline taxes—as well as the blocking by energy interests of a more complicated but arguably fairer tax initially proposed by the Clinton administration on all energy products other than wind, solar, or geothermal—only exacerbated another destructive aspect of American exceptionalism. Even adding the average of 28 cents per gallon of state taxes to the federal tax, Americans are taxed far less for gasoline than almost any other country in the world. Europeans and Asians typically pay three to ten times the tax that Americans pay on gasoline to fund their infrastructures.

President Obama's $787 billion stimulus plan to jump-start the economy in 2009 included $48 billion in transportation and other infrastructure projects. The relatively small portion was, itself, a sign of the times, given that about $288 billion of the stimulus money went for tax cuts meant to lure Republicans who ended up not supporting the bill anyway. After 2009, Obama repeatedly proposed infrastructure plans of the kind Republicans might have supported if a Republican had been in the White House proposing them—public-private partnerships, in which the government would establish an "infrastructure bank" to make loans to private investors to rebuild airports, for example, or repair and then maintain water systems, highways, and ports. The investors would then pay back the loans through management fees paid by local governments or from tolls or other fees collected from those who benefited from the improvements. Despite the need for these investments and the jobs they would create, and despite the abnormally low interest rates that would make the financing of such projects especially alluring, Republicans in Congress refused to consider them.

· · ·

In the heyday of the infrastructure boom, in 1971, the Port Authority of New York and New Jersey—which was responsible for much of the infrastructure in the New York metropolitan area and was soon to open the World Trade Center—announced plans to build a second train tunnel under the Hudson River. It was needed, officials said, to supplement a tunnel that would be clogged to a choking point by 1985 with fast-growing passenger and freight traffic running up and down the East Coast, as well as daily commuter rail traffic. Moreover, the original tunnel, which was built in 1910, was in danger of collapse from old age, a catastrophe that could kill thousands and freeze much of the American economy.

After the initial announcement in 1971, the project was planned and re-planned by the notoriously bureaucratic Port Authority, a bi-state agency, the structure of which allows the governors of New York and New Jersey to remain largely unaccountable for its performance. The plans and accompanying requests for partial financing from the federal government were never taken seriously by anyone in Washington during the Ford, Carter, or Reagan years. Even as the old tunnel's condition continued to deteriorate and the need for a new one began to take on some urgency, it failed to get funding during the Clinton and two Bush presidencies.

President Obama finally cleared the way for the federal government to fund most of the tunnel project. However, New Jersey governor Chris Christie, who was contemplating competing in the 2012 Republican presidential primaries, suddenly reneged in 2010 on committing his state's share of the funding, explaining that he feared being stuck with cost overruns.

By 2015, the old tunnel—which had been further weakened by saltwater damage in 2012 during Hurricane Sandy—was the subject of regular news reports about water seeping through and rail traffic being slowed to near standstills on the rotted tracks, causing train delays along the Washington–Boston corridor. In 2015, Christie came back to the table, and a new plan, called Gateway, was announced. Its scheduled completion: 2024. That assumes, however, that it survives repeated signals from the Trump administration that it might eliminate its funding. As of the beginning of 2018, construction on the project, announced in 1971, had not started, and the Trump administration had formally notified New York and New Jersey officials on

December 29, 2017, that there was no longer any federal funding commitment. If that position holds, a catastrophe under the Hudson River is inevitable.

The original projected cost of $8.7 billion had by 2017 increased to "just under 30 billion," according to *The Wall Street Journal*, with much of the increase due to delays and the demands added by the twenty-three state and federal agencies and seven municipalities that must approve some or all aspects of it. Christie had a point about how the tunnel might become a money pit. He and every other conservative, or any sensible taxpayer for that matter, had much to worry about given the historic incompetence and profligacy of those running government building projects, combined with the hurdles created when all those agencies applied their measure of due process to the project.

A simpler illustration was provided at about the same time by the travails of another, more modest Port Authority project.

The Bayonne Bridge carries traffic over a tidal strait called the Kill Van Kull from Bayonne, New Jersey, to Staten Island, New York. The Kill Van Kull is the waterway through which freighters coming into the New York harbor make their way to two terminals adjacent to Newark, New Jersey. To get to these Newark terminals, the freighters, therefore, have to pass under the bridge.

Together with two terminals on the other side of the Bayonne Bridge, including one in Brooklyn, the Newark terminals comprise the country's second busiest freight port. They are the lifeblood of the country's economy in the Northeast and beyond, delivering Middle Eastern fuel, German and Japanese cars, South American fruit, Asian-made clothing and furniture, and much more.

The bridge, which opened in 1931, was only 151 feet above the water. However, giant new freighters coming into use in the 2000s needed more clearance than that. If they could not come into the port, the port would only be able to handle smaller, older ships, making it less efficient than competitors. As they contemplated the problem in 2008, the Port Authority officials initially planned to build a tunnel or a new bridge and knock down the old one. However, in 2009, in a rare show of initiative at the Port Authority, a veteran project manager came up with a faster, cheaper idea: just raise the height of the existing bridge the required sixty-four feet. No new bridge or tunnel would have to be built, no new roadways approaching a new bridge or tunnel would be necessary, and no new zoning or environmental hurdles would have to be cleared to get the necessary approvals. Or so everyone thought.

The scaled-down project still required forty-seven permits from nineteen different government agencies. One agency was supposed to act as the lead in mapping out a building plan that all the others could sign on to. Getting one of them—in this case, the Coast Guard—to take on that responsibility took almost a year.

Typically, the plan is then used to write an environmental impact statement. As explained earlier, this summary of how the project—from temporary construction disruptions to permanent impacts after completion—might affect the environment now goes far beyond the "concise" statement that a 1978 regulation governing impact statements required. However, because this plan seemed so simple, the Coast Guard instead wrote an "environmental assessment." These are supposed to be still more concise, and are meant to be followed by a quick "Finding of No Significant Impact," after which the project can proceed.

The Coast Guard's shortcut assessment, published four years later in 2013, was 583 pages long and included 4,000 pages of appendices. It would be difficult to argue that it was not sufficiently painstaking. "The widening of the roadway would increase the area of overwater coverage and the associated shading of aquatic habitat within the project site," the assessors noted in Chapter 15 of the report. "However, given the changing daily and seasonal angles of solar illumination, light would be expected to reach the water under these structures during substantial portions of the day, reducing potential impacts to aquatic biota due to shading. Additionally, the generally high turbidities on the Kill Van Kull would limit any effect of the additional shading to the first few feet of the water column—benthic [flora or fauna] communities would be relatively unaffected by the increase in shaded habitat."

Nonetheless, the resulting Finding of No Significant Impact was quickly challenged in federal court by a coalition that included the Natural Resources Defense Council and groups representing homeowners and local businesses in Staten Island and New Jersey. They argued that the assessment's analyses were "inadequate," because its authors had not carefully enough considered the increased truck traffic that might come during the construction, the environmental damage that might be caused during the construction, and the fact that the raised bridge might result in the port becoming a destination for more freight, thereby increasing traffic permanently in nearby neighborhoods. It took until November 2015 for a federal judge to throw out the case and allow the raising of the bridge to proceed.

As of 2017, the $1.3 billion project was acknowledged to be 23 percent over-budget (with the final cost likely to climb still higher) and scheduled to be completed in 2019, with the delays and ballooning costs caused not only by the legal fights but also by engineering miscalculations and bad weather.

The cost overruns in raising the bridge—on paper a sensible, fiscally sound solution—are typical of the Port Authority of New York and New Jersey. The agency perpetually supplies ammunition to those who oppose spending money to have the government build or manage anything. It has the distinction of operating three of the world's lowest-rated major airports (JFK, LaGuardia, and Newark Liberty). At JFK, after it failed to win support from public officials to build the kind of high-speed mass transit line into the city center that travelers arriving at most other international airports take for granted, it proceeded to build a laughingstock $1.9 billion tram that deposits passengers about eight miles away in the center of Queens. The Port Authority's loose-money hijinks occasionally are so outrageous that they grace the pages of New York's tabloids, with tales ranging from a $4 billion replacement for the World Trade Center's subway terminal to some Port Authority police officers gaming the overtime system to make over $300,000 a year.

It was no surprise, then, that when the deal for the second Hudson River train tunnel was finally announced in 2015 to fulfill the promise the Port Authority began making in 1971, federal and state officials set the project up under a new agency. It was an additional sign that some measure of sanity was taking hold when the Obama administration launched a fast-track program to consolidate the approvals process for the tunnel project, with a goal of getting all the necessary go-aheads in two years instead of what had become the usual eight to ten years.

Expediting infrastructure because it has become an emergency—which the Hudson River project had become because it was clear that the old tunnel could become unusable any day—is the exception that proves the insanity of how the country has allowed non-emergency infrastructure responsibilities to be neglected.

After the bridge collapsed in Minneapolis, the federal government and Governor Pawlenty got a new one built in fifteen months—a performance reminiscent of how fast bridges and roads were rebuilt after earthquakes in California. But if rebuilding the Minneapolis bridge so quickly was a testament to American drive and ingenuity, what does the sixteen years it was allowed to rot even after the inspectors' designation of it as "structurally deficient" say about the country and its leaders?

This does not mean that projects should run roughshod over environmental concerns or community input. Celebrating the era of the 1950s and 1960s as the unalloyed heyday of infrastructure neglects the damage done to communities that did not have the power or the tools of due process to resist people like Robert Moses. As portrayed in Robert Caro's classic biography, *The Power Broker*, Moses was the brilliant but arrogant czar of New York's infrastructure in the middle of the last century. He developed a massive network of highways, parkways, parks, public housing, and beaches, but he destroyed innumerable neighborhoods and ghettoized the poor in the process. The environmental laws and the court decisions that began to take hold toward the end of his reign, starting with a 1971 Supreme Court ruling blocking a federally funded highway from cutting through a Memphis park, made sense—before they were carried too far and bottled up almost any significant construction. Beginning in the 1980s even routine projects became caught in bureaucracy and legal proceedings, which delayed them, made them more expensive, and contributed to the public's sense that government could not do anything on time or on budget.

In 2016, former treasury secretary Lawrence Summers gave readers of *The Boston Globe* the answer to a question many of them, like Summers, had been wondering about with increasing anger during the four years that they had been stuck in traffic squeezing past construction workers on a small bridge connecting Boston to Cambridge, Massachusetts, where Summers is a Harvard economics professor: Why was the rehabilitation of the 232-foot-long Anderson Bridge taking so long?

Summers and a research assistant discovered that the bridge, which had taken eleven months to build in 1912, was trapped a hundred years later in a process that required approvals from multiple agencies, including an historical commission that required specially made bricks to match the ones used in 1912. It was also disrupted by changes in design midway through the project and was generally undermined by lackadaisical management. What Summers called "bureaucratic ineptitude and the promiscuous distribution of the power to hold things up" had resulted in the project running $6 million over its $20 million budget and still not having a completion date four years after it had begun. The cost in time wasted by motorists and bus passengers sitting in traffic, Summers calculated, was an additional $40 million. "To collectively tackle the nation's crumbling infrastructure, citizens need to believe that the government is up to the task," the former treasury secretary warned.

The key is balance—balance focused on the common good. Instead, the country has walked away from the responsibility of keeping its arteries healthy and up to the challenges of a growing population and economy. As with so many of its broader policy challenges, when it comes to the simple act of maintaining or building roads or bridges, America now lurches from emergency to emergency, blocked by those who do not want to pay taxes to support even this most basic function of government, who do not want to work with politicians on the other side of the aisle, and who prefer to harp on the incompetence and waste at the public agencies that run these projects rather than dig in and fix them. With the added support of often overreaching environmentalists and those who might favor infrastructure projects generally but not in their neighborhood, and armed with overgrown requirements of due process that allow, as Summers put it, "the promiscuous distribution of the power to hold things up," they have been able to block America from investing in America.

INJECTING COMMON SENSE

In 1994, an unlikely champion emerged to make the case for restoring balance to the process of how the government fulfills its responsibility to keep the country functioning. Philip Howard's background and demeanor suggest anything but that he would shake the country by the lapels and argue that America was being paralyzed by those who had weaponized due process and other legal tools. But he did, and his role in trying to reverse America's tailspin is as important as the efforts of Democrats or liberals, whose political orientation he does not share. For those who listened to him, his "just do it" attitude and his ability to convey so effectively, if often hyperbolically, how his country had devolved into a place where the opposite approach had taken over were like a bucket of ice water being splashed over a hungover, slumping athlete.

When Howard graduated from the University of Virginia Law School in 1974, he joined the white-shoe Wall Street firm of Sullivan & Cromwell, helping to defend anti-trust suits and other claims against major corporations. Later, as the Wall Street firms took on the work pioneered by Joe Flom, he worked on corporate takeover fights.

Although Howard liked his job and it paid well, something about it bothered him. Everything he was involved in was buried in so much paper. Contracts and loan agreements were hundreds of pages long, as were the regulations his clients had to contend with. Decisions seemed to rest on nuances and technicalities instead of what made sense. Plaintiffs routinely asked for millions or hundreds of millions of dollars in damages for relatively minor claims, which he thought was like a prosecutor starting out by asking for the death penalty in a misdemeanor case.

"I just kept thinking about all the paperwork and posturing," he recalled. "It gnawed at me. What had happened to common sense?"

Howard, who was born in 1948 and grew up in Kentucky, and whose father was, he recalled, "a plainspoken" minister, became increasingly frustrated by what he thought was the way the legal system and government itself had become organized to "minimize human judgment and substitute the most complex rules and processes for everything." The law, he thought, "should be a framework for directing people to act responsibly, not a precise rule book that gives them no discretion to act and no accountability, because they can always hide behind some rule." In other words, Howard did not have much use for what had happened to due process, despite the fact that as a polished lawyer in a large corporate firm he was in the due process business.

In 1994, Howard, who had moved to a smaller, less stuffy law firm, turned his musings into a book. For a soft-spoken, always carefully attired lawyer who still looked like he belonged back at Sullivan & Cromwell, Howard flashed a surprisingly acid and accessible writing style. *The Death of Common Sense* quickly hit the best-seller lists and stayed there for nearly a year. Asserting that the "American legal community . . . has a tendency to overlook the obvious," Howard lampooned complex regulations that dictated the exact height of banisters on a workplace stairway, or every step a government supervisor had to take before firing someone.

"The EPA alone," he wrote, "has over 100,000 pages of regulations. . . . The result, after several decades of unrestrained growth, is a mammoth legal edifice unparalleled in history: Federal statutes and formal rules now total 100 million words." Business contracts, he added, had ballooned "to cover every situation explicitly. . . . There is no logical stopping point in the quest for certainty."

Like a lawyer addressing a jury, Howard captivated readers by assembling the anecdotes that clinched his case: Mother Teresa could not set up a homeless shelter in New York because the building code required that the tenement the revered missionary wanted to renovate had to add an unnecessary $100,000 elevator. The owner of a small meatpacking plant in Oregon had only four employees, yet one full-time federal government inspector and a second working half time were assigned to sit in his shop. An obviously incompetent government secretary kept her job by claiming racial discrimination. Showing especially intense scorn for how environmental protection laws had morphed into a playbook for anyone to block the building of almost anything, he sprinkled *The Death of Common Sense* with stories about senselessly blocked infrastructure projects.

Howard also targeted Charles Reich, the Yale Law professor and author who had been Exhibit A in Lewis Powell's memo decrying attacks on American capitalism. Reich's 1964 article in the *Yale Law Journal* evangelizing "The New Property" had powered a due process movement that, Howard wrote, gave everyone so many "rights" against government decisions that, "Rights became a fad. . . . Like termites eating their way through a home, 'rights' began weakening the lines of authority in our society.

"We should stop looking to law to provide the final answer," he wrote. "Law can't think, and so law must be entrusted to humans and they must take responsibility for their interpretation of it."

Howard became a fixture on the speaking circuit at business conferences. Conservatives treated him as a folk hero, although a close read of his work showed that he had no use for the way lawyers on their side had gummed up the works, too, by contesting commonsense interpretations of laws and regulations as violations of due process when those decisions went against them. (For example, if a corporation was fined for violating a vague rule that banisters simply had to be high enough to prevent stairway accidents, its lawyers might then have argued that due process required that the banister rule had to have a precise height requirement.) Howard was criticized by nonconservatives for, as a *New York Times* review put it, offering "no specific program. Only in his endless horror stories is he detailed."

A follow-on book in 2001, *The Lost Art of Drawing the Line: How Fairness Went Too Far*, offered still more anecdotes, this time about frivolous litigation, prompting the *Times*'s reviewer to conclude that Howard "has a weakness for horror stories—the lawsuit that shuts down a playground; the investment banker who posed for pornography magazines, then blamed racism for his firing—that are meant to be representative, but feel exceptional. . . . While his many sketches of institutions gone wrong point to specific problems, his responses stick to reproach and exhortation."

In 2002, Howard began to do more than write books describing problems. He started a New York–based non-profit called Common Good, whose mission statement promised that it would promote the idea that "Individual responsibility, not mindless bureaucracy, must be the organizing principle of government. We present non-partisan proposals to radically simplify government and restore the ability of officials and citizens alike to use common sense when advancing public goals."

With a small staff, he dug into the nuts and bolts of achieving that simplification, producing plans for state and local officials, including then–Republican governors Jeb Bush of Florida and Indiana's Mitch Daniels, and Democrat Zell Miller of Georgia. In Florida, for example, he helped Bush implement a more flexible, decentralized hiring system.

In 2014, he published *The Rule of Nobody*, which doubled down

on his anecdotes of paralyzed bureaucracy. He used as his opening
example the saga of how the commonsense solution attempted by the
Bayonne Bridge planners had to run a multi-year approvals gauntlet.
This time, however, Howard offered proposals, in the form of constitutional amendments, that would eliminate most protections from
dismissal for civil servants, require judges to be tougher on frivolous
litigation, including suits against infrastructure projects, and otherwise streamline government.

More important than these thought-provoking but hardly immi-
nent constitutional amendments, Howard and his organization began
producing white papers and specific legislative language aimed at
fostering the restoration of America's infrastructure. One mapped
out changes to the process of obtaining permits for infrastructure
projects—a process, Howard said, that typically takes eight years, but
can stretch to ten or more for major projects. Howard's plan would
shorten the process to two years or less. The chairman of the federal Council on Environmental Quality would have sole authority to
resolve any disputes among federal officials, or even among federal
and local officials, over the scope of the environmental review. If state
and local permits were delayed for more than six months beyond the
issuance of federal permits, the federal government would be authorized to grant final permits "for projects of interstate or national significance." Interference from the courts through subsequent appeals
would be "limited to the question of whether the initial review failed
to disclose material impacts and practical alternatives."

These changes would represent a significant advance beyond
a reform signed into law by President Obama in 2015. The Fixing
America's Surface Transportation (FAST) Act required only that the
environmental review of any priority projects be completed in no
more time than the average time it took such projects to be reviewed
in the prior two years. A classic case, as Howard put it, of "defining
deviancy down."

The Common Good white paper outlining Howard's plan, "Two
Years, Not Ten Years," exhaustively quantified the costs of the current delays, including how delays caused by opposition from environmentalists arguably hurt the environment. "Each year of delay,"
Howard and his staff wrote, "perpetuates the bottlenecks and inefficiencies that impede competitiveness and cause pollution. Delays cre-

ate uncertainties that drive up financing and construction costs. . . . Multi-year approval processes are not the price of good government; they are the enemy of good government."

Not attending to the congestion on U.S. roads and highways that could be fixed with repairs and new construction, the Common Good paper asserted, costs $160 billion annually in wasted time and wasted fuel. Transmission lines in America that need to be rebuilt "waste six percent of the electricity they transmit—the equivalent of 200 average-sized coal-burning power plants." Inefficient ports cause costly delays in the supply chain and often drive shipping elsewhere, requiring goods to be trucked longer distances.

The Common Good paper provided still more eye-catching numbers directly linked to the problem of project delays. Using an elaborate formula, Howard and his staff tabulated the cost—in terms of inefficiencies and pollution perpetuated, as well as extra financing and construction fees—of having various infrastructure projects take the current average of eight years to get the necessary approvals instead of his targeted two years. For road and bridge projects, the extra six years cost $428 billion. For fixing inland waterways, the tally was $227 billion.

Another Common Good white paper published in 2016 zeroed in on the just begun approval process for the revived Hudson River tunnel project. Howard's team presented a plan, which was an adapted version of their broader "Ten to Two" legislative proposal, for getting the remaining approvals for the project completed within eighteen months. They then compared the cost of the project, currently budgeted at $24 billion, if the approvals were to take three years (an extra $3.4 billion), five years (an extra $9.8 billion), and seven years (an extra $13.4 billion).

Presenting the numbers so starkly and persuasively had an impact. As of the end of 2017, the tunnel approvals process was adhering to a set of tight milestone deadlines that seemed likely to produce final approval by the spring of 2018 (although the project itself still depended on the Trump administration not aborting funding for it). And as of early 2018, the only specific aspect of President Trump's otherwise vague and unacted-upon infrastructure plan that had been announced was a virtual copy of Howard's "Two Years, Not Ten" framework—the result of multiple meetings Howard had had with

Trump administration officials. However, although Trump embraced the plan at a press event, by the end of his first year in office none of the essential changes Howard had outlined—including changing the law to authorize a centralized, one-stop-shop approvals process for major projects—had been implemented. "The Trump White House has been big on executive orders telling people to be more sensible, but has been reluctant to propose simple legislative changes that would create clear lines of authority," Howard told me.

For all of the pragmatic substance Howard had learned to add to his horror stories, it is worth remembering the lesson of Robert Moses. Howard's common sense can go too far. If unfettered, the rule of men applying their versions of common sense, instead of the rule of law under due process, is a threat, not a solution, to balancing interests in a democratic society. Environmental concerns are not inherently frivolous, even if they have become routinely deployed frivolously. Real people are affected when neighborhoods are torn up by construction. Howard's initial exhortations to let officials be free to use common sense ignored the danger that some measure of due process is a necessary safeguard against abuse or corruption. His careful blueprint for streamlining the permitting process, however, acknowledged that. He would not eliminate the process; it would still take two years. He would simply restore common sense to it.

Yet the story of the Minneapolis bridge is a reminder that the collapse of America's infrastructure is about much more than paralyzed bureaucracy. In fact, when the bridge fell and replacing it was an emergency, officials streamlined the approvals process more radically than anything Howard and his Common Good staff have ever suggested.

The more important issue is how the will to attend to this most basic common good had collapsed since that bridge was built in the 1960s. The paralysis caused by turf-conscious agencies, incompetent or slow-moving officials, and interest groups turning due process into rope-a-dope delay is part of the story. The bigger issue is how opponents of government spending (and, for that matter, government itself) took advantage of that paralysis, whereas proponents of responsible government want to end it.

Some of the best work sitting on the shelves of the Bipartisan Policy Center, whose activities we reviewed earlier, and articulated in op-eds by its leaders and at its conferences, has been its exhaustive analyses of the country's infrastructure needs and how they can be financed more efficiently, both by streamlining the approvals process with reforms similar to those suggested by Howard's group, and by attracting private sector investment through public-private partnerships.

Through loans from a government infrastructure bank, private businesses could be given the incentive to build and manage projects like airports or waterways, allowing them to repay the loans and earn profits through tolls and concession fees. Or they could take on more of the risk of fixing roads, airports, transit systems, or government facilities by being paid a set amount to build and also to maintain the facility over thirty or fifty years. That would reduce their incentive to skimp on materials because the maintenance costs they would then have to bear would increase. Except in the case of government facilities, like schools or courthouses, they might also be paid less to build and maintain a facility in return for a share of user fees or concession fees.

Although the Bipartisan Policy Center and other groups have developed a broad range of these alternatives, at their core none are new. Countries around the world have successfully engaged private companies to build and manage airports or highways. Some of those projects have even been initiated in the United States, and the Trump administration has rhetorically embraced expanding them. They have not been enacted because of opposition from those in Congress who are against any government spending. There has also been opposition from Democrats, who assert that the Republicans' plans are too much of a giveaway to businesses to reap excessive profits from expensive tollways or government-granted monopolies at airports, and that they ignore the need for the types of infrastructure that, unlike airports, cannot become profitable businesses and need direct federal grants of hundreds of billions of dollars. With President Trump having offered only $20 billion a year in actual federal funding when he announced an infrastructure plan in 2017, which Congress did not act on, they have a point.

In short, by 2018 there were lots of plans, just as there were lots of lists of long-overdue projects. Like the tax code, everyone seemed to understand that infrastructure is a mess. What was still lacking was the will in Washington among Republicans to make these projects happen—especially when the projects could not be done by harnessing the for-profit sector. No financial alchemy will ever get the private sector to build or rebuild common goods that by definition cannot be profit-makers—water and sewage systems serving the poor, public school buildings, rural broadband networks and highways, or mass transit that the poor and middle class can afford. These need government money. That is what government is for.

THE CURSE OF THE "LONG-TERM COMMON GOOD"

Infrastructure is what could be called the quintessential long-term common good. That is what makes addressing its needs in the America that evolved over the last fifty years almost unthinkable.

Long-term means it is not propelled by an emergency. The collapsed Minneapolis bridge was a crisis. The standing but rotting Minneapolis bridge was a long-term problem. The only way infrastructure, rather than one bridge, might become an emergency would be if three or four bridges or overpasses collapsed the same day or the same week, and then one or two more kept coming down every week thereafter—which, given the state of America's bridges, is possible sooner or later. Laws would quickly be passed. Money would quickly be appropriated.

We have also seen that long-term means that the issue will only be addressed by big-picture leaders, not partisan, hand-to-hand combatants. They have to be willing to work together and to look ahead and rally the people to spend money and pay attention to over-the-horizon issues for which they may not get immediate credit.

Common good means that unless, as with national defense, everyone has to worry equally about the problem, those who care more about their own interests will be ready and able to block the solution. In that sense, the only cause for hope lies in how bad things have gotten. Whether it is the collapse of the Minneapolis bridge or the D.C. Metro, the water main breaks, or the escalating daily indignities suffered at the airports, on subways, and in dilapidated public buildings, the once long-term problem may be on its way to becoming the kind of front-burner national scourge that will produce the kind of public uproar that forces public officials to act.

The shortsightedness and self-interest that have prevented infrastructure spending over the last four decades also explain why Washington has not dealt with climate change. Obviously, the need to protect the planet is another long-term, common good requiring an expensive, persistent response to a threat that is dire but slow moving. In addition, there are powerful interests, such as those arrayed across most of the energy industry, with an even greater stake in blocking major climate initiatives than those blocking infrastructure investments have had. In 2009, energy industry donors, led by David and Charles Koch, who own energy giant Koch Industries, began pouring money into candidates' campaigns almost solely on the basis of their willingness to deny climate science and even block solutions that had been championed by many Republicans—such as cap and trade, a plan to encourage clean energy by allowing corporations to trade carbon emissions credits and debits. As a result, when President Trump withdrew from the Paris climate accords in 2017, most Republicans were solidly behind him, even as headlines related to the warming planet—flooding in southeast Florida, abnormally severe hurricanes in the South, droughts and apocalyptic fires in the Southwest and West—were starting to become a staple of the day's news. True, a coalition that included some major oil companies as well as environmental groups had formed after the Paris accords withdrawal to push for a carbon tax; and many American states, cities, and corporations were proceeding with their own climate initiatives. But they were acting in a vacuum. The government of the United States was failing to act.

Protecting the Most Unprotected

Long-term common goods at least in theory have a chance to be addressed in a democracy because they involve something everyone benefits from, even if unequally. When things get so bad that the looming crisis becomes an actual crisis for more than a minority, it can ultimately become a priority that the majority demands be addressed. By then, as in the case of climate change, the cost of neglect may be catastrophic in terms of damage done and the capacity to undo it, but at least there is a possibility that long-term neglect will be reversed by the majority's anger or fear.

However, there is one core community function that always affects not only a minority, but the minority that has the least power—the poor. America's efforts to help the poor in the last five decades parallel how the country faced its infrastructure challenges: Visionary efforts in the 1960s gave way over the next forty years to unforgivable indifference and neglect.

To some degree, every functioning community regards providing some kind of safety net to help those most in need as a responsibility. No community with a conscience steps casually over people dying in the street. Nonetheless, sometimes that conscience needs to be awakened, especially because the poor are not visible to the larger community. Such was the case when democratic socialist and author Michael Harrington wrote *The Other America* in 1962. Harrington's book, written at the peak of American post-war prosperity and optimism, declared that there were forty to fifty million Americans living in poverty, but that "The millions who are poor in the United States tend to become increasingly invisible. Here is a great mass of people, yet it takes an effort of the intellect and will even to see them."

Harrington's description of the other America moved a nation. President Kennedy read it, and mapped plans to eradicate poverty. His successor, Lyndon Johnson, seized on it and declared a war on poverty with a parade of programs—Medicare, food stamps, Medicaid, Head Start, legal services for the poor. He also increased funding for a welfare program, Aid to Families with Dependent Children, or AFDC, begun in 1935 and aimed at children in the country's poorest households. Kennedy's brother Robert traveled through Appalachia as a senator and presidential candidate making the poor visible to the journalists who followed him as he vowed to surge Johnson's war.

Traveling with Robert Kennedy at the time was Peter Edelman, a gifted policy aide and speechwriter. The son of a successful Minnesota lawyer, he had been on his way from Harvard Law School and a Supreme Court clerkship to a Wall Street law firm before he signed on with Kennedy. Following Kennedy's assassination, Edelman, who married civil rights and children's advocate Marian Wright, would become one of the country's most articulate, impassioned anti-poverty policy experts.

In 2017, sitting in his office at Georgetown University Law School, where he was the director of the school's Center on Poverty and Inequality, Edelman explained the reaction to Harrington's book: "It came at a time when people were feeling great about the country. And then, Harrington comes along and says, Hey, there are all these poor people. It was a big surprise. So the country decided, We're America. We need to fix that."

In 2015, sociologists Kathryn Edin and H. Luke Shaefer published *$2.00 a Day: Living on Almost Nothing in America*. Their examination of the invisible poor was equally if not more compelling. Edin and Shaefer collected startling updates of the kind of data that Harrington had introduced to readers and mixed it with indelible personal stories of the struggles of people living hand-to-mouth in urban and rural areas throughout the country. The authors' message was that in modern America, where 46 million Americans were living below the poverty line, 1.5 million families with three million children were living in extreme poverty, with access to $2.00 or less in cash per day. Their only lifeline was the non-cash voucher program providing food stamps.

Some conservatives dismissed the book as overwrought. A review published by the American Enterprise Institute argued that the authors had not accounted for the value of the food stamps or cash that the families might be receiving ad hoc from friends or from off-the-books work. The complaints had the ring of climate change deniers pointing out that it had snowed a lot last week. While those reactions might have been predictable, what was more disappointing was that the book evoked nothing like the reaction *The Other America* had. It was widely praised by reviewers who seemed to agree that it was another "call to action." Sales were modest, however, and no president or presidential candidate declared war after it was published. The call was not answered.

"The reaction to their book says everything you need to know about how America changed since the 1960s," explained Edelman. "The stagnation of the middle class, beginning in the late seventies, totally changed the politics of doing something for the poor. . . . At least the middle class that was suffering and frustrated could still see that there were poor people below them. What politician is going to risk alienating them still more by saying he's worried about the poor or by doing anything for them? So, this is a problem that had pretty much stopped being talked about."

The reality is clear. As America became a knowledge-based, financialized economy that marginalized the working class, and as political money deployed by the winners in that transformation took over Washington and paralyzed the government's willingness or capacity to meet the country's challenges, America's impressive progress in ameliorating poverty stopped. And then it was reversed.

When Harrington's book was published in 1962, 38.6 million Americans, or 21 percent, were living at or below the poverty line. By 1973, efforts by Kennedy, Johnson, and Richard Nixon had produced change as dramatic as the building of the Verrazano Bridge. The number of Americans living in poverty had been cut nearly in half, to 22.9 million, or 11.1 percent of the population.

In 1974, the numbers started heading up again, and by 2015 the poverty rate had settled at between 13 percent and 15 percent for three and a half decades—including a poverty rate for America's children of 20 percent, which is the highest in the developed world and at least twice the rate in France, England, or Germany.

As with the country's pullback from grand visions for infrastructure investment, or Peter Peterson's ignored 1971 call for investing in training and retraining Americans to keep them in the middle class, the days of investing to move people from the "Other America" into the real America were over. The extreme poverty Edin and Shaefer documented had increased, too. In 1975, there were 7.7 million Americans living below 50 percent of the poverty level, or 3.7 percent. In 2014, there were 20.8 million, or 6.6 percent. People living in extreme poverty in the United States were now experiencing the kinds of perils and deprivation that one expected to see in the world's poorest countries: By 2008, life expectancy among low-educated black males in the U.S. was the same as it was in Bangladesh or Trinidad and Tobago.

Again, America has become exceptional in the wrong way.

In a broader low-income category—the poor, and those struggling to keep their families just above poverty—95.2 million people, almost a third of America, were living at or below twice the poverty level in 2016. It is an income level, $48,500 for a family of four, generally considered the minimum necessary to be able to pay consistently for basic necessities. That year, the Federal Reserve reported that 46 percent of all Americans did not have enough cash on hand to pay for a sudden $400 expense, such as a car repair or a visit to the emergency room, without borrowing.

Much of the economic angst of those barely living above the poverty line stems from the general marginalization of the middle class, which has pushed wages down for those not participating in the knowledge economy. The converse would also be true: Higher middle-class wages would trickle down to help the poor. However, a safety net of special programs to help the poor has always been there, too.

Support for these programs in the 1960s and first half of the 1970s was mostly bipartisan. After Presidents Kennedy and Johnson began the war on poverty following Harrington's book, President Nixon followed up in ways that might shock the next generation of Republicans. Even before he took office in January 1969, Nixon approved a proposal from his transition staff that called for a guaranteed national income—a set amount to be paid to every American as a floor of available funds to protect them from poverty.* He was unable to get Congress to approve it, but he did initiate a variety of other programs. His administration proposed—and his successor Gerald Ford pushed through—Community Development Block Grants to support local efforts to provide housing and community service assistance, such as Meals on Wheels, in poor neighborhoods. He passed what became known as Section 8 housing grants, providing rent vouchers so that people would not have to pay rents exceeding 30 percent of their incomes. He expanded and standardized a New Deal–era school lunch program that had already been upgraded by President Johnson. For millions of needy children it often provided their only solid meal of the day.

Beginning in about 1976, momentum began to shift. Ronald Reagan caused a stir that year attacking "welfare queens" in his unsuccessful bid for the Republican presidential nomination—an issue that seemed to resonate with a middle class that had become increasingly restive over wage stagnation and frustrated by much of the Democratic Party's continuing focus on civil rights, including affirmative action and forced integration through school busing.

During the Carter years, 1977–81, programs continued, but did not expand significantly when a flagging economy saw poverty rates rise. Meanwhile, it was becoming increasingly clear that the basic welfare program, Aid to Families with Dependent Children, was providing a safety net of cash but was not moving people out of poverty. Moreover, because a wave of due process and civil rights suits was forcing recalcitrant local officials, especially in the South, to end abusive and often racist programs that blocked people from getting the aid that the law mandated, millions more were being allowed to join the welfare rolls. They were almost never the "welfare queen" stereotypes whom Reagan, running a second time for president, told apocryphal stories about on the campaign trail, but they *were* tapping the taxpayers for billions of dollars more each year at the same time that the middle class was increasingly struggling.

Neither Reagan nor his Republican successor, George H. W.

---

* By the time he left office, Nixon had still not been able to get his plan through, despite results from pilot projects in 1973 that showed that the program did not dis-incent recipients from working.

Bush, was able to end Aid to Families with Dependent Children. It was Democrat Bill Clinton and Republicans in Congress who delivered on a 1992 campaign promise made by Clinton, a self-proclaimed "new Democrat," to "end welfare as we know it."

Clinton's plan, developed from the time he led a group of moderate Democratic governors in the 1980s, was to expand job training programs dramatically and even provide subsidized government jobs. In return, no adult or his or her family could get welfare if the adult did not take a job within a stipulated deadline. What Clinton got instead—in a deal he agonized over but ultimately agreed to with Republicans, led by Newt Gingrich, at the height of Clinton's 1996 reelection campaign—was the deadline and the work requirement, but none of the $9.3 billion in job training and backstopped government jobs he had sought. The program was also switched to one in which the states could decide how to spend a block grant for welfare, rather than have to dispense the money under federal guidelines. That would allow recalcitrant conservative governors to divert the money.

Peter Edelman, who had gone to work for Clinton as an assistant secretary in the Department of Health and Human Services, had become the administration's lead policy aide on welfare by the time Clinton negotiated the deal with Gingrich. When Clinton signed the bill, Edelman resigned in protest, rupturing a personal relationship that included a long bond between Hillary Clinton and Edelman's wife. The first lady worked for Marian Wright Edelman at the Children's Defense Fund following her graduation from Yale Law School and had maintained a close relationship with her and the Defense Fund through the years that followed.

Five years after Clinton signed the welfare law, Edelman contrasted Bill Clinton with Robert Kennedy in a memoir. The former Kennedy aide was still angry that Clinton had agreed to the Gingrich deal and even angrier that Clinton had quoted Robert Kennedy in explaining his support for it: "Kennedy envisioned . . . a national investment to assure that people actually had jobs," he wrote. "He also wanted to assure a decent measure of help for people unable to find work, and especially for their children. . . . He wanted to do something serious about poverty." Clinton, on the other hand, Edelman wrote, had

> hijacked RFK's words and twisted them totally. Instead of assuring jobs and a safety net, Clinton and the Republican

Congress invited states to order people to work or else, even if there are no jobs, and with no regard for what happens to them or their children. . . . By signing the bill Clinton signaled acquiescence in the conservative premise that welfare is the problem—the source of a culture of irresponsible behavior. President Clinton's misuse of Robert Kennedy's words highlighted a stark difference between the two young leaders. One pressed for social justice whenever he could. The other, originally projecting a commitment to renewing national idealism, ended up governing mainly according to the lowest common denominator.

Edelman then provided an apt summary of how America had changed since the tailspin had begun: "The America that permitted [Clinton] to sign a law shredding the sixty-year-old safety net for children is different in many ways from the America of Robert Kennedy's time. We are far richer materially, but too much of the increased wealth has gone to those at the top. Our politics has been corrupted by money and suffused with meanness."

The law that Clinton signed in 1996 did, indeed, end welfare as America had known it. That year, 12.6 million Americans received welfare aid; by 2016 just 2.8 million did, under what was now called Temporary Assistance for Needy Families, or TANF. Of those, 41 percent lived in California and New York, which have been relatively generous in implementing the program. The rest struggled to get by in states that have basically used the leeway of the TANF block grant rules to end cash assistance to almost all of the poor. In Wyoming, where 11 percent of 571,000 people lived below the poverty line in 2016, 727 children received TANF aid.

For a while it seemed that the Clinton-Gingrich reform aimed at eliminating the incentive-killing dependency of welfare had worked. Because the economy was so good in the years immediately following the 1996 change (fueled by the Internet bubble and then the run-up in debt, housing prices, and other speculation preceding the 2008–9 crash), overall poverty rates declined or remained steady. The number of single mothers—the unspoken targets of the reform—who were employed increased. However, when the economy turned down,

single mother unemployment returned to the old levels, and overall poverty rates went back to the 1996 level, or exceeded it. At the
same time, because cash assistance was now so much less available,
the $2.00-a-day economy that Edin and Shaefer wrote about became
a reality for millions, including single mothers who, as the authors so
vividly documented, spent their days trying to find jobs that would
take them and their children off a relative's couch or out of homeless
shelters.

Programs initiated by Clinton, George W. Bush, and Obama to
expand food stamps, school lunches, and Medicaid, to provide health
care to lower-middle-class and poor children, and to give earned
income tax credits to the working poor have been important factors
in staving off still more poverty in an economy that is so tilted toward
those at the top. Fifty-two percent of the nation's fifty million public
school students qualified for free or reduced-priced lunches in 2016,
and 44.2 million Americans received food stamps.

"We should not discount everything we've done," said Edelman.
"Were it not for all of these programs and for Social Security, America
would have ninety million poor people, not forty-three million, but
because of the changes in the structure of the economy, we're stuck
there, and it's only going to get worse, unless we do more."

The two principal dynamics that will inevitably drive more people
into poverty unless they are reversed are wages and housing costs. As
the same time that the economy of the last forty years has shed more
than a third of its nineteen million manufacturing jobs, it has replaced
them with lower-paying jobs in the service sector—fast food chains,
retail stores, hotels, customer service centers. Most who hold those
jobs work at the minimum wage, or at rates that use the minimum
wage as a benchmark. Many of these service workers struggle with
uncertain staffing schedules, working twenty to forty hours a week on
different days and at different times, depending on their employers'
always shifting needs. This makes providing for child care a weekly
challenge, and means the amount of the weekly paycheck is never a
sure thing.

Republicans in Congress have consistently blocked increases
in the minimum wage, which has not been raised since it was set at
$7.25 in 2009. It was raised only modestly in the four decades before
that, following a raise in 1968 to $1.60. Adjusted for inflation, the

$1.60 rate would be about $11 in 2018, or about 52 percent more than the actual $7.25. With the frozen minimum wage acting as a benchmark for so many large employers, more than one in four jobs pay below the poverty level, and 42 percent pay workers less than $15 per hour. Assuming the jobs are full-time, even $15 per hour, which had become by 2017 the goal of most advocates working to raise the minimum wage, only produces incomes of $30,000 per year. Although that $30,000 is earned through a wage that is more than double the current minimum wage, it is still barely 20 percent above the poverty level for a family of four. Put differently, Republicans, who claim to celebrate working Americans, have sat by while the law establishing the minimum allowable wage has produced a wage structure in the world's richest country that consigns more than 40 percent of its working citizens to live at or near poverty. The result, as *The Washington Post* put it, is that "Americans have the lowest national minimum wage, relative to the median wage, of any of the wealthy nations represented in the Organization for Economic Cooperation and Development."

Many states and cities have taken it upon themselves to raise their own minimum wages. Yet even those increases, when juxtaposed against the second factor, housing, have left a large percentage of people in a bind when it comes to finding a suitable, safe home for their families. Affordable housing is commonly defined as housing requiring rent (or mortgage) payments of no more than 30 percent of a worker's disposable income. By that standard, according to the Washington-based National Low Income Housing Coalition, no worker earning the federal minimum wage in any place in America can afford to pay the prevailing fair market rental rate in any state where they work. That generalization may not hold for families with two wage earners, but it does summarize the squeeze that low-wage earners face.

Other programs to help have been frozen or weakened. The federal government no longer builds housing for low-income families, which may not be a setback given the way these housing projects of the 1950s, 1960s, and 1970s shoved the poor into isolated, cheerless vertical communities. Successful alternatives, however, such as Nixon's Section 8 voucher program providing rental assistance for low- and middle-income families to live in residences built by the private sector and tax benefits to encourage private builders to add affordable housing units, have seen steady cuts, and, more recently, have been threatened with dire reductions by congressional Republicans and the Trump administration.

In 2007, 3.5 million families were renters who were characterized as living in "very low-income households," meaning they earned less than 50 percent of their area's median income. In 2015, there were 7 million of these renters. Yet housing programs had failed so badly to keep up that just one in four of these low-income renters was able to get assistance of any kind.

It is not that the government does not spend enough to help Americans pay for housing. The problem is that the government spends approximately 75 percent of its housing assistance dollars on middle-class and wealthy homeowners—by allowing interest on mortgages to be tax-deductible. That sacrosanct tax break costs the government about $70 billion annually. The cost of all housing assistance programs for the poor and lower middle class—who are unlikely to own homes or have mortgages, or even file tax returns that itemize deductions—is approximately $22 billion. The National Low Income Housing Coalition has calculated that limiting the deductions that the wealthy could take on jumbo mortgages, which in 2017 were capped at interest for mortgages of $1 million, to $500,000 would double the amount available for assistance to renters through rental vouchers. That would depend, of course, on whether the powers that be in Washington redirected the funds that way. The Republican tax bill passed in late 2017 lowered the threshold to $750,000 but used the money to pay for tax cuts that mostly benefited the wealthy and corporations. In fact, the Trump administration and congressional Republicans have repeatedly pushed to reduce low-income housing assistance that is already shamefully inadequate.

All of these numbers could numb us to the reality of what they really mean. Imagine being one of the 41 million poor living in America in 2017, or the eighteen million extremely poor, living at 50 percent below the poverty line, or the five or six million $2.00-a-day poor. Everything we know about what has happened to income mobility over the last fifty years has all but ordained that you would, indeed, be stuck in another America. The ads for vacations, for cars, for skin creams, or for fabric softeners that you see on television every night—assuming you found a place to stay that had a television, or had been able to pay your electric bill—would be ads meant for people living in a different country.

"The biggest disaster of the seventies and eighties," Edelman recalled, "was that we allowed working people to be split from the poor, when they were being victimized by the same forces. . . . We should have had the foresight to see that we needed to save the middle class. Instead we let the middle class become disillusioned by losing good jobs, by inflation, by unemployment, by thinking they were losing out to blacks from affirmative action or busing. So, they opted out, became totally cynical. That just gave the special interests more power, which left workers with lower wages and less protection, and left the poor even worse off, even while the middle class resented them still more."

FORCING A NEW ECONOMY

The most disheartening signs of America's breakdown are, obviously, these realities of life for the poor who live in the world's richest country. In the short term, the prospects for change are equally grim. The Trump administration and conservatives in Congress have made multiple attempts to take a wrecking ball to the programs—Medicaid, Meals on Wheels, food stamps—that have at least held off moving the poverty count closer to the 90 million that Edelman estimated would likely prevail if the American economy were left to its own devices. Yet poverty may also be one aspect of America's decline that presents the clearest path for reversal.

Edelman recalled that when the Great Recession came, "I thought that the poor and the middle class would be driven together" because so many in the middle class were suddenly facing the same pressures that the poor struggled with. "But I was wrong," he said. "Their reaction basically was, Don't put me in the same boat with those people." Fueled by Republican attacks on wasteful programs, resentment quickly mounted, Edelman added, over the considerable aid to the poor that Obama's stimulus plan proposed, and much of it was blocked or cut back when the stimulus money ran out.

Ten years later, however, the politics of poverty may be on the verge of changing. Most Americans are already charitable. They man sixty thousand soup kitchens and food pantries, and near-majorities have consistently responded in polls that more should be done to help the poor, even as those with the power in Washington push in the other direction. Now it seems possible that the political climate could become more aligned with these impulses to help the poor, if only because so many more Americans now have more than a hypothetical understanding of what it means to be financially squeezed.

Those formerly in the relatively comfortable middle class who are mired on the edge of poverty or have been driven over the edge may now be more receptive to political leaders who work to convince them that they have more in common with the poor than what was claimed in 2016 by the presidential candidate who promised to make their lives great again by driving away immigrants and driving down others below them on the financial ladder. Those promises no longer seem nearly as appealing, because the man who made them has worked with his Republican Party to attack the programs that so many in the middle class, or who were in the middle class, also now need.

Since 2008, lower-middle-class Americans have been the primary new recipients of food stamps. With the coming of the Great Recession, the program exploded. Food stamps, which are available to families with incomes as high as 30 percent above the poverty line, helped 48 million Americans in 2013, compared to 28 million in 2008. The number of recipients, which came down to 42 million by 2016, now surges during hurricanes and other emergencies, another indicator that the program has become a staple of working Americans now living on the edge. It is clearly a program for those seeking help, often temporary help, not life on the dole. During 2016, 32 percent of all food stamp recipients were in families where there was at least one employed worker, and most of the rest were either in families with workers who had lost their jobs and were looking for new work, or were elderly or disabled.

The dynamics behind these numbers are no mystery. While the unemployment rate that reached 10 percent in 2009 had come down sharply by 2017, the jobs that came back were typically lower-paying or part-time, and there were not enough to meet the needs of the more than seven million Americans who were still looking for work. Two thirds of Americans in one late 2016 poll agreed that "good jobs are difficult to find."

Much of the debate in recent years about poverty has included the term "working poor."* As the number of working people using food stamps or requiring housing assistance indicates, millions of workers *are* poor or are on the verge of poverty. Millions more who have dropped out of the workforce out of frustration would welcome the training and the work that would make them un-poor. These are the people who depend on food stamps, rental assistance, unemployment insurance, and Medicaid, or the premium subsidies on the Obamacare health insurance exchanges. A political leader with the right skills should be able to rally them—the poor and those hovering near the poverty line—to oppose those who are continuing to try to eviscerate food stamps and those other programs.

The last political leader with the vision and skill to bring the poor and working class together instead of playing them against each other was Edelman's boss, Robert Kennedy. Kennedy understood that the real and growing divide in America was between the protected and unprotected. Fifty years and one Trump presidency later, the time seems ripe for one or more political leaders to emerge who can rally a majority around the same message.

In short, to borrow Edelman's phrase, the crash of the American Dream for so many has thrown the working class into the "same boat" as the poor, and by now it is likely that they know it. That is why laws raising the minimum wage are being passed in states and cities across the country, energized by broad middle-class support. Polls show that Americans are repelled by the idea that someone can work a full, forty-hour week at a respectable American corporation for what is now a legal wage and still have to resort to food stamps and hope to get off the waiting lists for rental assistance.

With 42 percent of all American workers earning less than $15 per hour, a $15 minimum wage would cut sharply into the numbers of workers who can't find rental units costing less than a third of their incomes. So, too, would cutting back on the mortgage deduction and applying the new revenue to more rental vouchers, which, again, are increasingly needed by people living above the poverty line. Tilting housing assistance in this way, away from the affluent who benefit

---

* The plight of people working full-time but mired in poverty was highlighted as early as 2004 by David K. Shipler in *The Working Poor*, published by Alfred A. Knopf.

from the mortgage interest deduction, is another change that might also gain popular support if one or more politicians make it part of a platform designed to help both the poor and the working class.

THE NEW CAREGIVER ECONOMY

Edelman and his colleagues at Georgetown's poverty and inequality center support those changes. However, they have been thinking much bigger. While many Washington policy wonks spent 2017 debating the best approaches to financing the rebuilding of America's bricks-and-mortar infrastructure, they focused on a different kind of infrastructure problem: America's workforce is not aligned to fill two emerging, related gaps in the country's employment infrastructure.

With most families now lacking a stay-at-home parent and with mounting evidence that a lack of proficient early childhood education gives poorer children an almost insurmountable disadvantage by the time they get to kindergarten, the country faces a critical shortage of early childhood caregivers who are affordable and can provide more than baby-sitting. In addition, with Americans now living longer and with the baby boom generation entering the ranks of the elderly, there is an even more critical gap in affordable, competent workers who can care for aging Americans in their homes, at community centers, or at residential facilities.

In mid-2017, Edelman and his colleagues developed and published a comprehensive—indeed Marshall Plan–like—blueprint to fill these labor force infrastructure gaps. It is so necessary and so logical because it turns a problem into an opportunity that could become an unstoppable force if its prime beneficiaries, the poor and the middle class, can be brought together to demand it. It would allow economically challenged parents to obtain good care for their children while pursuing their own jobs, and allow economically challenged families to afford care for their older loved ones. At the same time, it could put millions of Americans otherwise facing low-wage jobs or no jobs to work at good wages filling these important responsibilities by creating a vital new sector in the American economy.

"The country needs jobs," Edelman explained, "and these are the jobs the country needs the most."

Published in June 2017, "Building the Caring Economy: Work-force Investments to Expand Access to Affordable, High-Quality Early and Long-Term Care" runs 160 pages, with 783 footnotes. It begins with a recitation of the facts, many of which would be familiar to most American families. Programs to provide financial aid to poor families to pay for child care reached only 23 percent of those who needed it as of 2012, the monograph explains, offering one of a series of surveys and data compilations to back the numbers. The cost of child care for those families who do not get aid and cannot find a relative to provide the care for free averages $9,000 a year, which presents a crushing burden for the average American family. As a result, many parents, especially those in low-wage, two-parent homes, are forced to stay out of the labor force or work part-time—which costs $96 billion annually in lost wages, Edelman and his team reported.

Those high costs only put children in the care of untrained, low-wage workers. Their median wage was a poverty-level rate of $10.60 an hour in 2012, which resulted in an annual turnover rate of 30 percent. Nearly half of the caregivers themselves receive some form of government support, such as food stamps or earned income tax credits. Yet, according to exhaustive studies cited by the monograph, paying more for better-trained caregivers is a high-return investment; quality preschool education by professional teachers and well-trained teachers' aides pays huge dividends in a child's future progress in school and in the job market.

As for long-term elder care, the demographics of what the blueprint called a "burgeoning crisis" are daunting. In 2012, 6 million of 43 million Americans sixty-five years or older needed help in caring for themselves on a daily basis. By 2050, there will be 83.7 million people sixty-five or older—a quarter of all adults. Approximately 59 million will need what the monograph calls "long-term services and supports."

As of 2016, the median cost of nursing home care was $80,000–$91,000 (depending on whether the resident shared a room). Medicaid covered the bills for the poor, at a cost of $158 billion annually. The care provided was often inadequate, and there was no aid available for those above the poverty line. Medicaid had a modest program to provide outpatient day care near a beneficiary's home, but the waiting list for those programs was already twenty-nine months long.

The cost for a home health care aide (including overhead and profit for the staffing agencies providing it) was $45,800 for forty-four hours of weekly care, which was significantly more than the median income of older Americans. The burden for families of those who could not afford to hire caregivers or who had to fill the other 124 hours of the week was such that, Edelman's researchers found, 19 percent of all Americans over forty years old were providing ongoing regular living assistance to a friend or family member. Caregivers reported spending an average of eighteen hours a week helping a family member or friend.

As with child care, the crushing economics for those families needing care hardly guaranteed the skilled caregiving that their loved ones needed. The 4.4 million full-time and part-time elder care workers in 2016 earned a median of $10.54 per hour. The quality of care depended on whether a family was lucky enough to find a low-wage worker who, despite the pay, had the skills and compassion necessary for the job. The annual turnover rate for these elder care workers was "over 60 percent," according to the monograph.

These growing crises, Edelman and his co-authors wrote, require a multi-pronged program, which they presented and costed out. It includes, among other steps, intensified caregiver training, an upgrade of that caregiver workforce, federally funded wage supports to pay them more ($15–$24.82 an hour in 2016 dollars, depending on the workers' training and education levels), and insurance for long-term care. The total bill for their caregiver infrastructure plan would be about $300 billion annually.

That may seem exorbitant. However, the blueprint persuasively calculated the savings and returns on every aspect of the program—including removing caregivers from the current financial supports (such as food stamps) that they receive because of their low earnings, the increased productivity, earnings (and taxes) coming from the parents of children and the children of the elderly who will be less likely to have to forgo or interrupt work because of their caregiving responsibilities, and the way that the proposed insurance for long-term care, would reduce Medicaid's current burden in meeting those costs. For example, better support for in-home and community-based care for the elderly, combined with that insurance to cover long-term care, would likely replace almost completely what Medicaid spends annually ($158 billion in 2015) for elder nursing home care.

Beyond that, there would be offsetting benefits from the overall stimulus to the economy stemming from higher wages for caregivers and so many new caregiver jobs, and the other dividends that will come from better early childhood education and moving what could be as many as ten million workers into quality, good-paying middle-class jobs. If, after accounting for all of these benefits, the net cost of the program is $75–$100 billion annually, it would constitute about 2 or 3 percent of the federal budget, be less than the annual cost of the tax cuts going mostly to corporations and the wealthy that the Republicans passed in late 2017, and arguably be the most sensible anti-poverty, pro–middle class jobs program since the New Deal. There is also the added benefit that none of the jobs would be make-work. It would be the kind of sensible, responsible long-term investment that America used to make.

The Edelman plan presents a solution that would resonate with the tens of millions of Americans who are struggling with these problems every day. As we have seen, there are also talented people working on the other issues that America has allowed to fester over recent decades—the corrupting power of political money, paralyzed government, the lack of corporate accountability, crumbling infrastructure, the lack of effective job training, and income inequality and the overall decline of the middle class caused by the financialization of the economy. Their solutions should also be broadly appealing, and the worse things get, the more compelling those solutions are likely to become. Whether they are acted on, however, depends on whether leaders can emerge in the American democracy who are willing and able to see beyond their own short-term interests, who can resist the temptation to win by dividing, and who have the capacity to think big and get their fellow citizens to think big—in short, whether they are willing and able to lead their country.

It also depends on those whom the leaders presume to lead. Americans have to get better at democracy.

CHAPTER 12

Storming the Moats

In his inaugural address on January 20, 1961, John F. Kennedy called on his countrymen "to bear the burden of a long twilight struggle . . . against the common enemies of man: tyranny, poverty, disease, and war itself." Americans, he famously said, should "ask not what your country can do for you—ask what you can do for your country."

On January 20, 2017, Donald Trump reminded Americans that "at the center" of the movement that had swept him into office "is a crucial conviction: that a nation exists to serve its citizens."

In between those two inaugurals, in 1979, President Jimmy Carter—addressing the nation with what came to be called his "malaise" speech, although he never used that word—scolded Americans for failing to answer Kennedy's call. "In a nation that was proud of hard work, strong families, close-knit communities, and our faith in God, too many of us now tend to worship self-indulgence and consumption," he said. "Human identity is no longer defined by what one does, but by what one owns."

What had happened between Kennedy's confident summoning of Americans "to bear any burden, meet any hardship" and Carter's speech about self-indulgence?

Kennedy's assassination.

Bloody Sunday on the Edmund Pettus Bridge in Selma, Alabama, and other violent civil rights confrontations.

The Vietnam War.

Urban riots.

The assassination of Martin Luther King, Jr.

The assassination of Robert Kennedy.

The Chicago Democratic convention riots.

Watergate.

Skyrocketing inflation.

A sharp increase in unemployment.

The beginning of the decline of the middle class.

There was also an energy crisis brought on by the country's dependence on foreign oil, which had resulted in motorists waiting on long lines that snaked around gas stations. That was what had prompted Carter to address the nation and warn that his country-men needed to regain their confidence and their sense of "common purpose," which Carter said included understanding that being less selfish about conserving energy "was an act of patriotism. . . . There is simply no way to avoid sacrifice."

The alternative, Carter warned, "is a path . . . that leads to frag-mentation and self-interest. Down that road lies a mistaken idea of freedom, the right to grasp for ourselves some advantage over others. That path would be one of constant conflict between narrow interests ending in chaos and immobility. It is a certain route to failure."

Sixteen months later, Carter lost to Ronald Reagan. The former California governor's most compelling message in an October 2, 1980, debate with Carter, offered in the form of a question, was, "Are you better off today than you were four years ago?"

In the immediate aftermath of the September 11 terrorist attacks, President George W. Bush was urged by some of his aides to tap the unity and sense of purpose that had swept the country in the fall of 2001 and call for a program of national service that all Americans would participate in, perhaps following high school. They thought it would be a good way to cement that unity, in addition to pro-viding manpower for a variety of needs. Bush's more conservative aides, however, nixed the idea as another intrusive big-government program. Although the president made repeated efforts aimed at calming the country and making sure that Americans did not turn against each other by blaming Muslims, his most memorable call to action following the attacks was that people should resume shopping as a way of keeping the terrorists from having destroyed the economy.

An influential, best-selling book published a year before the World Trade Center fell provided compelling evidence that Bush probably would not have succeeded had he asked for more. *Bowling Alone* by Harvard professor Robert Putnam traced the sharp decline in the United States of what Putnam and other social scientists called "social capital," which he defined as "connections among individuals—social networks and the norms of reciprocity and trustworthiness that arise from them." These networks were the essence of social capital, Putnam explained. They did not simply help individuals, such as by networking when seeking a job. They also produced a "public good," because they produced mutual obligations—a sense of being in a community that one derives benefits from, but also contributes to. In other words, social capital was all about balancing personal interests with the common good.

In the 1960s, America had been rich in social capital, Putnam wrote. People were heavily engaged in civic groups, such as the Rotary Club, the American Legion, and local political party organizations. They joined religious and social organizations, including bowling leagues, in droves. As a result, they had high levels of confidence in their fellow citizens and their elected officials. A 1964 poll reported that two out of three Americans believed that their elected officials were working to advance the interests of "all the people," while just three out of ten thought they were working to advance the interest of "a few big interests."*

However, by the end of the twentieth century, Putnam concluded, people were bowling alone. "Something important happened to social bonds and civic engagement in America over the last third of the twentieth century," he wrote:

> During the first two-thirds of the century Americans took a more and more active role in the social and political life of their communities—in churches and union halls, in bowling

---

* By 2016, those polling results would be more than reversed: 92 percent thought government favored the "few," and 8 percent believed government was working to help the "many."

alleys and clubrooms, around committee tables and card tables and dinner tables. Year by year we gave more generously to charity, we pitched in more often on community projects, and (insofar as we can still find reliable evidence) we behaved in an increasingly trustworthy way toward one another. Then, mysteriously and more or less simultaneously we began to do all those things less often. We maintain a facade of formal affiliation, but we rarely show up. . . . We are less likely to turn out for collective deliberation—whether in the voting booth or the meeting hall—and when we do, we find that discouragingly few of our friends and neighbors have shown up.

According to Putnam's survey data, between 1973 and 1994 the number of Americans who attended a public meeting on town or school affairs in the previous year declined 40 percent. In 1960, voter turnout in the presidential election was 63 percent. In 1996, it was 49 percent, far below that of most developed countries and often below that of less developed nations. That understated the actual decline because turnout rates of eligible voters prior to the passage of the 1965 Voting Rights Act did not account for the millions of Americans who might have wanted to vote but were not allowed to.

"Americans were roughly half as likely to work for a political party or attend a political rally or speech in the 1990s as in the 1970s," Putnam found. And despite decades of advances in education levels, Americans at the end of the twentieth century were so disengaged that "The average college graduate today knows little more about public affairs than did the average high school graduate in the 1940s." Instead of joining social or civic organizations, if Americans were active in any organizations they were typically groups focused on narrow interests, such as a professional trade association, or a group advocating for or against the building of a road.

Putnam considered whether this new American disengagement might have been caused by suburban sprawl and the hours spent commuting that gave people less time to devote to group activities; by the rise of television that made them still more likely to be homebodies; or by financial pressures on the average family that often forced both parents to work and required one or both to work longer and spend less time and money on civic or other group activities. He concluded that his data did not show any of the three to be a major cause. Instead, he cited what he called "generational change," the fact that a new generation of Americans had not faced the common danger, World War II, that their parents had. In other words, not enough Americans thought of themselves as being together in what Senator Bradley called the foxhole.

Near the end of *Bowling Alone*, Putnam picked up on that idea. He wrote that efforts to get Americans to become engaged again "would be eased by a palpable national crisis, like war or depression or natural disaster, but . . . America at the dawn of the new century faces no such galvanizing crisis."

A year later, on September 11, the crisis came. For a while Americans did seem to come together. Members of Congress from both sides of the aisle gathered hand in hand on the Capitol steps that night to sing "God Bless America." People flooded volunteer centers to help the injured and those who had lost loved ones. Hundreds of millions of dollars were donated to help the families of victims. Congress quickly passed bipartisan legislation setting up a victims compensation fund and revamping airport security. Police and other first responders were saluted by people on the left and right.

That mood soon faded. Divisions in Washington and cynicism across the country returned. If anything, the isolation from the larger community that Putnam had blamed, in small part, on television, intensified in the age of smartphones and social media. Polarization—which Putnam had attributed in 2000 to the "culture wars" of the 1990s, but at the time had cautioned "should not be exaggerated"—had also grown worse.

Putnam and a coauthor, Thomas Sander, wrote in a 2010 article, "Still Bowling Alone?" that there had been some increase in civic engagement among more well-to-do members of what they called the "9/11 generation"—people who were eighteen to twenty-nine years old by 2010. However, the authors were unsure how strong the trend was, and suspected it might be attributable to factors as unrelated to 9/11 as efforts to spruce up college admissions résumés, or the excitement generated by Barack Obama's presidential campaign. More important, they were certain that whatever uptick there had been in engagement among better-off younger people had not extended to older, better-off Americans or to the poor and middle class of all ages.

In fact, Putnam and Sander described what they called "an ominous larger and longer-term picture whose main feature is a growing civic and social gap in the United States between upper-middle-class young white people and their less affluent counterparts." Putnam would focus on that gap five years later. A new book, *Our Kids: The American Dream in Crisis*, published in 2015, documented the sad state of equal opportunity and income mobility. It also highlighted an issue Putnam had missed in writing *Bowling Alone* fifteen years earlier. In that book, he had discounted what he called "financial pressures" as the cause of Americans' estrangement—because he failed to notice how disproportionately those pressures had been distributed. He had concluded that squeezed family finances were not a likely cause because, he wrote, the decline in engagement had "continued unabated during the booms of the mid-1980s and late 1990s. The economy went up and down and up and down, but social capital only went down." What Putnam realized by 2015 was that those booms had been enjoyed by the rich but had bypassed most of the Americans he was writing about in *Bowling Alone*.

Surely, all of the assaults on the financial security of so many American families over the last fifty years drove the estrangement Putnam so convincingly documented. So, too, did the growing imbalance of political power driven by the rise of political money.

That raises a basic chicken-or-egg, cause-and-effect question. Did the phenomenon of so many Americans disengaging from civic life beginning in the 1970s allow those at the top to maximize their winnings, take over the political system, build their moats, and snuff out the dream of income mobility for everyone else? Or did Americans disengage as they began to realize the dream was becoming an illusion because everything it depended on—from secure middle-class jobs to actual power to influence a functioning democracy—was gone?

The answer, of course, is that disengagement was both a result and a cause. Why stay involved in politics if the system had been rigged by super PACs, lobbying, and gerrymandering? Why look to the government for help if government could not or would not fix the roads, protect unions, or hold bank CEOs responsible for crashing the economy? Yet how can democratic government be expected to work if those who depend on it do not demand that their leaders make it work? Democracy cannot work without the demos—the people.

For Americans to come together now to fix their country, they will have to overcome the forces that have broken their country: a meritocracy that has become the new aristocracy; the financialization of the economy and the resulting dominance of short-termism; the hijacking of the First Amendment that allowed money to take over Washington; the marginalization of the middle class that would have to rise up and support any resurgence; the polarization, entrenched incompetence, and cronyism that have soured most outsiders on the prospect of trying to get Washington to do anything productive; the moats that the winners have built to protect their winnings; and the success of political leaders serving those at the top in splitting the middle class from the poor, even as the middle class becomes poorer. In the face of these challenges and setbacks Americans could understandably give up on reversing their country's continued decline, for these forces have come together in a no-longer-silent storm to power a downward spiral that might seem hopelessly irreversible.

As the storm was gathering, Jimmy Carter saw that Americans were no longer heeding President Kennedy's call for engagement, but he was able to do little more than complain about it. Ronald Reagan saw it, but chose to exploit and exacerbate it by telling his countrymen in his inaugural address that government was the problem, not the solution.

Bill Clinton tried to finesse the divide between sacrifice and self-interest.

George W. Bush asked Americans to shop.

Barack Obama did re-engage millions with his campaign, and he did mix a call for shared responsibility with his bumper sticker message of hope and change. Indeed, he called for a "new era of responsibility" in his inaugural address. But, as we have seen, six hours later, leading Republicans were meeting over dinner to map plans to block anything he proposed. By then, Washington was so polarized and so much of the rest of the country was so frustrated and cynical that Obama was, as he put it in 2016, unable to "break the fever. . . . It just seems to get worse."

Obama undercut his efforts to break the fever with poor messaging and, sometimes, poor management, such as the debacle that accompanied the launch of Obamacare. He failed to accompany the programs funded by his stimulus program, such as infrastructure upgrades, with the kind of marketing that would have conveyed to people who drove by a repaved road or benefited from a refurbished sewer system that it was his initiative that was funding the improvements and the jobs created by them. He failed to drive home to poor and middle-class families how Obamacare was meant for them, something they only realized when the Republicans tried to take it away seven years later. There was little effort to showcase how his Dodd-Frank Consumer Financial Protection Bureau was retrieving billions for consumers cheated by banks. He was also ineffective in calling out the Republicans for their opposition to the job training programs he tried to upgrade, and insensitive to the damage done by free trade that he and his party had championed and that those programs were meant to address.

Then again, it is not clear that flawless management and the most stellar messaging could have overcome the forces of polarization, political money, and gerrymandering that enabled—actually, compelled—Obama's opponents. Nor is it clear that anyone could have broken through the cynicism that had built up over decades on the day he took office. It could be that the fever can only be broken when the public reaches a breaking point.

What is clear is that in 2016, Donald Trump rode that fever to the White House, promising Americans that they could sit back while he fixed everything. He would "drain the swamp" in Washington. He would take the coal industry back to the greatness it had enjoyed eighty years before. He would rebuild the cities, block immigrants with a great wall, provide health care for all, and make the country's infrastructure the envy of the world, while cutting everyone's taxes. Forty-six percent of those who voted figured that things were so bad they might as well let him try.

Yet in the spectacular collapse of Trump's flimflam act, there is hope. Those who voted for Trump committed the ultimate act of rejecting the meritocrats—epitomized by the hardworking, always prepared, Yale Law–educated, but seemingly cold and calculating Hillary Clinton—in favor of an inexperienced, never-prepared, six-time-bankrupted, vulgar, shoot-from-the hip heir to a real estate fortune. The debacle that their choice produced—the daily exposure of their candidate's lack of intelligence and integrity, his disgraceful personal conduct, and his disdain for the policies he promised, such as a fair tax code to help the middle class—may have broken the fever for enough of them so that the electorate will now settle in the middle: choosing leaders who are prepared and are intelligent, and who can connect with them and channel their frustration, rather than exploit it.

However, Americans must be willing to be led that way. In fact, they must re-engage and demand those kinds of leaders. That can only happen if Americans borrow some of Trump's bravado. The obstacles and all of their side effects must become energizing challenges, rather than excuses not to try.

For example, the new technology that produced targeted digital media represents one of those apparent breakthroughs during the fifty-year tailspin that produced unintended consequences and a valid excuse for people to remain at each other's throats or disengage altogether. It polarized the news that people consume, driving them further apart. Equally important, it resulted in newspapers—long hometown monopolies or oligopolies that advertisers had to use and readers had to buy—losing the subsidy that monopoly power gave them. Most then dug deeper holes for themselves by giving their content away online, in what became a fruitless search for equivalent digital advertising dollars. In 2016, newspaper advertising revenue was about a third of what it was in 2000. As a result, newspaper employment had dropped to 174,000 from 412,000 in 2001, and Americans could complain that they were less armed with the straight-shooting journalism necessary to hold their elected leaders accountable.

But that is not true. Today, the Internet and social media produce not just fake news or slanted news but infinite sources of solid news and information—if people choose to use them. Sheila Krumholz's OpenSecrets.org can tell any voter which donor from which industry has given how much to which member of Congress. Peter Peterson's foundation website produces up-to-the-minute reports on federal spending and the deficit. Other non-profits publish similarly solid information on every imaginable subject. Local websites do the same across the country, telling citizens what is happening at the town zoning board or the state utility commission.

Moreover, multiple print, online, and television news organizations are producing some of the best journalism ever. The importance of this surge in journalism cannot be overstated. The uncovered scandals of the Trump presidency, or the more routine work of reporters—stories about hospital price gouging or that collapsing lock that threatens the movement of freight along the Ohio River— demonstrate that every day. There is no excuse, other than the lame ones of being distracted or disheartened, for being uninformed.

The good news is that in the age of Trump fewer people were letting themselves be distracted. The Internet may have made the market for content more efficient by allowing people to customize their news, but the laws of supply and demand still applied. Demand grew for reliable substance—because that substance counts more to more people.

The New York Times, which decided to charge readers for online content in 2010, has seen a dramatic increase in revenue from readers, as have *The Wall Street Journal* and *The Washington Post*. Streaming video outlets, like Netflix and Amazon, have found strong audiences for documentaries, as have cable television channels. At the same time, non-profit news organizations, like *ProPublica* and National Public Radio and its local affiliates, have been fortified by an outpouring of new donations.

Similarly, every private organization working to counter the forces of the tailspin that has been described in this book—OpenSecrets, Issue One, the Bipartisan Policy Center, Better Markets, the Partnership for Public Service, the Coalition for Queens/Tech Equality, Year Up, Philip Howard's Common Good, the Aspen Institute's anti-short-termism American Prosperity Project—has seen a dramatic increase in support and in talent joining their cause. They are ready to step in and lead. And they may find followers. Americans may finally be ready to get into the same foxhole.

This will not be a revolution of those on the left against those on the right. It will be about the unprotected demanding that the protected become responsible and accountable, whether they are executives shielded by their corporate structures, their lawyers, their lobbyists, and their financial engineers; civil servants protected by work rules that need to be fixed and by the public's inattention; corporations hiding behind arbitration clauses or the First Amendment; or members of Congress protected by gerrymandering and PACs. It will be a revolution that demands that everyone be personally accountable for what they do and share in their responsibility for the common good.

Like the Boston Tea Party, or the abuse of a lone Tunisian merchant that set off the Arab Spring, and propelled by re-energized journalism organizations and the multiplying force of social media, the accountability and responsibility revolution could begin with a triggering event or series of events.

Coal miners who realize they will never get their jobs back could march on Washington and demand help in transitioning to an energy industry of the future. Victims of an arbitration clause as outrageous as the one that protected Wells Fargo might organize a Facebook group that floods the Capitol switchboard, or even camps out on Capitol Hill, to demand a change in the 1925 law that has been used to deny them access to the courts.

A particularly blatant scandal involving lobbyists or super PACs could, as Issue One's leader predicted, become that final gulp of alcohol that the liver rejects. Or, as suggested, one or more news organizations could finally generate broad disgust over the auctioning of American democracy by routinely attaching to the name of every politician, whenever he or she holds a hearing or votes on an issue, a tally of the campaign contributions received from the special interests involved.

Maybe an elderly woman's struggle to get the Social Security money she is owed will go viral and snowball into a meme that taps everyone's frustrations about broken government—and makes the Partnership for Public Service's wonky plans for civil service reform, agency performance metrics, and a rational budgeting process a cause that politicians have to latch on to. Perhaps one of the cable news networks could televise Stier's annual "Sammy Awards" dinner for stellar public servants to drive home the message that government can work if the right people are attracted to the mission.

A protest launched by a daughter who cannot get care for her elderly mother, joined by a mother who cannot get care for her toddler, could mushroom into a national caregiver movement that seizes on Peter Edelman's blueprint for a new caregiver workforce infrastructure.

Public fury over budget deadlocks and government shutdowns, amid the general failure of Congress to pass meaningful legislation, could break the fever of polarization and turn the Bipartisan Policy Center's work on infrastructure, job training, health care, and the deficit into an agenda, rather than the earnest musings of a shadow Congress. The paralysis that has made infrastructure little more than a political talking point could be overwhelmed by public fury if a bridge collapses on the same day or in the same week that two trains derail, a big city loses electricity, and a school system finds out that its water fountains are gushing lead.

Another banking scandal that victimizes millions but goes unpunished could produce demonstrations in front of thousands of bank branches, and make Dennis Kelleher's Better Markets lobbying team a driving force instead of a sidelines heckler.

Cutbacks at community colleges and public universities that force tuition raises and reductions in services that are too much to bear could send students and their families to the barricades.

Triggered by ever more stunning displays of the soaring fortunes and lifestyles of those at the top, at the same time that those in the middle continue to be pushed down, politicians and groups representing the poor and those in the middle could join to form a new advocacy group demanding the basic fairness—not equality, but just a fair chance at the Dream—that accountability and responsibility will produce.

My bet is that Americans will retake their democracy. Things may get worse before they get better, but the odds are that events like these will become trigger points that prompt Americans to reclaim the legacy of their country's historic resilience. When that happens, they will become the ground troops that propel the men and women we met in this book, and many others, who have been resisting the downward spiral and laying the groundwork for a revival.

Americans are going to answer the call of a new New Frontier. They are going to decide that enough is enough. That it is time to storm the moats.

Acknowledgments

This book would not have happened if two people hadn't endured two years helping to make a coherent story out of what I was finding and thinking about as I attempted to answer a simple question: How had the greatest country in the world fallen into a tailspin?

The idea was born when my wife, Cynthia, and I were stuck in traffic in a taxi one night on the Van Wyck Expressway coming from Kennedy Airport into Manhattan. As I thought about the grimy terminal where we had just arrived, and looked out at the snarled, dirty, pothole-filled road we were on, I asked Cynthia what a first-time visitor from another country would think about America upon landing at that airport and getting stuck on the ugly Van Wyck. How had things deteriorated so badly? And how did it happen that nothing else seemed to be working in our country—from politics (Donald Trump was on top of the 2016 Republican primary polls) to economic opportunity to health care to simple civility? When Cynthia said something about how maybe that could be a book, she didn't know she was volunteering to be a sounding board and a reader as I tested ways to wrestle that idea to the ground. But she never wavered—in critiquing, suggesting, reassuring, and pushing me from start to finish, through every draft. As with pretty much everything in my life, I don't know how I could have done this book without her.

Then there was Jonathan Segal, Knopf's vice president and senior editor. His heroics began when he somehow saw something in what reads two-plus years later as a half-baked, cliché-filled first try at a book proposal. He worked with me on multiple attempts to get close to a vision of the book that I wanted to write and that he wanted to edit and publish. Knopf editor-in-chief Sonny Mehta then provided a final breakthrough; he listened to me describe what I hoped to attempt, and warned, without missing a beat, that I would probably want to go back fifty years to get the real story.

That was only the beginning of the Knopf team's enormous contributions, led by Jon's hard-driving but patient input at every stage. Yes, editors get paid to edit. But not to edit and advise like this. From his focus on the big picture—and insistence that I do the same—to his attention to every word and punctuation mark (literally) in every sentence, Jon's care and talent permeates *Tailspin*.

Also at Knopf, Sam Aber helped coordinate the editorial process and many other details, large and small, while Maria Massey supervised the copyediting and production process with much-appreciated skill, efficiency, and good cheer. Copy editor Fred Chase reminded me once again of how valuable someone with his skills can be in saving a writer from himself. Soonyoung Kwon made the text and photo insert look as sharp as they do, and Tyler Comrie's remarkable inspiration and execution gave us the jacket design. The Knopf publicity and marketing team, especially Paul Bogaards, Abby Endler, and Danielle Plafsky, handled the book with consummate care and expertise. All in all, for any writer who wants a publishing partner that has fiercely high standards and endless reserves of enthusiasm and energy, Knopf can't be beat.

David Kuhn, my friend, former editing colleague, and agent proved again that he's still a wise editor, as well as a savvy adviser. I am also indebted to veteran journalist and longtime friend James Warren; to two former students in the journalism seminar I teach at Yale, Louise Story (a rising star at *The New York Times*) and Elise Jordan (an MSNBC and *Time* contributor); and to my son Sam and daughter Sophie for reading drafts and not sparing me their incisive comments. After the final draft was completed, two other former students, Sophie Haigney and Kendrick McDonald, fact-checked everything with great care and made important additional suggestions and comments along the way. Finally, my assistant Victoria Weiss helped from start to finish with valuable research and by coordinating everything, including the fact-checking and securing all of the photos.

Then there are the authors of books that came before *Tailspin* and covered major parts of this story. I have tried to credit them in the text or source notes where I drew directly on their material, but those listed below deserve special recognition and thanks because their work was so important in shaping my thinking and helping me assemble the facts:

Edward Alden, *Failure to Adjust: How Americans Got Left Behind in the Global Economy* (Lanham, Md.: Rowman & Littlefield, 2016).

Jeffrey Birnbaum and Alan Murray, *Showdown at Gucci Gulch: Lawmakers, Lobbyists, and the Unlikely Triumph of Tax Reform* (New York: Random House, 1987).

David Daley, *Ratf**ked: The True Story Behind the Secret Plan to Steal America's Democracy* (New York: Liveright, 2016).

Tom DeLay, *No Retreat, No Surrender* (New York: Sentinel, 2007), pp. 65–70.

Lee Drutman, *The Business of America Is Lobbying: How Corporations Became Politicized and Politics Became More Corporate* (Oxford: Oxford University Press, 2015).

Peter Edelman, *So Rich, So Poor: Why It's So Hard to End Poverty in America* (New York: The New Press, 2012).

Kathryn J. Edin and H. Luke Shaefer, *$2.00 a Day: Living on Almost Nothing in America* (Boston: Houghton Mifflin Harcourt, 2015).

Thomas Edsall, *The New Politics of Inequality: A Quiet Transfer of Power Has Taken Place in the Nation's Capital* (New York: W. W. Norton, 1985).

Rana Foroohar, *Makers and Takers: The Rise of Finance and the Fall of American Business* (New York: Crown Business, 2016).

Jacob Hacker and Paul Pierson, *Winner-Take-All Politics: How Washington Made the Rich Richer—and Turned Its Back on the Middle Class* (New York: Simon & Schuster, 2010).

Michael Harrington, *The Other America: Poverty in the United States* (New York: Macmillan, 1962).

Philip K. Howard, *The Death of Common Sense: How Law Is Suffocating America* (New York: Random House, 1994).

Mark Ingebretsen, *NASDAQ: A History of the Market That Changed the World* (Roseville, Calif.: Forum, an Imprint of Prime Publishing, 2002).

Brooks Jackson, *Honest Graft: Inside the Business of Politics* (New York: Alfred A. Knopf, 1988).

John B. Judis, *The Paradox of American Democracy: Elites, Special Interests, and the Betrayal of Public Trust* (New York: Pantheon, 2000).

Geoffrey Kabaservice, *The Guardians: Kingman Brewster, His Circle, and the Rise of the Liberal Establishment* (New York: Henry Holt, 2004).

Robert A. Kagan, *Adversarial Legalism: The American Way of Law* (Cambridge: Harvard University Press, 2001).

Jerome Karabel, *The Chosen: The Hidden History of Admission and Exclusion at Harvard, Yale, and Princeton* (Boston: Houghton Mifflin Harcourt, 2005).

Lawrence Lessig, *Republic Lost: Version 2.0* (New York: Twelve, 2015).

Michael Lewis, *The Big Short: Inside the Doomsday Machine* (New York: W. W. Norton, 2010).

Michael Lewis, *Liar's Poker: Rising Through the Wreckage on Wall Street* (New York: W. W. Norton, 1989).

Beth Macy, *Factory Man* (New York: Hachette, 2014).

Jeff Madrick, *The Age of Greed* (New York: Alfred A. Knopf, 2011).

Thomas E. Mann and Norman J. Ornstein, *It's Even Worse Than It Looks: How the American Constitutional System Collided with the New Politics of Extremism* (New York: Basic Books, 2012).

David Maraniss and Michael Weisskopf, *Tell Newt to Shut Up!* (New York: Touchstone, 1996).

Jane Mayer, *Dark Money: The Hidden History of the Billionaires Behind the Rise of the Radical Right* (New York: Doubleday, 2016).

John Micklethwait and Adrian Wooldridge, *The Right Nation: Conservative Power in America* (New York: Penguin, 2004).

Charles Peters, *We Do Our Part: Toward a Fairer and More Equal America* (New York: Random House, 2017).

Henry Petroski, *The Road Taken: The History and Future of America's Transportation* (New York: Bloomsbury, 2016).

Robert C. Post, *Democracy, Expertise, Academic Freedom: A First Amendment Jurisprudence for the Modern State* (New Haven: Yale University Press, 2012).

Robert D. Putnam, *Bowling Alone: The Collapse and Revival of American Community* (New York: Simon & Schuster, 2000).

Gillian Tett, *Fool's Gold: The Inside Story of J.P. Morgan and How Wall St. Greed Corrupted Its Bold Dream and Created a Financial Catastrophe* (New York: Free Press, 2009).

A Note on Methodology and Sources

Readers should know as much as possible about why an author thinks he knows what he says he knows. Although I often make it clear in the text what my source was, these notes are intended to supplement the text by providing information about sources where I decided that something in the text required an explanation or elaboration that would interrupt the narrative. The notes also make it possible for the reader to refer to the full text or a full set of data to ascertain that I quoted the text in context and used the data accurately.

In some cases where I thought an additional explanation or note was especially important and I did not want to count on readers finding it in this back-of-the-book section, I included a brief footnote in the text.

GENERAL METHODOLOGY

In no case is a thought attributed to someone directly unless that person told me about that thought or, in the case of historical events, unless there is a cited source that quotes the person directly.

In no case is a conversation or a discussion in a meeting quoted unless at least one participant in that conversation or discussion was my source or, in the case of historical events, unless there is a cited source that quotes the conversation directly.

Where I refer to interviews, these are always interviews that I personally conducted with the person cited.

All but a few of the interviews I conducted were done explicitly on the record. I tried not to rely on anonymous sources and, with few exceptions, succeeded.

Source references, such as books or newspaper articles, are listed below only where it is not clear in the text that I relied on the reporting of others.

References are not listed for general statements (about historical events or political developments, for example) if they are widely known and uncontroversial. Similarly, references are not provided for widely reported news events, or for unambiguous statements of fact, such as the date of a public event.

If the text quotes from a newspaper article or magazine, the reference is not cited here if the text makes the source and the date clear. However, I have provided links in these notes to documents if I think a reader might want to see them.

References to any company's revenue or profits are based on its publicly filed financial reports for the period in question.

Except when referring to historical trends, data cited is always the most recent data that was available as of December 2017. In cases where estimates are inexact or vary I tried to veer toward the more conservative estimates in order not to overstate a point.

DISCLOSURES

In reading references to Yale, you should know that I have been a long-time supporter of the university and that I teach journalism there (in an unpaid capacity).

After I had finished my reporting on Issue One, its president, Nick Penniman, became involved in a business venture I began exploring in fall 2017, and we also became friends.

As noted in the text, I am a board member (unpaid) and donor to the Coalition for Queens/Tech Equality.

As the text attempts to make clear, a small amount of the material in *Tailspin* (less than two percent) is taken directly or almost directly from books and magazine articles I have written over the years. More of it is drawn on what I learned researching the issues and people that were the subjects of this writing.

Additional note: Where newspaper articles are cited below without the name of an author, it is because the article had no byline.

Notes

3 *measures of public engagement:* Voter turnout in the U.S. is far lower than in most developed countries, according to data from the Pew Research Center: http://www.pewresearch.org/fact-tank/2017/05/15/u-s-voter-turnout-trails-most-developed-countries/. A 2017 Pew survey found that only 37 percent of Americans had faith that the next generation would have it better than the current one: http://www.pewglobal.org/2017/06/05/2-public-divided-on-prospects-for-the-next-generation/. Public trust in the government is near a historic low, according to other Pew survey data from May 2017: http://www.people-press.org/2017/05/03/public-trust-in-government-remains-near-historic-lows-as-partisan-attitudes-shift.

3 *46.1 percent of American voters:* Data from the Federal Election Commission: https://transition.fec.gov/pubrec/fe2016/2016presgeresults.pdf.

3 *657 water main breaks:* The American Society of Civil Engineers has estimated in its 2017 Infrastructure Report Card that there are an estimated 240,000 water main breaks per year, which averages to about 657 per day. The report card is available here: https://www.infrastructurereportcard.org/cat-item/drinking-water/. Note: The engineers society, of course, has an interest in emphasizing the need to repair infrastructure such as water systems.

4 *A child's chance*: Raj Chetty, David Grusky, Maximilian Hendren, Robert Manduca, and Jimmy Narang, "The Fading American Dream: Trends in Absolute Income Mobility Since 1940," *Science*, April 2017, 10.1126/science.aal4617.

4 *American middle class:* A *New York Times* analysis in 2014 found that after-tax middle-class incomes in Canada are now higher than those in

the United States: David Leonhardt and Kevin Quealy, "The American Middle Class Is No Longer the World's Richest," *New York Times*, April 22, 2014, https://www.nytimes.com/2014/04/23/upshot/the -american-middle-class-is-no-longer-the-worlds-richest.html.

4 *middle-class wages:* The Pew Research Center found that after adjusting for inflation, average hourly wages had the same purchasing power in 1973 as in 2014. This data can be found here: http://www.pewresearch .org/fact-tank/2014/10/09/for-most-workers-real-wages-have-barely -budged-for-decades/. It should be noted that from 2015 to 2017, median family *incomes* (as opposed to individual wages) increased by about 3 percent per year, after also being nearly frozen. However, that is because the improved economy has enabled more families to have one or even two wage earners working full-time, not because wages are higher.

4 *escalating out-of-pocket health care costs:* Health insurance premiums grew 61 percent between 2005 and 2015, according to data from the Kaiser Family Foundation, and worker contributions grew 83 percent. See http://www.kff.org/report-section/ehbs-2015-summary-of -findings/. For an analysis of the effect of health care costs on wages, see Gary Burtless and Sveta Milusheva, "Effects of Employer-Sponsored Health Insurance Costs on Social Security Taxable Wages," *The Social Security Bulletin* 73, no. 1 (2013), pp. 83–108, https://papers.ssrn.com /sol3/papers.cfm?abstract_id=2217486.

4 *earnings by the top:* Congressional Budget Office, "Trends in the Distribution of Household Income Between 1979 and 2007," October 2011, https://www.cbo.gov/sites/default/files/112th-congress-2011-2012 /reports/10-25-householdincome0.pdf.

4 *incomes in the three years:* This paper by economist Emmanuel Saez reported that from 2009 to 2012 incomes of the top 1 percent grew by 31.4 percent while bottom 99 percent incomes grew by 0.4 percent: Saez, "Striking It Richer: The Evolution of Top Incomes in the United States," University of California–Berkeley, 2013, https://eml .berkeley.edu//~saez/saez-UStopincomes-2012.pdf.

4 *Self-inflicted deaths:* This Associated Press report in 2016 found that drug and alcohol overdoses and suicides are on the rise: Mike Stobbe, "'Deaths of Despair' Drag Life Expectancy Lower for Whites," Associated Press, June 30, 2016, https://apnews.com/08c85b511f0245e5 ada2db8e3d7c33a5/deaths-despair-overdoses-drinking-suicides-hit -whites. Life expectancy declined by one month in 2015, according to the Centers for Disease Control: https://www.cdc.gov/nchs/products /databriefs/db267.htm, and by an additional month in 2016: https://www

.usatoday.com/story/news/2017/12/21/u-s-life-expectancy-drops
-second-year-drug-deaths-spike-cdc/970283001/.

4 *Household debt:* The Federal Reserve Bank of New York published this
   data in May 2017: https://www.newyorkfed.org/medialibrary/inter
   actives/householdcredit/data/pdf/HHDC_2017Q1.pdf.

4 *The world's richest country:* OECD Factbook 2015–2016. See the
   chapter titled "Poverty Rates and Gaps": http://dx.doi.org/10.1787
   /factbook-2015-21-en.

4 *"food insecure":* Alisha Coleman-Jensen, Matthew P. Rabbitt, Chris-
   tian A. Gregory, and Anita Singh, "Statistical Supplement to Household Food Security in the United States in 2016," U.S. Department
   of Agriculture, Economic Research Service, September 2017, https://
   www.ers.usda.gov/webdocs/publications/84981/ap-077.pdf?v=42979.

5 *highest infant mortality rate and lowest life expectancy:* Robert Pearl, *Mis-
   treated: Why We Think We're Getting Good Health Care—and Why We're
   Usually Wrong* (New York: PublicAffairs, 2017).

5 *American children rank:* See this 2015 report by the Program for International Student Assessment, which measures academic achievement
   in students every three years: http://dx.doi.org/10.1787/aa9237e6-en.

5 *twenty registered lobbyists:* Daniel Auble, a researcher for OpenSecrets
   .org, determined that there were a total of 11,165 registered lobbyists
   in 2016; there are 535 members of Congress, or 20.9 lobbyists per
   member.

10 *Republican economists:* See Peterson memo, detailed in Chapter 6.

2   MERITOCRACY BECOMES THE NEW ARISTOCRACY

17 *only about 5 percent:* This was told to me by school officials years later
   when, as an interested alumnus and supporter of the school, I inquired
   about Deerfield's history of financial aid.

19 *standardized aptitude tests:* http://www.pbs.org/wgbh/pages/frontline
   /shows/sats/where/timeline.html.

19 *Brewster, a member:* Ibid.

19 *Yale had accepted:* As recently as 1961, 53 percent of legacy applications were accepted, according to Geoffrey Kabaservice, who wrote an
   indispensable biography of Kingman Brewster, *The Guardians: Kingman Brewster, His Circle, and the Rise of the Liberal Establishment* (New
   York: Henry Holt, 2004). It was excerpted in the *Yale Alumni Magazine* as "The Birth of a New Institution: How Two Yale Presidents
   and Their Admissions Directors Tore Up the 'Old Blueprint' to Cre-

ate a Modern Yale," *Yale Alumni Magazine*, December 1999, http://
archives.yalealumnimagazine.com/issues/99_12/admissions.html.

19 *academic honors:* According to Kabaservice in *The Guardians*, private
school students made up more than 60 percent of the Yale Class of
1957, but accounted for less than half of the membership of Phi Beta
Kappa and one sixth of the membership of Tau Beta Pi, the national
engineering honor society.

19 *checklist of desired:* Kabaservice, *The Guardians.*

19 *"hesitate to admit a lad":* Jerome Karabel, *The Chosen: The Hidden History of Admission and Exclusion at Harvard, Yale, and Princeton* (Boston:
Houghton Mifflin Harcourt, 2005).

19 *He stunned:* Kabaservice, *The Guardians.*

20 *In Clark's first year:* Ibid.

20 *Markovits, who specializes:* Transcript: https://law.yale.edu/system/files
/area/department/studentaffairs/document/markovitscommence
mentrev.pdf.

23 *A student survey:* The survey can be found here: https://law.yale.edu
/system/files/area/department/studentaffairs/document/class_action
_report.pdf.

23 *First Generation Professionals:* Interview with Anna Gonzales, president
of First Generation Professionals. (According to other Yale students,
an earlier group had formed several years before but had disbanded.)

23 *"people could say":* J. D. Vance, *Hillbilly Elegy: A Memoir of Family and
Culture in Crisis* (New York: HarperCollins, 2016).

24 *American adults:* United States Census Bureau data on educational
attainment in the U.S.: https://www.census.gov/data/tables/2016
/demo/education-attainment/cps-detailed-tables.html.

24 *Harvard College:* In a survey conducted by *The Harvard Crimson*, 9.55
percent of students self-reported family incomes of below $40,000
annually, 18.54 percent reported family incomes of between $125,000
and $249,999, and 28.8 percent reported family incomes of over
$250,000 annually. The survey and accompanying article are available
here: http://features.thecrimson.com/2015/senior-survey/.

24 *college graduation gap:* "2015 Indicators of Higher Education Equity,"
The Pell Institute for the Study of Opportunity in Higher Education
and the University of Pennsylvania Alliance for Higher Education
and Democracy, http://www.pellinstitute.org/downloads/publications
-Indicators_of_Higher_Education_Equity_in_the_US_45_Year
_Trend_Report.pdf.

24 *middle-class family incomes:* This data comes from "The Poverty and
Inequality Report," published in 2016 by the Stanford Center on Pov-

erty and Inequality. Figure 1 in the "Wealth Inequality" section of this report, written by researcher Gabriel Zucman, illustrates these trends. The report can be found here: http://inequality.stanford.edu/publica tions/state-union-report.

24 *In 1970 the one-percenters' share:* Ibid.

25 *by 2007 the one-percenters' share:* Ibid.

25 *bottom 90 percent:* These numbers can be found using the last graph in Saez's 2013 paper, "Striking It Richer." Adding the three numbers from the graph representing the top 10 percent of earners, and sub-tracting the sum of those percentages from 100 percent, yields the income shares for the bottom 90 percent of earners in each given year.

25 *Incomes for the top:* Saez, "Striking It Richer."

25 *"children's prospects":* Chetty, Grusky, Hendren, Manduca, and Narang, "The Fading American Dream: Trends in Absolute Income Mobility Since 1940."

25 *The* wealth *of the upper class:* Two graphs released by the Center on Budget and Policy Priorities illustrate the trend: https://www.cbpp.org /research/poverty-and-inequality/a-guide-to-statistics-on-historical -trends-in-income-inequality.

28 *published an article:* http://science.sciencemag.org/content/349/6254 /aaboo96?sid=121580e9-c559-4974-883c-7b278eeboc07.

28 *Their study was attacked:* David Bernstein, "Fisman's and Markovits' Bogus 'Class War,'" *Washington Post*, September 27, 2015, https:// www.washingtonpost.com/news/volokh-conspiracy/wp/2015/09/27 /fisman-and-markovits-bogus-class-war/.

29 *"By the time we thought":* Interview with Markovits.

29 *number of lawyers:* See Richard H. Sander and E. Douglass Williams, "Why Are There So Many Lawyers? Perspectives on a Turbulent Market," *Law & Social Inquiry* 14, no. 3 (1989): 431–79, www.jstor .org/stable/828614.

30 *the legal industry was bigger:* Ibid.

30 *Cravath, Swaine & Moore jumped the starting salary:* Tamar Lewin, "At Cravath, $65,000 to Start," *New York Times*, April 18, 1986, http:// www.nytimes.com/1986/04/18/business/at-cravath-65000-to-start .html.

30 *By 2016, the going rate:* Sara Randazzo, "Law Firm Cravath Rais-ing Starting Salaries to $180,000," *Wall Street Journal*, June 6, 2016, https://www.wsj.com/articles/law-firm-cravath-raising-starting -salaries-to-180-000-1465241318.

30 *average household income:* United States Census Bureau: https://www .census.gov/newsroom/press-releases/2017/income-poverty.html.

30 *elite first-year lawyers:* Randazzo, "Law Firm Cravath Raising Starting Salaries to $180,000."

30 *the Yale Law class:* Fifth Year Career Development Survey conducted by the Yale Law School Career Development Office, available here: https://law.yale.edu/student-life/career-development/employment-data/5th-year-career-development-survey.

30 *At another top law school:* Columbia Law School employment summary for 2015 graduates, available here: http://www.law.columbia.edu/sites/default/files/microsites/careers/files/2015_aba_employment_summary.pdf.

31 *"66 of the 17,000 lawyers":* Joan Biskupic, Janet Roberts, and John Shiffman, "The Echo Chamber," Reuters, December 8, 2014, http://www.reuters.com/investigates/special-report/scotus/.

31 *Stanford law professor Robert Gordon:* Robert W. Gordon, "The Independence of Lawyers," *Boston University Law Review* 68 (1988), http://digitalcommons.law.yale.edu/fss_papers/1361.

34 *"The results for these kids"* and subsequent quotes: Interviews with Marx.

35 *about 8 percent:* Ibid.

35 *Amos Hostetter, Jr.:* This assessment of his reputation is based on my own experience in the cable industry.

36 *overall enrollment from 1,600 to 1,800:* Marx interviews.

36 *Harvard charges no student:* Harvard's financial aid office website: https://college.harvard.edu/admissions/choosing-harvard/affordability.

36 *Low-income students:* See Caroline Minter Hoxby and Christopher Avery, "The Missing 'One-Offs': The Hidden Supply of High-Achieving, Low Income Students," National Bureau of Economic Research, 2012, http://www.nber.org/papers/w18586.pdf.

37 *grade point averages:* Marx interviews.

37 *24 percent of the student body:* Interviews with Marx and Katie Fretwell, current dean of admissions at Amherst. In fall 2017, 22 percent of Amherst students were recipients of Pell Grants, and there was also an increase in aid for low-income international students, who are not eligible for Pell Grants.

37 *median family income of a Yale:* This data was published by *The New York Times* "UpShot" column: https://www.nytimes.com/interactive/projects/college-mobility/yale-university.

37 *At Amherst:* Ibid.

37 *At Yale, 16 percent:* Interview with Jeremiah Quinlan, dean of undergraduate admissions at Yale.

38 *Princeton embarked:* See Nick Anderson, "Princeton Draws Surge of Students from Modest Means," *Washington Post*, October 23, 2017.

38 *A Non-Elite Mobility Engine:* My information about Baruch comes from interviews with multiple students, college president Mitchel Wallerstein, and head of career services Ellen Stein. Other facts were provided by Suzanne Bronski, the director of public relations.

39 *There are 18,000 Baruch students:* Available on their online fact sheet: http://www.baruch.cuny.edu/about/by_the_numbers.html.

42 *Twenty-five thousand students:* Interview with Wallerstein.

42 *Seventy percent:* Interview with Wallerstein, checked by consulting the National Center for Education Studies Undergraduate Retention and Graduation Rates, published in April 2017: https://nces.ed.gov/programs/coe/indicator_ctr.asp.

42 *little or no loans:* 84 percent graduate with no federal student loan debt, according to information available on the Baruch website: http://www.baruch.cuny.edu/careers/scdc/outcomes.html.

44 *Baruch spends approximately:* Information provided via email by Suzanne Bronski.

45 *top three fifths:* David Leonhardt, "America's Great Working Class Colleges," *New York Times*, January 18, 2017, https://www.nytimes.com/2017/01/18/opinion/sunday/americas-great-working-class-colleges.html?_r=0.

3 CASINO COUNTRY

47 *Aspen Institute's New York office:* Visit to the office.

48 *"the disease of short-termism"* and subsequent quotes: Interviews with Samuelson.

48 *"The social responsibility":* Milton Friedman, "A Friedman Doctrine—The Social Responsibility of a Business Is to Increase Its Profits," September 13, 1970, http://www.nytimes.com/1970/09/13/archives/a-friedman-doctrine-the-social-responsibility-of-business-is-to.html.

49 *"Theory of the Firm":* Michael Jensen and William Meckling, "Theory of the Firm: Managerial Behavior, Agency Costs and Ownership Structure," *Journal of Financial Economics* 3, no. 4 (October 1976), https://doi.org/10.1016/0304-405X(76)90026-X.

49 *"Large corporations today":* Michael Jensen and William Meckling, "Can the Corporation Survive?," *American Institute for Economic Research* 17, no. 3 (March 1977), https://www.aier.org/sites/default/files/Files/Documents/Research/3292/EEB197703.pdf.

51 *In 1978, money began:* The Revenue Act of 1978 included a provision that became Internal Revenue Code 401(k).

51 *In 1960, $86 billion:* Report from the Employee Benefit Research Institute: https://www.ebri.org/pdf/publications/facts/0405fact.pdf, particularly Figure 7, titled "Retirement Plan Assets 1950–2003."

52 *By 2017, there was $26 trillion:* Total U.S. retirement assets were $26.1 trillion as of March 31, 2017, according to research done by the Investment Company Institute. Report: https://www.ici.org/research /stats/retirement/ret_17_q1.

52 *In 1950, institutional investors:* Note that the 1950 number represents all stock equity, whereas the 2009 number represents the 1,000 largest corporations. See Matteo Tonello and Stephan Rahim Rabimov, "The 2010 Institutional Investment Report: Trends in Asset Allocation and Portfolio Composition," The Conference Board Research Report, November 2010, https://ssrn.com/abstract=1707512.

52 *In 1960, stock was held:* PolitiFact used historical data from the New York Stock Exchange to compute these averages: Warren Fiske, "Mark Warner Says Average Holding Time for Stocks Has Fallen to Four Months," *PolitiFact,* July 6, 2016, http://www.politifact.com /virginia/statements/2016/jul/06/mark-warner/mark-warner-says -average-holding-time-stocks-has-f/.

52 *In 1980, the average:* Ibid.

52 *In 2016 the average:* Ibid.

52 *quantitative hedge funds:* Gregory Zuckerman and Bradley Hope, "The Quants Run Wall Street Now," *Wall Street Journal,* May 21, 2017, https://www.wsj.com/articles/the-quants-run-wall-street-now -1495389108?utm_source=newsletter&utm_medium=email&utm _campaign=newsletter_axiosfutureofwork&stream=future-of-work.

52 *estimated to account for roughly half:* Ryan Vlastelica, "High-Frequency Trading Has Reshaped Wall Street in Its Image," *Marketwatch,* March 17, 2017, http://www.marketwatch.com/story/high-frequency -trading-has-reshaped-wall-street-in-its-image-2017-03-15?mg =prod/accounts-mw.

53 *Joseph Flom:* I wrote about Flom extensively, beginning in 1976, and got to know him well. There is also an account of his life in, among other books, Malcolm Gladwell, *Outliers: The Story of Success* (New York: Little, Brown, 2008).

54 *a change in federal securities laws:* The Williams Act of 1968 amended the Securities and Exchange Act of 1934 to require mandatory disclosure of information regarding cash tender offers. See Section 13(d) of the act: https://www.sec.gov/about/laws/sea34.pdf.

54 *International Nickel:* Herbert Koshetz, "Inco Defends Its Tender Offer for ESB," *New York Times,* July 27, 1974, http://www.nytimes .com/1974/07/27/archives/inco-defends-its-tender-offer-for-esb -ingersollrand-to-acquire.html?_r=0.

55 *Flom was typically:* Steven Brill, "Two Tough Lawyers in the Tender-Offer Game," *New York,* June 21, 1976.

55 *Skadden, Arps, Slate, Meagher & Flom:* "The Am Law 200 List," published in 2017 by *The American Lawyer.*

56 *"What we've seen is the financialization":* Interviews with Lipton.

57 *Milken—who would go to prison:* Robert J. McCartney, "Milken Enters Prison Camp to Begin 10-Year Sentence," *Washington Post,* March 5, 1991, https://www.washingtonpost.com/archive/business/1991/03/05 /milken-enters-prison-camp-to-begin-10-year-sentence/0b56758a -707f-4f94-86a2-6f5c9d09b1a2/?utm_term=.d1400f3c2339.

60 *manufacturing of durable goods:* Reports from the U.S. Commerce Department, Bureau of Economic Analysis. The report for 1950: https://www.bea.gov/iTable/iTable.cfm?reqid=9&step=3&isuri=1 &904=1949&903=237&906=q&905=1987&910=x&911=0#reqid =9&step=3&isuri=1&904=1949&903=237&906=q&905=1987&910 =x&911=0. The 2016 report: https://www.bea.gov/iTable/iTable.cfm ?reqid=9&step=3&isuri=1&903=239#reqid=9&step=3&isuri=1&903 =239.

60 *Shad, pushed through a rule:* This was Rule 10b-18, which was adopted in 1982: https://www.sec.gov/rules/final/33-8335.htm.

61 *five million shares:* Interviews with multiple lawyers and bankers.

61 *"stock repurchases 'confer a material benefit'":* Richard L. Hudson, "SEC Eases Way for Repurchase of Firms' Stock," *Wall Street Journal,* November 10, 1982.

61 *By 1982, corporate boards:* Frank Dobbin and Jiwook Jung, "The Misapplication of Mr. Michael Jensen: How Agency Theory Brought Down the Economy and Why It Might Again," *Markets on Trial: The Economic Sociology of the U.S. Financial Crisis (Research in the Sociology of Organizations),* vol. 30b (2010) pp. 29–64, https://scholar.harvard .edu/dobbin/files/the_misapplication_of_mr._michael_jensen _dobbin_and_jung.pdf.

62 *In 1970, the ratio:* The Economic Policy Institute published a report in 2015 that detailed CEO compensation trends and compared them to average wages. The report can be found here: http://www.epi.org /files/2015/top-ceos-make-300-times-more-than-typical-workers .pdf. See Table 1 for ratios over time, and Figure C for a graph of the trend.

62 *drug makers Amgen and Pfizer:* William Lazonick, "Stock Buybacks: From Retain-and-Reinvest to Downsize-and-Distribute," Brookings Institution, April 2015. In particular, see Table 1 for ratio of buybacks and dividends to earnings: https://www.brookings.edu/wp-content/uploads/2016/06/lazonick.pdf.

62 *"449 companies":* William Lazonick, "Profits Without Prosperity," *Harvard Business Review,* September 2014.

62 *Economist Andrew Smithers:* Rana Foroohar, *Makers and Takers: The Rise of Finance and the Fall of American Business* (New York: Crown Business, 2016), p. 278.

63 *Other data Lazonick gathered:* William Lazonick, "Profits Without Prosperity," *Harvard Business Review,* September 2014.

63 *An executive compensation reform:* This is the compensation deductibility limit, or Section 162(m). Text: http://www.execcomp.org/Issues/Issue/tax-treatment-of-executive-compensation/tax-code-162m-deductibility-of-executive-compensation.

63 *the Clinton administration blocked a push:* Jay Mathews, "Congress Enters the Fray over Executive Stock Options Rule," *Washington Post,* August 13, 1993, https://www.washingtonpost.com/archive/business/1993/08/13/congress-enters-the-fray-over-executive-stock-options-rule/27b55e8e-ac13-47f4-9eee-e259632815a8/?utm_term=.c302d883232a.

63 *Buybacks have continued:* Letter from Larry Fink, chief executive of BlackRock, to his clients. Text: https://www.blackrock.com/corporate/en-us/investor-relations/larry-fink-ceo-letter. Also see Rana Foroohar, *Makers and Takers: The Rise of Finance and the Fall of American Business* (New York: Crown Business, 2016).

64 *Donald Trump publicly:* Nelson D. Schwartz, "Trump Cites Progress in Keeping Carrier Air Conditioning Plant in Indiana," *New York Times,* November 24, 2016, https://www.nytimes.com/2016/11/24/business/on-twitter-trump-cites-progress-on-restoring-indiana-jobs.html?ribbon-ad-idx=4&rref=homepage&module=Ribbon&version=origin%C2%AEion=Header&action=click&contentCollection=Home%20Page&pgtype=article.

64 *United Technologies:* Ted Mann and Ezequiel Minaya, "United Technologies Unveils $12 Billion Buyback," *Wall Street Journal,* October 20, 2015, https://www.wsj.com/articles/united-technologies-unveils-12-billion-buyback-1445343580.

65 *executives now routinely use buybacks:* Foroohar, *Makers and Takers.*

65 *a survey of 401:* John R. Graham, Campbell R. Harvey, and Shiva Rajgopal, "The Economic Implications of Corporate Financial Reporting," *Journal of Accounting and Economics,* vol. 40 (December 2005).

65 *Harvard Business School 2016 report:* Michael E. Porter, Jan W. Rivkin, and Mihir A. Desai, "Problems Unsolved and a Nation Divided, Harvard Business School, September 2016, http://www.hbs.edu/competi tiveness/Pages/default.aspx.

66 *an admiring profile:* Sandra Salmans, "New Yorkers & Co: Getting Rich by Enriching the Mortgage Pot," *New York Times,* November 7, 1984, http://www.nytimes.com/1984/11/07/business/new-yorkers-co -getting-rich-by-enriching-mortgage-pot.html.

66 *"Lewie Ranieri was the wild":* Michael Lewis, *Liar's Poker: Rising Through the Wreckage on Wall Street* (New York: W. W. Norton, 1989).

66 BusinessWeek *would crown Ranieri:* "Lewis S. Ranieri: Your Mortgage Was His Bond," *Bloomberg Businessweek,* November 29, 2004, https:// www.bloomberg.com/news/articles/2004-11-28/lewis-s-dot-ranieri -your-mortgage-was-his-bond.

69 *"Major firms and investors":* "The Financial Crisis Inquiry Report," January 2011, https://www.gpo.gov/fdsys/pkg/GPO-FCIC/pdf/GPO -FCIC.pdf.

69 *"IBGYBG":* The FCIC report, p. 17.

70 *Masters invented the credit default swap:* Gillian Tett, *Fool's Gold: The Inside Story of J.P. Morgan and How Wall St. Greed Corrupted Its Bold Dream and Created a Financial Catastrophe* (New York: Free Press, 2009).

71 *the biggest CDS player of all:* Ibid.

71 *AIG would get the largest:* U.S. Department of the Treasury report: https://www.treasury.gov/connect/blog/Pages/aig-182-billion.aspx.

71 *By 2005 the ten largest banks:* Hubert Janicki and Edward S. Prescott, "Changes in the Size Distribution of U. S. Banks: 1960–2005," *Federal Reserve Board, Richmond: Economic Quarterly* 92, no. 4 (Fall 2006): 291–316, https://ssrn.com/abstract=2186112.

72 *Depression-era Glass-Steagall:* This was the Gramm-Leach-Bliley Act: https://www.congress.gov/106/plaws/publ102/PLAW-106publ102 .pdf.

72 *report from the Boston unit:* Alicia H. Munnell, Lynn E. Browne, James McEneaney, and Geoffrey M. B. Tootell, "Mortgage Lending in Boston: Interpreting MHDA Data," 1992, https://www.bostonfed.org /-/media/Documents/Workingpapers/PDF/wp92_7.pdf.

73 *the* synthetic *credit default swap:* Tett, *Fool's Gold.*

73 *the notional value:* Lynn Stout, "Regulate OTC Derivatives by Deregulating Them," *Regulation* 32, no. 3 (Fall 2009), https://papers.ssrn .com/sol3/papers.cfm?abstract_id=1485518.

74 *Christopher Cruise:* Cruise was interviewed by the Financial Crisis Inquiry Commission in 2010. Audiotape of that interview is available

here: http://fcic.law.stanford.edu/interviews/view/48. This portion is drawn from minutes 4:50–7:20 on the tape.

75 *number three player was Countrywide Financial:* The FCIC report, which quotes extensively from his internal emails and details the rise and fall of Countrywide from the early 2000s through the financial crisis.

76 *Cash down payments were reduced:* FCIC report.

76 *Mozilo received:* Gretchen Morgenson, "Lending Magnate Settles Fraud Case," *New York Times,* October 15, 2010, http://www.nytimes .com/2010/10/16/business/16countrywide.html. See also William D. Cohan, "Wall Street Executives from the Financial Crisis of 2008: Where Are They Now?" *Vanity Fair,* April 2015, https://www.vanity fair.com/news/2015/03/wall-street-executives-2008-jamie-dimon -cancer.

76 *Mozilo was forced to sell:* Connie Bruck, "Angelo's Ashes," *The New Yorker,* June 29, 2009, https://www.newyorker.com/magazine/2009/06/29 /angelos-ashes.

77 *Mozilo was later sued by the SEC:* SEC complaint: https://www.sec.gov /litigation/complaints/2009/comp21068.pdf; also Morgenson, "Lending Magnate Settles Fraud Case."

77 *Mozilo testified:* Audiotape of his testimony before the FCIC is available online here: http://fcic.law.stanford.edu/interviews/view/67.

78 *value of stock buybacks and dividends:* Letter from Larry Fink, chief executive of BlackRock, to his clients. Text: https://www.blackrock.com /corporate/en-us/investor-relations/larry-fink-ceo-letter.

78 *"How Stock Options":* Michael Jensen, "How Stock Options Reward Managers for Destroying Value and What to Do About It," *Harvard Negotiations, Organizations & Working Paper,* 2001: http://dx.doi .org/10.2139/ssrn.480401.

78 *"perverse incentives":* Frank Dobbin and Jiwook Jung, "The Misapplication of Mr. Michael Jensen: How Agency Theory Brought Down the Economy and Why It Might Again," *Markets on Trial: The Economic Sociology of the U.S. Financial Crisis (Research in the Sociology of Organizations),* vol. 30b (2010) pp. 29–64. https://scholar.harvard .edu/dobbin/files/the_misapplication_of_mr._michael_jensen _dobbin_and_jung.pdf.

78 *"I was misunderstood":* Interview with Jensen.

79 *"short-termism is undermining":* Dominic Barton and Mark Wiseman, "Focusing Capital on the Long Term," *Harvard Business Review,* January–February 2014, https://hbr.org/2014/01/focusing-capital-on -the-long-term.

79 *"only on the short term":* Interview with Barton.

79 *"New Paradigm Roadmap":* Text: http://www.wlrk.com/docs/thenew paradigm.pdf.

80 *"Too many CEOs":* Alana Semuels, "How to Stop Short-Term Thinking at America's Companies," *The Atlantic,* December 30, 2016, https://www.theatlantic.com/business/archive/2016/12/short-term -thinking/511874/.

81 *"All too often":* Hillary Clinton, "Being Pro-Business Doesn't Mean Hanging Consumers Out to Dry," *Quartz:* https://qz.com/529303 /hillary-clinton-being-pro-business-doesnt-mean-hanging-con sumers-out-to-dry/.

81 *corporate charters began:* Lyman Johnson, "Corporate Law and the History of Corporate Social Responsibility," *Research Handbook on the History of Company and Corporate Law,* 2017. https://ssrn.com /abstract=2962432.

81 *Lipton asserted:* Martin Lipton, "Takeover Bids in the Target Board-room," *Business Lawyer,* November 1979.

83 *the New York Times Company did in 1969:* Joe Nocera, "How Punch Protected the Times," *New York Times,* October 1, 2012, http://www .nytimes.com/2012/10/02/opinion/nocera-how-punch-protected-the -times.html. See also Susan E. Tift and Alex S. Jones, *The Trust: The Private and Powerful Family Behind The New York Times* (New York: Little, Brown and Company, 1999).

84 *"Measuring and Managing":* Text: http://www.mckinsey.com/global -themes/long-term-capitalism/where-companies-with-a-long-term -view-outperform-their-peers.

84 *"a 65 percent chance":* Interview with Henderson.

86 *By 2008, Michael Pearson:* I consulted a number of news sources, academic papers, litigation documents, interviews, and a report by the Senate Committee on Aging on Valeant. Senate report: https://www .aging.senate.gov/imo/media/doc/Drug%20Pricing%20Report .pdf. I especially relied on an excellent article by David Crow, "Valeant: The Harder They Fall," *Financial Times,* March 28, 2016. https:// www.ft.com/content/dbc52fa8-f0d6-11e5-9f20-c3a047354386?mh q5j=e5.

87 *Ackman told stock analysts:* A transcript of a presentation that Ackman gave to investors was filed with the SEC. Text: https://www.sec .gov/Archives/edgar/data/850693/000119312514155081/d714446d 425.htm.

87 *Valeant's stock was up 4,000 percent:* James Surowiecki, "The Roll-Up Racket," *The New Yorker,* April 4, 2016, https://www.newyorker.com /magazine/2016/04/04/inside-the-valeant-scandal.

87 *stock and stock options:* Bethany McLean, "The Valeant Meltdown and Wall Street's Major Drug Problem," *Vanity Fair,* Summer 2016, https://www.vanityfair.com/news/2016/06/the-valeant-meltdown -and-wall-streets-major-drug-problem.

87 *"the Warren Buffett of the twenty-first century":* Bloomberg, "Bill Ackman Describes Valeant as Early Stage Berkshire Hathaway," https://www .bloomberg.com/news/articles/2015-05-04/bill-ackman-describes -valeant-as-early-stage-berkshire-hathaway.

87 *Pearson was fired:* Tracy Staton, "Valeant Hands Ex-CEO Pearson a Severance Package Worth Almost $12m," *Fierce Pharma* newsletter, May 31, 2016, http://www.fiercepharma.com/pharma/valeant-hands -ex-ceo-pearson-more-than-15m-severance-pay.

87 *nearly $100 million worth of stock:* Jacquie McNish and Charley Grant, "Valeant's Ex-CEO Michael Pearson Sells Nearly $100 Mil- lion in Company Stock," *Wall Street Journal,* July 14, 2016, https:// www.wsj.com/articles/valeants-ex-ceo-michael-pearson-sells-nearly -100-million-in-company-stock-1468446524?tesla=y.

87 *Ackman ended up losing:* Jen Wieczner, "Bill Ackman Lost $7.7 Million Per Day on Valeant Stock," *Fortune,* March 15, 2017, http://fortune .com/2017/03/15/valeant-stock-bill-ackman/.

87 *"Don't misunderstand":* Joseph Bower and Lynn Paine, "Managing for the Long Term," *Harvard Business Review,* May–June 2017, https:// hbr.org/2017/05/managing-for-the-long-term.

88 Fortune *editor Alan Murray:* "CEO Daily: Friday, 14th April," http:// fortune.com/2017/04/14/ceo-daily-friday-14th-april/.

88 *seventy thousand members*: Email exchange with Murray.

88 *Aspen's Samuelson:* She forwarded this exchange to me.

88 *Unilever's stock*: Historical New York Stock Exchange data.

88 *Polman had to fight off*: Martinne Geller and Pamela Barbaglia, "Kraft Heinz Bids $143 Billion for Unilever in Global Brand Grab," Reuters, February 17, 2017, http://www.reuters.com/article/us-unilever-m-a -kraft/kraft-heinz-bids-143-billion-for-unilever-in-global-brand -grab-idUSKBN15W18Y.

89 *"CEOs need not aspire":* http://www.nationalreview.com/article/446 342/corporate-social-responsibility-unilever-ceo-exemplifies-its -hypocrisy.

89 *Polman announced a plan:* Chad Bray, "Unilever to Sell Its Spreads Business and Restructure," *New York Times,* April 6, 2017, https:// www.nytimes.com/2017/04/06/business/dealbook/unilever-spreads .html?_r=0.

89 *"Do we choose":* Thomas Buckley and Matthew Campell, "The Fresh Scent of Success," *Bloomberg Businessweek,* September 4, 2017.

4 THE GREENING OF THE FIRST AMENDMENT

90 *we will call Jones:* I was there; interviews with Jones.

91 *"a cantankerous old guy":* Interviews with Redish.

91 *The Supreme Court came around: Texas v. Johnson:* https://supreme
.justia.com/cases/federal/us/491/397/case.html.

93 *landmark Supreme Court case: Griswold v. Connecticut:* https://supreme
.justia.com/cases/federal/us/381/479/case.html.

93 *"Toward a General Theory":* Thomas I. Emerson, *Faculty Scholarship Series*, 1963, http://digitalcommons.law.yale.edu/fss_papers/2796.

93 *"leading expounder":* Martin Redish, "The First Amendment in the Marketplace: Commercial Speech and the Values of Free Expression," *George Washington Law Review* 39, no. 3 (March 1971): 429–73.

94 New York University Law Review: Martin Redish, "Campaign Spending Laws and the First Amendment," *New York University Law Review* 46 (1971).

94 *amount spent on broadcast advertising:* Redish, "The First Amendment in the Marketplace."

94 *In 2016, TV and radio spending:* Erika Franklin Fowler, Travis N. Ridout, and Michael M. Franz, "Political Advertising in 2016: The Presidential Election as Outlier?" Wesleyan Media Project, February 22, 2017, https://doi.org/10.1515/for-2016-0040.

96 *The first case leading to* Citizens United: This was *Buckley v. Valeo*, https://supreme.justia.com/cases/federal/us/424/1/case.html.

96 *Campaign finance restrictions:* Federal Election Campaign Act, passed in 1971 and enacted in 1972. After Watergate, Congress amended the public finance laws and established the Federal Election Commission. The law and its amendments are available here: https://www.fec.gov/legal-resources/legislation/.

97 Virginia State Board of Pharmacy: https://supreme.justia.com/cases/federal/us/425/748/case.html.

98 *"Talk about boomerangs":* Interview with Nader.

98 *GM's clumsy attempts:* See Jerry T. Baulch, "GM's Head Apologizes to 'Harassed' Car Critic," Associated Press, March, 23, 1966, http://jfk.hood.edu/Collection/Weisberg%20Subject%20Index%20Files/N%20Disk/Nader%20Ralph/Item%2001.pdf.

98 *Donors contributed millions:* Robert N. Mayer and Stephen Brobeck, *Watchdogs and Whistleblowers: A Reference Guide to Consumer Activism* (Santa Barbara, Calif.: Greenwood, 2015).

99 *laws establishing price controls:* These were the Economic Stabilization Act of 1970; the Equal Employment Opportunity Commission Act

of 1972; Reorganization Plan No. 3 of 1970; and the Occupational Health and Safety Act of 1970.

99 *a manifesto:* The Powell Memo was sent confidentially to Eugene Sydor, Jr., the chairman of the Education Committee at the U.S. Chamber of Commerce, on August 23, 1971. It was titled "Attack of American Free Enterprise System." Text: http://reclaimdemocracy.org /powell_memo_lewis/.

99 *1964 report from the U.S. surgeon general:* "Smoking and Health: Report of the Advisory Committee to the Surgeon General of the Public Health Service," U.S. Department of Health, Education, and Welfare, https://profiles.nlm.nih.gov/ps/access/nnbbmq.pdf.

99 *The first law requiring warning labels:* The Cigarette Labeling and Advertising Act of 1965: https://www.law.cornell.edu/uscode/text/15 /chapter-36.

102 *the right of undocumented immigrant children:* This was the 1981 case *Plyler v. Doe.* Text of Powell's concurring opinion: https://www.law .cornell.edu/supremecourt/text/457/202#writing-USSC_CR_0457 _0202_ZC2.

102 *advanced corporate speech rights:* This was the 1978 case *First National Bank of Boston v. Bellotti,* https://supreme.justia.com/cases/federal/us /435/765/case.html.

103 *"A State grants":* Text: http://reclaimdemocracy.org/rehnquist_dissent _bellotti/.

103 *1819 decision: Dartmouth College v. Woodward:* https://scholar.google .com/scholar_case?case=7985814098766481295&hl=en&as_sdt =6&as_vis=1&oi=scholarr.

104 *The first PAC had been created:* "Labor Organizes Political Branch," *Washington Post,* July 8, 1943.

104 *seize industries important to the war effort:* This was the Smith-Connally Act of 1943. (President Roosevelt's veto was overridden by Congress.)

104 *"isolationist Republicans":* "C.I.O Leader Urges Support of Pro-F.D.R. Candidates Only," (Richmond, Ind.) *Palladium-Item,* August 23, 1943.

104 *That changed dramatically:* Brooks Jackson, *Honest Graft: Big Money and the American Political Process* (New York: Alfred A. Knopf, 1988).

105 *corporate America feared:* "Burke-Hartke Bill Opposed by the Chamber of Commerce," *New York Times,* April 10, 1972, http://www.nytimes .com/1972/04/10/archives/burkehartke-bill-opposed-by-chamber-of -commerce.html.

105 *enough lobbying power:* Edward Alden, *Failure to Adjust: How Americans Got Left Behind in the Global Economy* (Lanham, Md.: Rowman & Littlefield, 2016).

105 *Chamber of Commerce:* Lee Drutman, *The Business of America Is Lobby-*

ing: *How Corporations Became Politicized and Politics Became More Corpo-rate* (Oxford: Oxford University Press, 2015).

105 *National Federation of Independent Business:* Ibid.

105 *The Business Roundtable:* Ibid.

105 *"a domestic version of Shock and Awe":* Jacob Hacker and Paul Pierson, *Winner-Take-All Politics: How Washington Made the Rich Richer—and Turned Its Back on the Middle Class* (New York: Simon & Schuster, 2010).

106 *By 2016, approximately 1,400 companies:* Dan Auble, a researcher at OpenSecrets.org., estimated, based on filing data, that between 1,100 and 1,800 firms had physical offices in D.C.

106 *spending $3.1 billion annually:* Based on data from OpenSecrets.org, available here: https://www.opensecrets.org/lobby/.

106 *as much as double:* In a report available here: https://www.opensecrets .org/news/reports/shadow-lobbying, researchers from OpenSecrets .org estimated that there are at least as many unregistered lobbyists as registered lobbyists. It is safe to assume that these high-powered consultants, who are typically former officeholders, were paid the same or higher rates than registered lobbyists.

106 *300 PACs:* The number for 1971 comes from Hacker and Pierson, *Winner-Take-All Politics.* The numbers from 1980 and 2017 come from Auble at OpenSecrets.org, using data collected by his organization.

106 *in 1980, business PAC contributions:* This was computed by adding together the contributions of corporate PACs and trade associations and comparing these totals with contributions of labor PACs. See also Jeffrey Milyo, David Primo, and Timothy Groseclose, "Corporate PAC Campaign Contributions in Perspective," *Business and Politics* 2, no. 1 (2000): 75–88, http://www.sas.rochester.edu/psc/primo/corppac .pdf. See Table 1, titled "PACs and PAC Contributions by Type."

106 *Carter's push for new consumer protection:* Hacker and Pierson, *Winner-Take-All Politics.*

107 *proposal to make the National Labor Relations Board:* "Filibuster Kills Labor Law 'Reform' Bill," *CQ Almanac 1978*, 34th ed., 284–87, http:// library.cqpress.com/cqalmanac/cqal78-1238478.

107 *Carter's plan to change:* I used newsclips from the archives of *The Washington Post* and *The New York Times*, as well as the background provided on pages 15–17 by Jeffrey Birnbaum and Alan Murray in their sweeping, definitive narrative of the fight over tax reform during the Reagan administration, *Showdown at Gucci Gulch: Lawmakers, Lobbyists, and the Unlikely Triumph of Tax Reform* (New York: Random House, 1987).

107 *One law—passed in 2003:* This was the Medicare Prescription Drug

Modernization Act: https://www.congress.gov/bill/108th-congress /house-bill/1.

108 *contributions from the health care industry:* Dan Eggen, "Health-Care Firms Have Supported Lawmakers Debating Reform," *Washington Post,* July 21, 2009, http://www.washingtonpost.com/wp-dyn/content /article/2009/07/20/AR2009072003363.html.

108 *took a $2-million-a-year job:* Steven Brill, *America's Bitter Pill: Money, Politics, Backroom Deals, and the Fight to Fix Our Broken Healthcare System* (New York: Random House, 2015).

108 *highest profit margins:* GAO report: https://www.gao.gov/assets/690 /688472.pdf?utm_source=newsletter&utm_medium=email&utm _campaign=newsletter_axiosvitals&stream=top-stories.

108 *Trump frequently attacked:* Sarah Karlin-Smith, "Trump Tweets Up a Storm on Drug Prices, but Delivers Little Change," *Politico,* August 15, 2017, http://www.politico.com/story/2017/08/15/trump -drug-prices-medicare-241673. For the specific "rip-off" quote, see also: Rebecca Savransky, "Merck CEO Resigns from Presidential Council over Trump Remarks," *The Hill,* August 14, 2017, http:// thehill.com/homenews/administration/346437-merck-ceo-resigns -from-american-manufacturing-council-after-trump.

108 *spent $145 million on lobbying:* Jan Hancock, "Everyone Wants to Reduce Drug Prices. So Why Can't We?," *New York Times,* September 23, 2017, https://www.nytimes.com/2017/09/23/sunday-review /prescription-drugs-prices.html?action=click.

108 *"adverse circumstances":* Thomas Edsall, *The New Politics of Inequality: A Quiet Transfer of Power Has Taken Place in the Nation's Capital* (New York: W. W. Norton, 1985).

109 *Edsall recalled:* Interview with Edsall.

109 *spending per person on health care:* See this graph from the Peterson-Kaiser Healthcare System Tracker that follows health care expenditures per capita in the U.S.: https://www.healthsystemtracker.org /chart/per-capita-basis-health-spending-grown-substantially/#item -start.

109 *Profits and executive salaries:* Brill, *America's Bitter Pill.*

110 *"The Best Laws Money Can Buy":* Steven Brill, "The Best Laws Money Can Buy," *Time,* June 10, 2010, http://content.time.com/time/maga zine/article/0,9171,2001015,00.html.

110 *"We have three lawyers total":* Interview with Travis Plunkett at the time Dodd-Frank was being considered, as quoted in Brill, "The Best Laws Money Can Buy."

110 *a glossy "study":* Ibid.

111 *the number of lawyers:* John Judis, *The Paradox of American Democracy: Elites, Special Interests, and the Betrayal of Public Trust* (New York: Pantheon, 2000).

111 *The Administrative Procedure Act of 1946:* Text: https://www.gpo.gov /fdsys/pkg/USCODE-2011-title5/pdf/USCODE-2011-title5-partI -chap5-subchapII.pdf.

112 *quintupled in page length:* Philip K. Howard, *The Rule of Nobody: Saving America from Dead Laws and Broken Government* (New York: W. W. Norton, 2014).

112 *Katharine Gibbs secretarial school: Katharine Gibbs School (Incorporated), et. al, v. Federal Trade Commission:* https://openjurist.org/612/f2d/658/ katharine-gibbs-school-v-federal-trade-commission.

113 *Supreme Court decision about benzene: Industrial Union Dept. v. American Petroleum Institute:* https://supreme.justia.com/cases/federal/us /448/607/case.html.

113 *The first OSHA:* Interview and email exchanges with David Michaels, former assistant secretary of labor for OSHA under President Obama.

113 *"We had a team of people":* Interview with Michaels.

113 *579 to 796 deaths a year:* Combining the three major fatal health endpoints—for lung cancer, non-malignant respiratory diseases, and end-stage renal disease—OSHA estimated in the record it submitted for the silica ruling that it would prevent between 579 and 796 premature fatalities annually, with a midpoint estimate of 688 premature fatalities avoided annually, given a forty-five-year working life of exposure. Here is the text of the federal register on the silica ruling: https://www.osha.gov/laws-regs/federalregister/2013-09-12.

113 *more than twenty years:* Public Citizen report on OSHA inaction: https://www.citizen.org/sites/default/files/osha-inaction.pdf. For example, a proposed confined spaces standard has been delayed for more than thirty-one years.

113 *two new chemicals are introduced:* According to the Government Accountability Office, seven hundred new chemicals enter U.S. commerce each year, which averages about two per day. See John Stephenson, "Chemical Regulation: Options for Enhancing the Effectiveness of the Toxic Substances Control Act," GAO, 2009.

113 *OSHA has only been able to issue:* These are rules about hexavalent chromium, issued in 2006; silica, issued in 2016; and beryllium, issued in 2017.

115 *"I'll be leaving":* Steve Israel, "Confessions of a Congressman," *New York Times,* January 8, 2016, https://www.nytimes.com/2016/01/09 /opinion/steve-israel-confessions-of-a-congressman.html.

116 *"The most demoralizing thing":* Interview with Israel.

116 *Super PACs raised $1.8 billion:* OpenSecrets data, available here: https://www.opensecrets.org/pacs/superpacs.php.

117 *$250 million in "dark money":* Estimates provided by OpenSecrets.

117 *candidates raised directly:* OpenSecrets.org data compiled from FEC filings, available here: https://www.opensecrets.org/overview/index.php?display=T&type=A&cycle=2016.

117 *raised $4.4 million:* Data available on OpenSecrets.org: https://www.opensecrets.org/members-of-congress/summary?cid=N00033983&cycle=2016&type=C.

117 *gerrymandering results:* Based on estimates provided by Democratic and Republican congressional campaign staffs.

118 *Congressman Jones:* I attended this event.

121 *American Political Science Association's journal:* Martin Gilens and Benjamin I. Page, "Testing Theories of American Politics: Elites, Interest Groups, and Average Citizens," *Perspectives on Politics* 12, no. 3 (September 2014), http://citeseerx.ist.psu.edu/viewdoc/download;jsessionid=37EDA24D1D5DA87AEB950CEFE63883FF?doi=10.1.1.668.8647&rep=rep1&type=pdf.

123 *"develop systems to find conflicts":* Interviews with Krumholz.

124 *Funding had increased:* Ibid.

124 *organized by Chevron:* "Power Briefing" newsletter, *Politico*, April 4, 2017.

126 *"from the reality that this issue"* and subsequent quotes: Interviews with Bradley.

126 *"I saw that all the issues":* Interviews with Penniman.

126 *about $2.5 million:* Penniman; and Issue One filings with the Internal Revenue Service.

126 *Polls show:* Handout from Issue One lunch citing various polls.

127 *a lunch Issue One held:* I attended this lunch.

129 *five states had tried and failed:* Center for Public Integrity analysis of legislation in statehouses, available here: https://www.publicintegrity.org/2017/08/31/21146/statehouses-not-congress-hosting-biggest-political-money-fights. In addition to South Dakota, Virginia, Colorado, and Indiana, where reforms have failed in statehouses, voters in Washington State rejected a broad reform of state campaign finance laws. See election results from *The New York Times* here: https://www.nytimes.com/elections/results/washington-ballot-measure-1464-campaign-finance.

130 *amend the Constitution:* S.J. Res. 47 was introduced in 1996. In 2014, the Senate rejected it. Ramsey Cox, "Senate GOP Blocks Constitutional

Amendment on Campaign Spending," *The Hill,* September 11, 2014, http://thehill.com/blogs/floor-action/senate/217449-senate-repub licans-block-constitutional-amendment-on-campaign.

131 *The CBO has a well-paid professional staff:* The CBO director requested $49.9 million for the 2018 fiscal year. In 2017, its budget was $46.5 million: https://www.cbo.gov/publication/52785.

5   MAKING MARKETS EFFICIENT—
AND MARGINALIZING THOSE LEFT BEHIND

133 *"A more liberal trade policy":* Kennedy delivered this speech to Congress on January 25, 1962. Text: http://www.presidency.ucsb.edu/ws /?pid=8688.

134 *George Meany:* Earl V. Anderson, "Labor Looks at U.S. Trade Policy . . . And Doesn't Like What it Sees," *Chemical and Engineering News,* March 23, 1970.

134 *Labor Secretary Arthur Goldberg:* Ibid.

134 *Taft-Hartley Act:* John B. Judis, *The Paradox of American Democracy: Elites, Special Interests, and the Betrayal of Public Trust* (New York: Pantheon, 2000).The text of the statute, which was called the Labor Management Relations Act of 1947: https://www.casefilemethod.com /Statutes/LMRA.pdf.

135 *In 1946, there were strikes:* Bert Cochran, *Labor and Communism: The Conflict That Shaped American Unions* (Princeton: Princeton University Press, 1979).

136 *chairman of General Motors:* Charles Wilson testimony to the Senate Committee on Armed Services, January 15, 1953.

137 *Standard & Poor's 500 stock index:* The Standard & Poor's index on January 1, 1947, was 173.17, and on January 1, 1960, it was 484.81. See the inflation-adjusted Standard & Poor's 500 Index here: http:// www.multpl.com/inflation-adjusted-s-p-500/table/by-year.

137 *average family income:* Census Bureau Data, published in 1963. In 1963, the Census Bureau noted, "In terms of constant (1961) dollars, average family income increased from about $4,100 in 1947 to $5,700 in 1961." The report is available here: https://www2.census .gov/prod2/popscan/p60-039.pdf.

137 *42 percent:* Judis, *The Paradox of American Democracy.*

137 *In 1950, unions won:* Paul Weiler, "Promises to Keep: Securing Workers' Rights to Self-Organization Under the NLRA," *Harvard Law Review* 96, no. 8 (June 1983): 1769–1827.

137 *entire private workforce:* Ibid. See in particular Figure 1, titled "Union Density in the United States, 1935–1980."

137 *6.4 percent:* Data from the Bureau of Labor Statistics, available here: https://www.bls.gov/news.release/union2.nro.htm.

137 *charges of unfair labor practices:* Weiler, "Promises to Keep: Securing Workers' Rights to Self-Organization Under the NLRA." See footnote 34.

138 *By 1963, Stevens:* See Rudolph A. Pyatt, Jr., "For J.P. Stevens, 175th Anniversary Now a Requiem," *Washington Post*, July 3, 1988, https://www.washingtonpost.com/archive/business/1988/07/03/for -jp-stevens-175th-anniversary-now-a-requiem/7ae26e13-cfc0-49a3 -8ad7-285d5281802b/?utm_term=.72531eeeb74a. See also "Unionization of the Textile Industry: A Case Study of J.P. Stevens," The Heritage Foundation, August 3, 1977, http://www.heritage.org/jobs -and-labor/report/unionization-the-textile-industry-case-study-j-p -stevens.

138 *By 1980, the result:* Steven Brill, "Labor Outlaws," *The American Lawyer*, April 1980.

138 *A 1967 decision:* Ibid.

139 *"Not at all":* Interview with Jay Topkis, quoted in ibid.

139 *The 1967 case involved:* Text of the decision: http://law.justia.com/cases /federal/appellate-courts/F2/380/292/315016/.

139 *fired in 1963 from his $1.90-an-hour job:* Notes from interviews conducted during my reporting of "Labor Outlaws." Caveat: $1.90 is an estimate based on these interviews; I was never able to ascertain Mr. Aldridge's exact pay rate.

140 *It took three years and ten months:* Brill, "Labor Outlaws."

140 *if the employees had found:* Ibid.

140 *pay any fines:* Ibid.

141 *The company had invested:* Legal fees when I wrote "Labor Outlaws" for *The American Lawyer* were $2 million as of the beginning of 1980. I assumed that there would be an additional million dollars of fees during 1980. To get the rough amount saved over 17 years, I multiplied 34,000 employees by 48 weeks per year (probably a low estimate), by 40 hours per week, and then by 17 years. I then multiplied this number of hours by 25 cents, which yielded $277.44 million.

141 *"Contemporary American labor":* Paul Weiler, "Promises to Keep: Securing Workers' Rights to Self-Organization under the NLRA," *Harvard Law Review*, 96, no. 8 (June 1983): 1769–1827. Available at http://www.jstor.org/stable/1340809.

142 *After six tries, proponents failed:* "Filibuster Kills Labor Law 'Reform'

Bill," *CQ Almanac 1978,* 34th ed., 284–87, http://library.cqpress.com/cqalmanac/cqal78-1238478.

142 *By 1978, contributions to congressional candidates:* Jeffrey Milyo, David Primo, and Timothy Groseclose, "Corporate PAC Campaign Contributions in Perspective," *Business and Politics* 2, no. 1 (2000): 75–88, http://www.sas.rochester.edu/psc/primo/corppac.pdf. See Table 1, titled "PACs and PAC Contributions by Type."

142 *NLRB members appointed:* Judis, *The Paradox of American Democracy.*

142 *efforts to win union recognition:* Ibid. Judis writes, "In 1970 unions held about 8,000 elections to establish new locals; by the 1990s they were holding only 3,000 a year and were spending on average only 3 percent of their resources on organizing."

142 *a union-led boycott of Stevens's consumer products:* Ed McConville, "5 Years After Union Victory, Battle Goes On at J.P. Stevens," *Washington Post,* August 29, 1979, https://www.washingtonpost.com/archive/politics/1979/08/29/5-years-after-union-victory-battle-goes-on-at-jp-stevens/8a21141e-8187-460f-b049-235a255fa488/?utm_term=.6927659f0b42.

143 *17 percent of the company:* Robert J. Cole, "3-Month Battle for J.P. Stevens Ends," April 26, 1988, *New York Times,* http://www.nytimes.com/1988/04/26/business/3-month-battle-for-jp-stevens-ends.html?pagewanted=all.

143 *J.P. Stevens was sold off:* Cole, "3-Month Battle for J.P. Stevens Ends."

143 *the workforce of 45,000 had been reduced to 23,000:* Ibid.

143 *As* The Washington Post *put it:* Pyatt, "For J.P. Stevens, 175th Anniversary Now a Requiem."

143 *As of 2016, the larger textile maker:* Bloomberg News, "Company News; WestPoint Stevens Files for Bankruptcy Protection," *New York Times,* June 3, 2003, http://www.nytimes.com/2003/06/03/business/company-news-westpoint-stevens-files-for-bankruptcy-protection.html. See also "Icahn to Buy WestPoint Stevens," *Wall Street Journal,* June 27, 2005, https://www.wsj.com/articles/SB111983722528670112?mg=prod/accounts-wsj.

143 *Most of its manufacturing:* Jessica Stephans, "What Is Helping Icahn's Home Fashion Segment's Margins Rise?," *Market Realist,* May 14, 2016, https://beta.marketrealist.com/2016/05/icahns-railcar-segment-high-margin-business.

143 *textile workers in the United States:* Bureau of Labor Statistics employment data for both years. The data for 1973 is available here: https://fraser.stlouisfed.org/scribd/?title_id=4856&filepath=/files/docs/publications/bls/bls_1817_1974.pdf. The data for 2016 is available

here: http://www.bls.gov/iag/tgs/iag313.htm. The number in the text is from October 2016.

143 *the average hourly wage:* This calculation was done using Bureau of Labor Statistics data. In 1973, the mean hourly wage of a textile worker was $4.23 per hour (see Table 3 here: https://www.bls.gov /opub/mlr/2010/06/art3full.pdf). The mean hourly wage in 2016 was $14.82: https://www.bls.gov/oes/current/oes516099.htm. Using a CPI inflation calculator from the Bureau of Labor Statistics, $4.23 in January 1975 should have had the same buying power as $19.24 in January 2016.

144 New York Times *report:* Neil Irwin, "To Understand Rising Inequality, Consider the Janitors at Two Top Companies, Then and Now," *New York Times,* September 3, 2017, https://www.nytimes.com/2017/09/03 /upshot/to-understand-rising-inequality-consider-the-janitors-at -two-top-companies-then-and-now.html.

144 *the U.S. Postal Service has shed 300,000 jobs:* In 1999, there were 797,795 employees of USPS. In 2016, there were 508,098. Postal Service employment data: http://about.usps.com/who-we-are/postal -history/employees-since-1926.pdf.

144 *eliminated 108,000 coal mining jobs:* In 1960, there were 189,679 miners in the U.S. In 2016, there were 81,485. Data collected by the Mine Safety and Health Administration is available here: https://arlweb .msha.gov/stats/centurystats/coalstats.asp.

145 *fifteen million retail jobs:* See the "Retail Trade" category on this table of Bureau of Labor Statistics data: https://www.bls.gov/emp/ep _table_201.htm?-.

145 *Teamsters Union's division covering:* Steven Brill, *The Teamsters* (New York: Simon & Schuster, 1978). Also: http://www.nytimes.com/1978 /08/01/archives/national-drive-is-begun-by-dissident-teamsters .html. Current Teamsters membership numbers are listed on their website here: https://teamster.org/divisions/freight.

145 *tractor-trailer driver:* Brill, *The Teamsters.*

145 *truck driver wages had fallen:* According to the Bureau of Labor Statistics, the mean annual wage of truck drivers in 2016 was $43,590. That data is available here: https://www.bls.gov/oes/current/oes533032 .htm. Industry analyst Gordon Klemp, president of the National Transportation Institute, estimated that in 1980 truckers made $38,618 annually, which would be about $110,000 if adjusted for inflation; $43,590 is 60 percent less than $110,000. See http://www.overdrive online.com/trucker-pay-has-plummeted-in-the-last-30-years-analyst -stays/.

146 *seven million of its 19.2 million:* Bureau of Labor statistics data, available here: https://data.bls.gov/pdq/SurveyOutputServlet.

146 *"Add a few billion people":* Interview with Stiglitz.

146 *lost to trade:* One of the most credible estimates comes from a study published by economists at Indiana's Ball State University in 2015 (and noted by Claire Miller in *The New York Times,* December 21, 2016), blaming trade for 13 percent of the job loss. See Michael Hicks and Srikant Devaraj, "The Myth and Reality of Manufacturing in America," June 2015, http://projects.cberdata.org/reports/MfgReality .pdf.

146 *American steel industry:* Allan Collard-Wexler and Jan de Loecker, "Reallocation and Technology: Evidence from the US Steel Industry," *American Economic Review* 105, no. 1 (January 2015): 131–171, https:// www.princeton.edu/~jdeloeck/CWDL_AER.pdf.

6   "LIP SERVICE" FOR AMERICA'S WORKERS

148 *As early as 1967:* Earl V. Anderson, "Labor Looks at U.S. Trade Policy . . . And Doesn't Like What It Sees," *Chemical & Engineering News,* March 1970, pp. 86–89, http://pubs.acs.org/doi/abs/10.1021 /cen-v048n012.p086.

148 *There were some holdouts:* Edward Alden, *Failure to Adjust* (Lanham, Md.: Rowman & Littlefield, 2016).

148 *growing trade* deficit: Census Bureau data on U.S. international trade: https://www.census.gov/foreign-trade/statistics/historical/gands.pdf.

148 *the AFL-CIO circulated a paper:* AFL-CIO Economic Policy Committee, "World Trade in the 1970s," *American Federationist,* May 1970, pp. 9–15.

149 *Burke-Hartke anti-trade bill:* The bill, also known as the "Foreign Trade and Investment Act of 1972," died in the House Committee on Ways and Means. See Alden, *Failure to Adjust,* p. 87; and Judis, *The Paradox of American Democracy.*

149 *In 1971, Peterson:* For general background on Peterson, see Richard Nixon Presidential Library: https://www.nixonlibrary.gov/for researchers/find/textual/special/smof/peterson.php; Peter G. Peterson Foundation: http://www.pgpf.org/board/peter-g-peterson.

149 *the 133-page memo:* Peter G. Peterson, *The United States in a Changing World Economy* (Washington, D.C.: U.S. Government Printing Office, 1971), https://catalog.hathitrust.org/Record/006243860.

150 *"I had read the union's memo":* Interview with Peterson.

150 *"Peterson saw a storm":* Interviews with Alden.

151 *Trade Adjustment Assistance:* Special Message to Congress on Foreign Trade Policy, delivered January 25, 1962, http://www.presidency.ucsb .edu/ws/?pid=8688.

151 *The Kennedy program:* Ibid.

151 *L. Mendel Rivers: Congressional Record,* August 23, 1962, https://www .govinfo.gov/content/pkg/GPO-CRECB-1962-pt13/pdf/GPO -CRECB-1962-pt13-4-3.pdf. (Senator Strom Thurmond [R-S.C.] asked that Congressman Rivers's statement, previously published in a South Carolina newspaper, be included in the *Record.*)

152 *"The group will be afforded": Congressional Record,* September 17, 1962, https://www.govinfo.gov/content/pkg/GPO-CRECB-1962-pt14 /pdf/GPO-CRECB-1962-pt14-11.pdf. (Senator John J. Williams [R-Del.] asked that a September 11, 1962 *New York Times* editorial and Senator Prescott Bush's reply published the following day be included in the *Record.*)

152 *A search of the archives:* This search was conducted using ProQuest databases, which include extensive newspaper archives from the twentieth century. I separately searched the archives of several mainstream print news outlets, including *The New York Times, The Economist, The New Yorker, Time,* and *The Washington Post.* I define "substantive articles" as longer than three paragraphs and including an examination of how and whether the Trade Adjustment Assistance program was working.

152 *not a single worker received assistance:* See Alden, *Failure to Adjust;* and Anderson, "Labor Looks at U.S. Trade Policy . . . And Doesn't Like What It Sees."

152 *Applications were rejected because:* Alden, *Failure to Adjust;* and Anderson, "Labor Looks at U.S. Trade Policy . . . And Doesn't Like What It Sees."

153 *Many workers, especially older ones:* Alden, *Failure to Adjust;* and Anderson, "Labor Looks at U.S. Trade Policy . . . And Doesn't Like What It Sees." See also the various GAO reports cited below.

153 *three quarters of the workers:* See Alden, *Failure to Adjust.*

153 *six thousand jobs:* "Trade Adjustment Assistance: Experiences of Six Trade-Impacted Communities" (General Accounting Office, August 2001), http://www.gao.gov/assets/240/232601.pdf.

153 *A series of similar studies:* The General Accounting Office, later renamed the Government Accountability Office, published studies involving TAA in 1992, 2000, 2001, 2011, and 2012. These can be found at: www.gao.gov.

153 *The most exhaustive study:* Ronald D'Amico and Peter Z. Schochet, "The Evaluation of the Trade Adjustment Assistance Program," published by Mathematica Policy Research, December 2012, https://www.mathematica-mpr.com/our-publications-and-findings/projects/trade-adjustment-assistance-evaluation?MPRSource=TCSide.

154 *solar panel maker:* The decision on Kolmax Solar, Inc. can be found on the Department of Labor's website: https://www.doleta.gov/tradeact/taa/taadecisions/taadecision.cfm?taw=82074.

154 *"The very existence of trade adjustment":* Sallie James, "Maladjusted: The Misguided Policy of Trade Adjustment Assistance," Cato Institute, November 8, 2007, https://object.cato.org/pubs/tbp/tbp-026.pdf.

154 *The Reagan and George W. Bush administrations:* See Alden, *Failure to Adjust,* and this 2001 General Accounting Office report: http://www.gao.gov/assets/110/108928.pdf.

154 *"Socialist governments":* Paul Blustein: "Trade Bill to Help Laid-Off Workers; Victims of Imports Win Added Benefits," *Washington Post,* August 3, 2002.

154 *"I tried relentlessly":* Interview with Reich.

155 *In Germany:* Tamar Jacoby, "Why Germany Is So Much Better at Training Its Workers," *The Atlantic,* October 16, 2014, https://www.theatlantic.com/business/archive/2014/10/why-germany-is-so-much-better-at-training-its-workers/381550/.

155 *In the United States:* Ibid.

155 *"It's hard to find":* This data is collected by the Organisation for Economic Co-operation and Development: http://www.oecd.org/employment/activation.htm.

156 *"The economic benefits":* Robert E. Lighthizer, a trade lawyer who became President Trump's U.S. trade representative, referenced this data from the Cato paper in his testimony before the U.S.-China Economic and Security Review Commission on June 9, 2010. The Cato study was written by Mark A. Groombridge: https://www.uscc.gov/sites/default/files/6.9.10Lighthizer.pdf. A more extensive study, "China's Long March to a Market Economy," written by the same author, can be viewed here: https://object.cato.org/sites/cato.org/files/pubs/pdf/tpa-010.pdf.

156 *releasing a letter from a coalition:* Letter: https://clintonwhitehouse6.archives.gov/2000/04/2000-04-03-fact-sheet-on-granting-china-permanent-normal-trade-relations.html; March 29, 2000, press conference: http://www.presidency.ucsb.edu/ws/?pid=58305.

157 *From 2000 to 2009:* U.S. Census Bureau: https://www.census.gov/foreign-trade/balance/c5700.html.

157 *the U.S. lost 5.6 million:* Lighthizer testimony: https://www.uscc.gov
      /sites/default/files/6.9.10Lighthizer.pdf.

157 *$347 billion:* U.S. Census Bureau: https://www.census.gov/foreign
      -trade/balance/c5700.html#2016.

157 *debt crisis and financial collapse:* See Lighthizer testimony for a dis-
      cussion of this connection: https://www.uscc.gov/sites/default/files
      /6.9.10Lighthizer.pdf.

157 *American Enterprise Institute:* Judis, *The Paradox of American Democracy*,
      p. 210.

157 *$15.8 billion* deficit: U.S. Census Bureau: https://www.census.gov
      /foreign-trade/balance/c2010.html.

158 Factory Man: Beth Macy, *Factory Man* (New York: Hachette, 2014).

158 *rising enrollment in the disability program:* Ibid.

158 *Henry County voted:* 1960: http://historical.elections.virginia.gov/elec
      tions/view/79121/; 2016: http://historical.elections.virginia.gov/elec
      tions/view/80871/.

158 *"I find myself":* https://www.nytimes.com/2014/09/02/opinion/joe
      -nocera-the-human-toll-of-offshoring.html?mcubz=0&_r=0.

159 *Democrats were so opposed:* For example, see Congressman Peter De-
      Fazio's (D-Ore.) comments in the *Congressional Record* from June 12,
      2015, which appear under the headline "Stop Trade Adjustment As-
      sistance and Save America's Economy": https://www.congress.gov
      /crec/2015/06/12/CREC-2015-06-12.pdf.

159 *"burial insurance":* Ibid.

159 *"History shows":* Remarks delivered at the fiftieth reunion of the
      Yale University Class of 1966 and published in *The Wall Street Jour-
      nal* on March 25, 2016: http://about.van.fedex.com/wp-content
      /uploads/2017/03/How-Trade-Made-America-Great-WSJ-3.25.16
      .pdf.

160 *average family spent 6 percent:* From a talk given by Edward Alden at the
      Council on Foreign Relations in New York on December 13, 2016.

160 *"Consumer prices":* "How China Is Battling Ever More Intensely in
      World Markets," *The Economist*, September 23, 2017, https://www
      .economist.com/news/leaders/21729430-does-it-play-fair-how-china
      -battling-ever-more-intensely-world-markets.

160 *"Yes, trade has cut costs":* Interview with Stiglitz.

161 *"It is obvious":* Thomas Piketty, *Capital in the Twenty-First Century*,
      translated by Arthur Goldhammer (Cambridge: The Belknap Press of
      Harvard University Press, 2014).

161 *Coalition for Queens:* Information about Coalition for Queens/Tech
      Equality comes from a series of interviews conducted with the founder,

Jukay Hsu, and staff members and trainees in the spring and fall of 2017, as well as company materials that were provided to the board of directors, which I joined in 2016. More information about Coalition for Queens/Tech Equality can be found on its website: www.c4q.nyc.

164 *Year Up:* Information about Year Up comes from a 2016 annual report on the company's website, www.yearup.org, as well an interview with Year Up president Garrett Moran and a report on the "Prospectus for Philanthropic Investment," provided by Moran.

166 *hundreds of thousands of openings:* The Bureau of Labor Statistics has information about software developer jobs available here: https:// www.bls.gov/ooh/computer-and-information-technology/software -developers.htm. News organizations have used these numbers to produce a variety of estimates of how many coding jobs are unfilled now and will go unfilled in the future. Some are as high as one million, others are as low at 200,000. In addition, an industry organization called the App Association released estimates in a report titled, "State of the App Economy," which can be viewed here: http://actonline .org/wp-content/uploads/App_Economy_Report_2017_Digital.pdf.

166 *President Trump proposed cutting:* These cuts were discussed at length during a June 7, 2017, hearing before the House Appropriations Committee examining the administration's proposed budget for the Department of Labor, which can be viewed here: https://appro priations.house.gov/calendar/eventsingle.aspx?EventID=394897. The administration's proposed fiscal year 2018 budget, which includes the cuts, can be viewed here: https://www.whitehouse.gov/omb /budget.

166 *transitional income support program:* See Alden, *Failure to Adjust,* p. 123.

167 *"in 1967, the median income":* Patricia Cohen, "Bump in U.S. Incomes Doesn't Erase 50 Years of Pain," *New York Times,* September 16, 2017, https://www.nytimes.com/2017/09/16/business/economy/bump -in-us-incomes-doesnt-erase-50-years-of-pain.html?mcubz=0. The numbers in Cohen's article are an analysis of data from this paper: Bernadette D. Proctor, Jessica L. Semega, and Melissa A. Kollar, *Income and Poverty in the United States: 2015* (Washington, D.C.: U.S. Government Printing Office, 2016), https://www.census.gov/library /publications/2016/demo/p60-256.html.

167 *openings for skilled labor jobs:* Peter Coy and Matthew Philips, "Wanted: Forklift Driver," *Bloomberg Businessweek,* December 19–25, 2016, https://www.bloomberg.com/news/articles/2016-12-15/there-are -plenty-of-jobs-out-there-america.

167 *job participation rate:* From the Bureau of Labor Statistics. Unemploy-

ment: https://data.bls.gov/timeseries/LNS14000000; Job participation: https://data.bls.gov/timeseries/LNS11300000.

168 *"strong evidence that congressional districts":* David Autor, David Dorn, Gordon Hanson, and Kaveh Majlesi, "Importing Political Polarization? The Electoral Consequences of Rising Trade Exposure," NBER Working Paper No. 22637, September 2016, http://www.nber.org /papers/w22637.

7 DYSFUNCTIONAL DEMOCRACY

169 *Obamacare:* I wrote a book about Obamacare, *Bitter Pill: Money, Politics, Backroom Deals, and the Fight to Fix Our Broken Healthcare System,* published by Random House in 2015. Except for subsequent developments, almost all of the information about the law and how it was negotiated and implemented comes from the research and reporting undertaken for that book.

169 *Nixon had proposed:* Nixon's February 18, 1971, Special Message to Congress Proposing a National Health Strategy: http://www.presi dency.ucsb.edu/ws/?pid=3311. Nixon delivered two more speeches to Congress on the topic, also available on the same website.

170 *Heritage Foundation:* A copy of the report can be viewed here: http:// thf_media.s3.amazonaws.com/1989/pdf/hl218.pdf.

171 *Senate Republicans had initially:* These were members of the bipartisan "Gang of Six," including Chuck Grassley of Iowa, Mike Enzi of Wyoming, and Olympia Snowe of Maine. See *Bitter Pill*, Chapters 8 and 9.

171 *Frank Luntz:* Interview with Luntz. See also ibid., pp. 92–93.

171 *"government takeover of healthcare"* and *"death panels":* These two terms, and the rhetoric surrounding them, were awarded *PolitiFact*'s Lie of the Year in 2009 and 2010 respectively: http://www.politifact.com /truth-o-meter/article/2009/dec/18/politifact-lie-year-death-panels/ and http://www.politifact.com/truth-o-meter/article/2010/dec/16/lie -year-government-takeover-health-care/.

172 *plan to address the deficit:* The National Commission on Fiscal Responsibility and Reform produced this report: http://momentoftruth project.org/sites/default/files/TheMomentofTruth12_1_2010.pdf; *The New York Times* has a record of how the commission voted on the plan here: http://www.nytimes.com/interactive/2010/12/03/us /politics/deficit-commission-vote.html.

173 *"gutless":* Interview with Simpson in 2011.

173 *Budget Control Act of 2011:* The act can be read here: https://www.gpo .gov/fdsys/pkg/BILLS-112s365eah/pdf/BILLS-112s365eah.pdf. An

analysis by *The New York Times* of the automatic cuts is here: http://
www.nytimes.com/interactive/2011/07/22/us/politics/20110722
-comparing-deficit-reduction-plans.html.

173 *The fail-safe failed:* Members of the Joint Select Committee on Deficit Reduction did not reach an agreement by the required date of
November 23, 2011. This statement, issued two days before the
deadline, announced their failure: https://www.murray.senate.gov
/public/index.cfm/2011/11/statement-from-co-chairs-of-the-joint
-select-committee-on-deficit-reduction.

173 *modern proliferation of Senate filibusters:* Thomas E. Mann and Norman J. Ornstein, *It's Even Worse Than It Looks: How the American Constitutional System Collided with the New Politics of Extremism* (New York:
Basic Books, 2012). See also the Senate's record of calls for cloture,
the formal procedure for breaking a filibuster: https://www.senate.gov
/pagelayout/reference/cloture_motions/clotureCounts.htm.

174 *block judicial nominations and other actions:* George W. Bush nominated
Miguel Estrada for the U.S. Court of Appeals for the D.C. Circuit in
2001. Charging that Estrada's judicial philosophy was too far to the
right, Senate Democrats, led by Chuck Schumer of New York, successfully filibustered the nomination. Republicans could only muster
51 votes out of the required 60 for cloture, and failed to end debate
seven times. In September 2003, Estrada wrote to Bush request-
ing that his nomination be withdrawn, and Bush complied. See this
Congressional Research Service report on judicial nominations by
President Bush: https://fas.org/sgp/crs/misc/RL31868.pdf. See also
The New York Times coverage of these events: http://www.nytimes
.com/2003/03/06/politics/republicans-lose-bid-to-end-filibuster
-on-judge.html; http://www.nytimes.com/2003/09/05/us/stymied-by
-democrats-in-senate-bush-court-pick-finally-gives-up.html.

174 *nuclear option:* See this November 21, 2013, statement from Senate
Democrats: https://democrats.senate.gov/2013/11/21/reid-remarks
-on-changing-the-senate-rules/#.WdU1JhOPKAw.

174 *Neil Gorsuch:* Senate Republicans triggered this new "nuclear option"
on April 6, 2017, and Gorsuch was approved with a final vote of 54–
45, with one abstention. *Congressional Record,* April 7, 2017, p. S2442,
https://www.congress.gov/crec/2017/04/07/CREC-2017-04-07.pdf.

174 *the most uncontroversial hiccups:* See *Bitter Pill,* p. 194.

174 *John Boehner:* In this statement, for example, he moves from calling it a law to a bill and back again: http://abcnews.go.com/Politics
/video/john-boehner-obamacare-wreaks-havoc-american-families
-21085758.

175 *immigration reform law:* The Border Security, Economic Opportunity,

and Immigration Modernization Act (S.744) passed in the Senate with a 68–32 vote, but was never allowed a vote in the House: https://www.congress.gov/bill/113th-congress/senate-bill/744/actions.

175 *"With the Hastert Rule":* Interview with LaHood.

175 *Since 1994, Congress has failed:* Alice M. Rivlin and Pete Domenici, "Proposal for Improving the Congressional Budget Process" (Bipartisan Policy Center: Washington, D.C., 2015), https://cdn.bipartisanpolicy.org/wp-content/uploads/2015/07/BPC-Congressional-Budget-Process.pdf.

175 *approval ratings:* The website RealClearPolitics aggregates ratings from most major polls here: https://www.realclearpolitics.com/epolls/other/congressional_job_approval-903.html#polls.

176 *highway maintenance and construction:* First in October (H.R. 3819) and again in mid-November (H.R. 3996), Congress passed the Surface Transportation Extension Act of 2015 to extend funding through December. In the beginning of that month, Congress passed the Fixing America's Surface Transportation, or FAST, Act (H.R. 22).
H.R. 3819: https://www.congress.gov/bill/114th-congress/house-bill/3819
H.R. 3996: https://www.congress.gov/bill/114th-congress/house-bill/3996
H.R. 22, FAST Act: https://www.congress.gov/bill/114th-congress/house-bill/22

176 *gasoline tax:* Henry Petroski, *The Road Taken: The History and Future of America's Infrastructure* (New York: Bloomsbury USA, 2016).

177 *government dysfunction started:* Interviews with LaHood and Michel.

177 *The reformers:* Richard Pildes, "Two Myths About the Unruly American Primary System," *Washington Post*, May 25, 2016; Jeffrey H. Anderson and Jay Cost, "A Republican Nomination Process," *National Affairs* 33 (Fall 2017), http://www.nationalaffairs.com/publications/detail/a-republican-nomination-process. See also this April 2000 Congressional Research Service Report, which describes the process and history of presidential elections: https://www.senate.gov/reference/resources/pdf/RL30527.pdf.

178 *Instead they had to keep:* Judis, *The Paradox of American Democracy*, pp. 133–35.

179 *Gestapo-like tactics:* Tom DeLay, *No Retreat, No Surrender* (New York: Sentinel, 2007).

179 *DeLay soon became:* Hacker and Pierson, *Winner-Take-All Politics* (New York: Simon & Schuster, 2011), p. 207. See also a record of DeLay's fund-raising at the Center for Responsive Politics website Open

Secrets.org: http://www.opensecrets.org/members-of-congress/sum
mary?cid=N00005892&cycle=2006.

179 *"epitome of what was wrong":* DeLay, *No Retreat, No Surrender,* p. 77.

179 *Post-Watergate changes:* See Judis, *The Paradox of American Democracy,*
p. 133.

179 *Wright Patman of Texas:* Matt Stoller, "How Democrats Killed Their
Populist Soul," theatlantic.com, October 24, 2016, https://www
.theatlantic.com/politics/archive/2016/10/how-democrats-killed
-their-populist-soul/504710/.

180 *earmarks, which were special:* Joseph White, "Jimmy Carter's and James
Miller's Revenge: The Reasons and the Consequences for Presidential and Congressional Power of Measures to Ban Congressional
Earmarks," *Case Western Reserve Law Review* 65, no. 4 (2015), http://
scholarlycommons.law.case.edu/cgi/viewcontent.cgi?article=1011
&context=caselrev.

180 *shut down the government:* In late September, Senator Cruz filibustered for over twenty-one hours in opposition to Obamacare: https://
www.c-span.org/video/?c4466033/sen-ted-cruz-complete-remarks.
Gridlock over the health care bill caused a shutdown that began on
October 1 and ran through the 16th.

181 *"chaos syndrome":* Jonathan Rauch, "How American Politics Went
Insane," *The Atlantic,* July/August 2016, https://www.theatlantic.com
/magazine/archive/2016/07/how-american-politics-went-insane
/485570/.

181 *county-wide elections:* Stuart Taylor, Jr., "A Bad Place to Be," newrepublic
.com, February 16, 2010, https://newrepublic.com/article/73080/bad
-place-be. See also the book reviewed by Stuart Taylor, Jr., in that
article: Abigail Thernstrom, *Voting Rights—And Wrongs* (Washington,
D.C.: American Enterprise Institute Press, 2009).

182 *The Voting Rights Act was amended:* Ibid. See also David Daley, *Ratf**ked:
The True Story Behind the Secret Plan to Steal America's Democracy* (New
York: Liveright, 2016). The amendments may be viewed here: https://
www.gpo.gov/fdsys/pkg/STATUTE-96/pdf/STATUTE-96-Pg131
.pdf.

182 *The Court ruled: Thornburg v. Gingles,* June 30, 1986: https://www
.oyez.org/cases/1985/83-1968.

182 *"pushed us to agree":* Interview with Ginsberg.

183 *Southern Republican Leadership Conference:* The meeting took place in
Raleigh, North Carolina, and Ginsberg later met with the Congressional Black Caucus Foundation in September of the same year to
discuss redistricting. Interview with Ginsberg. See also Paul Taylor,

"GOP Will Aid Civil Rights Groups in Redistricting," *Washington Post*, April 1, 1990.

183 *African American 12th District:* This page provides a history of the district and the legal action involving it: https://www.senate.mn /departments/scr/REDIST/Redsum/ncsum.htm.

183 *Democratic Party lost:* The state's 2016 election results can be found on the Board of Elections website: http://er.ncsbe.gov/?election_dt =11/08/2016&county_id=0&office=FED&contest=0.

184 *"truly space-age" computer software:* See Daley, *Ratf**ked.*

184 *state senate district had been gerrymandered:* Ryan Lizza, "The Obama Memos," *The New Yorker,* January 30, 2012, https://www.newyorker .com/magazine/2012/01/30/the-obama-memos.

184 *money into state legislative races:* See Daley, *Ratf**ked.*

184 *Maptitude:* http://www.caliper.com/mtredist.htm.

185 *estimated 1.4 million more Americans:* According to the official 2012 election record on the House of Representatives website, Democrats received 1.6 million more votes than Republicans: http://history .house.gov/Institution/Election-Statistics/2012election/.   However, David Wasserman of *The Cook Political Report* calculated the number to be just under 1.4 million, taking into account "late December data from New York," according to *PolitiFact:* http://www.politifact.com /truth-o-meter/statements/2013/feb/19/steny-hoyer/steny-hoyer -house-democrats-won-majority-2012-popu/. This more conservative estimate is referenced in David Daley's *Ratf**ked* and in Senator Sheldon Whitehouse's book, *Captured: The Corporate Infiltration of American Democracy* (New York: The New Press, 2017).

185 *massive data analysis:* David A. Lieb, "Analysis Indicates Partisan Gerrymandering Has Benefited GOP," Associated Press, June 25, 2017, https://www.apnews.com/fa6478e10cda4e9cbd75380e705bd380.

185 *a group to fight:* The National Democratic Redistricting Committee is run by former attorney general Eric Holder: https://democraticredis-tricting.com/.

185 *bipartisan or independent commissions:* The National Conference of State Legislatures has a list of the states: http://www.ncsl.org/research /redistricting/redistricting-commissions-congressional-plans.aspx. See also Peter Miller and Bernard Grofman, "Redistricting Commissions in the Western United States," *UC Irvine Law Review* 3, no. 3 (August 2013), http://www.law.uci.edu/lawreview/vol3/no3/miller _grofman.pdf.

185 *In Washington State:* http://history.house.gov/Institution/Election -Statistics/2016election/.

186 *Anthony Kennedy:* See his concurring opinion on the 2004 case *Vieth*

v. Jubelirer: https://supreme.justia.com/cases/federal/us/541/267/con
currence.html.

186 *"To say that the Constitution"*: *Gill v. Whitford*, November 21, 2016,
Federal District Court Decision, http://www.scotusblog.com/wp
-content/uploads/2017/04/16-1161-op-bel-dist-ct-wisc.pdf; Supreme
Court Case: https://www.oyez.org/cases/2017/16-1161.

187 *Washington political intrigue:* Allen Drury, *Advise and Consent* (New
York: Doubleday, 1959).

188 *rise of Newt Gingrich:* David Osborne, "The Swinging Days of Newt
Gingrich," *Mother Jones*, November 1984, http://www.motherjones
.com/politics/1984/11/newt-gingrich-shining-knight-post-reagan
-right/; Julia Ioffe, "The Millennial's Guide to Newt Gingrich," *Politico*,
July 14, 2016, http://www.politico.com/magazine/story/2016/07/2016
-newt-gingrich-scandals-accomplishments-veepstakes-running-mate
-trump-gop-republican-214050.

188 *attacks on Flynt's integrity:* Gingrich seized on Flynt's relationship with
Ford Motor Company, whose chairman donated to Flynt's campaign.
Rex Granum, "Gingrich Labels Flynt 'Industry Watchdog,'" *Atlanta
Constitution*, October 3, 1974; Cliff Green, "Gingrich Is Tough One
for Rep. Flynt," *Atlanta Constitution*, November 3, 1974; David Morri-
son, "Avoids Misconduct Probes, Gingrich Says About Flynt," *Atlanta
Constitution*, October 13, 1976.

188 *Gingrich attacked Shapard:* Beau Cutts, "Newt Gingrich Prefers the
Underdog Role," *Atlanta Constitution*, September 22, 1978; "Shapard
Calls Flier 'Racist,'" October 31, 1978.

189 *"Newt totally stood out":* Interview with Ornstein.

189 *C-Span:* https://www.c-span.org/about/history/.

189 *talking to themselves:* John Micklethwait and Adrian Woolridge, *The
Right Nation: Conservative Power in America* (New York: Penguin,
2004), pp. 100–101. See also Osborne, "The Swinging Days of Newt
Gingrich"; and Ioffe, "The Millennial's Guide to Newt Gingrich."

190 *"Newt was different":* Interview with Michel; and: http://www.politico
.com/story/2017/02/bob-michel-dies-former-gop-house-leader
-234936.

190 *Jim Wright:* See Micklethwait and Woolridge, *The Right Nation*, pp.
100–101.

190 *to fine him $300,000:* See Gingrich's official congressional biography:
http://bioguide.congress.gov/scripts/biodisplay.pl?index=G000225.
See also https://www.govtrack.us/congress/bills/105/hres31 and https:
//ethics.house.gov/committee-report/matter-representative-newt
-gingrich.

191 *"Contract with America":* The contract can be viewed here: https://

web.archive.org/web/19990427174200/http://www.house.gov/house
/Contract/CONTRACT.html.

191 *welfare reform legislation:* The Personal Responsibility and Work
Opportunity Reconciliation Act of 1996: https://www.congress.gov
/bill/104th-congress/house-bill/3734/actions.

191 *Matt Drudge:* David McClintock, "Town Crier for the New Age,"
Brill's Content, November 1998. See also Jerry Lazar, "From a Little Corner of Hollywood, a Big Internet Success," *Los Angeles Times,*
March 24, 1997, http://articles.latimes.com/1997-03-24/business
/fi-41663_1_first-drudge-report.

191 *The* Drudge Report: http://www.drudgereportarchives.com/data/2002
/01/17/20020117_175502_ml.htm.

192 *Rush Limbaugh:* See Micklethwait and Woolridge, *The Right Nation,*
pp. 112–13.

192 *He attracted millions:* According to QuantCast, which measures website traffic, Drudgereport.com consistently gets over 2 million unique
visits per day, and reached a peak of over 4 million unique visits on
Election Day in 2016: https://www.quantcast.com/measure/p-e2qh6t
-Out2Ug.

193 *analysis of web traffic:* https://www.buzzfeed.com/craigsilverman/viral
-fake-election-news-outperformed-real-news-on-facebook?utm
_term=.wl5VDkorv#.xpvQEzvB3.

193 *75 percent of all American eyeballs:* Steve Waldman and the Working
Group on Information Needs of Communities, "The Information
Needs of Communities," Federal Communications Commission,
July 2011, https://transition.fcc.gov/osp/inc-report/The_Information
_Needs_of_Communities.pdf. Other sources put the number as high
as 90 percent.

193 *one poll reported that 89 percent:* https://www.axios.com/exclusive
-astonishing-poll-about-trump-and-media-2453120782.html.

193 *A 2016 survey found:* http://www.publicpolicypolling.com/main/2016
/05/gop-quickly-unifies-around-trump-clinton-still-has-modest
-lead.html.

193 *"very likely":* The poll, conducted by Scripps Survey Research Center at Ohio University, can be seen here: http://newspolls.org/surveys
/SHOH33/18911. A *Politico* story referencing Democrat-specific statistics is here: http://www.politico.com/blogs/ben-smith/2011/04/more
-than-half-of-democrats-believed-bush-knew-035224.

194 *"The misuse of big data":* https://www.nbcnews.com/meet-the-press
/video/is-big-data-is-destroying-the-u-s-political-system-90151
7891589.

195 *Bipartisan Policy Center:* The ten-year anniversary event described in the text took place on March 1, 2017. Information about the event can be found on the organization's website along with many of the reports mentioned: https://bipartisanpolicy.org. In addition, I interviewed BPC founder and president Jason Grumet.

8 MOAT NATION

197 *American health care economy:* According to the National Health Expenditure Projections prepared by the Centers for Medicare & Medicaid Services, U.S. health care expenditures accounted for 17.8 percent of the country's GDP in 2015 and is projected to grow at a faster rate than the GDP to make up 19.9 percent by 2025: https://www.cms .gov/Research-Statistics-Data-and-Systems/Statistics-Trends-and -Reports/NationalHealthExpendData/Downloads/proj2016.pdf. It should also be noted that the Centers' estimates of health care's share of the GDP are lower than those compiled by private researchers, such as Deloitte Consulting, LLP, which is why I am comfortable using "nearly one fifth."

197 *trust in the federal government:* From the Pew Research Center: http:// www.people-press.org/2017/05/03/public-trust-in-government -1958-2017/.

198 *Warren Buffett:* The investor has regularly used the term "moat" in his annual letter to Berkshire Hathaway shareholders. In 2007 he explained, "A truly great business must have an enduring 'moat' that protects excellent returns on invested capital": http://www.berkshire hathaway.com/letters/2007ltr.pdf.

198 *expedited access through airport security:* This was a company called Clear that I founded.

198 *leading growth industry:* See Drutman, *The Business of America Is Lobbying,* pp. 9–11.

199 *That is why that study:* Martin Gilens and Benjamin I. Page, "Testing Theories of American Politics: Elites, Interest Groups, and Average Citizens," *Perspectives on Politics* 12, no. 3 (September 2014), http:// citeseerx.ist.psu.edu/viewdoc/download;jsessionid=37EDA24D1D5 DA87AEB950CEFE63883FF?doi=10.1.1.668.8647&rep=rep1&type =pdf.

199 *The health care lobby:* As can be found at the OpenSecrets.org tally of lobbying by industry category, expenditures by Pharmaceuticals/ Health Products, Hospitals, Healthcare Professionals, and Health

Services combined are consistently higher than those of any other industry category or combined categories in related industries: https://www.opensecrets.org/lobby/top.php?showYear=a&indexType=i.

199 *risen by at least 30 percent:* I made this calculation using data from the Kaiser Family Foundation, which reports a 300 percent increase in the cost of health insurance per employee, and from the Bureau of Labor Statistics. Together they indicate that health insurance costs account for 10–14 percent of total costs per employee. See the KFF's annual Employer Health Benefits Survey: https://www.kff.org/health-costs /report/employer-health-benefits-annual-survey-archives/; as well as the Bureau of Labor Statistics' data on Employer Costs for Employee Compensation: https://www.bls.gov/news.release/ecec.nr0.htm.

199 *grew 460 percent:* Kalorama Information, "Out-of-Pocket Healthcare Expenditures in the United States," April 17, 2017, https://www.kalo ramainformation.com/Pocket-Healthcare-Expenditures-10781903/.

199 *no longer offered insurance:* See the Kaiser Family Foundation's report: https://www.kff.org/health-costs/report/employer-health-benefits -annual-survey-archives/.

200 *according to multiple studies:* John E. Kwoka, Jr., "Does Merger Control Work? A Retrospective on U.S. Enforcement Actions and Merger Outcomes," *Antitrust Law Journal* 78 (2013), https://ssrn.com /abstract=1954849. See also the April 2016 report by President Obama's Council of Economic Advisers, referenced later in the text: https://obamawhitehouse.archives.gov/sites/default/files/page/files /20160414_cea_competition_issue_brief.pdf.

200 *United Airlines:* Julie Creswell and Sapna Maheshwari, "United Grapples with PR Crisis over Videos of Man Being Dragged off Plane," *New York Times,* April 11, 2017, https://www.nytimes.com/2017/04/11 /business/united-airline-passenger-overbooked-flights.html?utm _source=newsletter.

200 *calls for a boycott:* James B. Stewart, "The Boycott That Wasn't: How United Weathered a Media Firestorm," *New York Times,* July 27, 2017, https://www.nytimes.com/2017/07/27/business/how-united-weath ered-a-firestorm.html.

201 *Yale New Haven Health System:* See this press release from Jones Day announcing its role in getting approval for Yale New Haven's 2012 acquisition of the Hospital of Saint Raphael, a competing hospital in the same city: http://www.jonesday.com/experiencepractices /ExperienceDetail.aspx?experienceid=28474.

201 *allowed to merge and buy:* The first page of the Yale New Haven Health System's 2016 Annual Report reviews "Highlights of the Past 20

Years." It is mostly a list of the hospitals it has acquired and new facilities it has opened: https://www.ynhhs.org/~/media/files/ynhhs/pdf/ynhh_system_annual_report_2016_4webfinal.pdf.

201 *$3.8 billion in revenue:* The 2016 annual report, cited above, includes an audit of the organization by the accounting firm KPMG: http://www.ct.gov/dph/lib/dph/ohca/hospitalfillings/2016/ynhav_2016afs_hospital.pdf. To calculate cash flow, I took the income from operations and added back depreciation, which is a non-cash accounting expense. This is a method that hospital finance officers I have consulted over the years say is the best measure of cash flow.

201 *President Obama's Council of Economic Advisers:* https://obamawhitehouse.archives.gov/sites/default/files/page/files/20160414_cea_competition_issue_brief.pdf.

202 *American income tax code:* Each year, Commerce Clearing House, a division of Wolters Kluwer, publishes the *CCH Standard Federal Tax Reporter,* which is widely referenced as the U.S. Tax Code. This is my source for the twenty-seven-page length of the 1913 tax code: https://www.cch.com/wbot2013/factsheet.pdf. The original code was printed in a 1913 book, which is available online: Thomas Gold Frost, *A Treatise on the Federal Income Tax Law of 1913* (Albany, N.Y.: Matthew Bender & Company), p. 131, https://archive.org/stream/cu31924020038711#page/n149/mode/2up.

202 *thousands of pages long:* The *CCH Standard Federal Tax Reporter* is described by Commerce Clearing House as a "25-volume service . . . containing the federal tax law and related materials." The "related materials" are largely composed of editorial commentary and court cases, which is why the tax code is often described as running over 70,000 pages in length. The statutory text of the code is between 2,500 and 3,000 pages; the exact number of pages is impossible to calculate because the amendments and editorial commentary are included throughout the statutory text, rather than at the end. Different formats also result in different page counts. The tax code is included in Title 26 of the U.S. Code, though it also includes large amounts of non-statutory amendment histories and court cases: http://uscode.house.gov/download/download.shtml.

202 *wealthy with tax rates:* See information published by the Organisation for Economic Co-operation and Development: http://www.oecd.org/tax/tax-policy/tax-database.htm.

202 *paid a lower share:* The U.S. paid 26.4 percent of its GDP in taxes, according to the most recent OECD data: https://stats.oecd.org/Index.aspx?DataSetCode=REV.

202 *In 1970, the income tax rate:* The Tax Foundation, an independent tax policy think tank, has a database of historical tax rates available here: https://taxfoundation.org/us-federal-individual-income-tax-rates -history-1913-2013-nominal-and-inflation-adjusted-brackets/. The 2017 rates can be seen in the 2016 1040 form available on the IRS's website: https://www.irs.gov/pub/irs-pdf/i1040tt.pdf.

202 *Social Security taxes:* Charles Peters, *We Do Our Part: Toward a Fairer and More Equal America* (New York: Random House, 2017), p. 212.

203 *lobbyists' reversal of Jimmy Carter's tax reform:* See Birnbaum and Murray, *Showdown at Gucci Gulch*, pp. 15–17.

203 *a loophole that allows the money:* IRS Revenue Procedure 93-27 (1993-27 C.B. 343): https://fortunedotcom.files.wordpress.com/2012/08/rp93 27.pdf.

203 *he wrote in 1924:* Andrew Mellon, *Taxation: The People's Business* (New York: Macmillan, 1924), p. 57, https://archive.org/stream /taxationthepeoplo33026mbp#page/n7/mode/2up. See also Ajay K. Mehrota and Julia C. Ott, "The Curious Beginnings of the Capital Gains Tax Preference," *Fordham Law Review* 84, no. 6 (2016), http:// ir.lawnet.fordham.edu/cgi/viewcontent.cgi?article=5205&context=flr.

203 *A bipartisan tax reform law:* The Tax Reform Act of 1986: https://www .congress.gov/bill/99th-congress/house-bill/3838?r=1. For the best description of the law and the process that produced it, see Jeffrey Birnbaum and Alan Murray, *Showdown at Gucci Gulch: Lawmakers, Lobbyists, and the Unlikely Triumph of Tax Reform* (New York: Random House, 1987). For a description of the rollbacks, see Lessig, *Republic, Lost: Version 2.0* (New York: Twelve, 2015); and Hacker and Pierson, *Winner-Take-All Politics*.

204 *armor-piercing bullets:* "Green-tip" bullets were previously exempted from a federal regulation banning armor-piercing bullets on the premise that they were only used in rifles for "sporting purposes." More recently, however, it has become possible to use these bullets in semiautomatic handguns, which would contravene the ban. In early 2015, the ATF confirmed this in a proposal for a new "framework for determining whether certain projectiles are 'primarily intended for sporting purposes.'" The ATF's proposal is located here: https:// www.atf.gov/resource-center/docs-0/download. After receiving over eighty thousand public comments, most of which were critical of the regulation, the ATF released a statement withdrawing the proposal: https://www.atf.gov/news/pr/notice-those-commenting-armor -piercing-ammunition-exemption-framework.

204 *Cerberus:* The private equity firm owns the Remington Outdoor

Group, formerly the Freedom Group, which is the parent company of a number of gun manufacturers, including Bushmaster, the maker of one of the guns used in the Sandy Hook massacre: https://www.remingtonoutdoorcompany.com/.

205 *Dodd-Frank Wall Street Reform and Consumer Protection Act:* https://www.congress.gov/bill/111th-congress/house-bill/4173/actions.

205 *the forty-three members:* This figure was reported by the Center for Responsive Politics on OpenSecrets.org at the time: https://www.opensecrets.org/news/2010/06/financial-reform-bill-to-be-finaliz/.

205 *"You can say that lobbyists":* Quoted in Steven Brill, "The Best Laws Money Can Buy," *Time*, July 1, 2010, http://content.time.com/time/magazine/article/0,9171,2001015-1,00.html.

206 *The 1935 Social Security Act:* Federal Trade Commission: http://legisworks.org/sal/38/stats/STATUTE-38-Pg717.pdf; Social Security: http://legisworks.org/sal/49/stats/STATUTE-49-Pg620.pdf.

206 *The lobbyist ranks:* According to the Center for Responsive Politics, from January to September 2009, "3,659 lobbyists worked for companies that explicitly lobbied on the Dodd-Frank bill": https://www.opensecrets.org/news/2010/11/lobbyists-newest-targets-in-wall-st/.

206 *243 regulations and conduct sixty-seven studies:* The Wall Street law firm Davis Polk & Wardwell tallied the number in a client memorandum published on the same day that Dodd-Frank was signed by President Obama: https://www.davispolk.com/files/files/Publication/7084f9fe-6580-413b-b870-b7c025ed2ecf/Presentation/PublicationAttachment/1d4495c7-0be0-4e9a-ba77-f786fb90464a/070910_Financial_Reform_Summary.pdf.

207 *the share of all banking assets:* Each quarter, the Federal Reserve publishes data on domestically chartered insured commercial banks with over $300 million in assets, which can be seen here: https://www.federalreserve.gov/releases/lbr/. I used this data to determine the top five banks and their total assets. Then, I used data from the FDIC to determine the total assets of all FDIC-insured commercial banks and savings institutions: https://www.fdic.gov/bank/statistical/. At the end of the second quarter in 2010, the top five banks controlled 42.33 percent of all assets with a total of $5.6 trillion. At the end of 2016, they controlled 43.37 percent of all assets with a total of $7.3 trillion. These market share percentages are probably more conservative than figures found elsewhere because of the inclusion of savings institutions in the FDIC's calculation of total assets.

208 *3,658 lobbyists:* From the Center for Responsive Politics: https://www.opensecrets.org/news/2010/11/lobbyists-newest-targets-in-wall-st/.

208 *implementing the Volcker Rule:* The five agencies involved were the Federal Reserve System, the Commodity Futures Trading Commission, the Federal Deposit Insurance Corporation, the Office of the Comptroller of the Currency, and the Securities and Exchange Commission. Here is the December 10, 2013, announcement of the rule: https://www.federalreserve.gov/newsevents/pressreleases/bcreg20131210a.htm.

208 *The first draft:* Proposed rule: https://www.federalregister.gov/documents/2011/11/07/2011-27184/prohibitions-and-restrictions-on-proprietary-trading-and-certain-interests-in-and-relationships-with. Final rule: https://www.federalregister.gov/documents/2014/01/31/2013-31511/prohibitions-and-restrictions-on-proprietary-trading-and-certain-interests-in-and-relationships-with.

208 *meetings with lobbyists:* Kimberly Krawiec, "Don't 'Screw Joe the Plummer': The Sausage-Making of Financial Reform," *Arizona Law Review* (2013), http://scholarship.law.duke.edu/faculty_scholarship/2445/.

208 *extended into 2019:* See this press release from the Fed: https://www.federalreserve.gov/newsevents/pressreleases/bcreg20170928a.htm.

208 *$171 billion: FDIC Quarterly* 11, no. 1 (2017), https://www.fdic.gov/bank/analytical/quarterly/2017-vol11-1/fdic-v11n1-4q16.pdf. The largest profits reported prior to the financial crisis totaled $145 billion in 2006 (see chart 3 in the cited report), a benchmark the industry passed in 2013.

208 *letter to shareholders:* The graph on page 3 shows the bank's profits back to 2004: https://www.jpmorganchase.com/corporate/investor-relations/document/ar2016-ceolettershareholders.pdf.

208 *22,000 pages of rules:* Based on an analysis by the Davis Polk & Wardwell law firm: http://www.volckerrule.com/infographic/july2015infographic.html.

209 *unfinished drafts:* See these progress updates from Davis Polk & Wardwell: https://www.davispolk.com/dodd-frank/.

210 *The phony accounts:* After a third-party review, the bank reported its findings in an August 2017 press release: https://newsroom.wf.com/press-release/wells-fargo-reports-completion-expanded-third-party-review-retail-banking-accounts. See also coverage from *The New York Times* from September 2016: https://www.nytimes.com/2016/09/09/business/dealbook/wells-fargo-fined-for-years-of-harm-to-customers.html; and from August 2017: https://www.nytimes.com/2017/08/31/business/dealbook/wells-fargo-accounts.html; as well as the original *Los Angeles Times* story from 2013: http://www.latimes.com/business/la-fi-wells-fargo-sale-pressure-20131222-story.html.

210 *After the $185 million settlement:* Information from the bank is located here: https://www.wellsfargo.com/commitment/. See also David Ng, "Judge Approves $142-Million Class-Action Settlement in Wells Fargo Sham Accounts Scandal," *Los Angeles Times,* July 9, 2017, http://www.latimes.com/business/la-fi-wells-fargo-settlement-20170709-story.html.

210 *"CEO of the Year":* From a January 2016 press release: https://news room.morningstar.com/newsroom/news-archive/press-release-details/2016/Morningstar-Hall-of-Fame-CEO-of-the-Year-Win ners/default.aspx.

210 *performance-related bonuses :* Stephen Gandel, "Wells Fargo Exec Who Headed Phony Accounts Unit Collected $125 Million," *Fortune,* September 12, 2016, http://fortune.com/2016/09/12/wells-fargo-cfpb-carrie-tolstedt/. See also Stacy Cowley and Jennifer A. Kingson, "Wells Fargo to Claw Back $75 Million from 2 Former Executives," *New York Times,* April 10, 2017, https://www.nytimes.com/2017/04/10/business/wells-fargo-pay-executives-accounts-scandal.html.

210 *Yet neither the executives:* A discussion of arbitration takes place around the 50:00 and 1:26:00 marks: https://www.banking.senate.gov/public/index.cfm/2017/10/wells-fargo-one-year-later.

210 *fifteen Democratic members:* The letter dated October 26, 2016, was signed by fifteen senators: https://www.sec.gov/comments/s7-07-16/s70716-74.pdf.

211 *lobbyists for Citigroup:* In 2013, *The New York Times* reported on the Citigroup lobbyists' involvement in writing seventy of eighty-five lines in a House bill from that year: https://dealbook.nytimes.com/2013/05/23/banks-lobbyists-help-in-drafting-financial-bills/?ref=politics. The bill was never considered in the Senate, but the lobbyists' key recommendations resurfaced in the 2014 spending bill: http://www.motherjones.com/politics/2014/12/spending-bill-992-derivatives-citigroup-lobbyists/.

211 *Closing Off the Courts:* An extensive overview of class action lawsuits and their history can be found in the 2017 rulemaking report prepared by the staff of the Consumer Financial Protection Bureau when the rule prohibiting clauses banning class actions was promulgated: https://www.consumerfinance.gov/policy-compliance/rulemaking/final-rules/arbitration-agreements/.

212 *In 1966, changes to federal court:* That year, Rule 23 of the Federal Rules of Civil Procedure was revised and amended. The rule, which is also discussed in the CFPB rulemaking report, may be read here: https://www.law.cornell.edu/rules/frcp/rule_23.

213 *Reform laws were passed:* The first was the Private Securities Litigation Reform Act of 1995: https://www.congress.gov/bill/104th-congress /house-bill/1058. The second was the Class Action Fairness Act of 2005: https://www.congress.gov/bill/109th-congress/senate-bill/5.

213 *class action arbitration proceeding:* See a trailblazing three-part series titled "Beware the Fine Print," published in *The New York Times* in late October and early November of 2015. See especially Part I: Jessica Silver-Greenberg and Robert Gebeloff, "Arbitration Everywhere, Stacking the Deck of Justice," *New York Times*, October 31, 2015, https://www.nytimes.com/2015/11/01/business/dealbook/arbitration -everywhere-stacking-the-deck-of-justice.html?_r=0.

213 *these clauses unenforceable:* The Fair Arbitration Act of 2011, for example, was introduced in the House and Senate but was never allowed to come up for a vote: https://www.congress.gov/bill/112th-congress /house-bill/1873. See also Amanlia D. Kessler, "Stuck in Arbitration," *New York Times*, March 6, 2012, http://www.nytimes.com/2012/03/07 /opinion/stuck-in-arbitration.html.

213 *Wells Fargo had exactly:* Initial complaint: https://assets.document cloud.org/documents/3114173/Wells-Amended-Cmplt.pdf. Motion to compel arbitration by Munger, Tolles & Olson: https://assets.docu mentcloud.org/documents/3114171/Wf-Motion-to-Compel.pdf.

215 *Federal Arbitration Act:* The statute, passed on February 12, 1925, can be found here: http://www.legisworks.org/congress/68/publaw-401 .pdf. The act is also discussed in the CFPB rule: https://www.consumer finance.gov/policy-compliance/rulemaking/final-rules/arbitration -agreements/.

216 *persuaded the Supreme Court: AT&T Mobility LLC v. Concepcion, Oyez*, April 27, 2011, https://www.oyez.org/cases/2010/09-893.

216 *the Supreme Court all but wiped out: American Express Co., et al. v. Italian Colors Restaurant, Oyez*, June 20, 2013, https://www.oyez.org /cases/2012/12-133.

216 *Chief Justice John Roberts:* Silver-Greenberg and Gebeloff, "Arbitration Everywhere, Stacking the Deck of Justice."

216 *Gretchen Carlson sued:* Noam Scheiber and Jessica Silver-Greenberg, "Gretchen Carlson's Fox News Contract Could Shroud Her Case in Secrecy," *New York Times*, July 13, 2016, https://www.nytimes .com/2016/07/14/business/media/gretchen-carlsons-contract-could -shroud-her-case-in-secrecy.html.

217 *Even American servicemen:* Christine Hines authored this report, titled "Armed Forces and Forced Arbitration," for Ralph Nader's group, Public Citizen: https://www.citizen.org/sites/default/files/armed-forces

-and-forced-arbitration-report.pdf. The Servicemembers Civil Relief Act passed in 2003: https://www.fdic.gov/regulations/compliance /manual/5/v-11.1.pdf. The Military Lending Act passed in 2006: https://www.fdic.gov/regulations/compliance/manual/5/v-13.1.pdf.

217 *a judge ruled:* The decision in *Beard v. Santander Consumer USA, Inc.* can be found here: https://www.gpo.gov/fdsys/pkg/USCOURTS-caed-1 _11-cv-01815/pdf/USCOURTS-caed-1_11-cv-01815-4.pdf. See also Christine Hines's report, "Armed Forces and Forced Arbitration."

217 *Nursing home patients:* The American Health Care Association, a trade association representing assisted living and other facilities for the elderly across the U.S., successfully sued the federal government in October 2016, before the new rule went into effect: https://www .documentcloud.org/documents/3144589-CMS-Arbitration-Rule -Complaint-10-16-16.html.

218 *Consumer Financial Protection Bureau:* https://www.consumerfinance .gov/policy-compliance/rulemaking/final-rules/arbitration-agree ments/.

218 *exposed the personal:* The company's press release about the findings of a forensic investigation into the breach can be found here: https:// investor.equifax.com/tools/viewpdf.aspx?page={CDB240BD-E470 -428F-A94C-49429222B5E3}. Former Equifax CEO Richard Smith testified before the Senate Banking Committee; his testimony can be found here: https://www.banking.senate.gov/public/index.cfm /hearings?ID=B61BB78D-CF34-4D54-B7F2-F7F982D77D6F.

218 *slipped an arbitration clause:* New York State attorney general Eric Schneiderman issued a statement a day after the breach was announced highlighting that the arbitration clause had been eliminated: https:// ag.ny.gov/press-release/ag-schneiderman-statement-equifax -arbitration-clause. Three days later, *USA Today* reported that at least twenty-three class action lawsuits had been filed: https://www.usatoday .com/story/money/2017/09/11/equifax-hit-least-23-class-action -lawsuits-over-massive-cyberbreach/653909001/.

219 *$264.4 million in fines:* These figures were calculated by reviewing reports on settlements by JPMorgan Chase from the Justice Department, the SEC, and other civil enforcement agencies. The estimates do not include class action settlements.

219 *the bank's Asia subsidiary:* See this Department of Justice press release and the attachments: https://www.justice.gov/opa/pr/jpmorgan -s-investment-bank-hong-kong-agrees-pay-72-million-penalty -corrupt-hiring-scheme.

221 *"concerned that the size":* The quoted comment begins at roughly the

2:19:00 mark: https://www.c-span.org/video/?311311-1/justice-depart
ment-oversight.

221 *"Too Big to Jail":* The Republican Staff of the Committee on Financial
Services, U.S. House of Representatives, "Too Big to Jail," July 11,
2016, https://financialservices.house.gov/uploadedfiles/07072016_oi
_tbtj_sr.pdf.

221 *"four years after":* See the senator's December 13, 2012, press release:
https://www.merkley.senate.gov/news/press-releases/merkley-blasts
-too-big-to-jail-policy-for-lawbreaking-banks.

222 *Justice Department press release:* https://www.justice.gov/opa/pr/hsbc
-holdings-plc-and-hsbc-bank-usa-na-admit-anti-money-laundering
-and-sanctions-violations. See also coverage from *The New York Times*
on the bank's profits, of which the $1.9 billion fine amounted to 14 per-
cent: https://dealbook.nytimes.com/2013/03/04/hsbc-annual-profit
-falls-on-money-laundering-charges/.

222 *as the Supreme Court put it:* Trustees of Dartmouth College v. Woodward,
Oyez, February 25, 1819, https://www.oyez.org/cases/1789-1850/17
us518.

222 *In the 1909 case:* Daniel R. Fischel and Alan O. Sykes, "Corporate
Crime," *The Journal of Legal Studies* 25, no. 2 (June 1996), https://
www.jstor.org/stable/724509. The case was *New York Central and
Hudson River Railroad Company v. United States,* which can be found
here: https://supreme.justia.com/cases/federal/us/212/481/.

223 *the prosecution of Ford:* Paul J. Becker, Arthur J. Jipson, and Alan S.
Bruch, *"State of Indiana v. Ford Motor Company Revisited,"* Ameri-
can Journal of Criminal Justice 26, no. 22 (March 2002), https://link
.springer.com/article/10.1007%2FBF02887826.

224 The Wall Street Journal *tallied:* Jean Eaglesham and Anupreeta Das,
"Wall Street Crime: 7 Years, 156 Cases and Few Convictions," *Wall
Street Journal,* May 27, 2016, https://www.wsj.com/articles/wall-street
-crime-7-years-156-cases-and-few-convictions-1464217378.

224 *paying $110 billion in fines:* Christina Rexrode and Emily Glazer, "Big
Banks Paid $110 Billion in Mortgage-Related Fines. Where Did the
Money Go?" *Wall Street Journal,* March 9, 2016, https://www.wsj
.com/articles/big-banks-paid-110-billionin-mortgage-related-fines
-where-did-the-money-go-1457557442.

224 *the federal commission investigating:* These are discussed at length
in a September 15, 2016, letter from Senator Elizabeth Warren
to the Department of Justice: https://www.warren.senate.gov/files
/documents/2016-9-15_Referral_DOJ_IG_letter.pdf.

225 *"If they ever sent a referral":* Interview with Rubin.

226 *"In some instances"*: Delivered at New York University on September 17: https://www.justice.gov/opa/speech/attorney-general-holder -remarks-financial-fraud-prosecutions-nyu-school-law.

226 *Angelo Mozilo:* See quotes included in Chapter 3, which come from the SEC complaint cited below as well as the FCIC report: https://www .gpo.gov/fdsys/pkg/GPO-FCIC/pdf/GPO-FCIC.pdf.

227 *the SEC sued Mozilo:* https://www.sec.gov/litigation/complaints/2009 /comp21068.pdf.

227 *$16.6 billion civil settlement:* https://www.justice.gov/opa/pr/bank -america-pay-1665-billion-historic-justice-department-settlement -financial-fraud-leading.

227 *A high-ranking Justice Department lawyer:* Interview. (The attorney, who was then still working for the government, declined to be named.)

228 *The Drug Makers' Corporate Plea-Bargaining Moat:* Throughout this section, I rely on reporting (and in a few sentences some text) that I did for a September 2015 series titled "America's Most Admired Lawbreaker" published by *The Huffington Post*'s "Highline" section about the pharmaceutical company Johnson & Johnson. The series is 57,500 words and includes links to most of the primary documents referenced in this section. It can be read here: http://highline.huffingtonpost .com/miracleindustry/americas-most-admired-lawbreaker/chapter-1 .html.

228 *The FDA labeling regulations:* These were the Kefauver-Harris Amendments: https://www.fda.gov/ForConsumers/ConsumerUpdates/ucm 322856.htm. See also "America's Most Admired Lawbreaker," Chapter 2.

229 *off-label promotion:* See Brill, "America's Most Admired Lawbreaker," Chapter 3.

230 *pediatric psychiatrists:* Ibid., Chapters 3 and 4.

230 *In a deposition conducted:* Ibid., Chapter 10.

231 *Alex Gorsky:* Ibid., Chapter 15.

231 *legal fees and civil suit payouts:* Ibid. $800 million is based on my estimates of legal fees and settlements.

231 *$2.2 billion in fines:* See this Department of Justice press release: https://www.justice.gov/opa/pr/johnson-johnson-pay-more -22-billion-resolve-criminal-and-civil-investigations; and Attorney General Holder's comments: https://www.justice.gov/opa/speech /attorney-general-eric-holder-delivers-remarks-johnson-johnson -press-conference.

231 *Profit from Risperdal:* See Brill, "America's Most Admired Lawbreaker," Chapter 15.

234 *Zane Memeger:* Ibid., Chapter 10; as well as his bio on his law firm's website: https://www.morganlewis.com/bios/zanememeger.

235 *the Supreme Court handed down: Sorrell v. IMS Health Inc.,* Oyez, June 23, 2011: https://www.oyez.org/cases/2010/10-779.

236 *tour guides be licensed: Edwards v. District of Columbia:* https://www.cadc.uscourts.gov/internet/opinions.nsf/E585CD5E522FBE9585257D04004F7891/$file/13-7063-1499657.pdf.

236 *dangers of tobacco: R.J. Reynolds Tobacco Company v. FDA:* https://www.cadc.uscourts.gov/internet/opinions.nsf/4C0311C78EB11C5785257A64004EBFB5/$file/11-5332-1391191.pdf.

236 *country-of-origin information: American Meat Institute v. USDA,* https://www.cadc.uscourts.gov/internet/opinions.nsf/A064A3175BC6DEEE85257D24004FA93B/$file/13-5281-1504951.pdf.

236 *overturned a local ordinance: Reed et al. v. Town of Gilbert, Arizona et al.,* Oyez, https://www.oyez.org/cases/2014/13-502.

237 *"robo" telemarketing calls:* Adam Liptak, "Court's Free-Speech Expansion Has Far-Reaching Consequences," *New York Times,* August 17, 2015, https://www.nytimes.com/2015/08/18/us/politics/courts-free-speech-expansion-has-far-reaching-consequences.html.

237 *"breakthroughs for freedom":* Interviews with Redish.

238 *the thirteenth most cited:* This was determined using the database HeinOnline at http://www.heinonline.org/.

238 *that scientific claims:* Martin Redish and Kyle Voils, "False Commercial Speech and the First Amendment: Understanding the Implications of the Equivalency Principle," *William & Mary Bill of Rights Journal* 25, no. 3 (2017), http://scholarship.law.wm.edu/cgi/viewcontent.cgi?article=1808&context=wmborj.

238 *a 1997 suit:* See Brill, "America's Most Admired Lawbreaker," Chapter 2.

239 *selling drugs off-label: U.S. v. Caronia:* http://www.hpm.com/pdf/blog/Caronia%202d%20Circuit%20Slip%20Opinion.pdf. See also Brill, "America's Most Admired Lawbreaker," Chapter 11.

239 *cholesterol drug to doctors: Amarin Pharma, Inc. v. FDA:* http://www.nysd.uscourts.gov/cases/show.php?db=special&id=478. See also Brill, "America's Most Admired Lawbreaker," Chapter 11.

240 *S&P paying more:* See this Department of Justice press release: https://www.justice.gov/opa/pr/justice-department-and-state-partners-secure-1375-billion-settlement-sp-defrauding-investors. See also coverage from *The New York Times* on Floyd Abrams's involvement in the case: http://www.nytimes.com/2009/07/19/business/19floyd.html.

240 *a two-day hearing:* Quotes are taken from the transcript of the first day of the hearing: https://www.fda.gov/NewsEvents/Meetings ConferencesWorkshops/ucm489499.htm.

241 *an American Enterprise white paper:* "The US Department of Justice's Targeting of Medical Speech and Its Public Health Impacts," American Enterprise Institute, December 2012, https://www.aei .org/publication/the-us-department-of-justices-targeting-of -medical-speech-and-its-public-health-impacts/.

241 *Coleen Klasmeier:* "Off-Label Prescription Advertising, the FDA and the First Amendment: A Study in the Values of Commercial Speech Protection," *American Journal of Law and Medicine* 37, nos. 2 and 3 (2011), https://papers.ssrn.com/sol3/papers.cfm?abstract_id =1793338.

242 *Joshua Sharfstein, a former FDA:* See the transcript from the second day of the FDA hearings: https://www.fda.gov/NewsEvents/Meetings ConferencesWorkshops/ucm489499.htm#transcripts.

242 *In a 2016 law review article:* "The New Lochner," *Wisconsin Law Review* January 2016, http://wisconsinlawreview.org/wp-content /uploads/2016/04/3-Shanor-Final.pdf.

243 *"This probably drives":* Interviews with Shanor.

244 *"I'm not a sound-bite kind of person":* Interviews with Post.

246 *"because too many brilliant people":* Interviews with Kelleher. Also, see Kelleher biography on the Better Markets' website: https://better markets.com/dennis-kelleher.

247 *$5.1 billion:* From an April 2016 press release: https://www.justice .gov/opa/pr/goldman-sachs-agrees-pay-more-5-billion-connection -its-sale-residential-mortgage-backed.

247 *"grossly inflated":* Nathaniel Popper, "In Settlement's Fine Print, Goldman May Save $1 Billion," *New York Times*, April 11, 2016, https:// www.nytimes.com/2016/04/12/business/dealbook/goldman-sachs -to-pay-5-1-billion-in-mortgage-settlement.html?ref=topics.

247 *Glass-Steagall allowed the banks:* Better Markets released this purported fact sheet in May 2017: https://bettermarkets.com/newsroom /fact-sheet-repealing-glass-steagall-contributed-2008-financial-crash -properly-reinstating-0.

248 *reverse a rule promulgated:* From a February 3, 2017, White House memo: https://www.whitehouse.gov/the-press-office/2017/02/03 /presidential-memorandum-fiduciary-duty-rule.

249 *eighteen-month delay:* The Department of Labor announced the delay of the Fiduciary Rule in August 2017: https://www.dol.gov/newsroom /releases/ebsa/ebsa20170831.

249 *Consumer Financial Protection Bureau:* The Democratic Staff on the House Committee on Financial Services released a July 2017 report on the CFPB, located here: https://democrats-financialservices.house .gov/news/documentsingle.aspx?DocumentID=400699.

250 *Rakoff made no such assumption:* https://www.leagle.com/decision /infdco20120717672.

251 *Second Circuit Court of Appeals:* On June 14, 2014, the court reversed Rakoff and approved the settlement: https://www.leagle.com/decision /infco20140604070.

251 *"It's so much easier":* and subsequent quotes from interviews with Rakoff.

251 *"egregious cases":* James B. Stewart, "S.E.C. Has a Message for Firms Not Used to Admitting Guilt," *New York Times,* June 21, 2013, http:// www.nytimes.com/2013/06/22/business/secs-new-chief-promises -tougher-line-on-cases.html.

252 *"offered one or another":* "The Financial Crisis: Why Have No High Level Executives Been Prosecuted?" *New York Review of Books,* January 9, 2014, http://www.nybooks.com/articles/2014/01/09/financial -crisis-why-no-executive-prosecutions/.

254 *McKesson Corporation:* Gretchen Morgenson, "Hard Questions for a Company at the Center of the Opioid Crisis," *New York Times,* July 21, 2017, https://www.nytimes.com/2017/07/21/business/mckesson-opi oid-packaging.html; "Consumers, but Not Executives, May Pay for Equifax Failings," *The New York Times,* September 13, 2017, https:// www.nytimes.com/2017/09/13/business/equifax-executive-pay.html.

256 *The job of enforcing:* Trump nominated David Zatezalo to be the assistant secretary of labor for mine safety and health on September 2, 2017: https://www.whitehouse.gov/the-press-office/2017/09/02/presi dent-donald-j-trump-announces-intent-nominate-personnel-key. *ProPublica* subsequently reported that his West Virginia mining company had been cited for illegal employment practices, including unsafe conditions: https://www.propublica.org/article/trumps-mine-safety -nominee-ran-coal-firm-cited-for-illegal-employment-practices.

9   WHY NOTHING WORKS

257 *jury duty reforms:* The occupation exemption is described on the third page of this New York Courts information sheet: https://www .nycourts.gov/admin/stateofjudiciary/stofjud9/2%20Jury%20reform .pdf.

258 *"The difference between us":* Interviews with Bradley.

259 *veterans were waiting months:* CNN's stories about the VA: http://www
.cnn.com/specials/us/va-hospitals.

259 *1998 GAO report:* "Veterans Health Administration: Performance and
Conduct Issues Involving Senior Managers at VA Medical Centers,"
April 30, 1998, http://www.gao.gov/assets/230/225604.pdf.

259 *by 2016 the GAO reported:* "Federal Workforce: Distribution of Performance Ratings Across the Federal Government, 2013," May 9,
2016, http://www.gao.gov/assets/680/676998.pdf?wpmm=1.

259 *every manager involved:* In September 2015, McKinsey & Co. published a lengthy report on the Department of U.S. Veterans Affairs,
which had been prepared at the request of the department itself.
Appendix L addresses leadership: https://www.va.gov/opa/choiceact
/documents/assessments/integrated_report.pdf.

259 *A 2010 report:* "Information Technology: Management Improvements
Are Essential to VA's Second Effort to Replace Its Outpatient Scheduling System," May 27, 2010, http://www.gao.gov/assets/310/305030
.pdf.

261 *performance bonuses:* Two years in a row, *USA Today* published reports
detailing these financial awards. First, in 2015: https://www.usa
today.com/story/news/politics/2015/11/11/veterans-affairs-pays
-142-million-bonuses-amid-scandals/75537586/; and again in 2016:
https://www.usatoday.com/story/news/politics/2016/10/28/more
-bonuses-va-employees-despite-ongoing-problems-agency/9283
7218/.

261 *government workers with a civil service:* Testimony of James Sherk of the
Heritage Foundation on July 30, 2014, before the House Committee
on Oversight and Government Reform: https://oversight.house.gov
/wp-content/uploads/2014/07/Sherk-Statement-IRS-Abuses-7-30
.pdf.

261 *President Carter in 1978:* The Civil Service Reform Act of 1978:
https://www.congress.gov/bill/95th-congress/senate-bill/2640.

262 *"The New Property":* Charles A. Reich, "The New Property," *The
Yale Law Journal* 73, no. 5 (April 1964), https://www.jstor.org/stable
/794645?seq=1#page_scan_tab_contents.

262 *overturned by the Supreme Court: Cleveland Board of Education v. Louder-
mill,* March 19, 1985, https://www.oyez.org/cases/1984/83-1362.

262 *Sharon Helman: Sharon Helman v. Department of Veterans Affairs,* http://
www.naus.org/wp-content/uploads/2016/07/Helman-motion.pdf.

262 *who was paid $169,000:* Craig Harris and Rob O'Dell, "Phoenix
VA Gave Out $10 Mil in Bonuses in Past 3 Years," *Arizona Repub-*

lic, June 16, 2014, http://www.azcentral.com/story/news/arizona
/investigations/2014/06/17/phoenix-va-gave-mil-bonuses-last-years
/10653263/.

263 *post office in Oklahoma : Eric S. Powell v. U.S. Postal Service,* https://www
.mspb.gov/netsearch/viewdocs.aspx?docnumber=1119146&version
=1123609&application=ACROBAT.

263 *General Services Administration: Prouty & Weller v. General Services
Administration,* https://www.mspb.gov/netsearch/viewdocs.aspx?doc
number=1120910&version=1125376&application=ACROBAT.

264 *Tully Rinckey:* The firm's website is located at: http://www.tullylegal
.com/.

264 *"We're the largest":* Interview with Cannon.

264 *fire a federal employees:* This is based on reporting I did for the book
Class Warfare, published by Simon & Schuster in 2011, and for "The
Rubber Room" (see reference below). I looked at data about the dismissal of tenured government employees for conduct or performance-
related issues in New York, California, and Illinois, as well as a white
paper by James Sherk: "IRS Abuses: Ensuring That Targeting Never
Happens Again," The Heritage Foundation, July 30, 2014, https://
oversight.house.gov/wp-content/uploads/2014/07/Sherk-Statement
-IRS-Abuses-7-30.pdf. However, other than the percentage of federal
employees removed for misconduct or poor performance, this is an
estimate because precise numbers for all state and local governments
are not available.

265 *signed a law supported by overwhelming:* The Department of Veterans
Affairs Accountability and Whistleblower Protection Act of 2017
was signed on June 23, 2017: https://www.congress.gov/bill/115th
-congress/senate-bill/1094.

265 *discovered the Rubber Room:* Steven Brill, "The Rubber Room," *The
New Yorker,* August 31, 2009, https://www.newyorker.com/magazine
/2009/08/31/the-rubber-room.

266 *Albert Shanker:* His biography can be found on the website of the
United Federation of Teachers: http://www.uft.org/who-we-are
/history/albert-shanker.

266 *the United States spends more:* Data from the Organization for Economic Cooperation and Development shows that Luxembourg
is the only country that spends more per student on education
than the U.S.: https://data.oecd.org/eduresource/education-spending
.htm#indicator-chart.

266 *student achievement scores:* Pew Research Center data shows that U.S.
performance in science, mathematics, and reading is well below that

of many other developed countries: http://www.pewresearch.org/fact-tank/2017/02/15/u-s-students-internationally-math-science/.

267 *The reformers:* Steven Brill, *Class Warfare: Inside the Fight to Fix America's Schools* (New York: Simon & Schuster, 2011).

267 *"Common Core":* See the Common Core website: http://www.core standards.org/about-the-standards/development-process/.

268 *Jeb Bush:* Caitlin Emma, "On Common Core, Jeb Bush Is a Party of One," *Politico,* May 28, 2015, http://www.politico.com/story/2015/05/chris-christie-denounces-common-core-testing-2016-election-118383.

268 *Rex Tillerson:* Alan Murray, "Exxon's Common Core Crack-Up," *Fortune,* December 23, 2015, http://fortune.com/2015/12/23/exxon-common-core/.

268 *public employee unions:* Adam Mertz, "A Century of Teacher Organizing," *The Labor and Working Class History Association,* https://www.lawcha.org/century-teaching-organizing/. See also information from the Bureau of Labor Statistics on Union Membership: https://www.bls.gov/news.release/union2.t03.htm.

270 *"The federal government is losing":* Paul C. Light, "The New Public Service," Brookings Institution, January 1, 2000, https://www.brookings.edu/articles/the-new-public-service/.

271 *national workforce was thirty-four:* Juliet Eilperin, "Trump Freezes Hiring of Many Federal Workers," *Washington Post,* January 23, 2017, https://www.washingtonpost.com/powerpost/trump-freezes-hiring-of-federal-workers/2017/01/23/f14d8180-e190-11e6-ba11-63c4b4fb5a63_story.html?utm_term=.116fddfeae6a.

271 *fifteen pay categories:* The General Schedule Classification and Pay is available on the Office of Personnel Management website: https://www.opm.gov/policy-data-oversight/pay-leave/pay-systems/general-schedule/.

271 *starting tech workers:* Interview with Max Stier.

271 *often impractical preference:* See the Veterans Services page on the Office of Personnel Management: https://www.opm.gov/policy-data-oversight/veterans-services/vet-guide-for-hr-professionals/.

271 *an average of ninety days:* Joe Davidson, "Federal Hiring Remains a Work in Progress After Many Fixes," *Washington Post,* October 4, 2016, https://www.washingtonpost.com/news/powerpost/wp/2016/10/04/federal-hiring-remains-a-work-in-progress-after-many-fixes/?utm_term=.a1f2a3047831&wpisrc=nl_politics.

272 *caregiver hiring spree:* Dave Philipps, "Did Obama's Bill Fix Veterans' Health Care? Still Waiting," *New York Times,* August 5, 2016, https://www

.nytimes.com/2016/08/06/us/veterans-health-care.html?rref=collec
tion%2Fsectioncollection%2Fus&_r=0.

272 *Salt Lake City center:* From an interview with Max Stier.

272 *"lacks any system at all":* Paul Light, "The New Public Service," Brookings Institution, January 1, 2000, https://www.brookings.edu/articles
/the-new-public-service/.

273 *Government Accountability Office:* Numbers were provided by a GAO
spokesperson via email.

273 *Lockheed Martin's F-35:* "F-35 Joint Strike Fighter: DOD Needs to
Complete Developmental Testing Before Making Significant New
Investments," Government Accountability Office, April 2017. See also
Steven Brill, "Donald Trump, Palantir, and the Crazy Battle to Clean
Up a Multibillion-Dollar Military Procurement Swamp," *Fortune*,
March 30, 2017, http://fortune.com/palantir-pentagon-trump/. Also:
https://armedservices.house.gov/legislation/hearings/update-f-35
-joint-strike-fighter-jsf-program-and-fiscal-year-2017-budget-0.

273 *"Get a 'Go' decision":* Interview with Mike Sullivan, director of Acquisition and Sourcing Management team.

273 *"I said, 'Who is running this' ":* Interview with Kendall.

274 *"We got thousands of pages":* Interview with Gates.

274 *A GAO report in 2010:* "Defense Acquisitions: Strong Leadership Is
Key to Planning and Executing Stable Weapon Programs," Government Accountability Office, May 2010, http://www.gao.gov/assets
/310/304106.pdf.

274 *The stocks of the contractors:* "Defense Acquisitions: Assessments of
Selected Military Programs," Government Accountability Office,
March 2016, http://www.gao.gov/assets/680/676281.pdf.

274 *757 lobbyists:* See data from the Center for Responsive Politics: https://
www.opensecrets.org/lobby/indus.php?id=D&year=2016.

275 *no discernable improvement:* Steven Brill, "Is America Any Safer?,"
The Atlantic, September 2016, https://www.theatlantic.com/magazine
/archive/2016/09/are-we-any-safer/492761/.

275 *The Pentagon spent:* This figure represents spending on outside goods
and services rather than overall Pentagon spending. See also this
December 2016 Congressional Research Service report on Department of Defense contracts: https://fas.org/sgp/crs/natsec/R44010
.pdf.

275 *D-FARS is a tribute:* Brill, "Donald Trump, Palantir, and the Crazy
Battle to Clean Up a Multibillion-Dollar Military Procurement
Swamp."

275 *A study by a Defense Department:* "Transforming DoD's Core Business

Processes for Revolutionary Change," January 2015, http://www.dtic.
mil/dtic/tr/fulltext/u2/a618526.pdf.

276 *Defense Acquisition University:* See the university's website: https://
www.dau.mil/. See also Brill, "Donald Trump, Palantir, and the Crazy
Battle to Clean Up a Multibillion-Dollar Military Procurement
Swamp."

277 *formal protests of bid awards:* Annual reports of bid protests are available
on the GAO website: https://www.gao.gov/legal/bid-protest-annual
-reports/about.

278 *the system was down:* See Brill, *Bitter Pill*, Chapter 20.

279 *Mikey Dickerson:* Interviews. See also the website for the U.S. Digital
Service, which details the projects mentioned: https://www.usds.gov/;
as well as Brill, *Bitter Pill*, Chapter 22.

280 *doubled down on a number of initiatives:* See this February 2016
White House press release: https://obamawhitehouse.archives.gov
/blog/2016/02/24/major-step-forward-category-management-
announcing-new-government-wide-category. See also the Office of
Management and Budget's exit memo from January 2017: https://
obamawhitehouse.archives.gov/sites/default/files/omb/reports
/cabinet_exit_memorandum.pdf.

282 *The Peace Corps:* According to the Peace Corps website, there were
7,213 volunteers and trainees in 2017: https://www.peacecorps.gov
/news/fast-facts/.

282 *Partnership for Public Service:* See the organization's 2016 annual
report: https://ourpublicservice.org/about-us/annual-report.php.

282 *"Policy fights and policymaking"* and subsequent quotes: Interviews with
Stier.

283 *"I used it as a key management benchmark":* Interview with Johnson.

283 *DHS had long languished:* See the Partnership for Public Service's
agency rankings website: http://bestplacestowork.org/BPTW/rank
ings/detail/HS00.

283 *"I was having trouble dealing":* Interview and email exchanges with
Kappos.

284 *Patent and Trademark Office:* See the office's 2013 annual report: https://
www.uspto.gov/sites/default/files/documents/USPTOFY2013PAR
.pdf.

284 *The agency's backlog:* The actual numbers are 34.6 months in 2009 and
29.1 months in 2013. See the U.S. Patent and Trademark Office's annual
reports for 2009 and 2013 respectively: https://www.uspto.gov/about
-us/performance-and-planning/uspto-annual-reports.

285 *Harvard Business School case study:* Dennis Yao and Hillary Greene,

"Rebooting the U.S. Patent and Trademark Office," *Harvard Business School,* March 26, 2017.

285 *"Sammy Awards":* Descriptions of the winners and finalists for the awards can be found here: https://servicetoamericamedals.org/.

286 *the appointment of an internship coordinator:* This was included in Section 1109 of the 2016 Defense spending bill: https://www.congress .gov/bill/114th-congress/senate-bill/1356.

286 *share their best job candidates:* The Competitive Service Act of 2015: https://www.congress.gov/bill/114th-congress/senate-bill/1580.

286 *"80 percent":* Interview with Stier. Also: Chapter 16 of the Analytical Perspectives Volume of the FY 2018 budget details these figures: https://www.whitehouse.gov/sites/whitehouse.gov/files/omb/budget /fy2018/ap_16_it.pdf.

286 *The most substantial proposal:* The Pre-Election Presidential Transition Act of 2010: https://www.congress.gov/bill/111th-congress/senate -bill/3196.

287 *fired the transition team:* In a joint project with *The Washington Post,* the Partnership for Public Service published a Political Appointee Tracker here: https://ourpublicservice.org/issues/presidential -transition/political-appointee-tracker.php. See also a press release covering the first one hundred days of the Trump administration: https://ourpublicservice.org/publications/viewcontentdetails.php ?id=1766.

287 *"I don't want to abolish":* Mara Liasson, "Conservative Advocate," *Morning Edition,* National Public Radio, May 25, 2001, http://www .npr.org/templates/story/story.php?storyId=1123439.

288 *happened to Social Security:* Interviews and email correspondence with representatives for the Office of Management and Budget. See also Kathleen Romig, "Budget Cuts Squeeze Social Security Administration Even as Workloads Reach Record Highs," Center on Budget and Policy Priorities, June 3, 2016, https://www.cbpp.org /research/retirement-security/budget-cuts-squeeze-social-security -administration-even-as-workloads?wpmm=1. Also see a report by the Office of the Inspector General of the Social Security Administration on wait times: https://oig.ssa.gov/sites/default/files/audit/full /pdf/A-04-17-50216.pdf; and the Social Security Administration website on hearings and appeals: https://www.ssa.gov/appeals/index.html.

288 *1.1 million citizens seeking:* See Social Security Administration website on hearings and appeals: https://www.ssa.gov/appeals/index.html.

288 *buyout incentives aimed:* Eric Katz, "Social Security Offers Nearly Its Entire Workforce Early Retirement," *Government Executive,* August 4,

2017, http://www.govexec.com/pay-benefits/2017/08/social-security
-has-sent-early-out-offers-nearly-its-entire-workforce/140008/.

289 *The funding of the Internal Revenue Service:* Interviews and email correspondence with Office of Management and Budget employees. See also Chuck Marr and Cecile Murray, "IRS Funding Cuts Compromise Taxpayer Service and Weaken Enforcement," Center on Budget and Policy Priorities, April 4, 2016, https://www.cbpp.org/research/federal-tax/irs-funding-cuts-compromise-taxpayer-service-and-weaken-enforcement; as well as this IRS report: https://www.irs.gov/newsroom/the-tax-gap.

10 BROKEN

290 *On April 21, 2017:* The fact-checking website *Snopes* wrote about the outages to disprove rumors of a cyber-attack: https://www.snopes.com/power-outages-la-sf-nyc/. Also major wire services and television news organizations ran stories, such as this one: http://newyork.cbslocal.com/2017/04/21/nyc-sf-outages-infrastructure/.

291 *657 water main breaks:* This is calculated by looking at the 2017 Infrastructure Report Card, an infrastructure review published every four years by the American Society for Civil Engineers. According to the 2017 report, 240,000 water main breaks occur each year, an average of 657 per day: https://www.infrastructurereportcard.org/.

291 *over fifty years old:* This figure comes from a study on water mains in both the U.S. and Canada. However, it should be noted that based on other infrastructure reports, including one done by McKinsey, Canada's infrastructure is in better shape than the United States' infrastructure, making this probably an understatement with regard to U.S. water mains. Stephen Folkman, "Water Main Break Rates in the United States and Canada," Utah State University Buried Structures Laboratory, April 2012, http://www.watermainbreakclock.com/docs/UtahStateWaterBreakRates_FINAL_TH_Ver5lowrez.pdf.

291 *air traffic control system:* "Air Traffic Control Modernization Progress and Challenges in Implementing NextGen," Government Accountability Office, August 2017, http://www.gao.gov/assets/690/686881.pdf.

291 *$8 million a day:* This estimate comes from a 2016 American Automobile Association report: https://westerncentralny.aaa.com/news-room/releases/2016-03/pothole-damage-costs-us-drivers-3-billion-annually. Another organization, Pothole.info, estimates that the cost

is $17 million a day, but I could not find any information about the bona fides of Pothole.info or its sources.

291 *surface transportation system:* Based on the 2011 Surface Transportation report published by the American Society for Civil Engineers: http://www.asce.org/uploadedFiles/Issues_and_Advocacy/Our _Initiatives/Infrastructure/Content_Pieces/failure-to-act-trans portation-report.pdf.

291 *In 2016, FedEx:* The increase in tire usage was included in CEO Frederick Smith's February 2017 testimony to the House Committee on Transportation and Infrastructure, available here: https:// transportation.house.gov/calendar/eventsingle.aspx?EventID =401047.

292 *Thirty-nine percent:* See the American Society for Civil Engineers report on bridges, from the Infrastructure Report Card cited above: https://www.infrastructurereportcard.org/cat-item/bridges/.

292 *"Choke Point of a Nation":* Tyler J. Kelly, "Choke Point of a Nation: The High Cost of an Aging River Lock," *New York Times,* November 23, 2016, https://www.nytimes.com/2016/11/23/business/econ omy/desperately-plugging-holes-in-an-87-year-old-dam.html.

292 *Department of Education survey:* "Condition of America's Public School Facilities: 2012–13," National Center for Education Statistics, March 2014, https://nces.ed.gov/pubs2014/2014022.pdf.

292 *lead or other contaminants:* The best-known case occurred in Flint, Michigan. *The New York Times* published a story in early 2016 detailing other examples from across the nation. Michael Wines, Patrick McGeehan, and John Schwartz, "Schools Nationwide Still Grapple with Lead in Water," *New York Times,* March 6, 2016, https://www .nytimes.com/2016/03/27/us/schools-nationwide-still-grapple -with-lead-in-water.html?smprod=nytcore-ipad&smid=nytcore-ipad -share.

292 *an eight-lane bridge:* See the accident report published by the National Transportation Safety Board in 2008: https://www.ntsb.gov/investi gations/AccidentReports/Reports/HAR0803.pdf.

292 *great American infrastructure:* See Petroski, *The Road Taken.*

293 *Net federal spending:* David Wessel, "Spending on Our Crumbling Infrastructure," Brookings Institute, March 10, 2015, https://www .brookings.edu/opinions/spending-on-our-crumbling-infra structure/. See also the Bureau of Economic Analysis's U.S. National Income and Product Accounts tables, which Wessel used to make his calculations: https://www.bea.gov/iTable/index_nipa.cfm.

293 *home to 70 million more:* See the Census Bureau's 2014 report on

population projections: https://www.census.gov/content/dam/Census /library/publications/2015/demo/p25-1143.pdf.

294 *It ranked fifteenth:* Based on the World Economic Forum's Global Competitiveness Report: https://www.weforum.org/reports /the-global-competitiveness-report-2017-2018. See also McKinsey's "Building Global Infrastructure Gaps" report: https://www.mckinsey .com/industries/capital-projects-and-infrastructure/our-insights /Bridging-global-infrastructure-gaps.

295 *"a state of emergency":* New York governor Andrew Cuomo signed an executive order, available here: https://www.governor.ny.gov/news /video-photos-rush-transcript-governor-cuomo-announces-1-billion -new-mta-funding-and-declares.

295 *"In the fifties and sixties":* Interview with Klein.

295 *higher marginal tax rates:* Available from the IRS here: https://www.irs .gov/statistics/soi-tax-stats-historical-table-23.

296 *The claims by proponents:* This 2017 *Washington Post* column by an architect of President Reagan's tax cuts sums up data and studies reporting no evidence of a relationship between raising or cutting tax rates and stimulating the economy: https://www.washingtonpost .com/news/posteverything/wp/2017/09/28/i-helped-create-the-gop -tax-myth-trump-is-wrong-tax-cuts-dont-equal-growth/?utm_term =.abd2b9c052bb.

296 America in Ruins: Pat Choate and Susan Walter, *America in Ruins* (Washington, D.C.: Council of State Planning Agencies, 1981).

296 *But at least he raised:* See Petroski, *The Road Taken.*

297 *a drop from 2000 to 2013:* The inflation-adjusted figures in the text are estimates based on the graph at the end of Nathaniel Popper and Guilbert Gates, "Rebuilding Our Infrastructure," *New York Times,* November 14, 2016, .https://www.nytimes.com/interactive/2016/11/15 /business/dealbook/dealbook-infrastructure.html. For nonadjusted revenue figures, see the data from the Federal Highway Administration: https://www.fhwa.dot.gov/policyinformation/statistics/2015/fe210 .cfm.

297 *Even adding the average:* According to data compiled by the U.S. Energy Information Administration, as of July 2017: https://www.eia .gov/tools/faqs/faq.php?id=10&t=10.

297 *pay three to ten times:* See data from the OECD: http://www.keepeek .com/Digital-Asset-Management/oecd/taxation/consumption-tax -trends-2016_ctt-2016-en#page149.

297 *$787 billion stimulus plan:* See the Department of Transportation's official report on the effects of the stimulus package on infrastructure:

https://cms.dot.gov/sites/dot.gov/files/docs/American%20Recovery%20and%20Reinvestment%20Act%20Final%20Report.pdf. See also an archived version of recovery.gov, which was the U.S. government's website that provided access to data related to Recovery Act spending: https://web.archive.org/web/20110919101840/http://www.recovery.gov/About/Pages/The_Act.aspx.

297 *"infrastructure bank":* Brad Plummer, "How Obama's Plan for Infrastructure Bank Would Work," *Washington Post,* September 19, 2011, https://www.washingtonpost.com/business/economy/how-obamas-plan-for-infrastructure-bank-would-work/2011/09/19/gIQAfDgUgK_story.html?utm_term=.322397877d54.

298 *heyday of the infrastructure boom:* In the 1971 Annual Report, the "Future Plans" section included "a new trans-Hudson rail tunnel leading to a new passenger terminal in mid-Manhattan": http://corpinfo.panynj.gov/files/uploads/documents/financial-information/annual-reports/annual-report-1971.pdf.

299 *"just under 30 billion":* Paul Berger, "Rising Gateway Tunnel Price Tag Could Cost Port Authority $800 Million," *Wall Street Journal,* September 27, 2017, https://www.wsj.com/articles/rising-gateway-tunnel-price-tag-could-cost-port-authority-800-million-1506510001.

299 *Christie had a point:* Patrick McGeehan, "Christie Halts Train Tunnel, Citing Its Cost," *New York Times,* October 7, 2010, http://www.nytimes.com/2010/10/08/nyregion/08tunnel.html?_r=0.

299 *hurdles created when all those agencies:* See the Hudson Tunnel Project Scoping Document from April 2016: http://www.njtransit.com/AdminTemp/weblibrary_esi_scoping.pdf.

299 *The Bayonne Bridge:* See the Port Authority website's information about the bridge: https://www.panynj.gov/bridges-tunnels/bayonne-bridge-history.html. See also Sam Roberts, "High Above the Water, but Awash in Red Tape," *New York Times,* January 2, 2014, https://www.nytimes.com/2014/01/03/nyregion/long-review-of-bayonne-bridge-project-is-assailed.html.

299 *second busiest freight port:* See the Department of Transportation's 2016 report to Congress on freight statistics: https://www.rita.dot.gov/bts/sites/rita.dot.gov.bts/files/PPFS_Annual_Report.pdf.

300 *Coast Guard's shortcut assessment:* Text: https://www.regulations.gov/docket?D=USCG-2012-1091.

300 *challenged in federal court:* The complaint is available here: https://www.nrdc.org/sites/default/files/air_13073101a.pdf. The court opinion is here: https://cases.justia.com/federal/district-courts/new-york/nysdce/1:2013cv05347/415617/135/0.pdf?ts=1448468993.

301 *As of 2017:* The bridge was raised and successfully opened to larger container ships by September 2017, although additional work on the bridge structure will continue until mid-2019. The most recent estimate put the project's cost at $1.6 billion. See Paul Berger, "Smooth Sailing as Port Opens to Larger Ships," *Wall Street Journal*, September 7, 2017, https://www.wsj.com/articles/large-container-ship-theodore-roosevelt-passes-under-bayonne-bridge-1504791695.

301 *lowest-rated major airports:* Skytrax, an aviation industry group, publishes airport rankings each year: http://www.worldairportawards.com/awards/world_airport_rating.html.

301 *New York's tabloids:* For instance, see Carl Campanile and Danielle Furfaro, "Port Authority Salaries Are So Out of Hand That the Average Worker Makes $100K," *New York Post*, March 22, 2016, http://nypost.com/2016/03/22/port-authority-salaries-are-so-out-of-hand-that-the-average-worker-makes-100k/. See also David W. Dunlap, "How a Commuter Rail Station Became a $4 Billion Colossus," *New York Times*, February 24, 2016, https://www.nytimes.com/interactive/2016/02/25/nyregion/world-trade-center-transportation-hub-history.html?rref=collection/sectioncollection/nyregion.

301 *second Hudson River train tunnel:* The agency that was created is called the Gateway Development Corporation, and the process to fast-track the approval of the tunnel is described in Hillary Russ, "Hudson Train Tunnel Between NY, NJ Gets Fast Environmental Review," Reuters, October 14, 2016.

302 *But if rebuilding:* Called the I-35 West Saint Anthony Falls Bridge, it was opened on December 24, 2008: http://www.dot.state.mn.us/i35wbridge/overview.html.

302 The Power Broker: Robert Caro, *The Power Broker* (New York: Alfred A. Knopf, 1974).

302 *1971 Supreme Court ruling: Citizens to Preserve Overton Park v. Volpe*, March 2, 1971, https://www.oyez.org/cases/1970/1066.

302 *Anderson Bridge:* Lawrence Summers and Rachel Lipson, "A Lesson on Infrastructure from the Anderson Bridge Fiasco," *Boston Globe*, May 25, 2016, https://www.bostonglobe.com/opinion/2016/05/25/lesson-infrastructure-from-anderson-bridge-fiasco/uKS6xQZxFBFofZd2EuTo6K/story.html.

304 *"I just kept thinking about":* Interviews with Howard.

305 The Death of Common Sense: Philip K. Howard, *The Death of Common Sense: How Law Is Suffocating America* (New York: Random House, 1995).

306 *"no specific program":* Christopher Lehmann-Haupt, "A Call to Dereg-

ulate Rules and Regulations," *New York Times*, January 19, 1995, http://
www.nytimes.com/1995/01/19/books/books-of-the-times-a-call-to
-deregulate-rules-and-regulations.html.

306 *A follow-on book:* Philip K. Howard, *The Lost Art of Drawing the Line:
How Fairness Went Too Far* (New York: Random House, 2001).

306 *"has a weakness for":* Jedediah Purdy, "So Sue Me," *New York Times*,
April 22, 2001, http://www.nytimes.com/books/01/04/22/reviews
/010422.22purdyt.html.

306 *Common Good:* Interviews with Howard. See also the organization's
website: https://www.commongood.org/.

306 *decentralized hiring system:* Common Good website: https://www
.commongood.org; and see, for example, Jonathan Walters, "Life
After Civil Service Reform: The Texas, Georgia, and Florida Experiences," *Governing* magazine, October 2002, https://sites.duke.edu
/niou/files/2011/05/Walters-Life-after-Civil-Service-Reform-The
-Texas-George-and-Florida-Experiences.pdf.

306 *In 2014, he published:* Philip K. Howard, *The Rule of Nobody: Saving
America from Dead Laws and Broken Government* (New York: W. W.
Norton, 2014).

307 *Fixing America's Surface Transportation:* See https://www.gpo.gov/fdsys
/pkg/PLAW-114publ94/pdf/PLAW-114publ94.pdf. This require-
ment can be found at p. 1745.

307 *The Common Good white paper:* "Two Years, Not Ten Years" : http://
commongood.3cdn.net/c613b4cfda258a5fcb_e8m6b5t3x.pdf.

308 *Another Common Good white paper:* "Billions for Red Tape" : http://
commongood.3cdn.net/e68919da002c4300cd_bzm6bxnb9.pdf. See
also the American Society for Civil Engineers' more recent estimate
of the cost of congestion: https://www.infrastructurereportcard.org
/roads/conditions-capacity/.

310 *shelves of the Bipartisan Policy Center:* See the organization's website
section on infrastructure: http://infrastructurecouncil.org/.

310 *announced an infrastructure plan:* See this White House fact sheet on
infrastructure funding in the 2018 budget, which pledges $200 billion
over ten years: https://www.whitehouse.gov/sites/whitehouse.gov
/files/omb/budget/fy2018/fact_sheets/2018%20Budget%20Fact%20
Sheet_Infrastructure%20Initiative.pdf.

312 *David and Charles Koch:* For one description of their influence on this
issue, see Coral Davenport and Eric Lipton, "How GOP Leaders Came
to View Climate Change as Fake Science," *New York Times*, June 3,
2017: https://www.nytimes.com/2017/06/03/us/politics/republican
-leaders-climate-change.html?hp&_r=0.

11   PROTECTING THE MOST UNPROTECTED

313 The Other America: Michael Harrington, *The Other America: Poverty in the United States* (New York: Macmillan, 1962).

314 *"It came at a time":* Interviews with Edelman.

314 $2.00 a Day: Kathryn J. Edin and H. Luke Shaefer, *$2.00 a Day: Living on Almost Nothing in America* (New York: Houghton Mifflin Harcourt, 2015).

315 *published by the American Enterprise Institute:* Robert Doar, "Are Americans Really Living on $2 a Day?," American Enterprise Institute, June 6, 2016, http://www.aei.org/publication/are-americans-really-living-on-2-a-day/.

315 *It was widely praised:* See this *New York Times Book Review* that referred to *$2.00 a Day* as a "call to action" : https://www.nytimes.com/2015/09/06/books/review/2-00-a-day-by-kathryn-j-edin-and-h-luke-shaefer.html. Other publications, including the *Los Angeles Times* and *The Boston Globe*, also published positive reviews.

315 *cut nearly in half:* See the Census Bureau's Historical Poverty Tables: 1959 to 2016: https://www.census.gov/data/tables/time-series/demo/income-poverty/historical-poverty-people.html.

316 *poverty rate for America's children:* See data on poverty rates published by the Organisation for Economic Co-operation and Development: https://data.oecd.org/inequality/poverty-rate.htm.

316 *50 percent of the poverty level:* Census Bureau's Historical Poverty Tables: 1959 to 2016: https://www.census.gov/data/tables/time-series/demo/income-poverty/historical-poverty-people.html.

316 *life expectancy:* H. Luke Shaefer, Pinghui Wu, and Kathryn Edin, "Can Poverty in America Be Compared to Conditions in the World's Poorest Countries?," National Poverty Center, August 2016, http://www.npc.umich.edu/publications/u/2016-07-npc-working-paper.pdf.

316 *twice the poverty level:* See the data on income-to-poverty ratio in the 2016 Census report on income and poverty in the U.S.: https://census.gov/content/dam/Census/library/publications/2017/demo/P60-259.pdf.

316 *a sudden $400 expense:* See the Federal Reserve's "Report on the Economic Well-Being of U.S. Households in 2016": https://www.federalreserve.gov/consumerscommunities/shed.htm.

316 *Nixon approved a proposal:* "Floor Under Income," *New York Times,* December 25, 1973, http://www.nytimes.com/1973/12/25/archives/floor-under-income.html?_r=0. See also Rutger Bregman, "Nixon's

Basic Income Plan," *Jacobin*, May 5, 2016, https://www.jacobinmag
.com/2016/05/richard-nixon-ubi-basic-income-welfare/.

317 *attacking "welfare queens":* See this 1976 article in *The New York Times*
discussing the issue of "welfare queens" in the election: http://www
.nytimes.com/1976/02/15/archives/welfare-queen-becomes-issue-in
-reagan-campaign-hitting-a-nerve-now.html.

318 *It was Democrat Bill Clinton:* President Clinton signed the Personal
Responsibility and Work Opportunity Reconciliation Act into law
in August of 1996: https://www.congress.gov/bill/104th-congress
/house-bill/3734. See also Judis, *The Paradox of American Democracy;*
and Peter Edelman, "The Worst Thing Bill Clinton Has Done," *The
Atlantic*, March 1997 issue, https://www.theatlantic.com/magazine
/archive/1997/03/the-worst-thing-bill-clinton-has-done/376797/.

318 *Edelman resigned in protest:* Interviews. See also Alison Mitchell, "Two
Clinton Aides Resign to Protest New Welfare Law," *New York Times*,
September 12, 1996, http://www.nytimes.com/1996/09/12/us/two
-clinton-aides-resign-to-protest-new-welfare-law.html.

318 *"Kennedy envisioned":* Peter Edelman, *Searching for America's Heart:
RFK and the Renewal of Hope* (Boston: Houghton Mifflin, 2001).

319 *12.6 million Americans:* These numbers are based on annual caseload data from the Office of Family Assistance of the Department of
Health and Human Services: https://www.acf.hhs.gov/ofa/resource
-library/search?area%5B2377%5D=2377&topic%5B2351%5D=235
1&type%5B3084%5D=3084.

319 *In Wyoming:* This data comes from the historical poverty tables published by the Census Bureau and the caseload data from the Office of
Family Assistance.

319 *The number of single mothers:* See Table 4 of the Employment Characteristics of Families annual survey by the Bureau of Labor Statistics:
https://www.bls.gov/bls/news-release/home.htm#FAMEE.

320 *free or reduced-priced lunches:* See Table 204.10 from the National Center for Education Statistics: https://nces.ed.gov/programs/digest/d16
/tables/dt16_204.10.asp.

320 *received food stamps:* See data on the Supplemental Nutritional Assistance Program (SNAP) from the USDA Food and Nutrition Service: https://www.fns.usda.gov/pd/supplemental-nutrition-assistance
-program-snap.

320 *nineteen million manufacturing jobs:* See data from the Bureau of Labor
Statistics: https://data.bls.gov/timeseries/CES3000000001.

320 *uncertain staffing schedules:* Patricia Cohen, "Steady Jobs, with Pay
and Hours That Are Anything But," *New York Times*, May 31, 2017,

https://www.nytimes.com/2017/05/31/business/economy/volatile-income-economy-jobs.html?_r=0.

320 *minimum wage, which has not been:* The Fair Labor Standards Act was passed in 1938 and has been amended several times since. The Bureau of Labor Statistics provides a summary of these changes: https://www.dol.gov/whd/minwage/coverage.htm. See also the BLS inflation calculator: https://www.bls.gov/data/inflation_calculator.htm.

321 *pay below poverty level:* This report from the American Policy Institute includes the data about the one in four jobs paying below the poverty level: http://stateofworkingamerica.org/fact-sheets/poverty/annet. This study provides the data about 42 percent of jobs paying near or at the poverty level: Yannet Lathrop, Paul K. Sonn, and Irene Tung, "The Growing Movement for $15," National Employment Law Project, November 4, 2015, http://www.nelp.org/content/uploads/Growing-Movement-for-15-Dollars.pdf.

321 *"Americans have the lowest":* Christopher Ingraham, "The U.S. Has One of the Stingiest Minimum Wage Policies of Any Wealthy Nation," *The Washington Post*, December 29, 2017: https://www.washingtonpost.com/news/wonk/wp/2017/12/29/the-u-s-has-one-of-the-stingiest-minimum-wage-policies-of-any-wealthy-nation/?utm_term=.05da49294512&wpisrc=nl_rainbow&wpmm=1.

321 *fair market rental rate:* See the National Low Income Housing Coalition's annual report, "Out of Reach: The High Cost of Housing": http://nlihc.org/oor.

322 *"very low-income households":* The ratios of affordable housing available to low-income renters include only those apartments that are physically adequate for renters, meaning the conditions of the unit would not pose a threat to its inhabitants. The inventory of units that are available and affordable, but not necessarily physically adequate, is higher. See the Department of Housing and Urban Development's "Worst Case Housing Needs" report to Congress: https://www.huduser.gov/portal/publications/Worst-Case-Housing-Needs.html. Previous years' reports are also available at www.huduser.gov. See also the National Low Income Housing Coalition's "Out of Reach" report (previously cited), as well as "The Gap: A Shortage of Affordable Homes," by the same organization: http://nlihc.org/research/gap-report.

322 *housing assistance dollars:* Here I compare the money spent on mortgage interest deductions to the Department of Housing and Urban Development budget for rental assistance programs: https://www.hud.gov/program_offices/cfo/budget. It should also be noted that the Center

on Budget and Policy Priorities reported in March 2017 that high-income households (over $200,000) received an average of $6,076 in housing benefits, four times greater than the $1,529 received on average by the low-income households that were fortunate enough to receive any assistance at all.

322 *interest on mortgages:* Data on the cost of the deduction, including a distribution of benefits by household income class, can be found on the Joint Committee for Taxation website for tax expenditures: https://www.jct.gov/publications.html?func=select&id=5.

324 *soup kitchens and food pantries:* This estimate comes from a non-profit called Feeding America: http://www.feedingamerica.org/need-help -find-food/.

324 *consistently responded in polls:* Jens Manuel Krogstad and Kim Parker, "Public Is Sharply Divided in Views of Americans in Poverty," Pew Research Center, September 16, 2014, http://www.pewresearch.org /fact-tank/2014/09/16/public-is-sharply-divided-in-views-of-amer icans-in-poverty/.

324 *48 million Americans:* Since 2000, the number of food stamp recipients with job-related earnings—as opposed to children, the disabled, and those whose income is Social Security—has more than tripled, and that ratio prevailed as the overall food stamp population grew with the coming of the Great Recession in 2008. Dottie Rosenbaum, "The Relationship Between SNAP and Work Among Low-Income House-holds," Center for Budget and Policy Priorities, January 30, 2013, https://www.cbpp.org/research/the-relationship-between-snap-and -work-among-low-income-households.

324 *at least one employed worker:* See data on SNAP from the USDA's Economic Research Service: https://www.ers.usda.gov/topics/food -nutrition-assistance/supplemental-nutrition-assistance-program -snap/charts/.

324 *"good jobs are difficult":* "The State of American Jobs," Pew Research Center, October 6, 2016, http://www.pewsocialtrends.org/2016/10/06 /the-state-of-american-jobs/.

325 *broad middle-class support:* See, for example, these Pew polls: http:// www.pewresearch.org/fact-tank/2017/01/04/5-facts-about-the -minimum-wage/.

326 *they get to kindergarten:* Roberto A. Ferdman, "Only in America: Four Years into Life, Poor Kids Are Already an Entire Year Behind," *Washington Post*, December 21, 2015, https://www.washingtonpost .com/news/wonk/wp/2015/12/17/how-your-first-four-years-of-life -affect-the-rest-of-it/?utm_term=.c9d43fa579e2&wpisrc=nl_evening &wpmm=1.

326 *Edelman and his colleagues:* For the remainder of Chapter 11, the data
is based on my interviews with Edelman, email correspondence with
him and his colleagues, and this report: Nina Dastur, Indivar Dutta-
Gupta, Laura Tatum, Peter Edelman, Kali Grant, and Casey Goldvale,
"Building the Caring Economy: Workforce Investments to Expand
Access to Affordable, High-Quality Early and Long-Term Care,"
Georgetown Law Center on Poverty and Inequality, Spring 2017,
http://www.georgetownpoverty.org/wp-content/uploads/2017/05
/Building-the-caring-economy_hi-res.pdf.

12 STORMING THE MOATS

330 *"to bear the burden":* Available at the JFK Presidential Library website: https://www.jfklibrary.org/Research/Research-Aids/Ready-Refer
ence/JFK-Quotations/Inaugural-Address.aspx.

330 *"at the center":* Available on the White House website: https://www
.whitehouse.gov/inaugural-address.

330 *"malaise" speech:* Delivered July 15, 1979, available through the
American Presidency Project: http://www.presidency.ucsb.edu/ws
/?pid=32596.

331 *October 2, 1980, debate:* Available through the Reagan Presidential
Library: https://reaganlibrary.archives.gov/archives/reference/10.28
.80debate.html.

331 *program of national service:* Steven Brill, *After: How America Confronted
the September 12 Era* (New York: Simon & Schuster, 2003), p. 616.

331 *people should resume shopping:* This was something Bush said a number of times. In late September 2001, he urged a crowd at Chicago's
O'Hare Airport to "Do your business around the country. Fly and
enjoy America's great destination spots. Get down to Disney World
in Florida": https://georgewbush-whitehouse.archives.gov/news
/releases/2001/09/20010927-1.html. See also Brill, *After.*

332 Bowling Alone: Robert D. Putnam, *Bowling Alone: The Collapse and
Revival of American Community* (New York: Simon & Schuster, 2000).

332 *"all the people":* See this report from Pew: http://www.people-press
.org/2015/11/23/1-trust-in-government-1958-2015/.

333 *In 1960, voter turnout:* See data at the American Presidency Project:
http://www.presidency.ucsb.edu/data/turnout.php.

334 *"Still Bowling Alone?":* Robert D. Putnam and Thomas H. Sander,
"Still Bowling Alone?," *Journal of Democracy* 21, no. 1 (January 2010),
https://sites.hks.harvard.edu/ocpa/pdf/still%20bowling%20alone
.pdf.

335 Our Kids: Robert D. Putnam, *Our Kids: The American Dream in Crisis* (New York: Simon & Schuster, 2015).

336 *"a new era of resonsibility"*: Available on an archived version of his White House website: https://obamawhitehouse.archives.gov/blog/2009/01/21/president-barack-obamas-inaugural-address.

336 *"break the fever"*: Jonathan Chait, "Five Days That Shaped a Presidency," *New York*, October 2, 2016, http://nymag.com/daily/intelligencer/2016/10/barack-obama-on-5-days-that-shaped-his-presidency.html.

338 *newspaper advertising revenue:* See the Pew Research Center's fact sheet on newspapers: http://www.journalism.org/fact-sheet/newspapers/.

338 *newspaper employment:* See data from the Bureau of Labor Statistics: https://www.bls.gov/opub/ted/2017/newspaper-publishers-lose-over-half-their-employment-from-january-2001-to-september-2016.htm?utm_source=newsletter&utm_medium=email&utm_campaign=newsletter_axiosam.

339 *dramatic increase in revenue:* See the 2017 third quarter results for *The New York Times:* http://investors.nytco.com/press/press-releases/press-release-details/2017/The-New-York-Times-Company-Reports-2017-Third-Quarter-Results/default.aspx; as well as Benjamin Mullin, "The *Washington Post* Is 'Profitable and Growing,' Publisher Says," *Poynter,* December 13, 2016, https://www.poynter.org/news/washington-post-profitable-and-growing-publisher-says. For *The Wall Street Journal,* see information from NewsCorp: https://newscorp.com/.

Index

page 1: (top left) Office of Public Affairs, Yale University, Photographs of Individuals (RU 686), Manuscripts and Archives, Yale University Library; (middle) Courtesy of Yale Law School; (bottom) Jason Torres

page 2: (top) Mathieu Asselin; (bottom) Courtesy of Harvard Business School

page 3: (top) *The American Lawyer*, vol. 1, no. 1, February 1979; (bottom) Courtesy Wachtell, Lipton, Rosen & Katz; photographer: Sasha Maslov

page 4: (top) Tom Toro, *The New Yorker* Collection/The Cartoon Bank; (bottom) Jimi Celeste / Patrick McMullan / Getty Images (Getty Image #: 591768566)

page 5: (top) Courtesy of Better Markets; (bottom) Keystone Pictures USA / Alamy Stock Photo (Alamy Image #: E0XDNK)

page 6: (top) Courtesy of Northwestern University Pritzker School of Law / Jasmin Shah; (bottom left) Harold Shapiro; (bottom right) Courtesy of Issue One

page 7: Washington and Lee University Library: Lewis F. Powell, Jr., "The Memo" (1971); Powell Memorandum: Attack on American Free Enterprise System, 1

page 8: (top) House.Sinema.Gov; (bottom) Alexei Agaryshev

page 9: (top left) Photograph by Diana Walker / Time & Life Pictures / Getty Images (Getty Image #: 53366136); (bottom) Courtesy of the Bipartisan Policy Center

page 10: (top) Visions of America, LLC / Alamy Stock Photo (Alamy Image #: AHTDJE); (middle) Ramin Talaie / Corbis / Getty Images (Getty Image #: 526380254); (bottom) Larry Downing / Sygma / Getty Images (Getty Image #: 590865840)

page 11: (top left) Scott J. Ferrell/Congressional Quarterly / Alamy Stock Photo (Alamy Image #: B6XWXF); (top right) Moviestore Collection Ltd / Alamy Stock Photo (Alamy Image #: BKGRNF); (bottom) Courtesy of Tech Equality

page 12: (top left) Dennis Wagner, *The Arizona Republic* / The *USA Today* Network; (top right) Kristoffer Tripplaar / Alamy Stock Photo (Alamy Image #: GW7E6A); (bottom) Aaron Clamage, https://www.clamagephoto.com

page 13: (top) U.S. Department of Justice; (bottom) Christopher Goodney / Bloomberg / Getty Images (Getty Image #: 801311338)

page 14: (bottom) Courtesy of Cornell University Library via Archive.org

page 15: Yale Law Journal

page 16: (top left) *The Washington Post* / Getty Images (Getty Image #: 137463204); (top right) Courtesy Philip Howard, www.commongood.org; (middle) Courtesy of Georgetown Law Center; (bottom) ZUMA Press, Inc. / Alamy Stock Photo (Alamy Image: CG1B2P)

DARK MONEY

The Hidden History of the Billionaires Behind the
Rise of the Radical Right
by Jane Mayer

Who are the immensely wealthy right-wing ideologues shaping the fate of America today? Why is America living in an age of profound and widening economic inequality? Why have even modest attempts to address climate change been defeated again and again? Why do hedge-fund billionaires pay a far lower tax rate than middle-class workers? In a riveting and indelible feat of reporting, Jane Mayer illuminates the history of an elite cadre of plutocrats—headed by the Kochs, the Scaifes, the Olins, and the Bradleys—who have bankrolled a systematic plan to fundamentally alter the American political system. Mayer traces a byzantine trail of billions of dollars spent by the network, revealing a staggering conglomeration of think tanks, academic institutions, media groups, courthouses, and government allies that have fallen under their sphere of influence. Drawing from hundreds of exclusive interviews, as well as extensive scrutiny of public records, private papers, and court proceedings, Mayer provides vivid portraits of the secretive figures behind the new American oligarchy and a searing look at the carefully concealed agendas steering the nation. *Dark Money* is an essential book for anyone who cares about the future of American democracy.

Political Science

VINTAGE BOOKS & ANCHOR BOOKS
Available wherever books are sold.
www.vintagebooks.com
www.anchorbooks.com